Portrait of Maurice Benyovszky, taken from the frontispiece of the 1790 edition of his *Memoirs*.

THE INTRIGUING LIFE AND IGNOMINIOUS DEATH OF MAURICE BENYOVSZKY

Published in 1790, Maurice Benyovszky's posthumous memoir was an instant sensation. A tale of exploration and adventure beginning with his daring escape from a Siberian prison and ending with his coronation as King of Madagascar, it was translated into several languages and adapted for the theatre and opera. This book explores the veracity of this memoir and, more broadly, the challenges faced by the explorers of the age and the brutality of colonisation.

The self-styled Hungarian Baron Maurice Auguste Aladar Benyovszky, Counsellor to the Duke of Saxony and Colonel in the service of the Queen of Hungary, was in fact only confirmed to have been an officer in a regiment of the Polish Confederation of Bar. While he did escape from Russian captors and subsequently travel to Japan, Formosa, China and Madagascar, many of his exploits were wildly exaggerated or simply invented. Andrew Drummond reveals an alternative picture of events by looking at statements from Benyovszky's travelling companions and sceptical officials as well as contemporary documents from the places he claimed to have visited, untangling the truth behind his stories and examining what these stories can nonetheless tell us about the era in which Benyovszky lived.

Witty and engagingly written, this book is fascinating reading for anyone interested in eighteenth-century colonial history and the story of early European and Russian explorers.

Andrew Drummond is based in Edinburgh, UK. He holds a degree in Modern Languages from Aberdeen University and a post-graduate degree in German Studies from King's College, London. His publications include *An Abridged History* (2004), *A Hand-book of Volapük* (2006), *Elephantina* (2008) and *Novgorod the Great* (2010), the first of which was short-listed for the Saltire Society's First Book of the Year award, and he has recently had several short stories published in anthologies.

THE INTRIGUING LIFE AND IGNOMINIOUS DEATH OF MAURICE BENYOVSZKY

Andrew Drummond

Routledge
Taylor & Francis Group

NEW YORK AND LONDON

First published 2018
by Routledge
711 Third Avenue, New York, NY 10017

and by Routledge
2 Park Square, Milton Park, Abingdon, Oxon OX14 4RN

Routledge is an imprint of the Taylor & Francis Group, an informa business

Library of Congress Cataloging-in-Publication Data
A catalog record for this book has been requested

ISBN: 978-1-4128-6510-4 (hbk)
ISBN: 978-1-4128-6543-2 (pbk)
ISBN: 978-1-315-11298-5 (ebk)

Typeset in Bembo
by Saxon Graphics Ltd, Derby

CONTENTS

ILLUSTRATIONS

Figures

Maps

PREFACE

Of Names and Dates and Places and Professors

A Researcher's Reliable Standby: Guesswork – Simply Add Eleven Days –
Simply Add or Subtract 156 Degrees – the Author Now Apologises to Everyone

Before you embark on this tale of high adventure and low deception, there are things of which you should be aware.

First, *names*: the eighteenth-century journals, chronicles and reports used as sources for this book all display a wonderful and confusing variety in their rendering of personal and place names. The spelling is largely dependent on the nationality of each writer, but even then nothing was fixed. Personal names can be written in half-a-dozen different ways. Where possible and desirable we have standardised spellings around a few simple rules – hopefully rational, but ultimately subjective. In preference to many other perfectly good alternatives, we have been persuaded to anglicise our hero's forename 'Moric' to *Maurice* and rendered his family name as *Benyovszky* – excepting those occasions when his name has been written in an interesting manner by others. In that spirit, anomalous spellings of absolutely everything have been retained in quoted text, to give a flavour of the original orthography.

A list of the people involved in the great adventure is provided in Appendix I of this book.

Given the patchy geographical certainties of the period, the actual locations of some of the places named by the primary sources can only be guessed at. This is particularly true of places in Japan and China. And even more true, as we shall see, when some locations are entirely fictitious. Frequently, therefore, we have resorted to that reliable standby: guesswork.

Second, *dates*: in the Russia of the 1770s, the 'old style' Julian calendar was still in use – and remained so until 1918. Much of Catholic Europe had adopted the 'new style' Gregorian calendar from 1582 onwards, with Protestant countries following in the early eighteenth century, and Britain, non-European as ever, in 1752; in those countries which had not adopted it by the late eighteenth century, the old style calendar was some eleven days behind the new style one. Hungary, birthplace of our main protagonist, was an early adopter of the Gregorian calendar. Since our chroniclers for the present book were largely Russian contemporaries of Benyovszky, old style dates are much in evidence. Mostly. But not consistently. To avoid utter confusion, we sometimes distinguish between old and new style dates using an abbreviation in brackets after the date (OS or NS, respectively); to convert from old style to new style simply add eleven days. Or not, according to taste.

Third, *latitude and longitude*: in the period described in this book, sailors and other travellers by sea were adept at establishing their latitude above or below the equator; but establishing longitude exercised them a great deal. We would refer readers to Dava Sobel's excellent book *Longitude* for further information.[1] Commonly, navigators would calculate their longitude as the number of degrees east or west of their last port of call; this calculation could be based on a number of different methods. Benyovszky used the Kamchatkan town of Bolsheretsk as his 'Greenwich', but readers will find that even the relative longitude from there was calculated with quite spectacular errors. We recommend that you ignore all longitude readings in this book. But those who wish to be pernickety are advised that Bolsheretsk lies at 156° 16′ East and 52° 49′ North; now away and do the maths.

And last, *sources and acknowledgements*: many of the sources used for this book date from the late eighteenth and early nineteenth centuries. These were generally written in Russian, Japanese, French or German. Some of the source material is readily available in digital format (OpenLibrary.org, Archive.org, Google Books, Hathi Trust, etc.), other material has been consulted in the National Library of Scotland. But I must specifically thank John Massey Stewart for his help in accessing material printed in Russian; Maria Bogomolova for her work in transcribing 'old Russian' documents into 'new Russian' text; and my sister Izzi Hazelwood for her translations from the Russian. I should also mention John Dundas Cochrane, the pedestrian traveller to Kamchatka, without whom I would probably never have heard of Benyovszky. And my gratitude to a whole galliot full of professors and doctors, in strict alphabetical order: Dr Ian Astley, for his explanations of Hungarian renditions of Japanese; Professor Hajo Eicken, for his timely guidance on ice conditions in the Bering Sea; Professor Ian Inkster, for his kind permission to reference his article on Benyovszky's visit to Formosa; Professor Roger Keys, for his translation work from poorly-written Russian; Dr Carol Padgham-Albrecht of Idaho University, for permission to cite from her dissertation on Austrian operas; Professor Luke Roberts, for his invaluable advice on giants, officialdom, diaries and dates in Japan, and permission to cite; and Professor Vilmos Voigt, for permission to quote from his detailed history of Benyovszkiana. My apologies here and now to all of these generous people: it is entirely possible that I have completely misunderstood any guidance they gave me.

A full bibliography has been provided at the end of this book, in Appendix III. The first section of the bibliography provides the details of all books cited in the notes at the end of each chapter; the reference to 'Benyovszky' is always to the two-volume edition of Benyovszky's *Memoirs*, published in London in 1790.

A sumptuous selection of digitised source materials – texts, maps, images – can be found on the author's website at www.andydrummond.net/benyovszky.

And now let us begin.

Note

1   Sobel, 1996.

I

MACAO

"A Vessel of Uncommon Appearance"

A Vessel Arrives at Macao – Great Excitement Amongst the European Merchants –
Strange Secrets – A Best-Seller

On the 23rd September 1771, Nathaniel Barlow, going about his daily business in
the merchant community of Macao, was much animated by the arrival in the port
of a small and bedraggled ship. It was, he reported later, "a vessel of uncommon
appearance." It had

> sixty five persons on board, most of them military. The Commanding
> Officer bore the rank of Colonel and the title of Baron de Benyorsky, which
> he held under the Queen of Hungary. There were in the vessel five persons
> in womens apparel.[1]

So great was the excitement created by the arrival of this ship and its curious crew
that Mr Barlow despatched a letter to London, where it was published in *The*
Gentleman's Magazine and Historical Chronicle for 1772. In a journalistic act of
caution worthy of marvel and respect today, the editor headlined it with the words:
"*The following extraordinary account, in a Letter from Canton, dated Nov 19, 1771, is*
said to be authentic." His caution, although unjustified for the letter in question,
could nevertheless be applied to several of the later accounts which emerged on the
same subject.

Barlow's letter contained a very brief statement from the uncommon vessel's
commanding officer, Baron Benyovszky, on the circumstances of the voyage that
had just been completed. Benyovszky said he had been sent into exile to Kazan in
Russia almost two years previously. Determining to escape, he and several companions
had overpowered their jailers, and "directed their rout to Kamschatka, on the sea
coast of Tartary, where the Colonel knew a friend, on whose assistance their hopes

depended." His most convenient friend most conveniently came up with the goods – a vessel on which the Baron could embark with eighty-five of his fellow-prisoners. They then set out on a lengthy sea-voyage which took them first down the coast towards China, then eastwards until he saw part of America, and then westwards again, towards Manila in the Philippine Islands, and finally, defeated by contrary winds, he arrived in Macao, "being five months on his passage from Kamschatka."

Barlow was also able to include in his report a later variant of this account, as supplied by Benyovszky "to a Gentleman in Canton." This second account was in fact an affidavit provided to the authorities in Macao; it stated that the Baron had sailed from Kamchatka on board the ship, with the intention of reaching the Mariana Islands. "A great tempest and very strong wind" drove them towards Japan, along which country they coasted until they reached Formosa and then crossed to China to reach Macao. The human cost of this voyage? "Went out with 85 men, came back with 62."

The factual basis of this voyage, the observant reader will note, was a little shaky from the very start. It was evident that Benyovszky was not telling the full story. There were perhaps many reasons for that – not the least of which was the danger of being extradited back to Russia as escaped prisoners, either by the Portuguese authorities in Macao, or the Chinese ones in neighbouring Canton. As the days went by, it became obvious that much of what went on in this lengthy voyage was not being divulged. What was the fate of the twenty-three members of the crew who never arrived? What was their actual route from Kamchatka? How on earth did such a large band of escaped prisoners cross four thousand miles of unforgiving land and sea, from Kazan to Kamchatka, without being apprehended? And, last but not least, what of the "five persons in womens apparel" – were they women or were they not?

Our man in Macao, Nathaniel Barlow, in a private letter that was published at a much later date,[2] offered a supplementary glimpse of Benyovszky's dealings there. Far from shedding further light on the route of the voyage, the Baron had become extremely secretive. He had been, he now said,

> as far north as 63 degrees; had with him Lord Anson's *Voyages*, translated into the Sclavonian language, which he repeatedly said was of greatest use to him, being guided in a great measure by them. In his apartment were several mathematical instruments, especially a quadrant, and a cross-staff. On requesting for a sight of his drafts [*of the log-books*], he with great reluctance produced one, but, unluckily, a gentleman in company telling him that one of us was a sea-captain, he immediately withdrew, and carried with him the draft, by which we lost the opportunity of knowing more particulars of this very extraordinary voyage. The vessel is fifty feet long, and sixteen broad, built entirely of fir.

This was indeed a very extraordinary voyage. The facts which later became evident were these: in May of 1771, just as the ice was beginning to recede from the shores of Kamchatka, in the far east of Russia's Far East, around seventy exiles, sailors, clerks and trappers had overpowered the military garrison, stolen a small ship, the *St Peter,* and set off for a better life. Over the course of the following five months, with almost no navigational guidance at all, ship and crew sailed in what could best be described as The Sea of Uncertainty, before edging their way south-westwards across the rim of the North Pacific. They endured violent storms, they suffered from hunger and thirst and scurvy, and they despaired of ever knowing where they were. Coming across the coast of Japan more by accident than by design, they attempted to trade peacefully for the bare necessities of life with the residents of small coastal towns. Their coin of exchange was a large smelly cargo of Siberian furs which, with some foresight, they had earlier liberated from the storehouses of Kamchatka. Eventually they reached Formosa and then the coast of China and were guided into the busy port of Macao. After a delay of three months, the majority of those who had survived took passage on ships heading for Mauritius and France. And, in a surprise move, a handful of those who reached France chose to return to Siberia.

It was a very extraordinary man who led them. In September 1771, Maurice Benyovszky was only 25 years old. He was the recognised leader of a motley band of seventy or more desperate men and women, possibly also a dog. The leaky ship in which they sailed was a galliot, a flat-bottomed boat of about eighty tons and with scarcely room to swing a cat. It was more suited to coastal trading than criss-crossing the North Pacific. To have sailed for almost five months in such a vessel, with so many people on board, with a bare minimum of navigational instruments, and a book of adventurer's tales in lieu of a chart, under the command of a young man with no obvious experience of the high seas – and yet to have arrived more or less unscathed is very extraordinary.

Extraordinary, finally, is the fact that, within days of the ship's arrival in Macao, some fifteen of the passengers and crew died a sudden death. Of those adventurers who remained alive after the voyage, several wrote their own accounts of their journey from Kamchatka. But their voices went largely unheard in the decades which followed. Those scraps, documents and reports which have come down the years tell only a rather brief tale of adventure.

A fuller and much more enthralling story of the voyage did not become public until almost twenty years later. Baron Benyovszky's *Memoirs and Travels,* which were also said to be authentic, were published posthumously in London in 1790. It became an overnight best-seller in Britain, France, Germany and beyond.

This, too, was very extraordinary because much of what was described in this book was simply untrue.

Notes

1   *Gentleman's Magazine,* 1772, p.272 (punctuation as in original).
2   Benyovszky, 1790, p.xx–xxii.

II

CHRONICLERS

"Short and Incomplete, it is Written with a Bias"

*A Meagre Inheritance – A Life of Adventure – Ippolit Stepanov's Misfortunes –
Ivan Ryumin's Observations – Everyone Entitled to an Opinion*

Before we join the extraordinary voyage of the *St Peter*, it is our duty to familiarise
ourselves with the main players in the two extraordinary stories. For there are two
intertwined stories here: the one of the escape from Kamchatka and subsequent
adventures of the participants; the other of the outrageous confidence-trick played
on the reading public of Europe and America by our Baron and his editor.

We shall delineate Benyovszky in more detail later. A short biography suffices
here: he was a Hungarian, born in 1746; because of straitened circumstances in his
family, the young Maurice found himself fighting as a mercenary in Poland during
one of its many disputes with Imperial Russia, something he quite enjoyed; he
found himself taken prisoner, something that was less enjoyable; least enjoyable of
all, he was shipped off to Siberia in 1770 as a prisoner-of-war. However, he rose
above this adversity and, on a stolen ship and in the company of a few dozen
others, sailed down the Kuril Islands, made two landfalls in Japan before reaching
Macao, from where he managed to find a way back to Europe. After he arrived in
France in 1772, he persuaded the French government to fund an expedition to
Madagascar, which, he promised, would result in a rich and vibrant colony for
exploitation. According to Benyovszky, his three-year residence resulted in him
being crowned King of Madagascar (the natives of that island might have begged
to differ, had they been asked). In 1774, he returned to Europe and spent some
years engaged in excellent money-making schemes in France and Croatia, but
always with an eye to returning to Madagascar. The French were having nothing
more to do with him; the British remained unmoved; finally he persuaded two
starry-eyed Americans of Baltimore to fund a second expedition. His arrival on
Madagascar in 1785 was inauspicious: he was believed to have been killed by the

native islanders almost as soon as his feet touched dry land; happily, he was not; less happily, he was killed a few months later by a troop of French soldiers sent from the neighbouring island of Mauritius. Murdered at the age of thirty-nine, he left behind in the fledgling United States a grieving widow and a child or two.

His *Memoirs*, which he had been touting around the publishers of Paris and London in the early 1780s, were finally published in 1790, four years after the author's death. While critics were sceptical of the veracity of the adventures laid before them, the reading public was far more appreciative, and several years of Benyovszky-mania followed. Translations of his *Memoirs*, extracts thereof, plays and operas all followed thick and fast; but the widow and her mites got not a penny in royalties.

So much for Benyovszky. We shall return to him in good time.

Amongst those who fled from Kamchatka were two others who kept a log of what they saw and did. The first was Ippolit Stepanov, a Russian army officer who had the misfortune – some would describe it as ill-judgement – to express his views about Catherine the Great at precisely the wrong moment: he found himself exiled to Kamchatka at the same time as Benyovszky. For a while, it is clear, Benyovszky and Stepanov were bosom-buddies, brothers in misfortune. It is probable that Stepanov played a leading role in the great escape from exile. Alas, by the time the ship had reached Macao, neither man trusted the other, and a bitter falling-out took place, very much to Stepanov's disadvantage: when all the surviving voyagers left Macao for Mauritius and France, Stepanov alone was left behind to fend for himself. He tried his luck by boarding a Dutch ship to Indonesia, but expired there in poverty. Before dying, he wrote down his own account of the escape; almost certainly, he expressed here an evaluation of Benyovszky which would have been less than complimentary. After dying, his account was acquired by a Dutchman, translated from Russian into Dutch, from Dutch into French and from French into German, and then was edited such that all trace of his original voice has been lost. All we have left is a short extract offered at third hand. But even these slops of an account contain some tasty chunks of information.

It should be observed here that Benyovszky in his account of events had nothing good to say of Stepanov; the best he could say of him was that Stepanov was "an unhappy man, who was rushing hastily to his destruction". So those who favoured the Benyovszkian world-outlook were also dead-set against anything Stepanov could come up with. It is a little unfortunate that Stepanov's account reaches us today through the editorial medium of one of Benyovszky's greatest admirers: Stepanov's account, we are assured, "is short and incomplete, it is written with a bias"; which is precisely why we will examine it closely.

Also on board the *St Peter* was a clerk from the chancellery in Kamchatka, Ivan Ryumin. Ryumin was always off Benyovszky's radar, and makes almost no appearance at all in the *Memoirs*; for later generations, this invisibility was providential. Ryumin kept his own journal of events, and Benyovszky knew nothing of it. It is raw and rough, it bursts with enthusiasm and vitality. He is daily captivated by flying fish, by fruits of every conceivable shape and colour, by the mysterious Japanese people, by wild beasts and enormous cannon. Where Benyovszky's style is flowery and decidedly pompous and self-aggrandising, Ryumin has no style at all: he rushes in, he counts and describes and he rushes onwards. Sadly, his journal did not see the light of day until 1822, and even now it is not readily accessible to anyone who might be interested. But his account of the voyage and its aftermath acts as a healthy counterpoint to Benyovszky's tales. Ryumin was hounded by good luck – with his wife in tow, he managed to survive the voyage, survive the heat and misery of Macao, survive the voyage back to France and survive an utterly dispiriting eight-month quarantine in a French port, before returning in 1773 under Imperial dispensation to Siberia, where he and his wife settled down to a very quiet life in Tobolsk.

The events of 1770–1772 did not go unnoticed by other travellers, either: we have corroborative evidence from Japanese officials; also from members of Captain James Cook's third voyage; and anyone who stepped ashore on Kamchatka in the 50 years that followed the Great Escape was sure to be button-holed by some tottering ancient who had much to say about 'the celebrated Benyovszky' – nothing so exciting had happened for years in that far outpost of the Russian Empire. If you happened to be French (in Kamchatka, by a twist of logic, Benyovszky was later regarded as French), then you were looked upon with considerable misgiving.

In the matter of Benyovszky's further adventures on Madagascar, we possess plenty of contemporary accounts of his actions – largely from Frenchmen of reputation and learning such as the polymath Abbé Rochon, the explorer Kerguelen and a swift succession of governors and administrators on the neighbouring island of Mauritius. All of whom could wield a critical pen dripping with Gallic scorn. "I do not draw back from telling you," wrote one of Benyovszky, "that, not only will this officer do nothing useful for the service, but that he will do it at the cost of many men and the King's gold. He has set no limits on his ambitions except those of his desires – and his desires have no limits."[1]

Everyone was entitled to their opinion. But it is our duty to examine Benyovszky's adequately intriguing life and his ignominious death by delving into all of these sources. Then we may sidle up to the truth and tap it on the shoulder.

But first: garlic.

Note

1   Cultru, 1906, p.64.

III

POLAND AND SIBERIA

"Iron and Garlick"

A Hungarian Baron in Poland – Laxity Amongst Russian Guards –
Betrayal and Exile – Interesting Travelling Companions – The Number of Furs
in Okhotsk – More Furs – A Dangerous Crossing – Nasty and Stupid Natives

An interested observer to the events in Macao was Simon Le Bon, the French 'Bishop of Mettelopolis' – a diocese which stretched from Turkey to Siam, challenging for even the best-travelled of bishops. On 23rd September 1771, the Bishop was introduced to

> the Hungarian Baron Maurice Auguste Aladar Benyofsky, Counsellor to Prince Albert, Duke of Saxony, Colonel (in the service) of her Apostolic Royal Imperial Majesty, the Queen of Hungary, and officer of a regiment of the confederation of the republic of Poland.

This Hungarian Baron was not a colonel. But his father had been one. Neither was he connected with the Duke of Saxony in any way. He was not a baron, except by virtue of his father's marriage to the daughter of a baron. In this period of his life, he also liked to be known as Count Benyovszky. He was not a count. At least, not at that time; he only became one in 1778 by order of the Empress Maria Theresa of Bohemia and Hungary. But his list of titles is not entirely misleading: he had probably been an officer of a regiment.

Maurice Benyovszky was born on 20th September 1746, the son of Samuel Benyovszky, a colonel of hussars who resided in the small country town of Vrbové, about 45 miles north-east of Bratislava. Samuel had married the daughter of a minor Hungarian baron, herself a widow with three daughters, all of whom subsequently married.[1] Maurice had three younger siblings – two brothers and a sister. His parents both died in 1760; resultant disputes with his brothers-in-law concerning the inheritance of the property escalated after a number of years into hot-headed actions by the young Maurice. He was brought before a judge in 1768 and handed a two-month jail-sentence for various imprudent acts; for reasons ill-defined but doubtless perfectly reasonable, upon his release the young man felt obliged to flee the country. Shortly before these troubles, he had married a lady named Anna Hönsch from the Szepes region of Upper Hungary, who bore him a son in December 1768; Benyovszky later claimed that Anna was of noble extraction; it appears she was not. Both wife and child were left behind in Hungary when he took himself off to Poland as a mercenary.

For a few months in 1768 and 1769, Benyovszky at the age of twenty-two fought with the aristocracy of Poland against the Russians. The huge Polish-Lithuanian Commonwealth was a splendidly colourful and disorganised aristocratic republic, which for some time had been in the decadent habit of electing its own 'King'. When the royal incumbent died in 1764, Catherine II of Russia managed to get her ex-lover Poniatowski installed as the new King Stanislaw II. Understandably, a fair number of the Polish nobility were not best pleased at this development, and, when Russia began to dictate domestic policy (including the granting of political rights for Protestant and Orthodox dissenters), the Poles clubbed together in 1768 in the 'Confederation of Bar' to organise an armed revolt.

After a distracted start, during which the rebels of the Confederation gained some military successes, Empress Catherine formally declared war on the Confederation in December 1768, and the Imperial Russian army moved into gear, slowly but surely regaining all lost towns and territory. The army of the Confederation was jam-packed with adventurers from all over Europe – Sweden, Hungary, France, Italy; young Maurice was only one amongst many. Just what his role was in the army of the Confederation is quite unknown; other than his own testimony, there is little contemporary confirmation. None of the official or unofficial histories mention the young Hungarian adventurer. He seems to have been captured near Ternopil in the Ukraine in May 1769 and hauled off to the town of Polonne, where he festered in a dungeon for several weeks, in the close company of around eighty other prisoners-of-war. In July, a large batch of prisoners was marched off to the city of Kiev. According to Benyovszky's account, 782 prisoners left Polonne, but only 148 arrived in Kiev, the majority having died under the cruel treatment of the commander of their guard. For the next two months, the prisoners were held in Kiev, before being sent a thousand miles further east to the city of Kazan – then, as now, a gateway to Siberia. During this period of captivity, Benyovszky became intimate friends with a Swede, like himself a mercenary fighting for the Confederation: Major August Winbladh, who remained Benyovszky's constant companion for the following three years.

Reader, be always circumspect! There is no independent verification of these events as they affected Benyovszky. There was plenty of scope for the Baron to invent episodes and characters, as we shall see. There is plenty of scope for us to

FIGURE 3.1 Benyovszky's parental home in Vrbové – functioning as a savings bank in 1891.

FIGURE 3.2 Benyovszky's parental home in Vrbové, as it is now – a museum and café.

disbelieve some of the detail. However, we should allow that the general flavour of events here is reflective of the truth.

A French mercenary, François de Belcour, had very similar adventures to those related by Benyovszky and he also passed through Polonne, Kiev and Kazan just a few months later, as part of another large group of prisoners-of-war.[2] He wrote an account of his adventures, which appeared in 1776. Benyovszky would almost certainly have read this book in Paris. Belcour proudly documented all the demands he placed on his Polish employers in respect of pay, number of horses "and all those things which are necessary to equip an officer of my rank for war". When all the *i*'s of his contract were dotted and all *t*'s crossed to his entire satisfaction, he arrived in Poland at the end of July 1769. Less than four months later, having done little but negotiate further terms and conditions from the Confederation, he became a prisoner-of-war. Just like Benyovszky, Belcour recounts appalling tales of brutality by the Russian officers – after his capture, ninety-seven of his comrades died on the journey from Prague to Kiev, and a further sixty-four died in Kiev; the survivors were then moved to Kazan – ten more died en route – and ultimately to Tobolsk, where they arrived in November 1770 and remained for several months until the Empress Catherine offered them release, dependent on signing abject confessions. With no honour or patriotism to engender second thoughts, they all signed immediately, and were then permitted to travel westwards under the close eye of Russian guards, before being shoved over the nearest convenient border out of harm's way.

In Benyovszky's account, further events during his captivity unfolded in rather an exciting and melodramatic manner; it seems ungenerous not to relate them here. In Kiev, the prisoners conspired to organise an escape, a plan based on the rather delusional supposition that the entire nobility of that part of Russia was about to take up arms against the Imperial power. Fortunately, an easier opportunity arose as a result of mistaken identity. Hearing a rumour that Benyovszky and other prisoners were about to make a bid for freedom, the Governor of Kiev sent a detachment of soldiers to Benyovszky's rooms to secure him; the Hungarian himself answered the door in his nightshirt. Supposing Benyovszky to be his own bleary-eyed man-servant, the soldiers rushed past him to make their arrest, leaving the door wide open. Benyovszky immediately repaired to the quarters of Major Winbladh. The pair hot-footed it out of Kazan, heading for St Petersburg, with a view to "passing by sea into another country."

All went well. They reached St Petersburg on post horses, travelling by night to discourage identification and arrest. In the port, they came to an arrangement with a Dutch sea-captain to take passage for Holland. Liberty was in sight. Alas! The pair were betrayed to the authorities by this same perfidious sea-captain. They were arrested and interrogated. Confessions were signed by the escapees, stating that neither would ever again bear arms against Russia and undertaking never to darken the doors of the Empire again, "under pain of death." Despite this commitment, which held out the promise of a slapped wrist and extradition, on 4th December 1769 the pair were promptly packed off to Siberia, under guard of an officer and seven soldiers. Passing through Moscow, they reached the town of Volodimir. Here they were joined by another sorry group of prisoners, who were under the guard of forty-six soldiers. Benyovszky names these fellow-prisoners: Vasilii Panov, Lieutenant of the Guards; Ippolit Stepanov, Captain of Infantry; Asaf Baturin, Colonel of Artillery; and Ivan Sofronov (or Solmonov), Secretary of the Senate of

Moscow. Like Winbladh, all four were Benyovszky's constant companions in the following months of exile. At Nizhney Novgorod, their guard was temporarily supplemented by no fewer than 150 horsemen, who gave them safe-passage as far as the town of Vyatka (present-day Kirov) before leaving them to make their way to Tobolsk, some distance towards Kamchatka, their ultimate destination.

This co-mingling of prisoners-of-war and standard Russian exiles should not surprise us. There was a constant and endless stream of exiles heading into Siberia from the cities of the Russian Empire. Given the travelling conditions of the time – appalling roads, barely-navigable rivers, independently-minded natives – there were good reasons not to have to organise separate transports for foreigners.

Benyovszky's group arrived at Tobolsk on 20th January 1770, where they rested for two weeks. Thence to Tomsk, arriving in April, then ever eastwards, scheming and plotting all the way, but unable to take advantage of any further opportunities for escape. Realising at length that it would be easier to escape eastwards from Kamchatka, than westwards from whichever bleak spot in which they might be stuck at the time, the prisoners made the best of their situation and travelled another 1,500 miles by horse, foot and dog-sledge, arriving in the port of Okhotsk in August (Benyovszky insists it was the 16th October, but we have good reason to doubt that). They had been travelling for a good eight months. Surprisingly, they arrived more or less intact.

It is a curious fact that many of the inhabitants of Siberia at that time were exiles of one degree or another. It was clearly not a place to which anyone went gracefully. It was also not a place anyone could leave with ease. A significant proportion of the exiles were foreigners – Germans, Swedes, Poles, French. Those who were not foreign were not at all happy. Those who were neither foreign nor exiles were usually the unhappiest of all. Many of the Cossacks under the command of the Governor of Okhotsk were perpetually on the verge of mutiny. However, despite the grim conditions, and weather always permitting, Okhotsk was flourishing. It was a trading-post at the very edge of the Empire, a rather dismal collection of wooden houses and warehouses, but vast quantities of furs were collected here from outlying areas – via Kamchatka – for forward export to European Russia or China. There are official figures of 310,000 animal skins being imported through Okhotsk in any given year. The Russian Far East was still for pioneers; the Russians had only gained a toehold on Kamchatka itself in 1700, with a proper colony established as late as 1740. A fine place, therefore, to which to send troublesome exiles: keep them out of the way and build up a lucrative fur-trade at the same time.

On 12th September 1770 our prisoners embarked on the supply-ship *St Peter and St Paul* (Benyovszky preferred to name the ship with both its saints rather than one, but since all other accounts kept simply to *St Peter,* we shall do the same hereinafter). En route, according to Benyovszky, the captain and crew got themselves drunk, became incapable or were otherwise inattentive. Benyovszky sensibly took command of the vessel and tried to bring it to the "coast of Korea"

– geographical knowledge was understandably vague; the island of Sakhalin, then under Japanese control, was the actual destination of choice. Winds and storms prevented them from landing here, and, in a final attempt to persuade the crew (now sober, capable and fully focussed again), to land on Sakhalin, he used an interesting stratagem. But "it was in vain that I made use of iron and garlick to falsify the compass."[3] The proverbial influence of garlic upon compasses had been disproved almost two centuries earlier,[4] but Benyovszky was clearly a desperate man. And alliaceous vegetables were all he had to hand.

The ship survived both storms and garlic. The prisoners were disembarked at the tip of Kamchatka, after a voyage of 800 miles, which had lasted twelve days. For a crossing of the Sea of Okhotsk this was really fast. The great "pedestrian traveller" John Dundas Cochrane made the same trip in 1821–1822 – the outward voyage took fourteen days, while the return took almost five weeks. Members of Captain Cook's expedition, who visited Kamchatka for three weeks in 1779, witnessed the arrival of the boat from Okhotsk, which had been thirty-five days in passage, of which a full fortnight was spent in sight of the coast, trying to enter a sheltered bay while passengers and crew rapidly ran out of fresh water.[5]

Kamchatka, wild frontier of the Russian Empire, was a land of active volcanoes, forests, fish, fog and lots of animals with fur. It is no different today – perhaps the number of furry animals is smaller. The peninsula is 800 miles in length and covers an area of around 100,000 square miles. There were a few tiny settlements scattered up and down its coastline. At this time, the principal administrative settlement was at Bolsheretsk, lying on the Bolshaya River 20 miles inland from the coast at the south-western tip of the peninsula; it contained thirty small buildings of various sorts, with a population of between 90 and 600 (depending on whom you believe), garrisoned by around forty-five to fifty soldiers. The civilian population of this pocket fortress comprised sailors, hunters, civil servants, boat-builders, priests, merchants and exiles. A very detailed official report of 1773 put the number of buildings at around fifty, with a garrison of 117, excluding officers. That the number of soldiers had increased was almost certainly due to the mass-escape led by Benyovszky in 1771.

In addition to the main settlement at Bolsheretsk, there were four smaller settlements on Kamchatka – one at Tigil Fort (Tigilskaya Krepost), further up the west coast; at the same latitude but on the east coast were Upper (Verkhne) Kamchatka and Lower (Nizhney) Kamchatka, and on a level with Bolsheretsk, and to the east, was the then tiny village of Petropavlovsk (now the capital of the peninsula). Together with a number of 'taxable' persons on the Kuril Islands, there were perhaps 400 individuals of interest to the government. "They send tribute annually of 279 sable, 464 red foxes, 50 Kamchatkan sea-otters, 1 female sea-otter, 38 young sea-otters; all of which yields 1530 roubles," explained an official report, with praiseworthy precision, in 1773.[6]

The total population of Kamchatka was around 4,000 at that time. A Russian geographer who stayed on Kamchatka in the 1730s, despite being moved to describe the natives as "nasty and stupid," documented their lives and works in tremendous detail. It was evident from his report that there was little commonality between natives and Russians, either in terms of religion, culture, social organisation or physical appearance. Trade was the only unifying factor. The clash of cultures bears uncanny resemblance to that between Native American peoples and Europeans in nineteenth-century America. The arrival of smallpox in 1768, brought from the mainland by soldiers and spreading like wildfire in native villages with little or no immunity, seems to have decimated the population – over the wider area of the Koriak lands to the north, Kamchatka and the Kuril Islands to the south, the death-toll was calculated at 20,000. In Kamchatka itself, official figures suggest that 5,767 natives and 315 Russians died (another contemporary account indicated 5,368 deaths in total, of whom 1,706 – crucially – were taxable). As a result of the epidemic, trading almost ceased and food supplies ran very low. Those who had been spared the smallpox began to succumb to starvation and despair. Many smaller settlements were ultimately abandoned in the face of depopulation. Captain Cook's expedition reported that

> no less than eight *ostrogs* [*were*] scattered about the bay of Awatska, all which [...] had been fully inhabited, but are now entirely desolate [...] At Paratounca *ostrog* there were but thirty-six native inhabitants, men, women, and children, which, before it was visited by the small-pox, we were told, contained three hundred and sixty.[7]

John Cochrane, who visited the peninsula some fifty years later, put the native Kamchadale population at 2,760 (plus, with a meticulousness over and above the call of duty, 2,808 dogs) and the Russian population at 1,200; he supposed – not without cause – that the native population had been, and still was, declining rapidly under assault from the triple evils of disease, alcohol and "the spirit of persecution."[8]

Animal life on Kamchatka largely comprised bears, other handsome furry creatures, salmon, lemmings and cows. An official report of 1773 advised that

> there are 587 cattle on the whole of Kamchatka. A cow costs [...] 25 to 50 roubles, a large ox 60 to 100, a pood [*ca. 36 pounds*] of fresh meat 4 to 6 roubles. These cattle eat tree-bark, the twigs of birch, aspen and willow, and will also happily eat fresh fish. Often they run to the river, place themselves in shallow water and catch exhausted fish from the raging torrent, without even bothering with the excellent meadow-grass on the bank.[9]

Fresh meat sold in Kamchatka at four times the price than was usual in St Petersburg or Moscow. Then, as now, the rivers of Kamchatka abounded in salmon, and it would have been more than possible for lumbering cattle to snap up fish as they ascended to their spawning grounds. All they had to do was avoid the bears. Other wildlife caused sporadic problems:

the whole of Kamchatka was plagued by mice in 1772. There were so many that some meadows were stripped bare of grass [...] In some places they stripped the trees of their bark and attacked the provisions [...] In Lower Kamchatka they caused a great deal of damage in the merchants' store-rooms.

"But," continues the 1773 report complacently, "this year there is no such plague."[10] Commerce was centred on the fur-trade in the Aleutian and Kuril Islands. Anything furnished with fur, tusks or blubber – ideally all three – was hunted down and killed, and the component parts shipped back to Russia. Many furs were transported laboriously to Khiakta on the Siberian-Chinese border, and there traded profitably with the Chinese: sale prices here were commonly twice those in Kamchatka. The native peoples of Kamchatka and of the outlying Kuril and Aleutian Islands contributed their share to the vast industry of slaughter, in exchange for tobacco, flour, trinkets and spirits. Captain Cook, in 1778, met some furriers who had come out from Okhotsk to the Aleutian Islands in 1776, and were not due to return home with their harvest until 1781; this was a serious and long-term business. Once a year, a ship would arrive in Kamchatka from Okhotsk in the autumn, over-winter near Bolsheretsk, and depart the following summer laden with furs. Frequently, other ships would take furs from the other Kamchatkan settlements.

The 1773 memorandum cited above makes especial note of the contribution to this economy of the merchant Ivan Popov: his ship

> returned from the American shores to Lower Kamchatka on 2 July 1772. Its main cargo was beaver and black foxes, and was divided into 55 shares. After the tax was paid, each share amounted to 18 beaver, 18 black foxes, 24 foxes with black bellies, 8 red foxes and 3 beaver-tails. A share could be sold on the spot for between 800 and 1000 roubles; the entire value of the cargo was probably around 55,000 roubles, but would probably fetch far more.[11]

If you consider that your best cow might be worth 50 roubles, and that this was only one ship out of several, the scale of the enterprise can be understood. The tax which Popov paid on this occasion was surrendered in furs to the value of 1,354 roubles and 48 kopeks.

But in 1770 all was not well in the fur-trade. There was a heavy cloud of discontent and open rebellion hanging over Kamchatka: one immediate side-effect of the catastrophic smallpox epidemic was a huge slump in the fur-trade, which in turn led to unemployment and dissatisfaction amongst the sailors and trappers of Kamchatka. Even amongst those who could still pursue their professions, morale was not high. One of the resident merchants of Bolsheretsk had sent out a small trading ship with a couple of dozen hunters aboard to harvest beaver on the Aleutian Islands in August of that year. But when the ship ran into trouble, barely having left the shore, the hunters and crew – although quite habituated to setbacks and hardship – simply refused to contemplate another attempt. The trip had to be abandoned.

Into such a powder-keg a match was dropped in the autumn of 1770. Between then and May 1771, Benyovszky and his companions managed to organise an audacious and successful mass-escape. We shall return to the details of that escape later. Before we do that, however, let us turn our sympathies on those in charge of civil authority in Kamchatka. They had much stress and tribulation to cope with.

Notes

1 Much of Benyovszky's early life and his activity in Poland is documented by Kropf, 1895, Vol.6, p.483 and Vol.7, pp.4–5; also by Voigt, 2007, pp.88–89. Brief genealogical details are provided in Appendix I (Section C) of the present book.

2 Belcour, 1776, pp.33–39 and *passim*.

3 Benyovszky, 1790, Vol.I, p.79.

4 See William Gilbert's work on terrestrial magnetism, *De Magnete*, 1600.

5 Cook/King, 1834, Vol.3, p.292.

6 Schlözer, 1780, p.351; also Coxe, 1780, pp.12–16.

7 Cook/King, 1834, Vol.3, pp.366–367.

8 Cochrane, 1825, Vol.2, p.46.

9 Schlözer, 1780, p.352.

10 *ibid*, p.356.

11 *ibid*, pp.346–347.

IV

KAMCHATKA

"Caviar and Cedar Nuts"

Some Unpleasantness Concerning the Government of Kamchatka – Smallpox
and Alcohol – A Fishy Diet – A Community of Exiles – Tales of Paradise

Grigorii Nilov had gone up in the world. His military career was at last worth something. He had been promoted out of Gizhiga, where he was chief of the small army garrison, and landed the job as Commander in Bolsheretsk. Bolsheretsk may have been a cold, wet, unwelcoming collection of thatched log-cabins huddled at the bottom of a vast and unforgiving wilderness. But Gizhiga?

Gizhiga could justifiably have been described as the back-end of nowhere. Founded in 1753, it was a tiny stockaded fortress situated near the mouth of the Gizhiga River, which flows into the Sea of Okhotsk at its north-eastern corner. Behind Gizhiga stretched hundreds of miles of mountains, snowy wastelands and recalcitrant native Koriaks and Chukchi. The climate was poor even by Siberian standards, and the residents had to put up with frequent sea-fogs and flooded streets. The harbour was difficult to access due to sandbanks. In the 1770s there were famine conditions due to the failure of crops. It was visited once a year (if you were lucky) by a supply-ship from Okhotsk. And not much else happened. The prime purpose of the fortress was to protect the land-route to Kamchatka from the natives but, since the sea-route was far more frequently used until the region to its north opened up to trade in the mid-nineteenth century, the land-route was only used in dire emergency. The fortress seems to have been retained purely as a deterrent to the unruly locals; there was a population of around 200 in 1770. Amongst them, Captain Nilov and his dependents.

Having established itself on Kamchatka in the early 1700s, Imperial Russia was faced with the near-impossible task of maintaining law and order there. Over such a vast area, and with a native population less than welcoming of the incomers – and the incomers less than welcoming of civic government, taxes and other burdensome interferences – a state of near-anarchy existed. The natives frequently rose up in rebellion. Energetic measures were required. St Petersburg, anxious for the spiritual well-being of its new children, sent in both soldiery and missionaries. As always happens, such actions only made matters worse.

Eventually, the Empire sent out a fixer. The man selected was a Latvian, Colonel Fedor Plenisner, until then stationed in Tobolsk. A seasoned Siberian explorer, he had been part of Vitus Bering's all-embracing second expedition from 1733 to 1743; Bering had sufficiently recovered from his first expedition which proved conclusively that Siberia and Alaska were not conjoined, being separated by the straits which now bear his name; the second expedition also yielded a lasting memorial for Bering, the island on which he died after being shipwrecked in 1741. Plenisner was subsequently assigned to other administrative and exploratory posts in the far east of Siberia. He was seconded to another expedition which had been despatched to survey the Aleutians and the Alaskan Peninsula in 1762. For his efforts, Plenisner was appointed Commander of the Okhotsk region in 1764. Until then, the original administrative centre of Kamchatka lay at Anadyrsk, to the north of the peninsula; it was Plenisner who argued that this place was now "useless" in the face of native Chukchi hostility and so it was abandoned in 1764. In his new appointment, based in Okhotsk, he had a brief to pacify as many native peoples as could be managed – a task beyond human powers, as he had already argued. Fortunately, his responsibilities also included the establishment of trading routes by sea and land, the promotion of agriculture, surveying, exploration, and all the other things a man might yearn to do at the very edge of the civilised world. Abuse of power, while not part of the job description, was undertaken in moderation. By order of the Governor of Siberia, part of Plenisner's territory included all of Kamchatka.

Alas, Plenisner's life was not made any easier by the decision of this same Governor to appoint another army man, Lieutenant-Captain Izvekov, to the post of Commander of Kamchatka a couple of years later. This appointment omitted to revoke Plenisner's responsibility for Kamchatka – something of an oversight. Izvekov was an interesting character: one report noted that "as regards immorality and harshness of manners [he] eclipses all his predecessors." Open robbery of the natives and atrocities perpetrated against the Russians were regular occurrences on his watch. Like Plenisner, he too had been granted unlimited power in re-establishing law and order amongst the population and in teaching them loyalty to their beloved Empress. And, like Plenisner, he was commissioned to explore any unknown "continents and islands" – something he was happy to undertake: he despatched a series of moderately catastrophic expeditions to the Kuril Islands to trade with the native Ainu people; these voyages all ended up in mutual distrust and bloody mayhem, and triggered a long drawn-out war of attrition between the Ainu and Russians.[1]

Clearly, these two men could not continue to govern Kamchatka in tandem for very long. Each man tried to treat the other as a subordinate, each refused to obey the other. Orders were received and scoffed at. Decrees issued by one party were annulled by the other. In the end, it all got too much for the residents of Kamchatka, who sand-bagged Izvekov and bundled him on to the next ship for Okhotsk. The Governor rolled his eyes and despatched a mediator to bang heads together. The Imperial Government had had enough of riot and chaos – after two prolonged uprisings by native peoples and Cossacks in 1711 and 1731, there was no appetite to become embroiled in yet another, this time of their own making. The Governor's man confined Plenisner to Okhotsk, and Kamchatka was removed from his area of responsibility, while Izvekov was placed under arrest for "follies committed and harsh measures employed" during his term of office. The town of Bolsheretsk was then named as the seat of government in Kamchatka. Finally Nilov was appointed as the new commander in August 1770, and the mediator went off home dusting his hands. Job done.

Captain Nilov, for his part, could not believe his luck. The commander's house in Bolsheretsk was a regular palace. Captain King of Cook's *Discovery* described it in 1779 as "much larger than the rest, consisting of three rooms of a considerable size, neatly papered, and which might have been reckoned handsome, if the talc with which the windows were covered, had not given them a poor and disagreeable appearance."[2] It was the most impressive building by far, larger than the log-cabins, than the "well-looking church," the court-room and the barracks. Another report rather revealingly states that in Bolsheretsk, in addition to the thirty or so houses, there was also "one publick-house for selling brandy, and one distillery." This was a small frontier town on the make. There was far more to do here than in Gizhiga. Boats from Okhotsk, after all, turned up two or three times a year. Trading expeditions to the Aleutian and Kuril Islands made this their base. And there was a flourishing community of exiles to look after, and they brought with them all their cultural baggage – distant and fading memories of polite society, theatres, books and conversation.

Most of which, apart from the distillery, was lost on Nilov. He was described by near-contemporaries as "poorly literate, broken by paralysis and eternally drunk."[3] But he is not here to defend himself.

Nilov arrived in these most comfortable of surroundings in the summer of 1770. He was not actually the Governor of Kamchatka, just the Commander. But it amounted to the same thing. His own Governor was some three thousand miles away, over sea, mountain and morass, and was unlikely to arrive unexpectedly, or often. Grigorii Nilov was accompanied by his young son, but not by his wife or any other children. It was perhaps intended that the rest of the family should ship out of Gizhiga at a later date – when the boat next called in from Okhotsk, for example; or perhaps they had seen sense and returned to some other part of Russia that they called home.

Barely had Nilov settled down to his rewarding responsibilities than a new shipload of trouble was dropped on his doorstep. The existing community of exiles had been quite tractable. Their leader at this time was one Pyotr Khrushchyov. Many of the exiles had been in Kamchatka for up to eight years, but some had been there much longer. Benyovszky mentions a Swedish gentleman aged 92 who had been living in exile in Kamchatka for twenty-two years. Another, Magnus Meyder, a physician of around 70 years of age, had been there twenty years. And there was Alexander Turchanin who had been exiled, along with his wife Anna, in 1742 for conspiring against the Empress Elizabeth (Anna was one of three exiles who was described as having "had her tongue cut out and her nostrils slit";[4] plotting against an Empress was no laughing matter). The remaining exiles were a hodgepodge of Poles, Swedes, court-officials, princes of obscure family, high-ranking army officers and so forth – in short, a typical cross-section of ordinary Siberian folk.

By the end of the eighteenth century, the tradition of sending political opponents to Siberia was already firmly established. It was difficult for your average Russian to guess quite how to position themselves politically, given the proclivity of their rulers to murder their predecessors or potential successors. With the help of the powerful Orlov family, Catherine herself ousted her own husband Peter III after his six-month rule, and made sure of his continued support by ordering his murder a couple of weeks later (officially, the cause of death was "haemorrhoidal colic" – a nasty complaint, as all will agree, though rarely fatal; unofficially, he was smothered between two mattresses and then strangled). It was all in the cosy family tradition, though: Peter had only come to power because his predecessor, Empress Elisabeth, had stepped in to prevent the accession of Ivan VI in 1741; Ivan, then barely eight weeks old, was locked up in a succession of strongholds, before being murdered by his guards during an escape attempt in 1764. Catherine's only legitimate son, Paul, was himself assassinated in 1801. Catherine managed to avoid being murdered, but her reign was peppered with plots and conspiracies of one sort or another.

A peculiar sideshow was the proliferation of suspicious characters who claimed to be the Emperor Peter III. It began in 1772 with a runaway serf and army deserter, calling himself 'Bogomolov' (the Pilgrim) who claimed to be Peter III and showed 'Tsar's marks' on his chest. He was quite reasonably arrested and sent to Siberia, but died en route. The following year, a Cossack named Pugachev did exactly the same thing, complete with the Imperial stigmata, with far more success; he kept the Imperial army at bay for 15 months, even captured and razed Kazan, before his defeat. By the end of Catherine's reign in 1796 up to two dozen impostors had appeared, all claiming to be Peter III. All were poor, illiterate, with stigmata. Even though he himself made no such pretension, one of the joint-rulers of the Adriatic principality of Montenegro in the 1760s was regarded as the born-again Peter III by his subjects.

Amidst all this, there were bouts of animosity against the Orlovs. In October 1763, Grigorii Orlov, occasional lover of the Empress, received a parcel from Moscow, containing a hollowed-out cheese filled with horse-dung and pierced with a truncheon. The symbolism is there for those who wish to see it. Seemingly untouched by it all, Catherine the Great stated, less than apologetically, that:

> It is not surprising that Russia has many tyrants amongst her sovereigns. The nation is naturally restless, ungrateful and filled with informers and men who

under the pretext of zeal try to turn everything in their path to their own profit.[5]

Naturally, all of this murder, seizure of power and other unpleasantness laid ungrateful and restless souls open to the twin threats of conspiracy and detection. In the small settlement of Bolsheretsk in 1770 there was now a fine collection of exiles, spanning three different reigns. At least four had been exiled by Elisabeth; more by Catherine. Asaf Baturin, who arrived in Kamchatka at the same time as Stepanov and Benyovszky, had more bad fortune than most. He had been holed up in a cell in the Schlüsselburg Fortress at St Petersburg since 1753, arrested for plotting against Elisabeth in favour of the Grand-Duke Peter Fedorovich, the future Peter III (no, the real one). On his accession in 1761, Peter stopped short of releasing Baturin, but did allow him better subsistence in his prison. Baturin, depressingly loyal, in his turn refused to believe that Peter died in 1762, and wrote notes to his guards and to Catherine, announcing that "scrutiny of the stars showed he [*Peter*] was alive, wandering in other lands, and he would return to Russia soon". When Catherine got her note, she ordered "the agitator and instigator" to be exiled to Kamchatka. There is a lesson for all of us here: best not to scrutinise the stars.

And then there was Khrushchyov. On 3rd October 1762, a mere 12 days after Catherine's coronation in Moscow, a "horrid conspiracy" was detected amongst the Izmailovskii Guards. Led by Pyotr Khrushchyov, they were plotting to install Ivan VI as Emperor (Peter III was by that time dead of his haemorrhoids, so Ivan was the next-best thing). An investigation was set up. Khrushchyov and others were beaten with sticks to get them to confess to further details – without success. Investigators concluded that it was all drunken posturing. It almost certainly had been. Catherine was outraged. Hurriedly, the investigators reviewed the evidence again and proposed death sentences for all those involved. The Senate duly confirmed death sentences on Khrushchyov and a man named Gusev. Catherine then played the always-popular leniency card and on 6th December 1763 commuted the sentences to "loss of rank, of status, and of surname, to have swords broken over their heads and then exile to Bolsheretsk forever." Two of Gusev's brothers, co-conspirators, were exiled to mainland Siberia. (Subsequently, all three Gusevs were pardoned because the first had not joined Benyovszky's escape from Kamchatka; they were allowed to return to their Russian estates west of the Urals. They pinched themselves all the way, unable to believe their good luck.)

The exiles who had been in Kamchatka for a while were resigned to their fate. But Commander Nilov was to find that Benyovszky and his party were altogether different.

Once he had cast his eye over the new arrivals, Nilov issued them with their equipment (to wit: food to last them three days, a hatchet and other tools for building their own cabins), and instructed them in the conditions of their exile (to wit: no cabins to be built closer than one league to the town, no absences from cabins to last longer than 24 hours, one day's unpaid *corvée* – forced labour – per week, one hundred roubles' worth of fur to be fetched to the chancellery per annum). Having clarified the rules to his own satisfaction, Nilov quickly passed them on to Khrushchyov and retired for a glass of something restorative. The leader of the exiles welcomed them warmly, and sat them in his 'yurt'. Here, Benyovszky says, "the women presented us with brandy and dried fish, and afterwards tea and butter; this breakfast was followed by a dinner, which consisted entirely of fish, and we were not without a dessert, composed of caviar and cedar nuts." Those who did not like fish were going to find it hard going: the new arrivals glumly noted that the statutory "provisions for three days" consisted of nine pounds of dried fish.

Billeted on Khrushchyov for the night, Benyovszky was delighted to find on the following morning that his host had contrived to maintain a library of sorts, "filled with French, Russian, English, German, and Latin books, placed in order." Mouldering in this treasure-trove was an edition of Lord Anson's *Voyage Round the World in the Years 1740–1744*. This had been something of a publishing hit 20 years earlier, relating in entertaining and colourful detail the story of George Anson's voyage into the Pacific; this book ("translated into the Sclavonian language") was the one which Benyovszky proudly brandished on his arrival at Macao – in all likelihood Khrushchyov's own copy. Anson had been sponsored and equipped by the British Admiralty, and his was a voyage of naked piracy against Spanish treasure-ships. One of the islands at which Anson's ship landed was Tinian in the Mariana Islands, described as a tropical paradise full of meadows, woods and valleys, water and fruits, coconuts and birds, cattle and hogs, limes and oranges. Khrushchyov admitted to dreaming of an escape to this heaven on earth, and Benyovszky stirred him up as best he could.

Over the next few weeks and months, the exile community got itself organised. The story of how this was done remains rather contentious. According to Benyovszky, it was achieved by his brilliance and personality alone, with Khrushchyov and the original exiles bowing (sometimes literally) to his greater energy, drive and authority; his sparkling personality also completely dazzled and wrong-footed Nilov, and rendered the civic and military authority helpless. Maybe so, maybe not; we shall examine these claims in more detail later. First of all, Ippolit Stepanov wishes to say something.

Notes

1   Lensen, 1971, pp.66–71.
2   Cook/King, 1834, Vol.3, p.215.
3   Sgibnev, 1876, p.528.
4   *ibid*, p.527.
5   Alexander, 1989, p.162.

V

STEPANOV'S ACCOUNT

"A Man Who Played an Active, but Unworthy Role"

Intrigue and Exile amongst Russian Officers – Misfortunes Come Not Singly –
Seventy in One Boat – Storms at Sea – Translations and Other Difficulties

Ippolit Stepanov was that most mundane of exiles – one who had done little wrong. A minor nobleman, he possessed extensive estates in the region around Moscow. His adult life was spent largely in military service, in the Preobrazhenskii Lifeguards, one of the oldest and most trusted infantry regiments in the Imperial Army. It was effectively the personal bodyguard of the Emperor or Empress of the day – up until 1762, Peter III, and then Catherine II, and all successors from then until 1917; at which point the guards, with equal enthusiasm, signed up to the February Revolution to overthrow the Emperor. Stepanov attained the rank of Captain in the regiment and then blew his chances of further progression by voicing the opinion that Catherine the Great should step down from power.

An account of Stepanov's career, passed down to us by Benyovszky's German translator Ebeling, suggests that the Captain had resigned from his regiment at the time of Catherine's seizure of power in 1762, and had then retired to his country estate. His rural retirement was rudely disturbed in 1768. New laws were being drafted and, in a passing fit of democracy, Catherine obliged the Governor of every region of Russia to send along two deputies to St Petersburg to vote through the legislation. The Moscow region elected Stepanov as one deputy; although it would seem that he had little say in the matter. After two months of sessional debate, Stepanov at last contrived to fall out with one of the leading members of the Congress.

Ebeling's version of the events must have come from Stepanov's own account; unfortunately, the original of that document has been lost. It is a version slightly at odds with another, drawn from the official Russian state archives. However, the two are not necessarily incompatible.

The official version states that Stepanov was one of four serving officers of the Preobrazhenskii regiment who attracted the notice of the secret police in 1769 by

> criticizing state policies, alleging that the Orlovs controlled Catherine, and advocating her overthrow in favour of Paul [...] A special court sentenced the four to death... [*But Catherine intervened and decreed that two of the group*], after "losing all ranks, noble status and calling, are to be sent eternally to Nerchinsk to factory work, but do not keep them together; Stepanov and Panov, after losing ranks and noble status, are sent to live in Kamchatka, where they will be fed by their own labour."[1]

Such ill-considered voicing of opinion was not uncommon in the early days of Catherine's reign. Later that same year, two other young guardsmen were denounced to the secret police for a similar plot. One was sent into exile in irons. Even in July 1772, another plot amongst the officers of the Preobrazhenskii regiment led to anything between 30 and 100 arrests.

Ippolit Stepanov's age at that time is indeterminate, but a reasonable guess might put him in his mid-thirties. Condemned for the same plot, and now in the same party that headed east into exile was his cousin Vasilii Panov, Lieutenant of the same guards regiment. It was something of a family affair.

We know of Stepanov's further adventures in Kamchatka and the North Pacific only from Stepanov himself – and, of course, from Benyovszky: the Hungarian kept a very special place for the noble Russian exile in his story, and it shall horrify and amuse us by turns. But have patience: we shall return to this later. There is no corroborating evidence of Stepanov's activities in any of the available official archives, many of which have been lost through the years due to revolution, wars and mice, not to mention a disastrous fire in Irkutsk in 1879, which destroyed the larger part of the town, including 4,000 houses, the Governor's residence, the archives of the Siberian government and a whole tinderbox full of municipal buildings, libraries and museums.

Stepanov's first misfortune was to get arrested and exiled. After his arrival in Macao at the end of the remarkable voyage of escape, Stepanov suffered a second misfortune, which was to fall out with Benyovszky. This did not leave him in a strong position, and when he then attempted to have Benyovszky arrested in Macao, he created for himself his third misfortune, which was to be left behind when his companions clambered hopefully aboard French ships bound for Mauritius. His other attempts at taking a ship to Europe having failed, Stepanov ended up booking passage on a Dutch East India Company boat heading for Batavia (now Jakarta) in Indonesia. Here he languished penniless and hopeless for a few short years before expiring in misery in June 1778. While languishing, however, he wrote up his own account of the events of 1770 and 1771.

His journal suffered as many misfortunes as the man himself. It was written in Russian. A Dutch preacher, resident in Batavia, acquired the diary from Stepanov

– probably after he had died – and took it back to the Netherlands. Here he translated it into Dutch and published extracts in a weekly newspaper printed in Amsterdam. These edited extracts attracted sufficient interest to be translated further into French[2] and finally to be rendered into German where they were included in a Hamburg edition of Benyovszky's own journal in 1791. Thus, all that is left to us of Stepanov's doubtless careful chronicle is a set of extracts, translated from Russian into Dutch, from Dutch into French, and from French into German (but never back into Russian), all posthumously. A further misfortune for Stepanov is that the man who published him in German, the schoolmaster Ebeling, was a die-hard opponent of the Stepanovian version of events.

"This remarkable essay came from a man who played an active, but unworthy role in the story of Count von Beniowsky," wrote our schoolmaster sternly. He continued:

> For all that this extract is short and incomplete, it is written with a bias: thus the author will already be known to the readers of [*Beniowsky's*] book and his words should be compared to Beniowsky's story, which he mostly confirms. Here the report is reproduced without any alteration, without considering whether both reports completely complement each other, or whether Beniowsky's credibility gains or loses by the comparison. Readers will of course not forget who Stefanov was, and what character he displayed throughout, however mercifully he was treated by the Count, who was always ready to forgive him.[3]

Herr Ebeling was being rather disingenuous when he assured us that Stepanov's report is reproduced without any alteration: by now Stepanov had suffered the indignity of having his diary pass through the mincer of threefold translation, and – somewhere along the line – rendered into a third-person narrative. Some of the facts about the exile's original arrest may also have been mangled along the way. But in order to tell Stepanov's story, we shall just heap one more indignity upon it, by translating into English Ebeling's version of the unfortunate Captain's diary. The story is not a long one, and begins thus:[4]

> After an extremely arduous journey lasting ten months, he finally arrived in Bolsheretsk in October 1770, a small town in Kamchatka. Here he lived for eight months in the greatest misery, and then he reached a bold decision with some of his comrades, to escape in a small vessel and sail to the Chinese coast which lay opposite to the Barscherevskisch Channel [*Bolshaya River*], and from there to travel to Europe. For this plan it was necessary to seize the first advantageous opportunity, and secretly steal one of the small two-masted vessels which were used here for hunting beaver. From there they planned to sail to the Spanish island of Guam.

So far, so Benyovszkian, albeit with the exclusion of the main man.

The Governor of Bolsheretsk then had the idea of treating his prisoners particularly harshly at the start of the Spring season. Stepanov therefore brought all those together whom he had involved in his plans. There were thirty-two of them, a sufficient number to overpower all the inhabitants of the place who might have been of any danger. Their enterprise had so few difficulties since the place had no fortifications and no other protection than three cannon and six soldiers. This plan was carried out on 18th April. First of all the plotters took possession of the Imperial coffers and all the supplies of food, disarmed the garrison, and then moved across country to Tschekavka, around forty *versts* from Bolsheretsk, which they reached on 1st May. The first thing they had to do was to free their ship, which already lay here at anchor, from the ice, for although the coast of Kamchatka is often free of ice earlier, sometimes at the start of April, the place where the ship lay often found itself in the shadow of towering mountains which catch the rays of sun until June and weaken its strength. After eleven days, all was ready and the ship, which they named *St Peter* was made ready with everything necessary for a long journey. They now elected a leader and set out to sea, cannon firing, on 12th May. The company now consisted of thirty-two free citizens, one merchant, one chancellor, one secretary, nine sailors, one pilot, seven inhabitants of Kamchatka, one Kuril, eight exiles or slaves, two Russian lads, four married women and two girls, the daughters of the pilot Tchurin, all in all 70 people.

It is evident from the extract above that Stepanov considered himself one of the ringleaders of the plot to escape; and also that he did not find it particularly difficult to arrange for it to happen. His statement that there were seventy people aboard the ship when it left is consistent with another account which we shall shortly examine. It was an interesting mix of voyagers, all united by a burning desire to leave Kamchatka. The main difficulty was that the 'pilot' really had no knowledge of the seas beyond Kamchatka, and none of those on board had much of a grasp of regional geography. One of Stepanov's several translators clearly had little idea either, as the next few sentences will demonstrate – bear in mind as you read them that the Kurils lie south-west of the Kamchatka Peninsula and what lies north and east are the Aleutian Islands. More specifically, what lies north and east of Chekavka, at the mouth of the Bolshaya River, is dry land: Kamchatka itself. But we can rest assured that it was indeed the Kurils that they presently reached.

> The voyage began in a north-easterly direction in strong winds, in an attempt to clear the coast; then because of the contrary winds and stormy weather they headed northwards, and finally eastwards. After two days they saw one of the Kuril Islands, which they left to starboard as they passed. On the third day they ran a great danger of shipwreck because of a mighty storm which was accompanied by thick fog; so they dropped anchor and immediately sent out a boat made of whale-skin, to take some people to the coast where they

could explore and try to find a safe harbour. They only found a small bay whose entrance was three fathoms deep, and anchored there. Here they lay from the 18th May to the 12th June, and in that time they made themselves ready again for departure, baked biscuit and bread and then continued their voyage south-south-eastwards before the prevailing east-wind. The sea was occasionally very calm and the currents and tides were advantageous. When they had reached a position, by their calculation, amongst the 'Thief' [*Ladrones*] or Marian Islands, their food supplies began to run out, for they had nothing left but stinking water and a little flour. The crew of the ship therefore began to get restless and displeased. So they had to steer in another direction and try to reach the mainland of China and Japan.

What Stepanov does not mention here, but other accounts do, was that a number of mutineers were abandoned on one of the Kurils. Amongst them was the sailor Izmailov, from whom we shall hear later. Having had their first taste of freedom upon the high seas, not all were anxious to continue. Those who did soon became twitchy, with good reason. We note the words "*a position, by their calculation*": since the Mariana Islands lie a good 2,500 miles from the Kurils, it was a calculation based solely on wishful thinking. Their goal, depending on whom you believe, was either Tinian or Guam in the Mariana Islands. But if they really supposed themselves to be close to their goal, the decision to head off in a contrary direction was odd, and probably based on an uncomfortable realisation that they had not the slightest inkling where they were. They sailed off before the wind and reached Japan.

In the beginning an uncommonly advantageous wind drove them along for two days, until suddenly a terrible storm came in from the south-west. Towards evening they reefed in all the sails, and left up only the single sail on the foremast, which was shredded an hour later by the wind. Now there was nothing else they could do except let the wind and the waves crash over them. The entire sky was covered with black clouds, the rain crashed down in torrents, the storm grew fiercer with every minute, wave upon wave towered up towards the clouds; the ship sprang a leak, a part of the cargo had to be thrown overboard, on the third day the gale tore down a pennant – the sailors took this as an unmistakeable sign that they were about to go down – and yet Providence rescued them once more from this terrible peril.

On the fourth day the sea became calm again, the wind vanished completely in place of the gale and on the following morning, after the air had cleared, they found themselves in a latitude of 33 degrees. Shortly after that they sighted land. As they believed themselves to be not far from Nangasaki, they hoisted their green flag, for they thought it wise to appear to be Dutchmen, and on the same evening they anchored in 40 fathoms of water close to the coast, where they saw various fires.

At that time, Nagasaki was the sole European trading-post in Japan, and it was permitted only to the Dutch East India Company to be there. Masquerading as Dutchmen was therefore well-advised.

> On the following morning before dawn, Stepanov, along with Major Windla [*Winbladh*] and eight men took a sloop to land on the coast to look for fresh water. It was impossible for them to land without being seen by the inhabitants by the light of their watch-fires. The Japanese came out in crowds and surrounded them. Since Stepanov and his people pretended to be Dutchmen, they were advised, by means of signs, to move further northwards up the coast; they became more trusting of each other, and the Japanese began to examine the clothes and weapons of our foreigners, from whom they received all kinds of presents of shirts, belts, silks and so on. But as the crowds increased, Stepanov decided it would be wise to get back on board again; however, he left six of his people behind. These men received from the inhabitants a good supply of rice and water, which they brought on board, whereupon they raised anchor and sailed northwards along the coast past several islands, to try and find a convenient landing-place. Towards evening they came across a flotilla of small boats who showed them a good harbour. Since they experienced a total lack of wind on the 10th July, they had to warp their ship, greatly assisted by the Japanese. Here they supplied themselves again with water and food. Four Japanese boats also stayed beside the ship, as protection, although they still kept a good eye on it.
>
> On the 11th July the commander and Stepanov left the ship to go ashore. They were met by various boats full of Japanese who, by means of signs and gestures, made it clear to them that they advised against this intention, since it would otherwise cost them their heads. The Russians therefore went back to their ship and sealed up their water-barrels. On the twelfth day the Japanese brought them some water, which was scarcely enough for one day; but they refused to hand over any more. The Russians nevertheless then sent their barrels on to land under the protection of several armed men, and the inhabitants came out and brought them rainwater to last them approximately two days. They contented themselves with that and made sail again, heading in a south-south-easterly direction.

We do not as yet have any clues as to where they were, but we shall find out later. Their next port of call was "an unknown land." This is unhelpful. However, latitude positions are provided – these, along with some specific depth-measurements, suggest that Stepanov had sight of the official ship's log, jealously guarded by Benyovszky.

> On the seventh day they discovered an unknown land and, when they approached the coast, found a bay where they lay at anchor until the 1st

August. This was the island of Usmaski which lay on the 28th latitude. Here they took on water and biscuit.

As with virtually every Chinese or Japanese place-name cited by the participants in this voyage, the place "Usmaski" is a little difficult of identification. Benyovszky rendered the same place as "Usmay Ligon," one of the "Lequeio Islands," and all evidence suggests it is one of the Ryükyü Islands, Amami-Oshima, to the south of Kyushu Island.

They then proceeded to "Termora" – Formosa (present-day Taiwan).

When they then continued on their voyage, they discovered land on the evening of the tenth day at 29 degrees north. They believed that they had now reached the island of Termora; just then they were becalmed; so they could only approach land three days later, and dropped anchor in forty fathoms of water. Since some sailors who had been sent in the boat to bring back news from the coast reported that the inhabitants had fired upon them, it was decided to sail on further. They went around the coast of the island and set their course southwards. A very blustery wind and strong currents drove them towards the promontory of an island, which they were quite close to when some of the inhabitants came towards them in small boats and showed them a bay which they entered and where they replenished their water. On the following morning, when they were trying to take on more water, some of the crew, who had decided to bathe in a small stream, were attacked and killed by the inhabitants. Stepanov immediately made a landing with thirty-three of his companions in order to avenge the death of his unhappy compatriots. Against him were ranged three or four thousand armed inhabitants; but the Russians who had divided themselves into three groups, advanced on the enemy with fearless courage, struck several parties of them about the head, dispersed the rest and, when they pursued them, burned down nearly a thousand of their huts. After this exceptionally fortunate victory, they went back on board again and on the 20th August continued their voyage. They wanted to get to Manila but were driven northwards by contrary winds. On the following day they sailed eastwards before a full wind and after a six-day voyage they caught sight of land. They followed the coastline and the first Chinese place that they reached was Tschinchina. Here they rested for five days and then sailed on, after they had taken on water and a coastal pilot.

The place named "Tschinchina" has bewildered many lively and enquiring minds. If the name refers to a place on the Chinese mainland then the most likely location is Dongshan Island, within striking distance of Formosa, and northwards along the coast from Macao.

After Formosa, they sailed to mainland China.

On the 22nd September they came without mishap to Macao, without losing a single one of the ship's company, apart from the aforementioned three people killed. Here they sold their ship for 3,960 Dutch guilders.

Stepanov had the misfortune that one of his companions, who had made himself out to be a Hungarian Baron, made so many difficulties for him in Macao that he ended up in prison; but he was released after a little time. It was in vain that he tried for a long time to be sent to Lisbon, in order to prove his innocence, but his hopes were disappointed. However, the Governor of Macao gave him a certificate of his good behaviour, with a permit to go to Batavia; which is where he went, but soon after his arrival he died in miserable circumstances.

Stepanov refers to Benyovszky in the end merely as "one of his companions." We get no sense here that Stepanov regarded the Hungarian as his superior, even though it is evident that Benyovszky was the one who had been elected the leader just before they sailed away from Kamchatka. And this is the man in whose close company Stepanov had spent most of the preceding two traumatic years of his life. Clearly, by now he was fed up with the Hungarian Baron, self-proclaimed or otherwise.

Another point we should note, because it is highly relevant when we examine a different account of this voyage: the date of departure from Kamchatka (12th May) is old style; the date of arrival at Macao is new style. The confusion is understandable, since Macao was under Portuguese control, and the Portuguese had been using that new-fangled Gregorian calendar for almost two hundred years. When the weary voyagers lurched off their stinking ship at Macao, they had no reason to doubt what date they were told. Eleven days gained or lost was largely irrelevant; it was enough that they were still alive. However, it is just as likely that Ebeling had changed the date given by Stepanov in order to make it chime with Benyovszky's account, according to which they arrived on 22nd September (NS): Stepanov's own chronology set out above suggests that they were at "Tschinchina," a mere 250 miles from Macao, not long after the 27th August. It did not take them – not even them – four weeks to make that short hop.

The "difficulties" in Macao which Stepanov complains about were caused by a disastrous dispute between Benyovszky and his crew. The Hungarian was keen to get shot of the ship and its remaining cargo of furs which had been liberated from government and private stores in Kamchatka. To this end he took it upon himself to sell the lot. Benyovszky himself reported later that the living expenses of his entire crew while in Macao would amount to 6,200 French *piastres* per month (rather bizarrely, he also ran up a tailor's account to have red and white uniforms made up for everyone: total cost 8,000 *piastres*). He therefore sold the furs (488 beaver, 500 sable, "180 dozen" ermines) through a Dominican priest, which brought in 28,440 *piastres*. "A scanty pittance!" fulminated Benyovszky – scarcely enough to live on. More seriously, however, the entire crew – who had not been consulted on the acquisition of the elegant red and white uniforms – were a little aggrieved at being cut out of the profits from the voyage. They then discovered that Benyovszky was also engaged in secret negotiations with the British, French and Dutch trading companies, all three simultaneously, with a view to selling to the highest bidder his log-book and all the supposedly profitable trading information contained therein. Attempting to seize the priceless log-book for themselves, Stepanov and Winbladh confronted him in the name of the rest of the crew. It did them no good, since Benyovszky was nothing if not a consummate schemer and had already squared things with the authorities. The two ringleaders found themselves briefly under house arrest.

When Benyovszky finally threw in his lot with the French, Stepanov saw an opportunity for revenge. He wrote to the Dutch agent and through him denounced Benyovszky to the Chinese Government as an escaped convict who had stolen both the ship and its cargo, and who, under utterly false pretences, had enticed his associates to leave Kamchatka. Bad news travels fast, they say – but perhaps not in the eighteenth century: it was almost a year later, at the beginning of August 1772, that the Government of Irkutsk received, through its frontier 'commissary' at Khiakta, intimation from Peking that the *St Peter* had arrived at Macao in September of the previous year, with valuable goods, and that the men in possession of her had declared her cargo to be Russian goods from the river Amur, intended for export to the East Indies.

But by this time the guilty voyagers were already half the planet away, in France.

Notes

1   Alexander, 1989, pp.162–164.
2   Ebeling, 1791, Vol.II, p.283.
3   *ibid*, Vol.II, p.283.
4   The quoted passages from Stepanov's story are all taken from Ebeling, 1791, Vol.II, pp.284–292.

VI

RYUMIN'S ACCOUNT

What Happened, and Other Things, and so on

Rebellion in Kamchatka – Mutiny on the Kurils – Deceit in Japan –
An Island of Infinite Bounty – Murder and Retribution – Untrustworthy Pilots –
Macao – Journey to Mauritius – The Singular Wonders of Paris

Ippolit Stepanov, swallowed up by poverty and disease in Batavia, had one tale to tell; it was short. Ivan Ryumin had another one; it was longer. Ryumin, a clerk by profession, was described by one contemporary as "that wily Cossack." He had at one time been a clerk in the Kamchatka Chancellery. But he fell foul of the Governor in 1766, after he had refused – for reasons doubtless pecuniary – to divulge to a governmental inquiry the details of certain fishy trading expeditions to the Fox Islands. When his deceit was discovered (sadly, he was unmasked by the very traders he had been covering up for), he was whipped, then demoted to a mere 'Cossack' in government service. Notwithstanding this setback, over time he managed quietly to re-enter the ranks of clerks, exploiting to the full the chaos surrounding the hotly-contested governorship.

Ryumin, with some assistance from two fellow-voyagers, Spiridon Sudeikin and Dmitrii Bocharov, put together a short account of his great adventure. On their arrival in Paris in April 1772 the document was handed to the Russian ambassador; the ambassador, with admirable good sense, immediately forwarded it to St Petersburg. On receipt of Imperial instructions, four months later, the ambassador bundled the small group of survivors aboard a vessel sailing for Russia.

Ryumin's chronicle was carefully squirreled away in the Russian Imperial archives, and gathered dust – until Mr Berg turned up.

The energetic Russian historian Vasilii Berg wrote a bewildering number of books and essays covering naval history (Russian and British), polar exploration, the history and geography of Russia, lives of admirals and Tsars – about anything, in fact, that twitched in a vaguely Russian or historical manner. In the early 1820s, while Berg was busily ransacking the archives in St Petersburg to stoke his literary boiler, he came across Ryumin's report which had been delivered nearly fifty years earlier. In 1822, he published the 'Papers of the Chancellery Clerk Ryumin Concerning his Adventures with Benyovszky' (*Flucht des Grafen Benjowsky aus Kamtschatka nach Frankreich*) in St Petersburg, and the full story (in nine chapters) of the great escape from Kamchatka could be read by an appalled Russian public for the very first time.[1]

In dramatic fashion, the subtitle of the first chapter of the account promises to describe:

> *The destruction of the town of Bolsheretsk and the capture of the Office of the Treasury and money and other things, and the murder of the local Commander, and the departure from the town to the sea, by boats on the river to the harbour, and the embarkation on board the government ship, and so on.*

The chapter headings could be the work of Berg, but are in much the same style as the words of Ryumin himself. The beauty of Ryumin's narrative lies in its unassuming and very direct approach to the subject matter. There is very little embroidery – except, as we shall see, when it comes to things to eat. He tells it like it was. For that reason, we shall simply follow his narrative to tell the full story of the escape from Kamchatka, only paraphrasing where required. (Note that Ryumin chose to spell his glorious commander's name as *Beysposk* – we have changed this wild spelling to avoid confusion.)

The First Chapter

The destruction of the town of Bolsheretsk etc.

"On the night of 26th to 27th April in 1771," he begins,

> the Polish rebel and vagabond Benyovszky, and the Swede Vinbland, together with other people, attacked the Commandant's government house without warning, and by force of arms broke into it, located the commander Captain Nilov in his bedroom and, in an attempt to capture him, killed him dead. Then they proceeded to the Kamchatkan government office in Bolsheretsk and attacked it as well.

The rebels thereupon looted the treasury, removing all the sable and fox furs which had been delivered up as tax payments. And finally they set up guns and a mortar, charged them with buckshot and placed a guard.

At dawn the following day, Benyovszky ("as it turned out," writes Ryumin in a rather surprised voice, "he was the main instigator and leader") consolidated his possession of the government buildings; he gave orders to the two clerks, Ryumin and Sudeikin, and to three apprentice sailors to collect all the alcohol from all the buildings in the town and to set a guard over it. At the same time, Benyovszky seems to have made a number of reparations to various merchants and traders of the town, distributing cash drawn from the governor's treasury. Ryumin's account does not explain this largesse, but one suspects it may have been a gentlemanly settling of gambling accounts.

On the 28th of the month, having arranged for the burial of the unfortunate Nilov in the Holy Church of the Assumption, Benyovszky ordered the Cossacks and residents to build rafts and boats on the river near the town; on the following day, eleven such boats were loaded with guns, gunpowder and ordnance, as well as wine, food and rye flour from the state-owned stocks, and all the furs they could lay hands on, and floated down the river. All the Cossacks and every other able-bodied man was rounded up to assist in this effort, leaving Benyovszky behind in Bolsheretsk with the sailor Vasilii Sofyin, the two of them guarding all the stocks of alcoholic liquor and spirits which remained in the town.

By the 30th, all of these supplies had safely arrived at the mouth of the river. The rafts and boats were drawn up on the bank of the river and everything was unloaded and stored in a large tent. Benyovszky then ordered the navigator Tchurin to arrange for the galliot *St Peter* to be made ready for sea. By the efforts of Tchurin and his crew, the ship, which had been encased in ice for the past few months, was ready for the voyage within a couple of days, taken out from the harbour and moored at the mouth of the river.

The Second Chapter

The exit of the galliot St Peter *from mouth of the Bolsheretsk river to the sea, and the arrival at the Kuril Islands, and what happened there, before the departure again to sea.*

"On the 12th May, Benyovsky ordered all available people at the mouth of the river to transport all the supplies and materials to the ship, and then for the crew to raise anchor." And off they went. Left behind on the banks were all those who had previously "been taken hostage" and obliged to carry out the hard labour of loading up the ship – these included the sailor Sofyin, several merchants, and a number of soldiers from the garrison. Sofyin was appointed as an unofficial interim commander, with the unenviable task of staying behind to present some plausible story for the investigation that was sure to follow.

> The sails were unfurled and they went to sea. They sailed on the sea from the 12th until the 16th May, and on the afternoon of the 16th they saw a small unknown island, which they passed. During the night they glimpsed a number of other islands and on the morning of the 17th they caught sight of a large island.

These were the Kuril Islands. It was evident that no one was entirely clear either where they were or what to do next, so the discovery of a "large island" was something of a blessing. On the 18th, they found a bay in which they could shelter, sailed in and dropped anchor. Benyovszky then sent some of the crew ashore with a small landing-party, with strict instructions to find out what the island was like and whether anyone was living on it. They returned some time later, reporting rather unhelpfully that they had found nothing at all – but lugging a small dog native to the Kurils. And, a little mysteriously given that no one but a dog could be found, they offered the intelligence that this was the seventeenth of the Kuril Islands, by the name of Goat Island (*Ikoza*); the seventeenth island from the north, now known as Simushir, was once named Marikan – conveniently, this is where other reports locate their landfall.

That night was spent aboard ship, but on the 19th May,

> people went ashore to the beach to make bread and ships-biscuit, and did repairs on board, and sewed English flags and pennants, which were set at the mast-head, and for all that we stayed on the island until the 29th of May.

Quite why the deceptive flags were to be English is not explained; the basic plan, outlined elsewhere by others, was to head for a Spanish island, and anyone who had read Anson would know that flying an English flag in Spanish seas would be tantamount to offering the ship up for target practice.

So there they sat, busily preparing for the longer voyage, for a period of eleven days. In that time, enthusiasm for the whole project cooled; mutinous feelings welled up to the surface. A plot was discovered. It had been instigated by "the apprentice sailor Gerasim Izmailov, the Kamchadale Alexei Parantsin and his wife Lukerya Ivanova." Benyovszky dealt swiftly and decisively with them, by ordering them to be flogged, taken ashore by boat and abandoned. "For food they were given some rye flour." Several of the crew who protested at this treatment were also flogged when it was established that, "as children of the fatherland, they had set out to capture the ship and head back to the mouth of the Bolsheretsk river." As the ship raised anchor, unfurled its sails and headed out of the bay, the passengers and crew could see Izmailov, Parantsin and his wife screaming and crying on the shore. Ryumin reported that "every decent person on board was filled with tears and regret."

The fellow-conspirators could count themselves lucky to be still aboard.

The Third Chapter

Follows the galliot St Peter *from the Kuril harbour to the Japanese coast, and their stay in the Japanese bay, and the things that happened, before leaving for sea again.*

After a week at sea, and despite the company of the small Kurilian dog, those aboard the *St Peter* were bored. There had been nothing of interest to observe, save, perhaps, a few more islands of the Kuril chain crawling past on their starboard side. But then Ryumin finds the excitement he so craved:

on the night of the 6th June, we suddenly saw fire or light in the air at the bow, and it lasted for a short time. The Europeans, being used to seafaring, took this as a good sign and praised the Mother of God. And again on the 9th, the same light was seen, lasting only a short time.

A week later, the voyagers "saw countless different kinds of fish in the sea, some of which were entire flocks flying above the water on wings." Luckily, someone had read Anson, who had also described shoals of flying fish, so it was understood that these fish could

> fly above the water for the distance of a hundred fathoms or more [...] fleeing the fish named the bonito, which chases after it and catches it for food. The bonito can weigh ten pounds or more, and is like a kind of carp, but fatter and the flesh is red, which we used as food. On the 16th, a not inconsiderable fish was caught in the sea, clinging to which we found two small fish, with considerable feathers, and we ate them. They had a very fair amount of flavour.

Apart from observing fish and the odd celestial miracle, the next three weeks were barely endurable. The sun and heat were intense, and the voyagers were suffering from a lack of fresh water. Their food supplies began to run out: by now they were subsisting on biscuit and rye bread which were already beginning to go mouldy. The flat-bottomed galliot flopped along on the high seas, heading steadily south-westwards. On the night of the 2nd July, a storm hit them and it lasted three days and nights:

> at which time, all were in despair of being saved. The storm grew worse and the ship was tossed about, with all the cargo below deck being thrown from one side to the other, and we were nearly overturned. But on the morning of the 6th, the weather changed and the storm subsided.

The next day, they caught sight of land to starboard, and directed their course to a small bay which they reached as evening fell. Here they saw a number of lights on the shore.

> And in the morning, that is, on the 8th July, we saw people standing on the shore, who waved their hands, advising us that we should not land on that island and pointing to us to move away to sea; but our appointed leader, the Hungarian Benyovszky, ordered the ship's boat to be let down, and sent the Swede Vinbland and Ippolit Stepanov with a strong landing-party on to shore.

When they had landed, they found themselves surrounded by people "who," Ryumin reported gravely, "were all Japanese." The landing-party were invited into the houses, and there provided with wine and rice, which they brought back to their boat. Accompanied by locals in their own boats, they returned to the ship. The Japanese were received warmly, and gave the voyagers to understand, through signs, that there was a bay to the north on their island, where the ship could anchor and take on fresh water. They then guided the ship there with a flotilla of their own boats. "The bay was overlooked on the starboard side by mountains and forest, and on the other side by the Japanese houses, which were much like those in our own Russian villages, being built of wood and stone."

Note, incidentally, the Russians' slightly uneasy nomenclature of new types of food. Rice was described by Ryumin as "*Sorochinskoe psheno*," that is, wheat from the Ukrainian village of Velyki Sorochyntsi. Rice, when it was first introduced into Russia, was known as 'Saracen wheat,' or *Saratsinskoe psheno*, but the first word was soon transmuted into a more homely reference to that popular Ukrainian fair which attracted buyers and sellers from far and wide – possibly even Saracens bearing sacks of rice. Ryumin here consistently refers to the Japanese staple food as "Sorochinsky wheat." But for simplicity we have adopted the more popular term 'rice.' Saracen wheat is, of course, one of the French names for buckwheat, (*blé sarrasin*) a completely different type of grain introduced to Europe by the Moors of Spain. Buckwheat, in Russian, is known as 'Greek wheat,' having been introduced into Russia by the Greeks; and so Russian buckwheat is not Saracen wheat, which was, if you are still keeping up, rice.

Despite the initial helpfulness of the locals, the Russians encountered difficulties when they attempted to land and take on fresh water; the ship's boat was prevented from landing, the Japanese indicating that it was forbidden.

> And so we rowed back to the ship, and in the evening they brought us some water and rice, and set a night-guard around the vessel, two boats at anchor with lighted paper lanterns, which kept guard day and night, until we went back to sea, so we were not allowed to land.

The next day, Benyovszky attempted to land again, and again met resistance. On this occasion, however, some priests or monks turned up and came to visit the ship. "These were lamas or monks," explained Ryumin carefully,

> who went on bare feet, and wore a dress made of light silk and paper, which they called '*azyamy*,' or robes of different colours – the lamas wore white and the monks black and white. All had shaved heads, but some wore Japanese swords and these were military men. They wore the hair on their heads with the front half shaved back – they called it 'the head of the moon,' since they worshipped the moon – and wore a sort of suit made of white bandages, which were wound so tightly that they could not get out, they do not wear caps, but rather pretty straw hats, carried fans, and umbrellas to protect them from the rain, and had boxes attached to patent leather belts, which contained tobacco and pipes, because they always smoke tobacco.

The women and girls are very beautiful, and they wear their hair like a tail, pinned up.

At this point, Benyovszky revealed to the Japanese that the *St Peter* was really a Dutch vessel and that they were heading for Nagasaki, which was said to lie about 50 *versts* or more from their present position. In reporting this entirely reasonable deceit, Ryumin's account agrees with that of Stepanov. The English flags, so carefully stitched together in the Kurils, had been quietly tucked away out of sight. "We gave them sables and other things, including Russian vodka, and they, in return, brought us water, rice and Japanese wine." The basic niceties of civilised trade had been satisfied: alcohol had been exchanged. On the 11th of the month, the Japanese brought more barrels of water, a barrel of wheat (or rice?) and a sack of salt. Benyovszky had composed a letter to the Dutch in their tiny depot at Nagasaki, and asked the Japanese to send it on.

This was such an interesting letter that the Dutch carefully sent it home to the archives. We shall see what it said – soon.

Since Ryumin can provide no place-name for this town, we must look for clues in the description. The place at which they were anchored was said (by someone) to be around 30 miles from Nagasaki. As they were leaving, the Russians were advised that a "most powerful" place described as "*Meakam*" was "not far away"; 'Meaco' is the old name of the city of Kyoto. Kyoto and Nagasaki are a long way apart by sea. Half-way between them is the island of Shikoku, which, for reasons to be explained later, we shall select as their location.

On the 12th July, Benyovszky gave the orders to raise the anchor, set the sails and prepare to depart. At the last moment, the Japanese asked them politely to stay one more night. With some alarm, the crew noticed that the boats that surrounded them that morning had weapons aboard. A few minutes of panic ensued, the Russians suspecting that the Japanese wished to kill them, they being "idolaters and haters of the baptised." It would seem that the locals had been in touch with higher authorities in Kyoto and had been belatedly instructed to detain the foreigners.

However, the foreigners retained enough sense to prime the ship's guns, and fire some warning shots. At this,

the Japanese were smitten with fear and made haste back to the shore. We then weighed anchor, unfurled the sails and went to sea. We learned later when we reached Macao that the Japanese people had burned two Spanish ships and a third one had barely escaped, while many of the people on board had been tortured and killed.

The Fourth Chapter

The departure of the galliot St Peter *from the Japanese bay and the arrival at the Bashinski islands, where people called Usmaitsi live, and of staying there and then continuing the voyage.*

After leaving the bay on the 12th July, the galliot sailed on for another three days; some more Japanese boats came up with them, and sailed alongside for a few hours. The following four days were spent at sea, seeing nothing, until, on the 19th, they spied land to starboard. This was

> a great island with high mountains and rocks, and to port was more land, a small island of the same appearance. We approached the big island at nightfall, and we saw no fires in the night, and stayed away from the shore. On the 20th, we approached the island and seeing that there was a decent entrance to a bay, brought the ship in safely, furled the sails and dropped anchor. As soon as we had done so, a boat approached us from the shore, carrying inhabitants of the island who were named the Usmaitsi, and they brought out to the ship rice, potato roots and some fresh sea fish.

This was a very different welcome from the one they had received further north. Benyovszky sent some of the crew to the shore, where they found a good place right opposite the ship to erect their tents, so that they could set up ovens and bake bread. Notwithstanding their warm reception, they took the precaution of establishing a strong guard around their camp, and loading their muskets with live shot.

The inhabitants of the island proved to be frequent visitors, although communication was tricky.

> Every day they came in crowds to visit us. But because of their lack of knowledge of the language, it was not possible to talk to them. They provided us with rice, potato roots and fish, and their wine was made from grain, which is no worse than our Russian grain vodka. These Usmaitsi people were generally all idolaters and, like the other Japanese, wore robes and gowns made of straw, and they have grass which grows like a tree, whose height was at least six yards with a thickness of five inches at the root, and the leaves were very long and wide, more than a yard long and the breadth was more than half a yard, the sheath of the grass being a very light blue [...] and when this was stripped and dried and spun, it was dyed in different colours and of this they make their clothes, and it is amazing that no one can tell that these are not silk gowns. In a place like Japan, there is no winter and it is always very warm, with seasonable and healthy air, so they make their shoes of the grass as well.

Ryumin was in his element here – he revelled in novelty and went on at great length to describe, not just the clothes of the inhabitants, but their hairstyles and their writing:

> they write letters, like the Japanese and Chinese, from top to bottom with brushes, and they have compasses and maps, and books about navigation, as

well as Chinese and Japanese ones, and they say that the Japanese often come to them on their ships and trade necklaces for goods. These residents have cattle, cows, goats, sheep, horses, pigs, poultry, chickens, ducks, geese and a lot of dogs, and in the sea and the bay where we were moored there were many different kinds of fish, which we could salt. Their houses were like the Japanese ones, but they did not have any wall around their village. And they had no weapons except their axes and knives and also small bows and arrows and they have cast-iron cooking pots.

Barely pausing for breath after this long catalogue of the islanders' possessions, Ryumin launches himself into the next list:

There are a lot of high mountains here, and these are clad in different fruit-bearing trees, grapefruit, bitter oranges, sweet oranges, palm and coconut and other trees which are unknown to us, and on the same island there are wild grapes, which are very small, not much larger than our red peas, and when they are ripe, they have a taste like a blackcurrant, very like Russian *kissel*, and on the same island there are trees on which grow a special little fruit that we did not know, the size of a small pumpkin, like an orange or a lemon, which is bumpy on the surface like our Siberian nuts, and when the fruit is gathered, in the middle there is something like a round yellow apple that has a sweet taste and tastes even better than a melon, and they say it is very healthy; Mr. Anson called it Tinian Bread because it is nutritious. And there are pineapples growing here, which is the best fruit, and there are sizable melons and ginger, and plenty of cinnamon and pepper.

Having regaled us with a list of all the comestibles, Ryumin proceeded to make an inventory of all the other stuff: "we saw wild beasts, such as pigs, goats, leopards, and also venomous reptiles, snakes and scorpions and others and locusts, also different stones, diamonds, sapphires and also pearls from oysters." The roll went on.

These same people sow grass called cane-sugar from which they get sugar and grows at least four yards high, very thick cane. It is very tasty and wine is made from it. And they have a lot of leaf tobacco, which they always smoked in small copper tubes, like the Japanese and Chinese.

The question of the actual location of island of the "Usmaitsi" needs to delay us. Cross-referencing this name, and the name of the people, with the description made later by Benyovszky himself, of the island of "Usmay Ligon," it seems that this is the island of Amami-Oshima in the Ryūkyū group, lying off the southern tip of the main Japanese archipelago. The island must lie between Japan and Formosa, as we shall see from the further voyages of Ivan Ryumin. Berg (or Ryumin), in his chapter-heading, notes that it is one of the "Bashinski" Islands;

there is no island named 'Bashinski', or anything remotely like it in that area of sea. There are islands in the Bashi Channel between Formosa and the Philippines which might suit, but even the wildest imagination – of which this ship inspired a few – cannot place our intrepid voyagers that far south. Stepanov's positioning of the same "Usmaski" Island, at a latitude of 28 degrees, places it in the precise location of Amami-Oshima, which could corrupt quite easily into 'Usmaitsi'. A seven-day sail southwards from their last-guessed location at Shikoku makes this location perfectly reasonable.

They stayed on this bountiful island for over ten days, and Ryumin wrote seven blissful pages describing all that was to be described (by contrast, Stepanov wrote two short sentences). "During our stay, the Usmaitsi were happy with us, and we lived without fear of them. On our arrival in Macao, the Europeans told us that these were good people, and gave shelter to Europeans." That the islands should be known about in Macao indicates that the Russians were not in completely new territory. As they were preparing for departure, the islanders presented them with a barrel of rice and a sack of sweet potatoes, along with sugar and wine. On the 31st of July, the islanders waved them off, accompanying them out of the bay in a great flotilla of boats, their elders having first brought aboard a final gift of bread and wine. Then they helpfully towed the ship out to sea – "and so we said goodbye to them."

A rather startling editorial observation on this description of Paradise was provided by Berg. In a review of Ryumin's journal prepared for the *St Petersburg Journal* in 1822, he wrote:

> I have quoted so much from this description of the island because until now no European travellers have brought back the slightest news of this place. The reader who realises what a surplus of food is on this island, and how close it is to the furthest and so scantily-provided frontier of Siberia will almost certainly be of my opinion that the hostile attitude of Japan to our Fatherland gives us a complete and indisputable right to take this island for ourselves. Thereby we would give an enormous advantage to the eastern frontier of Siberia, for which this support is almost indispensable.[2]

A naked exposition of the legal underpinnings of colonial exploration.

The Fifth Chapter

On the exit of the galliot St Peter *from Usmaitsi Bay and on reaching the sea, sailing to the island of Formosa, and our arrival there, and finding a decent harbour, and the murder of our three compatriots by wild Indians, and other circumstances, and coming to the Chinese coast.*

They sailed on until the evening of the 7th August, sadly with nothing remarkable to report until they saw an island to starboard. On the 8th they approached land, but could not find a safe mooring. They coasted up and down and finally anchored four miles off shore on the 9th. In the evening, the ship's boat was sent with armed men aboard to scout out the land, and see who lived there.

> They found a wild Indian people who joined our men in battle, and one of our people was wounded in three places by arrows. Our boat returned to the ship. We remained at anchor until the 10th and then we coasted along to the south side of this island, where we found a decent harbour, and landed the boat again and walked along the shore.

The "wild Indian" people, however, had been observing them and turned up en masse on the shore, brandishing bows and arrows and digging traps in the sand. Some of them then swam out to the ship and were captured while still in the water and brought aboard; but nothing unpleasant happened and they were taken back to the shore. Having met a hostile reception there, the voyagers spent the next six days coasting around the island to the north. On the 16th, about a hundred local people arrived in two large boats, some of whom came aboard, informed them that the island was called Formosa, and guided them to a good harbour, where they anchored. On the following day they were visited by the locals,

> who brought with them various good fruits, pineapples and more, there were pineapples that were very large and very tasty, and they brought chickens, pigs, and drink made of rice and some kind of milk which tasted sweet, and so the Indians traded with us for every little thing, needles, silk, silk fabric scraps, ribbons and so on and they traded different fruits, etc., and their wives and children came with them, and then they disembarked from the ship and went ashore to their houses, and no more came to the ship.

And suddenly, for no obvious reason, the mood changed again.

At around two o'clock in the afternoon of the 17th, the boat was sent ashore to find water and bring supplies back to the ship. This went well. The boat was then sent out a second time, with a different crew aboard. But when it returned, in some haste, the crew reported that "the Indians had killed Captain Vasilii Panov and Ivan Popov and Ivan Loginov, and with arrows had slightly wounded Vasilii Lapin, Andrei Kazakov and Ivan Kudrin." The boat brought the wounded back to the ship. At the same time, a native boat with seven people aboard approached the vessel, and was promptly fired upon from the ship's gun; five natives were killed and the boat was destroyed.

The ship's boat was sent back ashore, where the Russians found Loginov still alive. He was brought aboard, but died shortly afterwards from his injuries. Now a little more organised, the Russians sent back the boat along with another one captured from the natives, both crammed with men and guns, and set about exacting retribution. They found on the shore two natives who had survived the destruction of their own boat – and promptly put them to death. On the following day, they collected and buried the bodies of their three comrades; then, to demonstrate the mastery of a civilised nation, they set fire to the forest and grass next to the shore. Not content with this act of vengeance, they replenished their stocks of water, and sent ashore

> thirty people led by the Swede Vinbland, also Ippolit Stepanov, Krushchev and Kuznetsov, with guns and muskets, who followed the shoreline and carried on attacking Indians, of whom there was a large number, and they destroyed the Indian boats they found pulled up on the beach, and set fire to a larger boat that was under construction, and then went to the Indian village, killed one of them and wounded many more. But on our side, no one was killed or wounded. Those Indians had iron-tipped spears, some smooth and others jagged, with shafts made from thick cane, bows and arrows, and iron knives, and also protected themselves with shields made from thin wooden planks. The Indians fled and we entered their homes and burned them all down. From this battle we obtained bows, arrows, shields, wood and salt; but there was not much else in the Indian houses, as they had taken everything away beforehand. Then there was a signal from the cannon on the ship and the party returned to the ship.

Having blandly described this typical piece of shameful colonial savagery, in his very next sentence, Ryumin reverts to his usual role as fascinated tourist.

> The wild inhabitants of Formosa, whom nobody governs, are of a dark complexion, and almost all of them go naked, and while some do wear clothes, these are made from animal skins, and their skin is burned by the sun and they look quite savage. From the strong sun some people had cracks on their bodies, like a tree with the bark peeling off – it looks terrible. They sow grain and rice, and have cattle, cows, pigs, goats, birds, chickens, ducks, and salt. This island has mountains covered thickly with trees – lemon, orange, grapefruit, coconut, palm, lignum vitae, dogwood and plane, and other American trees unknown to us and fragrant trees, and there are different fruits, and large pineapples. There are also different kinds of wild animals of which we have seen the skins, and gold, silver, pearls and other precious stones.

(The adjective 'American' should simply be read as 'foreign'.)

With everything catalogued to within an inch of its life, and the natives back in their place, the Kamchatkan voyagers weighed anchor on the 21st August, set the sails and went back to sea.

The Sixth Chapter

The journey of the galliot from the bay on the island of Formosa and of being at sea, and what was worth noticing, and the arrival at the Chinese coast, and other things.

And now they approached the coast of mainland China.

> In the evening of the 21st August, the ship encountered a severe storm which lasted until the 23rd. In the morning of the 23rd, the weather changed and the storm subsided. The following day, we saw many islands in the sea but did not stop. On the 25th, we observed a lot of marine mammals floating in the sea and a large number of sea-snakes. On the 26th we caught sight of the Chinese coast and some Chinese fishing boats, and more of them on the 27th. On the 28th, two boats with Chinese people on them approached, and we gave them two roubles in Russian money, and two men came aboard and pointed out the entrance to a harbour. One of the men piloted us there and we anchored.

The voyagers then asked to be guided to Canton, "where the Chinese Emperor's viceroy lived," and then to the Portuguese city of Macao. They handed over another ten roubles to the Chinese as pilotage. To their disappointment, the pilot promptly left the ship with the cash, and was never seen again. Doubtless a cultural misunderstanding.

So they went back to sea on the 29th and, having encountered more helpful Chinese fishermen in boats, were pointed in the general direction of Canton and Macao. Chinese ships sailed past, looking – to Ryumin's delight – exactly like those which Anson had described, and then a small boat which had fish and crayfish for sale. A purchase was made to the value of one rouble, and when the cook cleaned the crabs, "we found in them bubbles of the purest ink with which we could write, and it was no worse than their Chinese ink." They sheltered from a contrary wind in another harbour and then, on the 31st August, they came to "a Chinese stronghold, where some people spoke Portuguese and promised to help us with the Cantonese authorities." The sea, it appeared to Ryumin, was at this point completely covered with Chinese fishing vessels. Another set of pilots put in an appearance and took then to the nearby city of Tasona (Dongshan Island?). Here they anchored and Winbladh and Kuznetsov were carried by a Chinese ship to land, in order to take on fresh water, for supplies had again run dangerously low. Two letters were also carried ashore, one in Portuguese and the other in Dutch, in the hope of finding Europeans there who would help the fugitives. But it seemed that the town only had Chinese residents. This did not greatly disappoint Ryumin, who joined the shore-party and eagerly described a Chinese temple.

A further attempt to seek aid was made on the following day, when the two Swedes, Winbladh and Meyder, went back to the city bearing gifts for the local mandarin. They were well received, admitted to the presence and given tea. In return, the Chinese sent aboard a barrel of rice, a cow, a calf and a goat. Four Chinese officials turned up, to whom a present was made of some of the Kamchatkan sable furs which had survived the journey. In the evening, there appeared a pilot who spoke Portuguese, "having been brought up," advises Ryumin, "in the Spanish city of Manila which lies 600 *versts* from Macao on Luzon Island, and he had lived there for several years. He would pilot our ship to Canton and Macao."

Before they set off on the final leg of their journey, however, they spent another two days in the port of "Tasona," and welcomed aboard crowds of Chinese merchants anxious to barter with them for all the furs which they had brought from the deep north. In exchange, they received "Chinese wine, food and various snacks, nuts, Chinese moss-tobacco and smoking pipes." At length, on the 9th September, they managed to extricate themselves and head south-westwards again. A decision had been reached – by the Chinese authorities – that they would not be allowed to visit Canton, where, Ryumin advises us, "there was a great commerce for the merchants from various European countries, and a great and noble port." Instead they would stop at Macao, with two Chinese pilots on board. For the next three days they sailed in a crowded sea, full of fishing boats, junks and other ships. In the afternoon of the 11th they sailed "past the city of Canton," and anchored for the night before they could reach Macao.

"And there we slept."

The Seventh Chapter

Arriving at the Portuguese city of Macao, which is on a small island in the sea, and entering the harbour, and of being in the city, and from there boarding the French ships for Europe, and so on.

By three o'clock in the afternoon of the 12th September, they had anchored safely off Macao. Benyovszky promptly clambered aboard the ship's boat and went ashore, where he was greeted by the Portuguese Governor. A Portuguese officer and pilot boarded and the ship was brought safely into the harbour. Here, as an additional precaution, some Portuguese soldiers were also put aboard, to "guard against theft by the Chinese and negroes." The Governor sent out supplies of bread and various fruits.

Ryumin's eyes missed nothing.

> In the harbour we saw different European merchant ships – Spanish, Portuguese, French, Dutch and English – about twenty of them. There were also about three hundred Chinese ships and boats, and many more fishing boats. On the morning of the 13th, the Macao Governor sent us, for our dinner, one cow and some bread, and then some Portuguese boats were sent out to the ship, like our own barges, with canopies of silk or European wool, to take people to the shore. We were assigned an apartment to live in and the Governor provided a feast.

They had arrived. At last. But all was not well.

> [*Benyovszky*], our leader, went to the house of the Governor, and there he
> sold our Russian ship, complete with all the rigging, anchors, cannons,
> muskets, gunpowder, lead and bullets, artillery and other supplies, and all our
> food – and we do not know what price they were sold for.

While the shipmates were stroking their chins at this secretive behaviour of their
trusted leader, Fate struck a heavy blow. "During our stay in the city of Macao,
fifteen of our men and women died of sickness and fever, and other diseases, and
there had been in all sixty-three men and seven women, seventy people in total."

It was a tragedy. But Ryumin never stood still in the face of tragedy and
mayhem. Ever the zealous sightseer, he proceeds immediately to describe the city
of Macao in the same kind of detail that he had already provided for the Usmaitsi
Island and Formosa. The people, the merchants, the buildings and, of course,

> the nice gardens, in which grow different American trees as well as fruit, two
> kinds of lemons, citrons, bitter oranges, sweet oranges, coconuts, and
> legumes like our Russian beans, only three times bigger and thicker, and
> several twisted things which have a nice sweet taste, grapes, and more sour
> fruit growing on trees, and other things we didn't recognise. They plough
> and sow grain for wheat rather like millet, also turnips, radishes, cabbages,
> lettuces, carrots, cucumbers and other vegetables. For livestock they keep
> cows, buffaloes, sheep, goats, pigs and horses, birds, geese, chickens, ducks,
> pigeons, a lot of those, and other supplies are brought to them from Europe,
> and also different drinks.

A brief history of Macao is then provided and a description of its fortifications.
Chinese religion is also dealt with, in a rather wistful tone:

> The Chinese have a few temples, in which their idolatry is celebrated every
> day morning and evening, with a ringing or beating of cast-iron pots, and
> music in the houses almost every night, launching rockets and firecrackers,
> and so on until midnight, having fun, leaving the afternoon free for
> commerce, and other craftwork.

The Russians, under their Hungarian and Swedish leaders, stayed in Macao for
three months. On the 4th of January 1772, they were taken on board three large
Chinese ships to meet up with two French merchant ships, the *Dauphin* and the
Laverdy coming from Canton. Benyovszky had booked passage on these ships for
those who wished to sail further. The new passengers found themselves divided up
between the two vessels – the French captains, sensibly enough, had no desire to
put all these suspicious characters together into one ship, given their inability to
explain just how they had come into possession of a Russian vessel.

The Eighth Chapter

About our voyage by sea on the French ship to the city of France, stopping on an island of the sea called St Maurice, and our arrival there and then further on to France, and from there to Russia, and so on.

The French ships set sail and reached the French-owned island of Mauritius on 6th March. The voyagers do not seem to have been astonished that, in comparison to their own painfully slow voyage from Kamchatka, such a vast distance could be covered by ship in such a short time. The ships moored in the harbour of Port Louis, the capital of Mauritius, and the Russians took up residence in a house provided by the French Governor-General.

> The city stands on the island and has a port, which is visited by French naval and merchant ships, and merchant ships from other countries, where they can take on fresh water and leave again within three days. The residents of the town are French and a considerable number of negroes, the buildings made of stone and wood, without stoves.

One begins to recognise some of Ivan Ryumin's preoccupations: "There are many high mountains, and good meadows for the cattle, and fruits such as pineapple and sweet peppers are grown." Disappointingly, however, his description of Mauritius ends here. Although Benyovszky and his surviving companions spent three weeks on the island before moving on, Ryumin's narrative merely reports that they left Mauritius on 24th March. On 4th May they "caught some sea-turtles on an empty island where there were four English frigates," landed at St Helena on the 11th May and then pressed on for France, where they arrived on 7th July 1772 at Port Louis (Lorient) in Brittany, the principal port for ships from the east. "There we were given an apartment and food, and a bottle of red wine a day, and some money from the Royal treasury, and we lived at Port Louis for eight months and nineteen days."

Ryumin clearly counted the passing of every single one of those 263 days. What they did there, apart from drinking themselves into a daily stupor, is not mentioned. It has to be said that, after the wonders of the east, Port Louis offered very little new to admire or taste. And – worst of all – nothing to count.

It was not until 27th March 1773 that Benyovszky obtained passports which permitted them all to travel to Paris. But the party split into two: those who went with Benyovszky, having no inclination to return to Russia; and the rest. Both groups set off for Paris separately. Ryumin's party – "sixteen people, including one woman" (this was Mrs Ryumin) – went on foot. "550 *versts*," complains our chronicler. 585 kilometers, give or take, in the French manner. Walking all the way. Remarkably, Ryumin's estimate of the distance is just about right. More remarkably, they made it in just under three weeks. On their arrival in Paris, they were welcomed by the Russian ambassador, Nikolai Khotyn, who "received us very well and found us an apartment, food and clothing and gave us seven *kopeks* of money per day, and made sure we wanted for nothing. On the 16th April," – the day after their arrival – "Sudeikin, Ryumin and Bocharov submitted to the Resident this report of our journey. He took it and sent it away by mail to Russia on the 18th."

Ryumin's eventual journey home will be described later. Let us leave him for now in Paris, where he penned his final chapter.

The Ninth Chapter

Description of the French capital city of Paris.

The ninth and final section is an unalloyed Ryumin-esque delight, which must have been appended at a later date to the original report of the voyage. It is the spiritual outpouring of a man who had been deprived of novelty for eight months and nineteen days. It reads in full as follows:

In the city there are:
   967 streets, excluding alleys.
   50,000 houses, including those of the nobles, in which there are very many rooms.
   40 cathedral churches.
   100 parish churches.
   53 male priories.
   70 women's nunneries.
   57 schools.
   15 workshops.
   26 hospitals.
   12 prisons.
   51 fountains.
   12 markets.
   30 bridges.
   26 river ports.
   8 squares and public promenades.
   12,500 coaches.
   6,200 street lights.
   12 sentries for the prison.
   160 cavalry and 412 infantry, deployed at night to look after the streets.
   225 soldiers, on guard duty at the gate.
In addition, there is a University, which is allocated 121,000 livres a year for maintenance from the Treasury.
In a year, the following food is consumed:
   Flour 112,000 quarters.
   350,000 measures of wine, excluding beer, also cider and other

beverages.

More than 100,000 bulls and cows.

More than 420,000 sheep.

126,000 calves.

140,000 pigs.

Its diameter is a walk of two hours.

The Paris Tourist Office of today could pick up a few marketing pointers from this goggle-eyed list of things to impress a visitor. Despite having seen the many wonders of the Kurils, Japan, Formosa, China and Mauritius, Ryumin in Paris must have thought he had died and gone to heaven. Here there were so many things to count! So many measures of wine! So many sheep consumed! Incredible!

Notes

1   All the quoted passages here are taken from Ryumin, 1822.

2   Berg, 1822, p.203.

VII

MAURITIUS

"Captain St Hylaire... Weighs, Calculates, Forsees the Danger"

Grumbles and How They Might be Suppressed – Mutineers and How They Might be Suppressed – Disgustful and Unpleasant Passages – Sunshine and Scurvy

Let us now tear ourselves away from the dazzling delights of Paris and retreat half-way back round the world, for there is yet another account of the later stages of the voyage.

Those who had the good fortune to reach Macao and not drop dead were not at all happy. They convened in dark corners, grumbled, plotted and wrote letters of complaint. Having smoothly disposed of all their assets, Benyovszky now found himself obliged to pen the following formal declaration to his fellow-voyagers:

> From Baron Moritz August Aladar de Benyovszky, colonel of His Imperial Majesty, and chamberlain and counsellor to His Highness Prince Albert, Duke of Saxe-Teschen, and part of his highest cabinet etc., to all the officers and the entire company.
>
> It has come to my notice that you have been grumbling and holding meetings against me. All this leads to disagreement amongst yourselves, brings me and the Emperor into dishonour, and finally disturbs the discipline of the company. [...]
>
> You know the sincerity of my heart: you can see that I, although in a foreign land, have provided for all your needs. As I promised you, you can make demands on me when I am back in my native country. But to be scheming here is ridiculous and is dangerous for you. This letter is to remind you to come to your senses, do not be deceived by people whose scheming is already well-known to you. That is why I am writing to you. If you really love me and respect me, then I swear to you before God that my fervour towards you will be evident every day; if, on the other hand, I perceive that

your hearts have hardened and that you no longer respect me, then you can
conclude for yourselves what to expect.[1]

Having fired off this stern but paternal note, Benyovszky sensibly took the
precaution of looking for a swift escape-route. The longer he remained in Macao
with a bunch of ingrates, the better the chance of being arrested, deported or
worse. He therefore wooed Simon Le Bon, the Bishop of Mitelopolis, made
friends with anyone who worked for any of the European East India Companies,
and towards the end of November signed a contract with Messieurs de Robien and
de St Hilaire, Manager and Captain respectively of the French Company, for
passage back to France with the remaining four dozen refugees. The fee paid was,
according to Benyovszky, 115,000 French *"livres Tournois"* – no mean sum, we
suppose. It is entirely possible that Benyovszky exaggerated the amount, but we
have no confirmation from any other source and very little with which to compare
it: paying passengers to and from the Far East were few and far between in that era.
At all events, the only funds available to them were the proceeds from the sale of
ship, equipment and furs, and it is reasonable to suppose that all that money went
on purchasing passage to France.

With their tickets westwards safely in his pocket, Benyovszky felt more
confident in his next letter to his companions: "My dear children!" he wrote
grandly,

> You know that I have always worked hard for your enjoyment and have
> defended you to the very last, and you can be sure I make every effort for
> your well-being. The truth is that I was greatly insulted to hear about your
> complaints and hostility towards me, but I am now informed that you were
> deceived by flattery and false hopes, and so I do not blame you anymore, and
> I wish to forget all of that.
>
> Have faith in me! With the help of God I will protect you, and will allow
> no attacks on you. We will have food and clothing and, if Almighty God
> permits, we will come to Europe. I promise you that you will be free and
> will be happy for the rest of your lives, and confirm this in my own hand.[2]

Most of the crew seems to have fallen for this piece of graceless flannel. In any
event, they all had a stark choice before them: either they signed up with Benyovszky;
or they rotted sick and penniless in Macao. So, few complained. Only the
unfortunate Stepanov, who had already fallen out with Benyovszky by this time,
was left out in the cold. Benyovszky was busy trying to sell him off to the Portuguese.
Benyovszky's comrade-in-arms, August Winbladh, had made the mistake of
supporting Stepanov early on in the proceedings, but even he was handed a one-way
ticket to France. It was several weeks before they sailed, setting out on 22nd January
1772 on board the two French ships: the *Dauphin* and the *Laverdy*.

Captain de St Hilaire on the *Dauphin* was horrified by the passengers he had
taken on. He reported his nervousness to a traveller he met in Mauritius,

Alexis-Marie de Rochon. Despite being an ordained priest, the Abbé Rochon was also a member of the Academies of Sciences of Paris and St Petersburg, Astronomer to the French Navy, Keeper of the Royal Cabinet of Natural Philosophy, Inspector of the Machines of the Mint, "*etc*" – in short, the archetypal Enlightenment Frenchman.

Rochon's account of his visit to Mauritius and Madagascar appeared in his 1791 book *Voyages á Madagascar, á Maroc, et aux Indes Orientales*, which was translated into English two years later (*Voyage to Madagascar and the East Indies*). (Rochon's translator, Joseph Trapp, MA, was evidently of the Old School of Honourable Translation: "The Translator finds it necessary to premise," he stated firmly at the outset, "that he has been obliged to omit in his version many tedious passages and uninteresting digressions which crowded the original, and must consequently appear disgustful and unpleasant to every judicious English reader.")[3]

In those portions of his book which survived Trapp's moral filters, Rochon has much to say about Benyovszky and his followers. After a lengthy passage in which he called into question practically every aspect of Benyovszky's claims about the voyage from Kamchatka to Macao, he then dramatises Captain de St Hilaire's dilemma:[4]

> Benyowsky, having escaped from the prisons of Kamchatka, sails to China with thirty or forty fellow-prisoners. No sooner is he arrived at Canton, than he finds among the French, individuals who commiserate his misfortunes. This is matter of fact, and Benyowsky has never denied it; the merchants and officers of the East India Company granted considerable supplies to him and to those of whom he called himself the chief. The generous French made a still greater effort in his behalf, they invite, persuade Captain St Hylaire to take the chief, Benyowsky, and all his men on board his ship, and to carry them to Isle de France. Captain St Hylaire being entrusted with a rich cargo belonging to different private individuals, made some objections in the beginning; he hinted some apprehensions in granting hospitality on board his ship to so great a number of strangers, just broke out from the prisons of Kamchatka; yet the sentiment of compassion surmounted in him every other consideration. No sooner had the captain set sail, than his uneasiness was revived with more power and reason: they gave him occasion to repent his imprudent generosity.
>
> These adventurers, at the time they embarked, had taken care to conceal their arms; Captain St Hylaire, apprised of this insidious cunning, was much grieved to see himself surrounded by men, perhaps more disposed to command him than he was to command them. Thirty or forty gaol-birds, armed in a formidable manner, could well alarm him about the fate of a cargo worth some millions. In a situation so delicate, so difficult, what shall he do? Shall he make use of his authority to disarm those strangers? Consider: his crew is weak, his ship badly armed; should he in this case have put at stake the fortune of his employers, risked his life and liberty with a set of stout,

resolute, enterprising fellows, who had all to gain and nothing to lose? The slightest pretence could give birth to a quarrel, to an insurrection which it was prudent to avoid.

The reader is on tenterhooks. Will there be a bloody outcome? Can the good French sailors survive, or will the nefarious Russians feed them to the sharks? Ah! All is well.

Captain St Hylaire, as a man of prudence, weighs, calculates, forsees the danger, and resolves to watch secretly the ways and proceedings of his passengers. He does more, he feigns to show great honours, respect and deference to Count Benyowsky. From that moment our adventurer gives himself all the airs of a great man, he uses every trick in the book to make himself appear greater; and by the most ridiculous bravadoes, he even dupes the companions of his misery. He loudly proclaims himself their chief; his orders are rigorously executed; henceforth he commands as master, and the people obey as slaves. He would suffer no person to speak to him but a nobleman.

These honours so adroitly conferred on Benyowsky; by flattering his pride, restored order and calm to the ship. Subordination so necessary to the safety of the navigator, was no longer troubled by those dangerous men. Finally, after a short and fortunate passage, they were landed at Isle de France.

Rochon and St Hilaire may well have been taking liberties with their descriptions; but the latter felt with some justification that he had made a mistake in taking on board this particular set of passengers. The sigh of relief as they dropped anchor at Mauritius on 4th March 1772 was audible on shore, where Rochon was observing through a telescope.

Benyowsky, surrounded by a numerous suite, waited on the governor of the colony. Their appearance of wretched prisoners, was suddenly changed into a procession or parade, consisting of a General, decorated with several ribbons, followed by a brilliant staff of officers, whose rich uniforms announced their bearing high commissions. What an astonishing metamorphosis! Or rather what a ridiculous farce! Had I not been a spectator, I should be afraid of giving this account. As soon as the real history of these adventurers was known at Isle de France, the general and his splendid retinue, became the objects of derision of all the sensible people of the colony. [...] The more he prolonged his stay, the less consideration was shewn him. At his departure for old France, he dropped the name of Baron Aldar, and took that of Count Benyowsky; but it really deserves notice, that [...] he gave out publicly, that he was going to solicit the Government General of Madagascar at the court of Versailles.

Benyovszky's parting shot about governing Madagascar certainly caused a stir on Mauritius, and it marks the opening of another chapter in the Hungarian's colourful life, as we shall see. His credibility amongst the trading and voyaging fraternity gathered on Mauritius dropped to a low ebb. But those who waved him on his way to France a few weeks later were not all sniggering behind their hands. The Governor of Mauritius, the Chevalier du Dresnay, had been greatly impressed by his guest's stirring speeches and, in a letter of recommendation handed to Benyovszky as he set off for France, he wrote to his superiors.

> He is covered with wounds, and some of them disfigure his gait, which is very laboured. Nevertheless, he retains both health and physical strength and has a pleasant appearance, reflecting a great mind. He is very discreet and restrained [...] It seems to me that he is naturally inclined to pride and authority, but if someone confides in him, he accepts with extraordinary courtesy [...] Superficially he knows almost all sciences and knowledge, which is quite unusual in the military calling and is sure to help him in the difficult circumstances of his life.[5]

When the party sailed for France, left behind in Port Louis on Mauritius were four corpses, victims of scurvy, and fifteen survivors who clearly had had quite enough. Four had already died en route from Macao, including Baturin, the exiled astrologer who had originally set out with Benyovszky from Moscow, three long years earlier. Either the cuisine aboard the *Dauphin* was not as good as the travel-brochures had promised, or these men were still suffering from their earlier deprivations. Scurvy was deemed to be the cause of death of the other four who died after they had reached Mauritius. Amongst those who were easily persuaded to extend their residence on this island in the Indian Ocean was August Winbladh, who pleaded illness and later went home to Sweden; the veteran exile Pyotr Khrushchyov, who now hitched up with the widow of one of his fellow travellers; and probably also two exiles – the Swedish doctor Meyder, and Grigorii Kuznetsov. A good number of the others may well have stayed behind simply because they were likely to die if they got on another boat – although at least one of those left behind subsequently reached France and joined his fellows.

The voyage from Mauritius to France lasted from 24th March to 7th July 1772. A stop was made at St Helena in the South Atlantic to top up with water and fresh supplies. By now, Captain St Hilaire must have felt a bit more comfortable with his remaining two dozen passengers, although it is unlikely he took his eye off them for more than a minute. At length, they reached Lorient in Brittany, the main port of arrival and departure for the East. The passengers were swiftly off-loaded, given a couple of rooms, furnished with bottles of cheap wine and left to rot – for "eight months and nineteen days," as we have heard Ivan Ryumin lament. Benyovszky alone, armed with his letters of recommendation from both Robien, the French

East India Company's man in Macao, and from Chevalier du Dresnay, skipped past passport-control and made his way to Paris.

Here he began a campaign of self-promotion, boasting of his exploits on the *St Peter* and announcing great geographical discoveries in the mysterious Orient. Articles about him began to appear in the newspapers and journals. In response, the far-distant Russian government conducted a campaign against Benyovszky and the other fugitives, through articles in the *Petersburg Gazette* in which he was accused of having taken the Bolsheretsk fortress by storm.

The purpose of Benyovszky's PR campaign was not simply self-aggrandisement. He had a serious purpose – selfish, certainly, but practical all the same: initially he offered his services to the French government to lead an expedition to Formosa, to conquer that island and bring it under French control. He handed over to the Foreign Minister some early version of his memoirs. When this approach failed to find any takers, he switched tack and proposed to mount an expedition to Madagascar, to impose control over the island, and govern it as a large and bountiful French possession. Until then, Madagascar had failed dismally in its historic duty of being subjugated by one of the colonial powers, and was still governed very efficiently by native families. Some isolated coastal colonies were tolerated by the Madagascans – those established by pirates and various European trading nations, including the French. But these were only toeholds, and the French were obliged to observe the island forlornly from their distant outlooks on Mauritius and Réunion.

In Paris, Benyovszky at last found some people willing to listen to him. Several important agreements in principle were reached with the government, and plans were laid for an expedition to the great African island, to begin the task of founding more settlements. It was a busy time. As a result, he was able to stay in Paris for some months, and had all but forgotten the people he had left behind in Lorient. At length, a pathetic letter arrived from Brittany: five more of the dwindling band had died of illness as they waited out their time in the French port; the rest were getting pretty twitchy. In a nakedly condescending letter dated 1st February, their absent leader replied: "My children! I received your letter. Just stay put until I return. When I do, you can let me know your intentions. Until my arrival, stay happy. I am your friend. Baron de Benyovszky."[6]

It was not, perhaps, the letter the weary exiles had hoped for. But what were they to do? They stayed unhappy. However, a few weeks later, on 19th March, Benyovszky came back to Lorient. His achievements in eight months were hard to measure, but he had at least managed to obtain some kind of passport for the entire band, which allowed them all to cross over to mainland France and head for Paris. As Ryumin had reported, they split into two groups – those who wished to return to Russia, and those who did not. In the latter group were a handful of souls who yearned for yet more adventures and were intending to seek them with Maurice Benyovszky. While we have no definitive documentation, we can suppose that these were members of the trapping fraternity, whose normal life saw them taking risks far from home, for months, or even years, at a time – a bit longer away from home would be nothing to them. Many of their colleagues had, after all, already taken that decision and had stayed on Mauritius. When Benyovszky embarked on his first expedition to Madagascar in February 1774, these men – by then only a couple – went with him. The only one of his companions here whose subsequent fate has been documented was young Ivan Ustyuzhinov, the priest's son, who returned to Siberia in 1789. He was reportedly employed thereafter in the mines in the Nerchinsk district, a popular destination for Tsarist exiles, some ways east of Lake Baikal: perhaps not as balmy as Madagascar.

For those who expressed a desire not to have any more adventures, their leader granted one last favour – an excellent reference for the good life in Hungary. A completely valueless pro-forma was carefully composed:

> We, Maurice Baron Benyovszky, colonel, commander of the Volunteer Corps of our name, in the service of France, certify to all whom it may concern, that the person called [*insert name here*] is of good character, that he served us very faithfully as a volunteer, that, wishing to withdraw to Hungary, our homeland, we ask all those who are able to lend him aid and assistance, for which we will be grateful.
>
> In witness whereof, we have issued this certificate and do affix the seal of our arms.

His reluctant followers remained unimpressed with this magnanimous offer. They were, for the most part, of independent mind – otherwise they would not have ended up in Paris. It was not by the efforts of one man alone that they had arrived in the foremost city of the world; they had all played their part.

And Ivan Ryumin will catalogue them all.

Notes

1   Stein, 1908, Vol.II, p.599.
2   *ibid*, p.599.
3   Rochon, 1793, p.ix.
4   *ibid*, pp.229–235.
5   Stein, 1908, Vol.II, p.600.
6   *ibid*, p.601.

VIII

GENTLEMEN

"Who They Were and What Happened to Them and Where They Are Now"

Seized with a Dangerous Illness — Adventurers and Voyagers —
Exiles, Hostages, Traders and Hunters — The Troubles of the Merchant
Kholodilov — Thirty-two Dropped Dead

In a letter dated 24 September 1771 from Macao, Bishop Le Bon described the arrival, on the preceding day, of a vessel "under Hungarian colours." This would have been that same ship which belonged to the Russian state, and had set off with English flags aloft, then Dutch ones. Benyovszky had dined with Le Bon on the night of his arrival, so his Right Reverend host had first-hand knowledge of the adventurer's account. Much of the Baron's narration to the Bishop appears to have confirmed other rumours which were already flying through the merchant quarter of Macao. But Le Bon reported that all was not well on board the ship:

> Out of fifty-four men of his equipage, there remains no more to this Captain than eight men in health; all the rest are confined to their beds. For two months past they have suffered hunger and thirst. He has twice been shipwrecked and twice they have repaired their vessel.[1]

Within a few days, at least fifteen of these survivors had died. Benyovszky himself (after listing twenty-three names) described their deaths as a result of being "seized with dangerous illness." Ivan Ryumin's account was more precise: the dead had been afflicted with "sickness and fever." Neither diagnosis is entirely illuminating. Most likely, the illness was a fatal overloading of the digestive system with fresh food and water after several weeks of deprivation. Malaria may also have been involved. It was an unhappy end to a singular journey.

But before the final echoes of this voyage had faded away, thirty-two died out of a total of seventy people, all of them as a direct result of having boarded the *St*

Peter in Kamchatka. Compared with other well-documented sea-voyages in the eighteenth century, the death-toll was acceptable (the magnificent Lord Anson lost almost three-quarters of the crews of his ships, mostly to scurvy); nonetheless, for a disparate collection of quite ordinary people unused to travelling, such attrition was an unimaginable tragedy.

Who were all these people – the ones who died and the ones who survived? By good fortune, we have names. Too many names, admittedly. But names nonetheless, and occupations. And in an adventure of this kind, it is unforgivable to focus solely on the main players. So let us dig deeper.

When Ivan Ryumin and his small band of friends turned up in Paris, they passed two documents to the Russian ambassador. One was their narrative of the voyage, which we have examined already; the other was a confused justification for their sudden and unexpected appearance on French soil, which we shall examine quite soon; and accompanying this document was a full "list of the number of people who sailed from Kamchatka on board the galliot *St Peter* with the Hungarian Benyovsky on the sea voyage and who they were and what happened to them and where they are now."[2] One could not ask for more from our trusty chronicler Ryumin. At around the same time, at the far end of Asia, another list of the people involved was being put together by the investigating authorities in Kamchatka. There is a reasonable concordance between these two lists, which is a comfort; for there is a third register compiled by Benyovszky himself, which has but a very tenuous relationship with the other two lists.

Stepanov and Ryumin agree on a total figure of seventy who eagerly clambered aboard the *St Peter* when it left Kamchatka. En route, six of these were left behind – three as castaways on the Kurils, three as corpses stuck with arrows on Formosa. Sixty-four, therefore, arrived at Macao, of whom six were women.

Benyovszky's numbers are more flexible: according to his account which was published some years later, ninety-six people embarked on the ship from Kamchatka. Twelve of those are described, a little inexplicably, as "passengers." Allowing for the documented natural wastage on the voyage, we might expect ninety to have arrived in Macao, of whom eight were women. That still leaves a large gap in the Benyovszkian roll-call – discounting women, mere passengers and the much-lamented dead, there should have been seventy able-bodied men left, not the fifty-four reported to the Bishop. No matter: fifty-four from Benyovszky's earliest statement to Le Bon almost agrees with the fifty-eight men counted by Ryumin and Stepanov. (At least, it would have agreed, had Benyovszky not drawn up another document just a few days later which stated that he had "gone out with 85 men, and come back with 62." Sometimes it is best not to examine statistics too closely.)

Appendix I to the present book provides a register of all the individuals named by Ryumin, by the Kamchatkan authorities and by Benyovszky himself. With the reader's mental welfare in mind, we shall stick to the list compiled by Ryumin: anything else will lead into uncertainty, fruitless speculation and outright despair.

Given the curious mix of prisoners and exiles, free citizens malcontent with their lot, alleged hostages, and a covey of hangers-on, we cannot simply name the ship's complement as 'escapees.' Neither were they all 'adventurers' – unless we understand 'adventure' in the light of its original etymology: 'people to whom things happened,' or indeed 'people who arrived.' So they might best be described as 'the voyagers.'

These voyagers can be categorised under five main headings:

• Escaping exiles
• Hostages (alleged)
• Soldiers and sailors
• Traders, workmen and hunters
• Wives and girlfriends

We will look at the wives and girlfriends shortly and separately – seven in total; all on the journey, sadly, only because their men were. Some did not fare well. The captain of the ship, Maxim Tchurin had his wife and daughter with him. All three members of the family died in Macao.

In the group of escaping exiles, there were nine men. Ryumin lists those who survived under two distinct categories: "Sent into exile" and "Russian exiles." Since the latter category included a Swede, the distinction must have been between those who had recently arrived in Kamchatka ("sent into exile") and those who had been there a while. The official report classified the exiles in much the same way: on the one hand, "Polish insurgents and the vagabond Benyovsky" and, on the other, those "sent earlier into exile." It is rather an academic distinction. The entire group included the original gang of five, who had been shipped to Kamchatka the previous year: Benyovszky himself, with his Swedish friend Winbladh, the ever-unfortunate Stepanov, his cousin Panov whose mortal remains were left on Formosa and Baturin. Also notable in this group were: another Swede, Magnus Meyder, an Admiralty doctor who had been exiled in December 1765; Pyotr Khrushchyov, the erstwhile leader of the Bolsheretsk exiles; Alexander Turchanin, exiled in 1742; and a man described as a "peasant from Ustyug," Grigorii Kuznetsov – Ustyug being a province in north-west Russia: for what crime he had been exiled, is unknown; it is bad enough that he was merely a peasant.

At least five of the voyagers either were, or made every effort to represent themselves as, unwilling hostages. This group included Ryumin himself – who evidently made a good job later of persuading the Russian authorities of his innocence – and his fellow-clerk, Spiridon Sudeikin. The official report describes Ryumin as "the disgraced Cossack," and Sudeikin as "the former secretary to Nilov." Our wily Ryumin himself classifies these people as "in the party of the Hungarian Benyovszky" As what? As guests? Three sailors made up the numbers in this group: Dmitrii Bocharov, Filipp Zyablikov and Gerasim Izmailov – the defence-case of the last-named was cast-iron, since he had been turfed off the boat early at the Kurils.

Around ten men described by both sources either as soldiers or sailors made up a distinct group. They included the three "apprentice navigators" mentioned above, the captain of the ship, Tchurin, and a couple of soldiers from the garrison at Bolsheretsk – these latter were clearly fed up with the common soldier's lot and had gone over to the other side.

Another ten men seem to have joined the voyage of their own volition, seeking adventure or a better life. The official report classifies these men variously as "townsmen," "workers," "Kamchadals" or "merchants," while Ryumin has a slightly obscure category of "assistants and workmen of the merchant Fyodor Kholodilov" – and this group is quite distinct from "the workmen of the merchant Kholodilov" whom we examine next. Included in this group by Ryumin are two wives and at least one sailor. They were surely there to seek their fortune in the time-honoured manner: by running away to sea. This group included Ivan Loginov and Ivan Popov who were killed on Formosa. Also here was Alexei Parantsin, who was abandoned on the Kurils with his wife.

By far the largest group seems to have comprised "twenty-five workers employed by Kholodilov." This description is the one used by the Kamchatkan authorities. It is a little difficult to identify these twenty-five on Ryumin's list with any precision: the list does name eight men from that same group, but the rest are lumped in with all the others in the section labelled "those who died."

But who was Kholodilov?

In the autumn of 1770, the Kamchatkan merchant Fyodor Kholodilov had contracted a trader named Tchuloshnikov to sail to the Aleutian Islands to gather in the usual harvest of furs from the islanders. The usual gang of hunters was also on board to assist in the effort. The boat was a small vessel of around 150 tons. But, it seems, not a very good one. They did not get far. They left the Bolshaya River, almost immediately encountered a storm and found themselves drifting helplessly to the shore. The ship ran aground without injury or loss of life and the crew was eventually able to refloat it. They limped back to the Bolshaya for a stiff drink. It was already late in the season when this occurred, so traders and men settled down for another Kamchatkan winter. In early April of the following year, Tchuloshnikov unearthed the men from their winter hibernation and announced that they were going to make a second attempt to get out to sea and start on the business of trading. This time, citing a total lack of confidence in both the skill of their captain and the condition of the boat, most of the hunters ("people not accustomed to the sea") refused point-blank to leave dry land. Kholodilov was outraged. He had invested good money in this voyage. So had the new commander of the garrison, the "ever-tipsy" Nilov – his investment was to the tune of 5,000 roubles, from which he might have expected a tidy return. The merchant banged his fist on Nilov's desk, and the commander responded immediately by summoning the twenty-five mutineers before him and shouting at them. They remained unmoved. Nilov locked them up in the colony's small prison for a few days, in the vain hope that they would see sense. It did little good. The rebels folded their arms and looked sullen.

The plotting exiles – men such as Benyovszky, Stepanov and Khrushchyov – got wind of this, and saw in the situation an opportunity for escape. A brief discussion in prison with the mutinous crew was quite enough for both parties to agree to capture Kholodilov's vessel and head off for a safe port – doubtless Lord Anson's Tinian. Everyone was very enthusiastic about the plan. However, someone sensibly sought the advice of Maxim Tchurin, an experienced sailor whose sympathies lay with the exiles. He took one look at the leaky boat and declared her unfit for purpose. She required, he announced, a complete overhaul to repair the damage done in her last abortive expedition. With that bucket of cold water, the flames of their enthusiasm were extinguished for a few days. But the glowing embers of rebellion amongst Kholodilov's "workmen" did not cool, and when the chance came to take ship with the *St Peter* in May, they were to be found queuing up at the shore, kitbags over their shoulders, and a couple of their women in tow. The same Tchuloshnikov, who had been embroiled in the original fiasco, was of their number.

Having gone to sea a second time, some of those twenty-five disgruntled contractors almost immediately regretted their enthusiasm. So when Izmailov and Parantsin planned to seize control of the *St Peter* when they stopped off in the Kurils, "ten of Kholodilov's men" signed up to the plot. When the plot was discovered, they were flogged until they saw sense, but were not left behind as castaways.

Let us look again at the numbers: of seventy individuals, only nine were actually exiles. In the popular literature, the Benyovszkian adventure is commonly viewed as a mass-escape of bold and desperate exiles. This was simply not the case. True, it was the exiles who had the gumption and energy to organise the break-out. But the great majority of those on board the galliot were not trying to regain civic liberty: they left because they actively wanted a better life than the one offered in the Russian Far East. Many were hunters and trappers by trade, and were almost certainly fed up to the back teeth with the grim coldness of hunting down furry mammals on wet and windy islands. They wanted to see the world.

Seventy voyagers set out, then. Let us now mark off the dwindling numbers:

- Three were abandoned on the Kurils, but subsequently made it safely back to Kamchatka;
- Three were killed by the inhabitants of Formosa;
- Fifteen died in Macao of "the sickness and fever";
- One (Stepanov) died in Indonesia, of poverty and heartbreak;
- Four died en route from Canton to Mauritius, probably of scurvy;
- Another four died in hospital on Mauritius, with scurvy named as the cause of death.

And then there were forty...

- Thirteen remained on Mauritius, for the sea and the sunshine;
- Two, according to Ryumin's list, went AWOL – "where they are, is not known." One of them, however, was later officially listed as having returned to Russia, so he must have turned up in Paris in good time;
- One was left sick in Mauritius, but also made it to Paris;
- According to Ryumin, three – apart from Benyovszky – joined "the French service": it is unclear whether they did so by remaining on Mauritius, or travelled to Paris – but we will assume the latter. Another who "joined the service" did, however, remain on Mauritius;

Twenty-six, therefore, reached France.

- Five more died at Lorient, the island off the coast of France, while waiting for passports to the mainland.

Twenty-one reached Paris.

Since the Russian government – which is unlikely to have got the numbers wrong in this matter – named the seventeen individuals who returned to Russia,[3] this left Benyovszky with three faithful companions in France. Two or three later accompanied him to Madagascar.

Our man Ryumin listed all those who expired en route – Formosa, Macao, Mauritius, France – under one pithy heading: "Dropped Dead." Three of these were women.

Notes

1 Benyovszky, 1790, Vol.I, p.xx.
2 Stein, 1908, p.605.
3 Sgibnev, 1876, p.546.

IX

LADIES

"Five Persons in Womens Apparel"

*A Strange Interment – How Many Women Sailed? – Upwards of Fifty Women
Offer Their Services – The Most Perfect Works of Living Nature*

Nathaniel Barlow had had certain doubts about the women who arrived in Macao aboard the *St Peter*. "There were in the vessel five persons in womens apparel," he noted. This is caution taken to an extreme. Why did he not just come out and say what was on his mind? Perhaps there is a clue to his scepticism in a postscript to the report sent to London, concerning the newly-arrived ship, its passengers and crew. It described a most curious incident.

> P.S. Since I wrote the above, the following strange account has reached me from Macao (every day brings forth new matter concerning these people): One of the persons dressed like a woman died a few days since. The body was sent on shore, with the following very extraordinary request to the governor, that the corpse should be interred where none had lain before, and in an honourable spot; that the baron might have liberty to attend the funeral to pay particular honours to the deceased. This remarkable request producing that never-failing curiosity peculiar to the Romish Priesthood, two *worthies* of the Franciscan order, taking advantage of the night, *peeped* into the coffin and discovered the body of a man. This deception disgusting the Portuguese exceedingly, the body was ordered common interment. Various are the accounts we have of the rank of the deceased: some say the Baron declares he was a Prince of the empire; others report him a Bishop. This account has produced many conjectures, not very favourable to remaining petticoats.[1]

From our safe twenty-first century perspective, we can only wonder at the behaviour of all concerned – at Benyovszky, claiming a man was a woman; at the

Franciscans who, for reasons we should not examine too closely, peeped at the body; at the Portuguese authorities, outraged at the deception; and at Barlow and his colleagues who spent some jolly hours poking fun at the remaining female voyagers. The general surprise that the commander of a foreign ship should wish to bury a passenger on Macao soil is not too irrational. The Portuguese authorities were, to a man, Catholic, and refused to let adherents of any other religion be buried in their cemetery. It was not until 1821 that the Protestant traders – mostly British – won the right to bury their own dead. Before that, Protestant bodies were either secretly buried in Chinese territory, or were slipped overboard into the water from ships. The Chinese authorities just over the wall were even more sticky about this issue – Western corpses buried outside the Macao jurisdiction were sometimes dug up again and sent back. So a ship full of Russians who would be understood to follow the Orthodox religion, even if accompanied by the odd Catholic, would have to plead a special case for an "honourable" burial. Ideally in a spot not previously occupied.

But, these minutiae of obsequies aside, just what was going on here? Who was this man who was not a woman?

The Governor of Mauritius, in his memorandum of March 1772, manages to confuse us even further regarding this mysterious burial at Macao. The story is similar to the one recounted by Barlow, but with a significant difference.

> At Macao, something happened which is worthy of report, but which may not ever be clarified until they reach Europe. A young girl of eleven or twelve years of age, who had been with M. de Aladar [*Benyovszky*], died at Macao. The Baron wanted her to be buried with ceremony in the ground attached to the church, and he had several initial letters engraved on the tombstone. This event attracted a lot of attention, especially from the English, for Mr. Russell told me recently that it was a young and beautiful woman disguised as a priest, and her gender was only realised during the burial. He sticks by his story, nevertheless, and the priest Surida, a Spanish Dominican, also assured me yesterday that it had been a child which he saw dressed according to her gender.[2]

Reconciling the "female child dressed as a priest" with the "man dressed as a woman" is difficult, but perhaps no more difficult than understanding some of the other quite odd things that went on. There may have been two completely separate burials. If we were to put a name to this child, we might opt for the daughter of the ship's captain: Tchurin. There is another possible candidate, but we would prefer to discount that one completely: "Miss Aphanasia" as discussed below.

The number of women who sailed with the *St Peter* is a matter for debate; their names, even more so.

Ippolit Stepanov's diary had noted that there were six women aboard when they sailed – "four married women and two girls, the daughters of the pilot Tchurin." A list of all the passengers and crew provided by crew-member Ivan

Ryumin indicates seven women, of whom only one was the daughter of Tchurin. Benyovszky, on the other hand, mentions "nine women," of whom eight were married, and the ninth – well, the ninth is a bit of a surprise.

Since the surviving extract from Stepanov's diary does not provide us with any names for the women, we must turn to Ryumin.[3] Here we have:

- Yuliana Zakharyina, the wife of "a navigator" – presumably Filipp Zyablikov, who died in Macao. Yuliana continued from Macao to Mauritius, and remained there in Port Louis, where she married the veteran exile, Pyotr Khrushchyov.
- Agafya Egorova Andreyanova, the wife of Alexei Andreyanov, both of whom went to Mauritius and remained there.
- Ivana Ryumina, the wife of Ryumin who reached Paris with her husband, and returned from there to Tobolsk.
- Stepanida Fedorova Tchurina, the wife of navigator Maxim Tchurin, both of whom died in Macao.
- Nastasia Fedorova Tchurina, the Tchurins' daughter, who also died in Macao.
- Praskovya Mikhailova Bocharova, the wife of Dmitrii Bocharov, who died in Macao; her husband returned to Irkutsk.
- Lukerya Parantsina, the wife of the Kamchadal Alexei Parantsin, both of whom were abandoned on the Kuril Islands, along with Izmailov.

Ryumin's record may not be completely accurate. We have the report, in the same Governor's memorandum referenced above, that:

> the woman who arrived at Île de France with the Baron is the widow of the captain who commanded the ship from Kamchatka, and she has voluntarily followed the fortune of M. de Aladar. This captain died in Macao and the Baron felt he had to take care of this woman like a sister or a daughter. One suspects that he has gone slightly further than that, although the widow is neither very young nor pretty.[4]

Disregarding the prurient Gallic speculation on this relationship, we have the problem of whether this was, or was not, Stepanida Tchurina. If it was her, then Ryumin's account of her death in Macao is wrong. But we have no other record of her subsequent fate: she certainly does not appear to have reached Paris. If it was not her, then it might well have been Yuliana Zyablikova, the widow of the sailor who also died in Macao.

Benyovszky's naming of the women aboard gives us a significant problem. To put it bluntly, he does not name any of the women at all, unless they happen to have died in Macao. There are a few – very few – places where he does make mention of "the women" on board. The first is when he records the abandonment on a desolate island of "Mr Ismailow and the Kamchadale Parenczin, with his wife."

The second mention was his record that, sailing towards the Aleutian Islands, "the women and sick, who were shut up below during the storm, were carried upon deck. They at first found themselves faint, but afterwards grew better." There are no more than eight other references to "the women" in his narrative, almost invariably in the close company of "the sick." Now and again, these females make themselves useful by sorting out damaged furs in the cargo-hold, or making biscuit, and – on one colourful occasion – "one of our lady passengers" (note the change of status) found herself "greatly interested" in the singing and dancing of Japanese women. A notable event seems to have occurred just three days before the ship entered the harbour of Macao: "This night one of the women who was attached to Mr. Csurin was brought to bed." By this, we are to suppose that she gave birth. Who was she – Tchurin's wife? Why not say so? We have no idea what this is about. It is just a drifting sentence in a rollicking sea of narrative.

It is only when Macao is reached that Benyovszky names three women – and only three. They have expired. First, "the wife of Perevalow": her husband was "John Perevalow" who also died – according to Benyovszky – in Macao. A slight problem here in that no one by the name of Perevalov appears on any other list of those involved in the great adventure. The nearest match might conceivably be Mikhail Perevanov, a Cossack from Bolsheretsk, who is named by Ryumin amongst the Macao dead. But his wife is not mentioned anywhere.

Second, "Miss Aphanasia du Nilov," hypothetical daughter of the Governor of Kamchatka. Now, we will have much to say about young Miss Nilov later in our book, as we begin to unpick the story woven by Benyovszky. Suffice it to say here that this young lady does not appear to have existed, let alone to have sailed to Macao for the purposes of dying. But we should at least honour her with a funeral address before we discount her entirely – the words are Benyovszky's own:

> On the 25th, Miss Aphanasia paid the debt of nature. Her premature death affected me greatly, and more especially as it deprived me of the satisfaction of repaying her attachment, by her marriage with the young Popow, son of the Archimandrite, to whom I had given the surname of my family.[5]

This disappointed young man and ersatz son was all of 13 years old, Ivan Ustyuzhinov. A contemporary described him as Benyovszky's "pet"; he followed the Hungarian to Madagascar and then, unexpectedly, he made his way home to find employment in Siberia.

Third, "Catherine Kuzmika." If we state simply that "Miss Kuzmika" was the lady's maid of "Aphanasia du Nilov," we have stated enough.

This general silence about the female passengers is not a matter for surprise. This was, after all, the late eighteenth century. Women were useful, but decidedly not part of the narrative. Even when giving birth, they are not worth identifying. The only exception to this general rule in Benyovszky's account was Afanasia who was, we fear, quite fictitious. What is a surprise, however, is his rather racy inclusion of a number of female persons and events concerning women which were purely imagined.

The first such risqué thread was Benyovszky's supposed romantic liaison with the Governor's daughter, the doomed Afanasia Nilova. This was a girl of perhaps 15 or 16 years of age who had fallen head over heels in love with the dashing Benyovszky. Her mother had pushed the star-struck girl into Benyovszky's bed and had, in all but name, married the girl off. As the final preparations were being made to leave Kamchatka,

> Miss Aphanasia presented herself in the dress, and with the arms of a man, and the company named her *Achilles*. Her figure in this dress was charming, and she certainly had as much courage as it is possible for a woman to have.[6]

This was actually the last time Afanasia was mentioned until her death in Macao – a deafening silence lasting 240 pages and four months.

When the adventurers were preparing to embark on their ship, Benyovszky

> received a request from more than thirty women and girls, who were desirous of following the fortune of their friends, but as it was impossible for us to take so large a number of people on board, three only were accepted, and the others were refused, with the promise, that on our arrival at the first island, we would send the vessel for them.[7]

And again, that was the last we ever hear of these brave women. Quite how the three chosen ones fitted in to the total of "nine women" whom Benyovszky mentioned as being on board, is not known.

In his most entertaining tale of women flinging themselves panting at the adventurers, Benyovszky reported that, when the ship was moored off one of the Aleutian Islands, "upwards of fifty women" had been aboard for two nights, having previously turned up unannounced to "offer their services"; they had to be put ashore, "after the distribution of presents among them," before the crew weighed anchor. What the three (or nine) voyaging "women" thought of this on-board debauch going on around them is not recorded.

At a later stage in the voyage, when the ship had stopped off at Benyovszky's island of "Liquor" (his version of the Elysian island of Tinian), there was a debate between the entire male crew, who wished to settle on the island, and Benyovszky, who wished to move on. The decision finally went the commander's way after he had pointed out

> that our company consisting of a great number of men, and only eight women, the disproportion would hinder our union; and that, in fact, it was merely this want of women which had prevented me from making the proposal to them of fixing our residence upon the island.[8]

As the crew hummed and hawed about this, Benyovszky then pitched in with the killer argument: "I then declared, that my intention was to sail for Japan, and there make a descent near a town, from which we would carry off as many women as we could seize, together with cattle and grain." That did it. "They all exclaimed, 'Long live our Chief, long live our General'; and they came one after the other to kiss my hand."[9]

Two days later they set sail to find a supply of women and cattle. All in a day's work for eighteenth-century adventurers.

Finally, there is a curious episode on Formosa when Benyovszky found himself 'married' to a local girl. The islanders were friendly. Very friendly indeed. A string of seven young women, "some of whom were real beauties," was paraded before Benyovszky, and he was asked to select one as a wife. "The choice would have been rather difficult, if it had really been incumbent on me to decide; for there were three among them who might have disputed the preference with the most perfect work of living nature." At last he made up his mind, and the islanders declared themselves delighted. But that good old-fashioned European morality kicked in:

> I informed my companions of my adventure, and several of them determined to pass the night with me, in order to avoid certain embarrassments; and to answer this purpose more effectually, I requested all the female companions of our voyage to be present, to amuse those who might come from the village.[10]

An unseemly one-night stand was thus averted for the man who, with a perfectly good wife waiting back home in Hungary, had recently found himself promised to Afanasia Nilova and was now apparently hitched to a nice Formosan girl.

So much for all the voyagers. We return now to Ivan Ryumin and his fidgety friends sitting on their thumbs in Paris.

Notes

1 *Gentleman's Magazine*, 1772, p.272.
2 Cultru, 1906, p.162.
3 Stein, 1908, pp.605–609.
4 Cultru, 1906, p.163.
5 Benyovszky, 1790, Vol.II, p.79.
6 *ibid*, Vol.I, p.261.
7 *ibid*, Vol.I, p.263.
8 *ibid*, Vol.I, p.378.
9 *ibid*, Vol.I, p.378.
10 *ibid*, Vol.II, p.14.

X

RETURN FROM PARIS

"Wild, Empty Land in Hungary"

Deceptions – An Inadvertent Escape – Confusion –
A Deception Had Been Perpetrated – Forgiveness – Return to Siberia

Having walked all the way to Paris (550 *versts* – 585 kilometres – walking all the way, in case you had forgotten), the small group of unwilling exiles threw themselves on the charity of the Russian ambassador. They begged him to lobby on their behalf with the government back home, to which end they delivered up Ryumin's journal, a map of the voyage from Kamchatka to Macao and a list of all who participated. Sadly, the map has not survived. Even more importantly, they also produced a lengthy explanation of the circumstances of those regrettable events in Bolsheretsk. This last item had to look good, because upon its reception in St Petersburg rested the group's chances of a return to liberty. The document turned up in the Imperial Archives, so we can be sure it was delivered safely.[1] Ill-written and in places quite obscure of meaning, the words are most likely Ryumin's, and the document is worth some careful consideration: it provides an alternative view of how Benyovszky managed to win over the exiles and the disaffected to his plans for escape. It begins,

> In 1770 five prisoners had been sent from Petersburg, two of them foreigners, but what kind of people they were was not indicated in the order, and we did not know. They said, however, that they had been exiled to Kamchatka on account of the Grand-Duke Pavel Petrovich. One of the foreigners called himself a baron; everyone treated him with respect, and especially those who had been exiled and the commanding officer treated him with the highest regard.

A somewhat garbled explanation followed, which boiled down to this: that Benyovszky had been acting on behalf of the Holy Roman Emperor (Josef of Austria) who was attempting to arrange a marriage between his daughter and the Grand-Duke Paul of Russia. We will recall that Paul – the future Tsar – was the son of Catherine the Great (and possibly of her husband Peter – or possibly not). In 1770, at the time of Benyovszky's arrival in Kamchatka, Paul was 16 years old and the rightful heir to the throne of Russia, which his mother had occupied since disposing of the Emperor Peter. Naturally, Catherine was having none of that nonsense about succession rights, and continued to reign until her death in 1796. She made some small concessions to promote her son Paul, largely in reaction to endless conspiracies and palace plots. But many, traditionalists and opponents alike, still silently favoured Paul over Catherine.

Benyovszky seems to have latched on to this; rather than presenting himself to the community of Russian exiles as a mercenary Polish-Hungarian prisoner-of-war, he made up a story about his devotion to the lawful heir-apparent. The curious tale of "letters" carried to the Holy Roman Emperor was a complete fiction; but a rather pretty one nonetheless. So, said he, he had been caught red-handed with incriminating letters between the Holy Roman Emperor and the Grand-Duke Paul, and had been duly packed off to Kamchatka. By great good fortune, he had managed to preserve one of the letters, which of course proved it all. All of this was quite acceptable to the exiles, many of whom were in Kamchatka precisely because of Catherine. His audience swallowed the story whole. Even those who were not exiles would have found some attraction in the story. And no one in Kamchatka would have had access to any other sources of information.

> As soon as we found out about this, in our innocence we requested to know of him by what means we might serve the prince, and at the same time we asked the exiles about him, and especially Stepanov who, as it seemed to us, was friendly with him and whom we believed. And all equally assured us that he was a nobleman and had apparently sworn before God in their presence that he had been genuinely sent from the Emperor to the Grand-Duke Pavel Petrovich. And upon hearing this we were satisfied.

The document presented to the Russian ambassador describes this tale of deceit; an added twist was that the 'so-called Baron' used the fiction of his loyalty to Grand-Duke Paul as blackmail to ensure that the escape plan went smoothly. At the first sign of dissent on board ship, he

> summoned us and said that the secret was out and that things would work out badly for us, and furthermore that the Grand-Duke would be distressed; we did not know what to do, and said: as you wish, we are happy to obey and are ready to die for the Grand-Duke.

This stratagem worked well until they reached Macao, where the Baron promptly jettisoned the story told so far:

> However, on arriving in Macao, the so-called Baron exerted himself with the Governor and began to beat us and reprimand the officers, forbidding us to pray to the icons and make the sign of the cross in our customary way, and calling us Hungarians – we put up with everything; finally he began to inveigh against the Grand-Duke and said [...] that he considered the previous oath to be of no consequence.

Well, here was a fine pickle, and no mistake. They were mired up to their necks in trouble, and had no one to pull them out of it – until Stepanov stepped up to the mark, claiming that Benyovszky was actually in the pay of the French:

> We did not know what to do, but one of the Russian exiles – his name was Captain Stepanov – stood against him, and he finally told us that everything had obviously been a deception; he [*i.e. Benyovszky*] had wanted to travel to the Spanish territories, but had now changed his intention; he was travelling with the French, and the French were about to have a war with the English, and for that reason the French needed men, and at the same time he would surrender the log-book to them and they would cause harm to our motherland, and that it was bad to fight against friends of one's motherland and that we had been deceived and had fled Kamchatka inadvertently, which the Empress, since she was magnanimous and reasonable, would, of course, forgive; but if we began to fight against the motherland, then we could not hope for mercy and we would be deeply ashamed; but we were free men, and it was up to us whether we went with him or not.

An "inadvertent flight"?[2] Benyovszky working for the French? Confused? Everyone was even more confused when the Baron turned quite nasty and threatened them with re-location to "wild, empty land in Hungary."

> After that he [*Benyovszky*] berated his companion, who was called Major von Vinblat, and placed him under arrest, meanwhile going on to violate the Kamchatkan serving-girl of [*the ship's captain*] Churin's. At this act of rape, people began to voice disapproval, but the Major told the Captain [*i.e. Stepanov*], and the Captain then told us that he did not regard him as a nobleman, but knew him to be a captain in the hussars, and through his deceptions he had brought misfortune upon him, too; he had not been sent by the Emperor at all, and it was all lies in order to save himself and wanted this whole company to be settled on wild, empty land in Hungary. At this point we begged the Major to deliver us from his clutches. Although he [*the Major*] was a foreigner, he was obviously an honest person, and he promised, as he had sworn, to help us regain our freedom and return to our motherland,

and he explained as much to the English. The so-called Baron still wanted to take away the log-book, however, but we would not give it to him; and the Captain said that we should not surrender it until someone from the Senate in Macao would be in favour of informing everyone about the rape, and for that reason the Governor would be obliged to send us all to the King in Portugal, and there we would seek out a translator and be able to explain the deception that had been perpetrated.

While they dreamed up increasingly desperate plans for self-preservation, the Baron was several steps ahead of them.

It turned out that our rival had given false testimony about us, to the effect that we wished to capture the city, with the result that the entire city assembled to place us under guard, including the Captain [*Stepanov*], and the Bishop took the Major away with him. And on the following day the so-called Baron came to our quarters and said to us that he would starve and torture all of us to death in the prison, if we did not give a signed statement to the effect that we were travelling under the protection of the Roman Emperor, and that he would send the Captain and the Major into exile. We could see that he had the ear of the Governor and, in fear, we signed the statement as he wished, and all of us were released, and the Governor placed us under his command; the Major was kept under arrest for two months, but the Captain was stubborn, did not travel with him and remained in Macao, for which reason he was compelled by force to pass his life in misery there.

This entire curious story, which may or may not have had some basis in reality, was leading up to the Grand Petition. It must be said that using devotion to the Grand-Duke Paul was a risky tactic to employ when seeking forgiveness from Catherine the Great. But there was no other way:

And now that we have had the occasion to come upon you, we most humbly beg you, as a person of Russian nationality, to offer us your hand in assistance, to deliver us from brute force; we wish to return to our motherland, knowing the magnanimity of the Empress, and that she will pardon us our naivety and, if she should punish us, then it would be better for us to suffer it from our Empress, than from the enemy of our motherland.

This defence was delivered on 16th April 1773. It contained several points of interest – not least the charge of rape against Benyovszky, along with lesser charges of deception. The events in Macao are just as unclear as many of the other events of the escape, notwithstanding the fact that there were more – and more reliable – witnesses in China. No other account makes any accusation of rape: it may be pure embroidery on the part of the authors, to blacken Benyovszky's name even further; or it may have had some element of truth. In their precarious position in

Paris, surviving on seven *kopeks* per day, the authors had a deep interest in painting the worst possible picture of treachery on the Baron's part. On the other hand, the falling-out of Stepanov, Winbladh and Benyovszky certainly did take place, for reasons which vary according to perspective. We note that this account states that Benyovszky lost possession of the ship's log for a period – a period in which both Ryumin and Stepanov would have been able to take notes for their own later accounts. Possession of that log was crucial – it would represent the incontestable proof to anyone interested that certain places had been visited.

Two days later, the Russian ambassador, Khotyn, sent all the relevant documents off to Russia by diplomatic bag, with a note of the exiles' petition to return. Despite the fugitives' confession of a preference for the Grand-Duke Paul over Catherine, a favourable answer eventually came back and, on the 26th August, the band of seventeen hopefuls made their way from Paris to Le Havre. We hope they did not walk all the way, but Ryumin had by now put down his pen, so we will never know. At Le Havre they boarded the vessel *Brigitte Marguerite*, which arrived in St Petersburg on 30th September. The authorities there were keen to pack them all off to a dark corner of the Empire, and not have them cluttering up the boulevards of the capital.

The Empress herself wrote a letter to the senator and Privy Councillor Prince Vyazemski on 2nd October, forwarding Khotyn's notes and explaining:

> Seventeen people from those who were deceived by Benyovszky have returned here today and I promised them a pardon, which I will grant them. They have already been fairly punished for their sins by undergoing a long journey and suffering sea-sickness and a harsh road on land. You are to decide their fate as soon as possible and give them a quiet habitation. Do not delay, if you please, to ask Count Panin, since they are now being looked after by the Foreign Office, to make them swear an oath of fidelity and ask each of them, where they are willing to live. Apart from the two capitals, they may go to whatever place they choose.[3]

Such was the efficiency of the government and such was the strength of Catherine's will that, within three days of their arrival, the returning voyagers were en route to Siberia under the watchful eye of two Senate couriers. Taking the Empress' offer at face-value, Ivan Ryumin and his wife chose to stop off in Tobolsk, far enough from the west to please the government, far enough from the east to please the former chancellery clerk. The couple (and one other) settled down to an existence in anonymity, having had more than enough excitement for one life. Nine men settled in Irkutsk, three in Okhotsk – and two returned to Kamchatka: the Imperial government quite encouraged this, with the perfectly sound logic that the travellers' tales of woe would cause other hotheads to think twice about escaping.

However, it was not just the Kamchatkans who were fated to listen to these tales. Captain Cook had to listen as well.

Notes

1   All the quoted passages in this chapter are taken from Stein, 1908, Vol.II, pp.602–610.
2   *ibid*, p.603. The Russian word *neumyślenno* can translate as *not deliberately, unintentionally, not wilfully, inadvertently.*
3   *ibid*, pp.608–609.

XI

IZMAILOV

It Made His Story a Little Suspicious

Captain Cook Explores the North Pacific – A Russian Character –
Tall Tales of Exploration and Adventure – The Aleutian Postal Service –
Justified Fears Concerning the French – Another Captain Is Lost

In the summer of 1778, Captain James Cook with his ships the *Discovery* and the *Resolution* made two attempts to break through the Bering Strait and into the northern sea. Repulsed in the first attempt, which found him exploring the coastline of Alaska, he retreated down to the Aleutian Islands, and found a comfortable harbour on the largest of these, Unalaska. After a second attempt, which this time took him along the coast of north-east Siberia, the ships returned to Unalaska in October, and anchored in the bay of Samganooda, on the north side of the island.

And here an interesting gentleman introduced himself. As Captain Cook wrote[1]:

> On the 15th, in the evening, while Mr. Webber and I were at a village at a small distance from Samganoodha, a Russian landed there, who, I found, was the principal person amongst his countrymen in this and the neighbouring islands. His name was Erasim Gregorioff Sin Ismyloff. He arrived in a canoe carrying three persons, attended by twenty or thirty other canoes, each conducted by one man. I took notice, that the first thing they did after landing, was to make a small tent for Ismyloff, of materials which they brought with them; and then they made others for themselves of their canoes and paddles, which they covered with grass, so that the people of the village were at no trouble to find them lodging. Ismyloff having invited us into his tent, set before us some dried salmon and berries, which, I was satisfied, was the best cheer he had.

This person, who evidently knew how to make an entrance in style, was none other than Gerasim Izmailov, he who in June 1771 had been abandoned on the Kuril Islands by the commander of the *St Peter* on its glorious voyage to Liberty and the Island of Paradise. Cook judged that

> He appeared to be a sensible intelligent man, and I felt no small mortification in not being able to converse with him, unless by signs, assisted by figures, and other characters, which however were a very great help. I desired to see him on board the next day, and accordingly he came, with all his attendants. Indeed, he had moved into our neighbourhood for the express purpose of seeing us.

Cook found that Izmailov possessed a great wealth of useful information about the geography of the islands; the Russian spent his time on the *Discovery* in criticising all the 'modern maps' which Cook possessed, obliterating islands here, shifting them there, adding in one or two others. He claimed to have accompanied the Russian explorer Synd, in his expedition to the north in 1762, and pointed out places on Cook's charts which Synd had also visited.

> To what place Synd went after that, or in what manner he spent the two years, during which, as Ismyloff said, his researches lasted, he either could not or would not inform us. Perhaps he did not comprehend our enquiries about this, and yet, in almost every other thing, we could make him understand us. This created a suspicion that he had not really been in that expedition, notwithstanding his assertion.

But Gerasim Izmailov was only just getting into his stride with his polite British audience. The garrulous Russian had one other story to tell, which Captain Cook seemed greatly inclined to take with a large pinch of salt:

> But a voyage which he himself had performed, engaged our attention more than any other. He said, that on the 12th of May, 1771, he sailed from Bolscheretzk, in a Russian vessel, to one of the Kuril islands, named Mareekan, in the latitude of 47°, where there is a harbour and a Russian settlement. From this island he proceeded to Japan, where he seems to have made but a short stay. For when the Japanese came to know that he and his companions were Christians, they made signs for them to be gone, but did not, so far as we could understand him, offer any insult or force. From Japan he got to Canton, and from thence to France, in a French ship. From France, he travelled to Petersburg; and was afterward sent out again to Kamtschatka. What became of the vessel in which he first embarked, we could not learn, nor what was the principal object of the voyage. His not being able to speak one word of French, made this story a little suspicious. He did not even know the name of any one of the most common things that must have been

in use every day, while he was on board the ship and in France. And yet he seemed clear as to the times of his arriving at different places, and of his leaving them, which he put down in writing.

Captain Cook did not realise it, but this story was remarkable for two reasons: first, we have independent verification that Izmailov went no further with Benyovszky on the *St Peter* than the Kuril Island on which he was abandoned in late May of 1771. So his story – heading off to Japan, Canton and France, and thence back the long way to Kamchatka – was untrue from the second sentence onwards. Second, however, the story which he told was an accurate summary of what actually did happen to those on board the galliot. Izmailov can only have had this story from one of the small number of people who made it home in 1773. This would have been his friend Dmitrii Bocharov, who trained with him as navigator and had also been involved in the Benyovszky adventure, returning to Kamchatka via Paris and Irkutsk. And so, as with any other good story in that part of the world, Izmailov had adopted it for his own autobiography and dined out on it with passing explorers.

Having dined, Izmailov retired to his tent. A few days later, he arrived back on the ship with an armful of charts for Cook's officers to copy. One of these covered the "Penshinskian Sea" (the north-eastern part of the Sea of Okhotsk), the "coast of Tartary" (which covered the coast down to the mouth of the Amur River, the island of Sakhalin and beyond), the Kurils and Kamchatka; this contained much information that was to prove useful to the British expedition in the following year. The second chart "was to me the most interesting, for it comprehended all the discoveries made by the Russians to the eastward of Kamtschatka, toward America." The Captain quite rightly did not accept these charts as definitive, and took pains, in his journal, to point out that they could well be erroneous. But the fact that they existed at all and were in his possession suggests that Izmailov was busy carving out a little empire for himself, just out of sight of the Russian government. Cook's final summing up of the man's character was that he

> seemed to have abilities that might entitle him to a higher station in life, than that in which we found him. He was tolerably well versed in astronomy, and in the most useful branches of mathematics. I made him a present of an Hadley's octant; and though, probably, it was the first he had ever seen, he made himself acquainted, in a very short time, with most of the uses to which that instrument can be applied.

Captain Cook and Gerasim Izmailov parted the very best of friends. The Russian even offered to post a letter.

> Mr. Ismyloff remained with us until the 21st, in the evening, when he took his final leave. To his care I entrusted a letter to the Lords Commissioners of the Admiralty; in which was enclosed a chart of all the northern coasts I had

visited. He said there would be an opportunity of sending it to Kamtschatka, or Okotsk, the ensuing spring; and that it would be at Petersburgh the following winter. He gave me a letter to Major Behm, Governor of Kamtschatka, who resides at Bolscheretzk; and another to the commanding officer at Petropaulowska.

So the letter for London was not going to get there any time soon. However, on the following morning, a man in possession of a small boat turned up. He explained to the British naval men that Izmailov had commissioned him to take the letter to Petropavlovsk the following May. Cook gave the postman a small spyglass to present to the Kamchatkan commander, Major Böhm. Then, four days later, realising that another trip northwards was ill-advised so late in the season, the expedition raised anchor and set off southwards, returning to a warmer winter station in the Sandwich Islands and beyond. It was a winter break from which Cook never returned. He met his end in Hawaii in February of the following year.

When Gerasim Izmailov met Cook, he was in the middle of forging himself a career as a leading explorer in the Russian-Alaskan region. Born in Yakutsk in 1745, he had been trained as a navigator in Okhotsk before shipping out to Kamchatka. When, along with the Kamchadale ship's carpenter Alexei Parantsin and his wife, he was abandoned on one of the Kuril Islands by Benyovszky, the three of them spent a nervous day or two wondering what was to become of them, before stumbling across the remains of an old trading settlement which gave them shelter. There is some debate about which Kuril Island was now their home. Izmailov declared it to have been the inhabited island of "Mareekan"; 'Marikan' appears on older maps of the Kurils at the same location as the island now known as Simushir – at 47°, as per his account to Cook. Any inhabitants at that time were probably native Ainu. (According to the official Russian report on the whole unfortunate saga, the island was most definitely uninhabited – but then, it named the completely unrelated island of Makanrushi.[2]) All three castaways appear to have spent a further year on the island, eating a healthy diet of "scallops, cabbage and roots," until at last, in June of 1772, a passing Russian trading vessel took them back to Bolsheretsk – just in time to be arrested. In Izmailov's absence, the authorities had been vexing themselves with an official inquiry into the events at Bolsheretsk in April and May of 1771. Our friend Plenisner, blameless in Okhotsk, found himself in the spotlight again, accused of "weak supervision of the criminals" while they were awaiting ship to Kamchatka and – worse still – of delaying his reports to his Governor on the events concerning the peninsula. Unsurprisingly, Izmailov was soon caught up in this, and found himself facing charges of insurrection. More surprisingly, when the inquiry finished in March of 1774, he was found to be blameless, and set loose.

Making best use of this singular piece of luck, he schooled himself in the twin Siberian disciplines – exploration and the fur-trade. Between 1775 and 1781, he commanded a boat named *St Paul*, gradually working his way along the Aleutian

Islands, establishing contacts with the natives, drawing up charts of the waters. After his encounter with Captain Cook, he continued his exploration eastwards, eventually hitting the Alaskan coastline and, with others, securing Russian rights to that vast region. Where possible, the explorers and traders would erect large wooden crosses proclaiming the territory to be the property of Russia.

In the years 1783 to 1786, Izmailov was in command of the galliot *The Three Saints, Basil the Great, Gregory the Theologian and John Chrysostom* (it was *de rigueur* that every ship in that part of the world should be named after one or more Christian saints: a wise precaution, given the weather conditions), sailing from Okhotsk to chart the Aleutians all the way up to Kodiak Island and back. In 1788, he and his friend Bocharov charted Prince William Sound and then, in June, they called in at Yakutat Bay in Alaska, where they settled down to trade furs with the native Tlingit people. In return for business transacted, the Tlingit chief was deeply honoured to receive an Imperial crest; it probably looked good on the wall of his dwelling, but it is unlikely he realised that he agreed thereby to become subject to the Russian Empire. Izmailov had two large copper 'possession plates' marking "the extent of Russia's domain" buried nearby. Safely out of sight of any curious passer-by, this was clear evidence that Russia had established colonisation rights.

In 1789, we find him on the galliot *St Simeon*, exploring and mapping the south-east coast of the Kenai Peninsula (to the south of what is now Anchorage). Three years later, in the employment of the Russian-American Company, he was in command of this same ship. In the following years, he sailed in the Bering Sea, and visited the Aleutians on several occasions. The story of the Russian-American Company is a depressing one of atrocity and tragedy: by turns trading with the local peoples and killing (or being killed by) them; Izmailov himself was accused of shooting dead at least two unarmed Aleuts.[3] In 1794, he delivered some thirty settler families (described by an astute observer as "unfortunate ones") and a clutch of missionaries to Yakutat in Alaska, captaining a new *Three Saints*, the earlier one having fallen from saintly favour and been wrecked. Izmailov died in Okhotsk between 1795 and 1797, but two small islands in Alaska are named after him – one in Cook Inlet (Ismailof Island in Halibut Cove) and one in the Gulf of Prince William (Izmaylov Island in the Strait of Latouche).

For his part, Dmitrii Bocharov remained active in the Aleutian trade until his death on Unalaska in 1793. He gave his name to Lake Becharof in Alaska, as well as a tiny island. Not bad for an ordinary boy from Kamchatka.

In April of 1779, the ships *Discovery* and *Resolution* from Cook's third voyage were back in Siberian waters, now under the leadership of Captain Charles Clerke, with Captain James King as his second-in-command. They headed, this time, straight for Kamchatka, without attempting to renew their acquaintance with the up-and-coming Izmailov or the residents of the Aleutians. Arriving amidst snow and ice, they made use of Izmailov's charts to get them into the harbour of Petropavlovsk; they found some of the information provided not to be quite accurate.

According to the accounts given in Oonalaska, we had conceived [*it*] to be a place of some strength and consideration. At length we discovered, on a narrow point of land to the North North East, a few miserable log-houses, and some conical huts, raised on poles; which, from their situation [...] we were under the necessity of concluding to be Petropaulowska.[4]

Welcome to Kamchatka.

However, once they had got themselves ashore – Captain James King plunging through the ice into the sea and then floundering about in the snow – and after some initial difficulties of communication, they found a warm welcome from the garrison and residents. King was placed in front of a roaring fire and set to steam, while the commander of the fortress suspiciously eyed Izmailov's letters of introduction. One of the letters was sent off to Bolsheretsk for closer inspection. (The British got to Kamchatka – via the South Pacific – long before Cook's letter to London which had been sent with the help of Izmailov. The letter reached London in January 1780, while the ships got back to London in October of the same year. Given that the Russian naval authorities were able to publish charts based on Cook's data in 1781 – three years before the British Admiralty – dare one suppose that this letter had been opened by the mail service? But at least it got there – the hazards of the Siberian postal service were documented by John Cochrane in 1821, when the year's mail from Kamchatka to European Russia was stolen by a bear. On his return journey westwards across Siberia, Cochrane's party "met the post from Yakutsk, and in the course of an hour we were overtaken by that from Okotsk: the latter had been encountered by a bear, which had destroyed most of the letters and papers. The Journal of Captain Vassilieff's Expedition, in particular, had suffered much."[5] The postman was fortunate to escape with his life).

In Petropavlovsk a meal was served to the British, one far better than the exiles had received in 1771: on the menu was

cold beef sliced, with hot water poured over it. We had next a large bird roasted, of a species with which I was unacquainted, but of a very excellent taste. After having eaten a part of this, it was taken off, and we were served with fish dressed two different ways; and, soon after, the bird again made its appearance, in savory and sweet *patés*. Our liquor [...] was of the kind called by the Russians *quass*, and was much the worst part of the entertainment.[6]

After a couple of days of relentless hospitality, a merchant and a senior army officer arrived from Bolsheretsk; both appeared greatly alarmed at the size and war-like appearance of the British ships. "We afterward found," wrote King "that Ismyloff, in his letter to the commander, had misrepresented us, for what reasons we could not conceive, as two small trading boats." This little misunderstanding was soon sorted out, and both visitors and hosts settled down to a couple of weeks of amiable co-habitation.

The Kamchatkans turned out to be extremely welcoming hosts, plied them with food and drink and gave them the grand tour of the surrounding countryside. Subsequently, the British engaged in further explorations of the eastern seaboard of Siberia, returned to Kamchatka at the end of August, undertook some hunting and fishing, then set off down the Kurils, following much the same route as the *St Peter* had taken nine years before. The difference was that the British ships took only six weeks to reach Macao. Here "we received a farther corroboration of the facts, from the gentlemen of the English factory, who told us, that a person had arrived there in a Russian galliot, who said he came from Kamtschatka."

By then, the leaders of the expedition were in rather a sticky position: Cook having been killed on Hawaii in February 1779, Captain Clerke had then died at Petropavlovsk and was buried at the end of August of the same year, succumbing to tuberculosis previously contracted while stranded, as proxy for his brother, in a debtors' prison in London. James King in the *Discovery* may have begun to fear for his prospects when he returned to London with the bad news: to lose one captain might be regarded as a misfortune; to lose both was beginning to look like carelessness.

Notes

1   All the following quotations from Captain Cook are taken from Cook/King, 1821, Vol.2, pp.455–463.
2   Sgibnev, 1876, p.544.
3   For more on the Russian-American Company see: Matthews, 2013.
4   Cook/King, 1834, Vol.3, p.184.
5   Cochrane, 1825, Vol.2, pp.94–95.
6   Cook/King, 1834, Vol.3, p.188–189.

XII

SCAPEGOATS

"The Rampaging Rapaciousness of Robbers"

Colonel Plenisner Finds Himself in Trouble – The Authorities Take Decisive Action –
Captain King Considers it Well That He Is Not a Frenchman –
Monsieur de Lesseps Perhaps Wishes He Were Not – Commander Cochrane's Aunt

Carelessness, too, was Colonel Plenisner's crime – carelessly losing his commander of Kamchatka and carelessly allowing seventy people to make off with a precious supply-ship.

It is the first rule of government that, after each inevitable embarrassment to the structures of state, one should point fingers at officials who are already unpopular, or – even better – tainted by some misdemeanour. It was no different in Russia in the aftermath of the escape from Kamchatka.

One of the first scapegoats was Plenisner, the rather luckless one-time Governor of Kamchatka. Fate, not content with despatching him to the farthest reaches of Siberia so that he could recommend the closure of the government fortress there, and not content with embroiling him with the rival 'Governor' Izvekov, and finding himself grounded in a rather dismal port on the edge of nowhere – Fate now dealt him a third blow, which was to place him in Okhotsk just as Benyovszky escaped. Since Commander Nilov, actual head of civil government in Kamchatka, was rather inconveniently dead, the next available figure of authority was Plenisner, who had been blamelessly mouldering away on the far side of the Sea of Okhotsk while the rebellion was brewing.

In June of 1772, a month after the setting sail of the *St Peter*, a ship named the *St Catherine* brought to Okhotsk an interim report on the events in Bolsheretsk. The captain of this ship was Sofyin, the man who had been left behind by Benyovszky and Stepanov to sort out the mess they had left behind. For reasons best known to himself, Plenisner chose not to pass the report up the line to his Governor in Irkutsk until December; instead he initiated his own investigation – in all probability, the intervention of the Governor in the preceding year still rankled. To this end, he sent a veteran military man to Bolsheretsk, to act as interim commander and clear up the mess. Irkutsk got to hear of the events from a different source, and was greatly annoyed that this veteran "in his old age and folly" had been sent out. But events dragged on remarkably slowly, as they seemed to do in Siberia, and it was not until October that a younger man, Captain Schmalev, was despatched to Okhotsk and then Kamchatka to take up the reins of government.[1]

Schmalev's instructions were set out quite clearly: first, he was to take with him a reasonable number of soldiers, in case the "villains" returned to Kamchatka; second, he was to ensure that said "villains" did not attempt to make a return elsewhere in the province, by the careful issue of "wanted" posters; third, he was to re-stock all the forts with artillery, muskets and gunpowder; fourth, he was to make a map of the area around Bolsheretsk; fifth, and only fifth, he was to investigate why "the outrage" happened; and sixth, root out any remaining "accomplices." The instructions may have been clear; the road to Kamchatka was less so. Schmalev spent two months getting to Yakutsk, arriving in mid-December, where – wisely, given the season – he fell sick. Accompanied by thirty-five soldiers, he finally reached Kamchatka in July 1773.

In the meantime, the Governor in Irkutsk had sent a report to St Petersburg. A letter signed by the Empress Catherine herself eventually came post-haste back down the road; it was, noted the archives,[2] "delivered by the courier at 12 o'clock midnight, February 14, 1772." "We," began the letter in the prescribed regal manner, "judge it necessary in this matter to instruct you as follows..." First, "all means and methods conveniently possible" were to be used to restore "order and obedience"; second, a reward of 200 roubles was to be advertised for any information leading to the apprehension of any of the guilty parties (the Governor was explicitly authorised to draw on his own treasury to fund this); and third, fourth and fifth, the Governor was instructed to make sure no other malcontents in Siberia were tempted to embark on similar escapades.

Spurred on by this declaration of the Imperial interest, a second investigator was despatched to Kamchatka to join Schmalev; but this one, when he arrived, found the inhabitants rather reluctant to discuss the matter; their excuse for having said nothing previously was that they were afraid even to mention it in private letters back to mainland Russia.

While one set of authorities was carefully counting out funds from the treasury, in order to despatch troops and investigators to Kamchatka, another group got to work on establishing a fall-guy for the whole fiasco. One figure stood out head and shoulders above the rest: Colonel Plenisner, who had made the fatal mistake of not informing his superiors within the statutory three days (as per Imperial codes and decrees of 1730 and 1762). Accordingly, Plenisner was summoned to Irkutsk, and placed before a tribunal. The hearing began on 7th February 1772 and was completed three weeks later. Plenisner's line of defence seems to have been rather disingenuous – that he had really wanted to send a message to Irkutsk, but "the mud and the expense" had prevented him from doing so until the roads cleared and someone would be travelling that way anyway. It was not perhaps the most robust of excuses. So he was quite pleased when the tribunal found that he was not guilty of any criminal intent, merely of making "a mistake," occasioned by "his ignorance of the duties of his office, or from weakness and negligence." The charge of negligence stuck nicely, and Plenisner was relieved of his post.

This judgement was reached swiftly – far more swiftly than the act of sending staff out to Kamchatka. The Empress was kept informed. Already in his sixties, Plenisner was eventually allowed to retire to Tobolsk, on a pension of 200 roubles. He died a few years later in St Petersburg. He had removed himself there in 1776 clutching, as his final and positive contribution to the consolidation of government in the east, a portfolio of the first maps of the Chukchi territory which were then incorporated in the Academy's definitive atlas of the Russian Empire.

As for a handful of possible "accomplices" and "villains" – mostly innocent bystanders who had got caught up in the whole sorry mess – they too were thoroughly investigated. A total of thirty-six people were rounded up and sent to Irkutsk in June 1772, and kept there under strict guard until the authorities had finished interrogating them – a process which continued for over a year. Of these thirty-six, the most likely to be found guilty of anything were the three castaways, Gerasim Izmailov, Alexei Parantsin and his wife Lukerya; but they had a pretty watertight case having fallen out big time with Benyovszky, and in due course they were absolved from all liability by Imperial decree at the end of March 1774. Also held for investigation was the Kamchatkan priest, Ustyuzhinov, "who had incurred the suspicion of a friendly relationship with the traitors"; worse still, the priest had made the mistake of presiding over Governor Nilov's funeral rites; worst of all, his 13-year-old son Ivan had run off to sea with Benyovszky. But the priest, too, was forgiven on the basis that he had been punished enough by "everlasting separation" from his son.

Bizarrely, while those who had been left behind in Kamchatka were being closely investigated, some fugitives who had made it all the way to France with Benyovszky were blithely returning home unpunished. This was the group of seventeen who had asked to return to Russia from Paris, and, having arrived in St Petersburg at the end of September 1773, were given an immediate pardon by the Empress and quickly shoved out the back door in the direction of Siberia and Kamchatka. Doubtless the Empress – always the realist – calculated that anyone actively wishing to return to the farthest reaches of Siberia was unlikely to be intent on stirring up further trouble. This group must in fact have passed through Irkutsk (some even took up residence) while their friends and neighbours were languishing there under lock and key.

Long after Benyovszky's shipload of malcontents had disappeared over the horizon, the legacy and the legend of the break-out flourished. It was just about the most exciting thing that had ever happened in Bolsheretsk in the very short history of that place, and no one was inclined to forget it.

Amongst the first outsiders to run up against the collective memory of the great escape were members of Cook's expedition. We saw earlier that the ships *Discovery* and *Resolution* had returned to the Far East of Russia in April 1779, and had sailed into the bay of Petropavlovsk in Kamchatka. When word reached the fort at Bolsheretsk that foreigners had landed, two members of the community were sent hot-foot across the peninsula to have a good look at them. One was a merchant, who had been misinformed in a letter from Izmailov that the newcomers were traders; the other was the second-in-command to the Governor, a Major Böhm, who had the gravest of concerns that these were Frenchmen. "It had required," observed Captain King, "all the Major's authority to keep the inhabitants from leaving the town, and retiring up into the country; to so extraordinary a pitch had their fears risen, from their persuasion that we were French."[3]

And what had caused this fear of the French?

> Their extreme apprehensions of that nation were principally occasioned, by some circumstances attending an insurrection that had happened at Bolsheretsk, a few years before, in which the Commander had lost his life. We were informed, that an exiled Polish officer, named Beniowski, taking advantage of the confusion into which the town was thrown, had seized upon a galliot, then lying at the entrance of the Bolschoireeka, and had forced on board a number of Russian sailors, sufficient to navigate her: that he had put on shore a part of the crew at the Kourile islands; and, among the rest, Ismyloff, who, as the reader will recollect, had puzzled us exceedingly, at Oonalaska, with the history of this transaction [...] Most of the Russians had returned to Europe in French ships; and had afterward found their way to Petersburg. We met with three of Beniowski's crew in the harbour of Saint Peter and Saint Paul; and from them we learnt the circumstances of the above story.

The most logical nation for the Kamchatkans to hide from would have been the Hungarian, or the Polish, or maybe even the Swedish, given that the ringleaders of the escape plot were men of those origins. For once, the French were blameless – they had not yet imbibed the devil's brew of Liberty, Fraternity and Equality. So the only way the French could have come into the picture was as a result of the tales told by those who had returned – such as the three men, unfortunately not named, whom King met. It must have seemed obvious to these people that the French were behind it all: did they not, after all, take Benyovszky away from Macao and deposit him with his close followers in various pleasant spots such as Mauritius and Paris? To a group of people largely ignorant of the fine distinctions between distant European powers, France might have lurked large in the shadows.

And it was an entirely blameless Frenchman who experienced local truculence when he arrived on Kamchatka eight years after Captain King. Monsieur Barthélemy de Lesseps was the French Vice-Consul in Russia who, by a series of happy accidents, found himself aboard an expedition to the north-west Pacific led by the Count de la Pérouse. He had been taken on as an interpreter; he ended up on a journey that was considerably more fraught than he had bargained for. Having pitched up in Petropavlovsk in September 1787, La Pérouse suddenly received instructions to proceed to Australia to investigate what the perfidious British were up to in Botany Bay. The report and logs of his voyage to date, however, had to go back to France. So M. de Lesseps was despatched overland to Bolsheretsk – a journey that took a mere two weeks for a hundred miles – with the aim of crossing to Okhotsk and hot-footing it westwards. Anyone could have told him that that was not going to happen. Sure enough, bad weather prevented their ship from sailing before the ice locked it in. Plan 'B' was then adopted: go the long way round, overland by dog-sleigh. But that did not go too well either since Lesseps' travelling companion, the Governor of Okhotsk, had to stop off at every way-station and yurt en route and perform gubernatorial duties. Four months after leaving Bolsheretsk, Lesseps finally reached Okhotsk in early May 1788: he might have done better just to hang around at the pier at Bolsheretsk and wait for the next ship. It took him a further four months to drag sledges and broken horses across the vast tract of mud and mosquitoes that defines Siberia in summer, before he stumbled into St Petersburg in September. Just your average Siberian journey – one year door to door.

A couple of years later, Lesseps wrote the book. It bore the utilitarian title *Journal Historique du Voyage de M. de Lesseps*, and appeared in Paris in 1790 (the same year as Benyovszky's *Memoirs* – Lesseps may even have used material from the latter). This is what he had to report about the image of France in Kamchatka:[4]

> The disadvantageous opinion that the people of Kamchatka have of the French, that we are a terrible, disloyal nation, stems from the infamous Benyovsky. This Slav represented himself as a Frenchman, and behaved like a true barbarian.
>
> His story is well-known. We know that he served in the Condottieri in the Polish unrest of 1769. Because of his fearlessness, he was counted as a leader of a hastily-collected band of foreigners, or rather robbers, like himself, whom the Condottieri had unwillingly taken into their service. He roamed through the land at their head, and pulled everything down which lay in his path. He harried the Russians incessantly and was feared by them as much as by the Poles. They soon saw the necessity of disposing of such a dangerous enemy; and they were fortunate to take him prisoner in the end. One can readily imagine that they did not treat him gently. He was exiled to Siberia and then to Kamchatka, and his dangerous mind and vengeful spirit accompanied him to that part of the world. Suddenly he came out of the snow where the Russians thought they had buried him, popped up unexpectedly in Bolsheretsk at the head of a mob of exiles, whom he had been able to influence with his boldness. He attacked the garrison, confiscated their weapons; the commander, Herr Nilov, was killed by Benyovsky's own

hand. There was a vessel in the harbour; Benyovsky took possession of it; everyone shook under his gaze, everyone felt obliged to obey him. He forced the poor Kamchadals to deliver food to him, and did not content himself with the sacrifices they brought, but also handed over their dwellings to the rampaging rapaciousness of the robbers who accompanied him, and in all this he stood out as a model of crime and wild cruelty. At last he went to the ship with his comrades and sailed, so they say, to China. The curses of the inhabitants of Kamchatka followed him. Since then, not long ago, the exact details have been learned of the fate of this infamous adventurer. He was the only so-called Frenchman who has ever been seen on this peninsula, so the inhabitants of Kamchatka cannot be blamed for not liking us, but rather fearing us.

It is curious that Lesseps did not question why the Kamchatkans had regarded Benyovszky as a Frenchman ("so-called" or otherwise). However, he was not greatly exercised by that, since he judged that his impeccable French manners had made a good impression:

> I tried to destroy this prejudice [*against Frenchmen*] by my conversation and my behaviour towards them: I do not dare flatter myself that I succeeded, but it seemed to me that in the end their way of thinking had utterly changed in our favour.[5]

Another foreign visitor turned up in Kamchatka in 1821. This one had the good sense not to be French, and was accordingly made very welcome. So welcome, in fact, that he married Ksenia Loginova, a local girl just a few days short of her fifteenth birthday, before whisking her back to London. This romantic traveller was John Dundas Cochrane, whose astonishing "pedestrian journey" across Russia and Siberia was detailed in his book of 1823. It was now over fifty years since the escape of the exiles, but still Kamchatka had not forgotten. While Cochrane was touring the south of the peninsula in the company of various Kamchatkan luminaries, he heard

> strange stories of the celebrated Benjofsky, who made his escape hence to Canton, having previously murdered some people and fomented an insurrection. I heard nothing in his favour, although an old lady, afterwards my aunt, was a companion of his.[6]

The reference to his "aunt" is intriguing. Clearly, this was some sort of elderly relative of his beloved Ksenia, whom he married in January 1822. We note that Ksenia's family-name was Loginov. Ivan Loginov was one of the three crewmen on the *St Peter* who were killed by natives on Formosa. An 'aunt' however, need not be a relative – the lady could have been a friend of parents or of grandparents. Assuming she was perhaps between twenty and thirty years of age when she sailed with Benyovszky, she would have been into her seventies by the time young Cochrane presented himself for inspection at her door. Who was she?

The best candidate is easy to spot. From Ryumin's list of seven women, three died in Macao, two returned to Siberia, and two settled in Mauritius. How likely is it that reasonably impoverished women would want to – let alone pay for – travel back to cold Kamchatka from Mauritius? Stranger things have happened, but surely not that strange. Ivana Ryumina returned to Siberia, but settled in Tobolsk which lies several thousand miles from Kamchatka. This leaves only Lukerya Parantsina, one of the three castaways.

But, given the quality of contemporary records, the aunt might have been someone else altogether. In 1823, Cochrane's readers could consult Benyovszky's book published thirty years earlier, and come up with a veritable swarm of aunts.

Notes

1   Sgibnev, 1876, p.530.
2   *Ibid*, pp.531–532.
3   Cook/King, 1834, Vol.3, p.193.
4   Lesseps, 1790, pp.154–156.
5   Two historical footnotes: Barthélemy de Lesseps was the uncle of Ferdinand de Lesseps, the developer of the Suez Canal. As for the luckless French explorer Count de la Pérouse – he arrived in Botany Bay just a week too late to claim Australia for the French. Disappointed, he set sail for New Caledonia. Neither he nor his ship was ever seen again. Barthélemy had had a lucky escape.
6   Cochrane, 1825, Vol.2, p.6.

XIII

BENYOVSZKY'S ACCOUNTS

"Written by Himself"

Sumptuous Woodcuts – August von Kotzebue's Strange Year –
Several Possibilities for the Truth – A Bit of Straightening and Correcting

The year of 1790 saw the publication of Benyovszky's *Memoirs* by William Nicholson. It was an instant best-seller. French, German, Dutch, Swedish and Polish translations followed within a year; several further German editions were printed during the next decade, Slovak and Hungarian editions soon appeared.[1]

Alas! For the author, fame came too late: by 1790, Benyovszky was four years dead.

His posthumous literary triumph bore the following full and self-explanatory title:

> *Memoirs and Travels of Mauritius Augustus Count de Benyowsky, Magnate of the Kingdoms of Hungary and Poland, one of the Chiefs of the Confederation of Poland etc., etc. Consisting of his Military Operations in Poland, his Exile into Kamchatka, his Escape and Voyage from that Peninsula through the Northern Pacific Ocean, touching at Japan and Formosa, to Canton in China, with an Account of the French Settlement he was appointed to form upon the Island of Madagascar.*

The editorial subtitle continues: *Written by Himself and Translated from the Original Manuscript.* The manuscript had been written in the French language, and its publication was largely thanks to two men closely associated with the Royal Society of London, Messrs Magellan and Nicholson. And this was no slim monograph. The original edition ran to two volumes, each of around 400 pages octavo, complete with maps (sketchy at best) and woodcut illustrations (of varying quality).

And why have we not subjected this massive document to closer examination before? Why have we sneaked up on Baron Benyovszky from behind? Just like

Stepanov's and Ryumin's accounts, it was "written by himself." To ignore it would be manifestly unfair. After all, the immediate success of the book, and the number of its many admirers over two hundred years, suggest it is more deserving of our attention. And so it shall be.

But first: August von Kotzebue. Kotzebue was, in the late eighteenth century, a hugely popular German author and playwright. He had a colourful career, managing to squeeze into the fifty-eight years of his life the writing of around 200 stage-plays; the production of around eighteen children; a career as an Imperial civil servant in St Petersburg; and his own unfortunate death at the hands of a German theology student who strongly resented Kotzebue's mockery of German liberalism. (By a happy coincidence for students of the Russian Far East, one of those eighteen children grew up to be an explorer who spent much time in the seas east of Kamchatka – it is after young Otto that the town and Sound of Kotzebue in Alaska are named.) On his retirement from the Russian Civil Service in 1795, August von Kotzebue had returned to Germany to devote himself to writing, when a falling-out with Goethe prompted him to return to St Petersburg in 1800. It was one of those journeys not fated to go well. No sooner had he reached the border than he was arrested on suspicion of being a French revolutionary, and transported to Siberia. Evidently, this was some kind of bureaucratic foul-up; barely had he managed to settle in to polite society at Tobolsk than he was hauled back to civilisation by the Emperor Paul (for whom, by happy chance, Kotzebue had once written a charming comedy), presented with an estate in Estonia, and appointed director of the flourishing German Theatre in St Petersburg. And all would have ended well had the Emperor Paul not continued the fine tradition of the rulers of Russia by getting himself assassinated the following year; at which point Kotzebue took the sensible precaution of retreating once more to Germany.

What had triggered this arrest and brief exile, the strangest year of his life, as Kotzebue gleefully described it in a later book? It was his play entitled *Count Benyowsky; or, the Conspiracy of Kamtschaka*, first performed in 1792 and published three years later.[2] This play was remarkable for two things: first, the breathless tenor of its dialogue (each speech is on average two lines long, and there are enough exclamation-marks to populate a good-sized Russian forest); second, its uncritical adulation of Benyovszky. Undoubtedly the two primary themes of the play – spiritual liberty and the pursuit of good taste – and its headlong melodramatic pace made it a great success. It had performances all over Europe, from Berlin to London. In Russia, all public reporting of the events in Bolsheretsk had been carefully suppressed for two decades; so the publication of this new play even attracted the attention of Catherine II, who asked the Governor of Tallinn, where Kotzebue was living in 1795, what motives the author had. Small wonder, then, that Kotzebue's arrival at the border-post in 1800 caused consternation amongst the guardians of the public weal. (Despite all this fuss, the play was later performed at the German Theatre in St Petersburg, and was even translated into Russian, much to the outrage of Tsarist commentators.)[3]

BENYOWSKY.—"*There you have her, old Father!—Emilia! my Wife!—Away on board!*"

Count Benyowsky, Act 5. Scene last.

FIGURE 13.1 Benyovszky suddenly remembers his wife and bids farewell to Afanasia Nilova – as imagined for an English translation of Kotzebue's play.

In Kotzebue's play, Benyovszky sparkles as a highly sympathetic and sensitive lover, a man of the greatest morality and intellect, beloved by all his comrades, cherished almost as a son by the silver-haired Commander Nilov of Bolsheretsk, and adored by Nilov's soulful daughter "Athanasia." Kotzebue took several liberties with the story as it had been told by Benyovszky himself – not least in the ending of the play, where there is a tearful scene of farewell between Nilov (upset, but very much alive), his swooning daughter, and Benyovszky (who at the last moment remembers his wife "Emilie" and leaves "Athanasia" in Kamchatka to care for her grateful father). In 1798, theatre critics of the London production of the play noted these deviations from the official story and commented instructively: "It was with sorrow we remembered that Athanasia and her Father met with a severer fate; but, in deviating from the history, the Author has done wisely. He has produced an admirable tragedy."[4]

But here was a slight problem: not only had Kotzebue deviated wisely from the official history provided by Benyovszky; but Benyovszky himself had, in his history, deviated from the actual events. The development of his deviation invites closer scrutiny.

The very first account of Benyovszky's travels had appeared in a report we have already noted – that of the merchant Nathaniel Barlow, who was at Macao when the *St Peter* limped into port:

> The following account is taken from the Count: he was sent by the Queen of Hungary with a body of five thousand men in May 1769, to join the Catholic Confederates in Poland against the Polish Protestants, who were strongly supported by the Russians. A battle soon ensued, in which the protestants defeated and took prisoners the greater part of their enemies. The Colonel, with many of his countrymen, was carried to Casan. They were closely confined and cruelly treated, which determined them to resolve on an escape. An opportunity soon favoured their design, by their guard being reduced, which they overpowered; and, having taken their arms, they directed their rout to Kamschatka, on the sea coast of Tartary, where the Colonel knew a friend, on whose assistance his hopes depended. On his arrival at Kamschatka his friend furnished him with a vessel, in which he embarked with eighty-five of his fellow-prisoners. As he had been formerly in the marine service of the states of Malta, he knew something of navigation, by the assistance of which he determined to sail to China; but, being scantily provided, he resolved to keep near the coast. A strong gale of wind, which he soon met with from the Westward, defeated his purpose. The Colonel then giving up all thoughts of regaining the coast, sailed to the Eastward and Southward till he saw part of North America, in Lat 57.00 N. Here he refreshed his people, having encountered every difficulty Nature is able to sustain. From hence he endeavoured to go to Acapulco, but contrary winds prevented him. This obliged him to sail for the Philippine Islands, intending

to go into Manilla, but was again disappointed by contrary winds. He proceeded then for Macao, having once more experienced suprizing difficulties, being five months on his passage from Kamchatka.[5]

So far, so implausible. These unlikely details were then almost immediately contradicted by Benyovszky in another document which was reported by Barlow – the "*Copy of a Paper sent by Baron de Benyorsky from Macao to a gentleman at Canton*":

> Became prisoner in the year 1769. Carried away into exile with the Princes P. Szolti, Bishop of Cracowia, P. Szangusko, P. Rzseviusky, P. Paez, Bishop de Kiowe. Kamschatka, under 63rd degree of north lat. 175 deg. longitude, month of May 1771, sailed on board the S. Peter Galliot in order to pass as far as 238 N deg. of long and 57 N degree of lat. from whence sailing we were to pass to the isle of Marian; with a great tempest and very strong wind came to Japan; rounded that place from the port of Namgu; went on shore; from thence came to the isle of Tonza and Bongo [*Tosa on Shikoku and the Bungo Channel?*]; from thence proceeded as far as Nangeasaki; from which place, after taking in wines, sailed out again and passed by the isles of Ulsina, as far as Formosa and the isle of Bastee; lastly took the straight course to Makaw, where I arrived in the month of September, 1771.
>
> Signed, Baron Maurice Aout of Aladar and Benyorsky, Colonel in her Imperial Majesty's service, and Regimentary General of the Confederates.
>
> Went out with 85 men. Came back with 62.[6]

While the second account provided far more detail of the voyage from Kamchatka (and some nonsensical latitude/longitude figures), it immediately posed the problem – which version was true? A later report by Barlow, which were certified as being "the Colonel's own words," confirmed much of what had been claimed by Benyovszky, with very little difference in the narrative of the Great Escape from Kazan, and the voyage to America from Kamchatka.[7] Further questioning of Benyovszky by the merchants at Macao, noted Barlow, prompted the adventurer to clam up completely.

A letter written to London by the supercargoes at Canton in November 1771 reeked of frustration: the gentlemen of Canton noted that Benyovszky had arrived, but that the voyagers,

> being at Macao, and cannot obtain permission to come to Canton, we are deprived of the means to procure the intelligence which we might possibly otherwise do, had we an opportunity of discoursing with him; it seems, beyond doubt, he is come from Kamschatka, but by what track, or his motive, we have only what he pleases to say, being the only person who speaks about their concerns, and he very reserved. We could wish it were in our power to give you a particular account of this affair, but cannot do more

than send you the accounts we have received from others, and one that he gave himself, and signed by him.[8]

Even Bishop Le Bon could not get Benyovszky to confess to anything more; he noted only that

> He has been twice shipwrecked and twice they have repaired their vessel. He is not acquainted with the Portuguese or the Spanish, but he speaks Latin, French, and German. He came from the North and has coasted the island of Japan, &c.[9]

That final "&c" in the report of Le Bon's narrative is tantalising – was it Le Bon's own or a dismissive one provided by his editor?

So, by the time Benyovszky sailed away to Mauritius, no one – outside of Stepanov and Ryumin – had had sight of the log-books; the only information which had been offered up as facts were as follows:

- Benyovszky had fought in Poland, been captured, and had escaped from Kazan to Kamchatka (with or without some Bishops in tow);
- On arrival in Kamchatka, he had immediately been provided with a ship and had set sail with eighty-five companions (but no Bishops);
- He may have sailed to North America or – indeed – he may not have done;
- He had veered around the North Pacific until he came across Japan, whose coastline he followed until he reached Formosa;
- From Formosa he had sailed to Macao.

When he reached Mauritius, Benyovszky felt the need to open up a little more. In a letter to the Governor there, M du Dresnay, which was quoted in its entirety by the scientist and geographer Alexis Rochon,[10] Benyovszky had much to say, mostly about himself, but also about his voyage. He addresses his letter as follows "*From Baron Aladar, now known by the name of Count Benyowski, [to the] Governor of Isle de France*" – his name, like his story, was undergoing a certain metamorphosis. As we shall see, so was his nationality. The letter, dated 21st March 1772, is rendered below, in the translation of Joseph Trapp MA: it represents the first coherent account of his travels by Benyovszky, and lays the groundwork for his later *Memoirs*.

> It is with the utmost pleasure and eagerness flowing from the zeal and affection I feel in serving you, I am induced to comply with your commands.
> Born in Hungary, descendant of the illustrious house of the barons of Benyowski, I am a general in the service of the armies of the Empress our Sovereign. My father descended from Aladar XIII, and my mother from the family of Reray; I am therefore of Polish extraction.

In 1765, the King of Poland, Elector of Saxony, being dead, and his kingdom invaded, I retired to Warsaw, to espouse the cause of a prince surrounded with troubles, and the overthrow of the celebrated Constitution of the first members of the state. By a secret warrant the grandees of the kingdom were seized, a partisan of the Prince Bishop of Cracow, and other great men; I was to be secured by order of Prince Repnin, minister of Russia.

Much name-dropping now ensues. It would be tedious for everyone to repeat every name thus dropped, so we will not. However, the use of names does actually suggest that Benyovszky had indeed been in Poland, doing his bit for Freedom. We then embroil ourselves in a wildly improbable story about manly warfare, capture and release; the Pasha of Anatolia takes a personal interest in our hero; he becomes a Colonel and then a General; he is re-captured; and so on. While yet a prisoner for the second time, he undertakes a secret mission from Kazan to St Petersburg on behalf of dissident Russian princes; he succeeds; but is arrested (not once, but twice).

Gradually, however, the breathless narrative comes to a halt. Having been arrested for the second time, he is interrogated in St Petersburg and forced to sign an oath never again to take up arms against Russia:

A few days after, being again brought before the commissioners, violent means were made use of to make me write and sign what follows:

> I, the undersigned, do acknowledge, that I have not only broke my engagements, but even committed murder, and became guilty of blasphemy against her Imperial Majesty; and should my sentence be mitigated through the natural clemency of her Majesty, I do hereby bind myself, after having recovered my liberty, never to put my foot on the territories subject to her Majesty, and less still to carry arms against her.
>
> *Baron Maurice-Augustus Aladar de Benyowksy.*
> *General of the first Confederation. Petersburgh, Nov. 22nd, 1769*

Signing this document appears to have done no good at all: Her Majesty's natural clemency did not deliver. He was bundled off eastwards:

> After having drawn up and signed this piece of writing, I was again put under arrest, and finally on the 24th of November, at midnight, an officer came at the head of twenty-eight men, and threw me in a carriage. We took the road of Moscow. One Major Winblat was the companion of my misfortune. [...]
> On the 28th December of the same year, a soldier informed me, that five posts further, some horsemen had conducted people, who had stopped at a certain distance from us. As they were so near us they were extremely desirous of seeing persons as unfortunate as themselves, and they persuaded their officer to conduct them to us at night. I then recognized the most Serene Prince Bishop of Cracow, his tears prevented him from speaking, we

were only permitted to be together for a little while, and then separated. We travelled together, but in different carriages, as far as Tobolski, the capital of Siberia.

We made but a very short stay in this town. We were dragged by dogs across the deserts of Tartary, without hearing any thing from other quarters of the earth. We suffered much from hunger, and having traversed Siberia, we met with exiled officers of different nations. Finally on 2nd of May [sic] 1770, we arrived at the port of Ochozk. The governor received us kindly. A few days after two Russian officers arrived, who called themselves guards of their Highnesses the Princes detained at Kaluga. I became intimate with them. On the 3rd of September we embarked and sailed to the harbour of Bolsao [*Bolsheretsk*]. On the 24th of December I received, by a merchant, a letter from the Bishop of Cracow. I learned from the contents that the captive princes had been removed to the North of Tartary, towards Anadyr, and that a troop of Russian soldiers were preparing to rise and set them at liberty. I gave to Major Winblat written instructions how to behave, so that we both might recover our liberty.

Again, let us pause for breath and reflection: this tale of the Bishop and other princes of note shivering in Siberian exile does not make it to the final cut of the *Memoirs*; possibly because it was so demonstrably untrue. The real Bishop, although imprisoned, never went east of the Urals. And the very idea of receiving a letter from the mainland in deepest, darkest midwinter on Kamchatka is mind-boggling. All of which is a pity, because it had the makings of a good adventure story. But Benyovszky had only just got started: a bizarre story follows of mysterious exiled noblemen in irons, and of plans formed for escape. "Being the only person that understood how to manage a ship, I was made chief of the enterprise."

When the plot was discovered, Benyovszky demonstrated all the military prowess he had acquired in Poland. It makes riveting reading.

The plot was discovered on the 21st of April, the governor gave orders to a detachment to carry me off a second time, to another place. My associates, frightened at the stroke, came to me on the 26th, imploring my assistance. It was no easy matter. The lieutenant upon duty about me, had secretly conveyed some arms to his house, which he distributed among my companions, at the head of whom I rendered myself master of the fort in the night of the 27th. In the beginning of this action, the governor and several officers and privates were killed. There was but a few of my party slightly wounded. The next morning the soldiers and Cossacks attempted, arms in hand, to enter the town of Bolsao, when the inhabitants, frightened at the first and second discharge of our musquetry, surrendered on the 29th of April. I entered in triumph the town of Kamschatka, and found not the smallest opposition. I sent instantly people to seize the ships in the harbour, and marched with the rest of the men to Zamiecka, where I took prisoner the secretary of the Senate, arrived from Petersburgh, and forced him to deliver up all the letters of Chancery. Having taken all that belonged to me, and to two hundred inhabitants of Kamschatka, I entered the harbour, where I seized thee ships, I took the strongest for myself, and dismasted the rest. I caused the ice to be cleared from the ship St. Peter, and having provided myself with all necessaries, set sail on the 12th of May 1771. The crew of my ship consisted of sixty-seven persons, *viz.* eight officers, eight married women and a girl surnamed the Princess; the rest were all mariners. I left the harbour of Kamschatka, passed under the 52nd degree 52 minutes, and sailed down the canal of the islands call Jedso [*the Kurils*].

And now his description of the voyage takes an odd turn – figuratively and literally. Benyovszky reverts to Version One of his story – heading north-eastwards towards America. On the way, he encountered his spiritual brother, an outlaw – Polish, no less – of whom we shall have more to say later.

Steering my rout North-east, I landed at the island of Bernighiana [*Bering Island*], situate in the 55th degree of Eastern latitude, and in the 9th meridian from the harbour whence I had sailed. Here I found Mons. Ochotinsky with eighty men. This Polish officer told me he had effected his escape in a manner very similar to mine, and settled with his crew in the American islands, called Aleutis. He had entered into an alliance with the natives, and riveted that alliance by marrying some of their women. I left him three of my men, and he gave me letters to produce wherever it should be necessary. On the 26th of May, steering my course far from that island, I found the sea covered with ice; I found myself obliged to land at the island of Aladar, situated under the 61st degree of latitude, and the 22nd meridian from Kamschatka. I left that island on the 9th of June, and sailed South-east. I descried, in my opinion, the point of the continent of America, under the 60th degree of latitude, and the 26th meridian from Kamschatka; and sailing afterwards towards the 51st degree of latitude, on account of a heavy gale, I changed my direction, and steered again South-east.

On the 20th of June I saw myself off an island known to the Russians by the name of Urum Sir, or the island of Christi, situate in the 53rd degree 45 minutes latitude, and distant 15 degrees 28 minutes longitude from Kamschatka. I had a great deal of friendly intercourse with the Americans, who persuaded me to make some stay among them. Finally, on the 27th of June, I set sail West-south, and kept at sea till the 30th of the same month. I discovered in the 46th degree 6 minutes of latitude, and 10 degrees longitude from Kamschatka, a country likewise occupied by the Russians, where I could not land, on account of contrary winds, which bore me far away. Having, therefore, taken the resolution of steering my former course, after having suffered as great deal from the inconstancy of the winds, having seen all our fresh water exhausted, and been obliged to drink the brine, which may be rendered potable with spermaceti and flour, we landed on the 15th of July, at an island in the 32nd degree 45 minutes of latitude, and 354 degrees 45 minutes longitude of Kamschatka. Its beautiful site, and other natural amenities, induced me to give it the name of Liquoris. It is [un]inhabited.[11]

The island of "Liquoris" takes on a life of its own in the published *Memoirs*. It is, of course, the exact equivalent of Lord Anson's Tinian. And from here on, Benyovszky's version of events more or less chimes with those of Stepanov and Ryumin.

I heaved anchor on the 22nd, and steering to the westward, I moored on the 28th at Kilingur, a Japanese harbour, situated at 34 degrees of latitude and 343 degrees of longitude from Kamschatka. This port is joined to a town and a citadel, where we met with a very good reception from the inhabitants, who supplied us with fresh provisions. On the 1st August I sailed from this harbour, and landed on the 3rd at Meaka, where the Japanese became very intractable and insulted us. Hence, wishing to seek the Philippine islands, I continued my rout southwards, and coasting for several days the other islands, I went on shore at Usma, in the 27th degree 28 minutes of latitude, and 335 degrees of longitude.

The natives of this island received us with great hospitality, and I staid for some days among them. They supplied us plentifully with provisions, and after a mutual treaty, I set sail to the island of Formosa. I reached it fortunately, and entered the harbour which lies eastward, in the 23rd degree 15 minutes of latitude, and 223 degrees of longitude. The inhabitants attacked us, and three of my men were killed. Having however avenged their death, the winds being always contrary, I was forced to steer towards the continent of China, coasting along the little islands called Piscatoria; at last all our fresh water being exhausted, we were forced to enter Tanasoa, arms in hand, to repulse the Chinese who would not suffer us to fill our casks. I then bore away for Macao, a town belonging to her most faithful Majesty, where I went on shore September 22, 1771. Seignor de Saldanha, the governor, received me with great friendship and cordiality. He granted permission to all the ship's company to come on shore, and I ordered them to leave their arms on board, to remove all kind of mistrust. In this town I was informed, that a treaty of friendship and alliance was subsisting between our august sovereigns, and wishing to keep a secret which concerned them, I begged leave to hoist the colours of his most Christian Majesty, and my request was granted.

One is struck by several things in this narrative. Not least is the preponderant usage of the first person singular, the voice of a man assured of his own importance, hobnobbing with the Great and the Good of his era. But it is clear that this was still a work-in-progress: significant points from the original sketches had either been ditched altogether (the escape from Kazan? Being shipwrecked twice?), or changed radically (eighty-five on board, or sixty-seven?); and a number of new facts had been introduced (the meeting with the Polish gentleman-adventurer on Bering Island; a more detailed account of his voyage into the Far North; the presence of a young lady named "the Princess"; the deaths of three voyagers on Formosa).

These new elements now introduced by Benyovszky were the grit around which the pearls of his later *Memoirs* would grow.

At the time of the publication of the German translation of the *Memoirs*, the German satirical writer Heinrich von Bretschneider had something revealing to divulge about an early meeting with Benyovszky:

> When he showed me his papers in the year 1780 and asked my advice in setting them in order, there was nothing there at all of these beautiful descriptions; but there were other things and other tales which do not appear in his edited diary. So he must have chopped and changed everything. There was already something unbelievable in those papers, and some things quite suspicious: but relating to quite other events than the ones described. He himself confessed that he felt some embarrassment about correcting the data and straightening out his tale in relation to some of the events he had mentioned.[12]

Given the large number of "tales" which ended up in the published *Memoirs*, one feels cheated now that other ones had been left out. The reading public surely has a right to these alternative facts? But Bretschneider's comments are useful, for they tell us just how much time Benyovszky spent in preparing his manuscripts, right up to the last moment.

The creation of a beautiful fiction is a fascinating thing to observe.

Notes

1 For more information see: Voigt, 2007, pp.94–104.
2 Kotzebue, 1795, play.
3 Berg, 1822, pp.56–57.
4 Critical Review, June 1798, p.162.
5 Gentleman's Magazine, 1772, p.272.
6 *ibid*, pp.272–273.
7 Benyovszky, 1790, Vol.I, pp.xx–xxii.
8 *ibid*, p.xxiv.
9 *ibid*, pp.xxvi–xxvii.
10 Rochon, 1793, pp.208–224.
11 Joseph Trapp MA, the translator, lets us down here, by rendering Rochon's French word *inhabité* as "inhabited": it is precisely the opposite. That could have been a bombshell for later travellers.
12 Meusel, 1816, pp.112–113.

XIV

EXILED TO SIBERIA

"A Pack of Lies"

Mr Kropf's Disapproval – A Young Soldier Takes up Arms for Liberty –
Adventures in Poland – Escape from Kazan –
Treachery at the Hands of a Dutchman – Journey Across Siberia –
Brandy and Storms Are Not Good Companions – Safe Arrival in Kamchatka

Captain Samuel Pasfield Oliver, who produced an edition of Benyovszky's *Memoirs* in 1893, thought that perhaps the Hungarian had overdone the beauty of the fiction. He was not a man to beat about the bush: "The Memoirs open with a lie," he wrote in severe tones.[1] A Hungarian by the name of Lajos Kropf went a shade further: "Why, Capt. Oliver ought to have written, 'with a pack of lies.'" Kropf had no patience with the book at all:

> The Memoirs, to my mind, have a very much smaller substratum of truth than that which either the editor [*Oliver*] or his reviewer [*in the London Times*] are inclined to admit, and there is very little in them that is not 'romantic embellishment' or 'exaggeration,' not to use stronger terms.[2]

What was it that had upset them so much that any polite Victorian reserve was jettisoned? Kropf was an excitable foreigner, and naturally could not be expected to have any decent manners; but Captain Oliver? He was a military officer of some experience, son of a rector, handy geographer (Fellow of the Royal Geographical Society), antiquary (Fellow of the Society of Antiquaries), and a gentleman of solid British uprightness.

What offended them both was the first sentence in the *Memoirs*, which ran as follows: "The Count Mauritius Augustus de Benyowsky, Magnate of the kingdoms of Hungary and Poland, was born in the year 1741 at Verbowa, the hereditary lordship of his family."[3]

It is an unfortunate fact that he was born five years later than 1741 and was never a "Magnate" of Hungary, far less of Poland. This was no misprint, nor was it the work of some anonymous editor. All the words which appeared in the *Memoirs* came from the hand of Benyovszky himself: despite the curious affectation of writing an introductory section in the third person, nobody else could have documented in detail what Benyovszky claimed to have done in Poland. When he ran off to the Polish wars in 1768, he was barely twenty-one years of age; when he reached Kamchatka, he was only twenty-four; and when he turned up at the French court in 1772, he was still only twenty-six. In Paris, he aimed to attract some serious money from investors attached to the French court. He reasoned, almost certainly, that investors would look for age and experience: experience he had, in bags; age, he did not, if he told the truth. Even when he was preparing his *Memoirs* a decade later, he was still on the look-out for investors for his schemes, and his rationale would not have changed.

An additional convenience of having been born five years earlier soon becomes apparent in the *Memoirs*. He was able, at the admittedly still-young age of fourteen, to sign up with the Austro-Hungarian army and take part as a lieutenant in the Seven Years War, from 1756 onwards, participating in four battles until his war was conveniently interrupted by "an invitation from his uncle, the Starost of Bieniowsky, to repair to Poland, in order to secure the inheritance of his Starostie."[4] The uncle and his estate were, it so happens, entirely fictitious. But that matters little, since Benyovszky barely had time to settle into his new country seat before he had to return to Hungary to take up cudgels with his brothers-in-law who had possessed themselves of his father's estate. Defeated in his rightful cause, the young Baron found himself fleeing back to Poland soon after 1760. He therefore "repaired to Dantzick, with the intention of applying himself to navigation, and made several voyages to Hamburgh, and from thence to Amsterdam and to Plymouth." On the point of sailing to the East Indies in 1767, however, he received communication from the "magnates and senators of Poland" to join them in the Confederation of Bar. He hastened to Poland, signed up to the cause, made one brief and abortive return to Vienna to press his claim on the inheritance, headed back to Poland, fell ill en route, stopped off at "a gentleman's castle," married his daughter, got her pregnant, and then hastened (again) to Poland to take up arms against Russia. It was all a bit of a whirl.

Even more of a whirl was his triumphant military career in Poland. Now aged, for the purposes of his chronicle, twenty-six, he was in July 1768 given command of a regiment of five hundred men to lead to Krakow, "a commission he performed with honor." It would be an imposition to share with the reader the number of glorious deeds performed by, and honours heaped upon, the young Benyovszky over the next few months: there is too great a number and in any case they had little basis in fact. We can perhaps summarise in a couple of sentences: charmed all of his military companions, galloped about, undertook admirable feats of arms, was taken prisoner by the awe-struck Russians who offered to take him into service (he refused with disdain), and then released on a ransom raised by "his friends." After returning to the Confederation HQ, he galloped about, harried the Russians, took hundreds of them prisoner, was promoted to "Commandant-General of Cavalry," and generally made the Russians regret their offer of ransom. Then he allied with various Turkish troops, took more Russian prisoners in skirmishes, and blazed like a meteor across the theatre of war, before finally succumbing to

> two wounds with the sabre and a wound in the body by the shot of a cannon, loaded with old iron and other destructive rubbish. His fate decided that of his party and the Russians had at last the satisfaction of seeing him their prisoner.[5]

So ended Benyovszky's glorious career in Poland on the 20th April 1769. It had lasted thirty pages (about nine months).

Kropf remains entirely unmoved by Benyovszky's tale, pointing out a number of chronological anomalies in his account. Not the least of these was Benyovszky's surprise to learn, at the end of November 1768, that the town of Bar had fallen to the Russians, when, as Kropf points out,[6] "everybody else in Poland must have been in possession of that intelligence many months before, as Bar was stormed and taken by the Russians on June 9, O.S., i.e., probably before Benyowszky set foot on Polish soil." To be fair, Benyovszky would have been writing his account a good dozen years after the event, and may have slipped up on a few dates. But his critic inserts the knife one last time: "In addition hereto he commits the indiscretion of coveting for himself the laurels and fame gained in the defence of Zwanietz and in the skilfully conducted retreat across the Dniester into Turkish territory, which honours, with his sole exception, all chroniclers have assigned to Casimir Pulawsky." It would seem that the Hungarian adventurer was a little too free in the matter of covering himself with glory.

The next phase of his life was spent as a prisoner-of-war. It will come as faint surprise to learn that he covered himself in glory here as well. Benyovszky and his fellow-prisoners were put in the charge of a "cruel and base" Russian General (our chronicler has the decency to replace this fiend's name with four asterisks, to prevent identification), a man

> who, contrary to every sentiment of humanity, insulting the misfortunes of the Count, not only forbad the surgeons to dress his wounds, but likewise, after reducing him to bread and water, loaded him with chains, and in that state transported him to Kiow.[7]

Before Kiev, the prisoners were marched to Polonne, where the 'Count' (as he calls himself) was admitted to hospital and cured of his wounds, before settling down to a relatively easy internment. Until another Russian fiend came along, "caused him to be loaded with chains, and conducted to the dungeon with the rest of the prisoners." In these conditions, thirty-five of the eighty prisoners in this dungeon died of infection in the three weeks they were kept locked up. On release, they were immediately put in the tender hands of yet a third Russian monster, "an ancient Captain of Infantry" who marched them to Kiev: of the 782 who left Polonne, only 148 reached Kiev, "the rest being either dead, or abandoned in the forests in a dying state."

This account sits ill with a memorandum written by Governor du Dresnay of Mauritius, from notes made from an interview with Benyovszky. Here, the Hungarian warrior states that, after being taken prisoner in Poland, and until he reached Kazan, "he was treated with great respect and humanity."[8] But it is by no means impossible that the conditions of the prisoners were much as Benyovszky later described them. There was no international treaty governing prisoners-of-war in those days, and few armies of any allegiance were ever noted for their humanity towards the defeated. The journal of the French mercenary Belcour, which has already been mentioned, also testifies to harsh treatment and the deaths of large numbers of prisoners.[9]

Scarcely had Benyovszky and his comrades found time to recover from the harsh treatment than the order was received from St Petersburg to move them all on to Kazan, jumping-off point for Siberia. Only once they had all reached Kazan was there a respite. Benyovszky is a little skimpy with facts and dates, but we must suppose that they reached the town in late August or early September 1769; here they stayed until late November. Many were the plots which Benyovszky engaged in during that time, with disaffected Russian "men of quality" – our Hungarian only ever moved in circles "of quality" – who were debating the pros and cons of throwing off the despotic yoke of the Empress (etc.). Benyovszky pointed out that the plotters had no chance, unarmed against the garrison. Having stated the blatantly obvious, he was thenceforward treated as a master-strategist and asked to organise something more realistic, namely a joint uprising by prisoners and seditious Russians.

> The Count de Benyowsky was entrusted with the management of this affair, which he pursued with [*as we might expect*] the greatest zeal, prudence and sagacity, in such a manner as not to endanger any of the prisoners, even on the supposition that government should discover the conspiracy. The malecontents, on the other hand, entered into their pursuit with so much spirit, that they succeeded in bringing over to their party the nobility of the governments of Voronicz, Bielogorod, Kiow, and the greater part of Moscow, the capital of Russia. They only waited for the appearance of the Tartars of Cazan, who had engaged to present themselves before the town of Cazan with nine or ten thousand horse.

It is a little difficult to grasp the scale of this plot, which in the space of a few weeks had encompassed not merely the local malcontents, but those of Moscow, some 600 miles distant. But let us not tarnish this account of proceedings with any modern scepticism – we were not there: Benyovszky was.

He continues:

> Such was the state of affairs on the 6th of November (1769) when a sudden change was produced by a quarrel between two Russian lords, one of whom informed the governor, that the prisoners, in concert with the Tartars, meditated a design against his person and the garrison. This apostate accused the Count, in order to save his friends and countrymen. On the 7th, at eleven at night, the Count, not suspecting any such event, heard a knocking at his door. He came down, entirely undressed, with a candle in his hand, to enquire the cause; and upon opening his door was surprized to see an officer, with twenty soldiers, who demanded if the prisoner were at home. On his replying in the affirmative, the officer snatched the candle out of his hand, and ordering his men to follow him, went hastily up to the Count's apartment.
>
> The Count immediately took advantage of the mistake, quitted his house, and repaired to the quarters of his intimate friend, Major Wynbladth, who was likewise a prisoner. After relating the adventure to him, and engaging him to make his escape together with him, they quitted Cazan, and repaired to the nearest village, where they took horses of the countrymen, with the intention of hastening to Sebuksar. On their arrival at this place they apprized several Russian gentlemen of the discovery of their plot, who having the strongest reasons to fear the consequences of the Count's being arrested, gave him a *podruschna*, or order for post horses, with money and clothing. From Sebuksar they passed to Kusmoden Janskoy, where they took post, and continued their route as far as Nizney Novogrod, where they gave out that they were officers returning from Kizlar to Petersburgh, charged with dispatches from the governor.[10]

Far-fetched as this escape may seem, it is not strictly impossible. Equally unlikely escapes have happened under the noses of authoritarian regimes in every century. And yes, it may seem surprising that two men with heavy foreign accents could pass themselves off as Russian officers, even to the extent of being invited to dinner with the Governor of Novgorod, who was sufficiently taken in as to give them a letter of safe-passage to help them on their way. Surprising, but also not impossible.

Two weeks after leaving Kazan, our escapees arrived in St Petersburg on the 19th of November.

> The Count took lodgings in a hotel, causing his Major to pass in the character of his valet de chambre. Upon his first going out he met a German tradesman, by profession an apothecary, who being given to understand that the Count was desirous of passing by sea into another country, directed him to the lodgings of a Dutch Captain.

The Dutch captain turned out to be a rogue: having agreed to take the pair to Holland on the solid promise of 500 ducats upon arrival, he promptly turned them over to the Russian authorities. Arrested at midnight, they were soon subjected to interrogation and imprisonment in a dungeon, on a diet of bread and water. After three days he was brought before the Empress Catherine's Minister, Count Panin, who asked him many questions and revealed himself to be well disposed to his prisoners – not entirely implausible, given Panin's soft spot for Poland. Shortly afterwards, they were hauled up before a Privy Council who were determined to get Benyovszky to name names of the Russian conspirators of Kazan; a thing which Benyovszky naturally did not do. At length, seeing they were getting nowhere, they obliged him to sign a "resignation," worded as follows:

> I, the undersigned, do acknowledge, that having been seized in my flight from Cazan, and her Imperial Majesty of all the Russias having pardoned me by her natural clemency, I have entered into the present renunciation, never to serve any power against the arms of her Imperial Majesty; and that, upon becoming in possession of my liberty, I promise for ever to quit her dominions, obliging myself, under pain of death, not to enter them again under any pretext whatever.
>
> Done at Petersburgh, the 22d of November, 1769.[11]

Whereupon, in a final demonstration of Russian duplicity, he and Winbladh were returned to prison, where they languished for two weeks, before being taken out at midnight, given sheepskin garments and whisked off southwards on a sledge in the snow. The nocturnal journey might at first have seemed romantic; but it soon became clear that they were not dashing towards freedom.

A long and arduous journey had begun, across Russia from west to east.

Their guard was changed when they arrived near Moscow, and onwards they raced to Volodomir, which they reached nine days after quitting St Petersburg, on the 13th of December. Here "they were joined by four sledges with four exiles, likewise destined to pass the remainder of their lives at Kamchatka." Of these four, three were destined to be bound up closely with Benyovszky's adventures over the next two years: Ippolit Stepanov, Vasilii Panov and Asaf Baturin. The fourth member of this miserable group was a man named Ivan Ivanovich Solmanov, designated by Benyovszky as the "Secretary of the Senate of Moscow"; this gentleman is slightly mysterious, since he is only mentioned three times by Benyovszky in his entire book, despite his manifest social importance; we can find no independent verification of the Moscow Senate Secretary having been exiled at this time – but, again, nothing is more likely in the conditions of the time. The group of six prisoners were now conducted, under a guard of forty-six members of the Volodomir garrison, to Nizhney Novgorod, after which their guard was boosted by no fewer than 150 horsemen,

> to pass more securely through the government of Cazan, at that time disturbed by the incursions of the Tartars, who, since the departure of the

Count, had already committed several acts of hostility, and with whom a party of the prisoners deserted from Cazan had taken refuge.[12]

So, 200 of Imperial Russia's finest surrounded six exiles, gliding through the snows of the darkest midwinter, all the way to the town of Malmyzh on the Vyatka River; this route carefully avoided the town of Kazan itself. At Malmyzh, the 150 horseman breathed a sigh of relief and galloped back westwards, leaving the smaller group to trek the remaining 700 miles or so, over the Urals, to the town of Tobolsk, then the most prominent town of Siberia. Here they could admire the famous Bell of Uglich, one of the first exiles to Siberia, flogged, mutilated and exiled for having rung in 1591 at the time of the murder of the young Crown Prince Dmitri, yet another victim of a long line of impatient Tsars.

The party arrived in Tobolsk on 20th January, and stayed for a pleasant fortnight. The local governor was

> a man equally estimable for the humanity and generosity of his disposition, caused my fetters to be taken off the first day of my arrival, and, after providing me with a lodging, heaped many favours upon me and Mr. Wynbladth, the companion of my misfortunes.[13]

But they were bound for Kamchatka, so "the governor, after having loaded me with marks of his favour, which was likewise extended to my five companions, dispatched us for our place of destination"; a mere twenty-four men now guarded them. They were now truly into exile territory. Benyovszky tells of meeting Hungarians, Swedes, Russian exiles, in every village and every town. They consumed mare's milk and horse flesh. They were blocked in for days on end by snowdrifts. They drank brandy. They passed "through immense woods and over lofty mountains." They wore furs. They drank more brandy. On 17th March, they finally reached Tomsk, where they were permitted to rest for almost two months to avoid the rainy season. They hobnobbed, as always, with the Governor: this one was a Frenchman by the name of Villeneuve, a man whom the French diplomat Lesseps was later overjoyed at finding in the middle of this wilderness; other travellers of the period – Siberia was crowded with adventurers who returned home to write their memoirs – also encountered this jovial man who claimed to be the son of the Duc d'Orleans. They drank brandy. Benyovszky also struck up a friendship with "the Tartars," the native Siberians, one of whom proposed that the prisoners escape to China. If we recall that Benyovszky's very first account of his journey was of an escape across Siberia to catch a boat at Kamchatka, then his reaction to this daring proposal was a little out of character, but quite understandable: "I should have accepted his proposal with joy, if the difficulty, or rather the impossibility, of travelling at least three hundred leagues on foot had not detained me."

Yes, indeed: the whole point of Siberia was that it was a vast open prison; it was almost impossible to escape.

A curious feature of the account of this journey across Siberia is the Case of the Missing Bishops: the Bishops of Krakow and Kiev, to be precise. We will remember that, in his first accounts of his adventures, Benyovszky insisted that he had been taken off into exile in the company of the Bishops of Krakow and of Kiev along with a generous sprinkling of Polish magnates. At Tobolsk, the two groups had become separated, and the Bishops had apparently been transported to Anadyr, to the north of Kamchatka. This story is also set down in Benyovszky's letter to Dresnay and in the latter's memorandum. But in the *Memoirs* the entire story has vanished completely, leaving us to wonder what it was all about. Certainly, the Bishops and their supporters had been arrested by the Russians, very early on in the war, in 1767, and had been locked up for the duration in Kaluga, just south of Moscow – where Benyovszky claims first to have met them. But they were never sent to Siberia, let alone Anadyr. Possibly the fact that they had all been released from prison by 1781, and had given public report of their experiences, had some bearing on Benyovszky's change of tack.

The Bishops had been lost to the story: no matter, we have much else to occupy us. Let us proceed.

The next stage of the journey was relatively normal for a trip across Siberia, if a little depressing:

> On the 11th of May we at length quitted the town of Tomszky, and passed through a desert country covered with woods and mountains, always encamped in the snow, and after fourteen days most painful march we were necessitated to reduce our allowance to half a pound of biscuit per day. Being thus exhausted by hunger and fatigue, after losing eight Cossacks and twelve horses on the road, we at length arrived on the 18th at Juska Krasnoiarszk, a town situated on the banks of the great river Jenisea: it consists of about thirty houses, inhabited by Russian exiles; the fort, more properly called the miserable intrenchment, in which the house of the *Voivode* [*governor*] is built, is a raised square surrounded with palisades, and the garrison which defends it is composed only of twenty soldiers, who are likewise exiles.
>
>   The *Voivode* of this province, famous for its misery, lodged us in his fortress, and did not condescend to see us till our conductor had informed him that we intended making him a present. This news, which our conductor likewise communicated to us, occasioned the Governor to invite us to supper; and he did not disdain the acceptance of sixty roubles as a present, and for a like sum he sold us a small barrel of brandy, containing about eighteen bottles.[14]

The governor, having profited a little from the passing exiles, was quick to wave them on their way. The journey went downhill from here: snow, snow, mountains and snow. The remaining horses began to fall by the wayside. The party was reduced to chewing birch-bark steeped in water. After four weeks of this, they fell in with "a horde of Tungus Tartars" who exchanged four elks and some dried fish for brandy and tobacco (the Governor of Tobolsk had generously donated 500 pounds of the leaf to the group. Presumably he knew of the problems that would arise with provisions. Alcohol and narcotics went a long way in Siberia). With these supplies they staggered on to the next town, passing out tobacco and brandy with one hand, taking in elks, fish and flour with the other. At length, on 26th August, they reached Yakutsk. Not a big place.

> It is composed of 130 houses and a fortress, the whole built of wood, and inhabited either by exiles or Cossacks, a kind of military which the government has formed by enrolling all the male children of the Swedes and Germans formerly exiled into Siberia.

They stayed here for four days. It was enough time for Benyovszky to prove, yet again, his leadership qualities.

The exiles met up with a surgeon who also passing through Yakutsk. He went by the name of Hoffman. Hoffman apparently was on his way to Kamchatka to take up a medical post there, at the very generous salary of 1,500 roubles per annum. He was a man of quality, worthy of Benyovszky's notice: "At our first meeting I perceived, from his conversation, that he possessed a penetrating mind and a worthy and amiable disposition." No sooner had Dr Hoffman sat down with the Hungarian than he proposed that, upon arrival in Kamchatka, the exiles should seize a ship and escape to China or Japan. He foresaw no difficulties with this. For his part, Benyovszky assured Hoffman that he was quite capable of navigating the vessel, given his wide and extensive experience of the high seas. Garlic may have been mentioned. Subsequent to this,

> the company elected me their chief; it was composed of Mr. Hoffman, Major Wynbladth. Captain Panow, Captain Hippolite Stephanov, Colonel Baturin, and Secretary Sopronow. The ardent desire which we all had to carry our design into execution, induced us to use our endeavours with the *Voivode* to dispatch us to Ochoczk, a sea port in Siberia, from whence we were to embark for Kamchatka.

The governor almost certainly had no problems with this urgent request, given that these were precisely the orders from St Petersburg. So off they went on the 29th August. This next stage of the journey was entirely uneventful, apart from the small matter of the mutiny of the Cossacks of their guard, who took it into their heads to strip their commanding officer naked and apply three hundred lashes of the whip. This "afforded us some diversion."

However, they were almost undone. En route, news reached them from Yakutsk that Dr Hoffman, who had remained behind due to transportation difficulties, had upped and died. The Governor had come upon papers in possession of the deceased which implicated the six exiles in an escape plot, and he was forwarding these letters to Okhotsk, for the attention of Governor Plenisner, with a recommendation not to send the prisoners to Kamchatka. The Cossack bearing the package of papers arrived post-haste in the camp. For some reason, he knew every detail of the papers he was carrying and blabbed all of this information to the exiles, but not to the guards nor to their sore and stripy officer. This tactical error was fortuitous. Given that they had in their number the Secretary of the Senate of Moscow, it was a simple matter to remove the letters, re-write them, and replace them in the satchel. The switch was considerably helped by the merry pranks of the Cossacks: while they were crossing the River Aldan,

> the boat in which our conductor was placed with his dispatches was overset by the malice of the Cossacks; who, after having well flogged him, were desirous of playing another trick, to disembarrass themselves entirely of his company. It was a happy circumstance for him that he was a good swimmer, and quickly reached the shore.

The completely revised letter which was subsequently delivered to Plenisner now praised the exiles as "men of honour, especially the two foreigners," and urged the Governor to give them a certain degree of liberty, to "preserve them from scurvy." The letter made a further request:

> the surgeon Hoffman, who was about to repair to Kamchatka, is dead, and I have no person to appoint in his place. One of these prisoners is of the same profession. I see no inconvenience in recommending him to the governor of Kamchatka, who being unprovided will, doubtless, be glad to avail himself of his services.

Given the professions of the six exiles (two mercenaries, three career-soldiers and one secretary) we must assume that Benyovszky saw himself in the role of surgeon.

Package re-sealed, crisis averted, officer dried out, Cossacks exhausted with laughing: they continued on their way, stopping briefly at the crossing of the River Inna to haul in a "prodigious quantity of fish," before passing over "very lofty mountains and dreadful precipices. The cold was so extreme near the summits of the mountains, that two of our conductors were frozen to death." They fell down crevasses, dogs, sledges and all. Travellers across Siberia prior to the convenient railway consistently reported terrible conditions; astonishing tales of self-preservation and survival were *de rigueur.* (Fifty years later, John Dundas Cochrane experienced similar, and worse, detailing his hair-raising brushes with an icy death with the greatest glee.)

On the sixteenth day of October, the party arrived in Okhotsk.

Let us take a brief pause to catch our breath and consider the dates.

They arrived in Okhotsk, by Benyovszky's calculation, in mid-October. They then took ship to Kamchatka on 22nd November, some seven weeks later, and arrived in Kamchatka, slightly the worse for wear, on 2nd December 1770. This timetable gives us a puzzle: first, it is probable that any reference to dates by that group of exiles would have been based on the old-style Julian calendar, which was a good eleven days behind the calendar as we now use it. Even if, as a good Hungarian, Benyovszky had been using the Gregorian calendar at an early point in his adventures, it is most unlikely that some internal clock would have maintained that calendar over so many months of deprivation and travel. Therefore, he would have arrived in Okhotsk, by his own account, in late October (NS), and arrived by ship in Kamchatka mid-December. Second, regardless of any calendar, no ship ever made the crossing from Okhotsk to Kamchatka any later than September. The weather would have been impossible, and both shoreline and sea subject to ice. All other journals and reports from that period note that the ships to and from Kamchatka had a very limited window of opportunity to make the voyage – April to early October at the extremes. Other accounts, both official and from Stepanov, suggest that the ship left Okhotsk on 12 September 1770, over two months earlier.

Remember also that Benyovszky, in his earlier deposition to the Governor of Mauritius, had stated that he had reached Okhotsk on 2nd May, and had sailed to Kamchatka on 3rd September.

And if those later dates are wrong, then there is something amiss with Benyovszky's account of his journey from Yakutsk into Okhotsk. Freezing almost to death in the snow and ice is a perfectly acceptable thing to do in a Siberian winter, maybe even in a very late autumn; but not in the latter half of the summer. Additionally, although a couple of mountain-ranges are crossed, the road for the most part passes through swamp, over rivers and along valleys. And the mountains, even at that season, were unlikely to be covered with snow. If we accept Benyovszky's timetable as correct, then we could accept that there had been perilous snow-based activities; but as we know his timetable is late by over two months, then we have, with regret, to suppose that at least some of his Siberian adventures were not true.

Okhotsk was not much to look at, being a collection of wooden houses, but the exiles were "very commodiously lodged in the houses of the towns-people, who were in very good circumstances."[15] The Governor Plenisner himself treated them "with goodness," surely as a result of the forged letter. Benyovszky had a rather prejudiced view of Siberia: he regarded almost everyone as an exile, governors, Cossacks, the lot. Plenisner was therefore introduced to us as "an exile from the time of the Empress Elisabeth." He was not: a predecessor of his, appointed in 1731, was a one-time commandant of the naval academy and then a 'state felon,' before his elevation. The 480 soldiers in the fort were all exiles from European regiments. The town, comprising 322 houses, was inhabited by exiles. Some attempt had been made to cultivate respectability, learning and civic government, but Benyovszky remained unimpressed, describing the leading citizens of the town as "brutes, whose only merit was placed in continual licentiousness and debauchery."[16]

To while away the time until the ship was ready to sail to Kamchatka, Benyovszky busied himself with finding out all about the fur-trade, and made sure, in his *Memoirs*, to detail the number of furs passing through the port on an annual basis. We shall not repeat the figures here. Suffice it to say that there were a lot. But his socio-economic investigations did not last long: there was always the chance that another courier would turn up, hot-foot from the west, bearing another set of incriminating letters. He therefore,

> persuaded my companions unanimously to request orders for our departure, and to engage the governor to dismiss us for Kamchatka as soon as possible. This officer was likewise urged by its being the season to dispatch vessels to Kamchatka, and accordingly embarked us on board the packet *St. Peter and St. Paul.*

As we have noted, it was no season at all to be sending ships out into the Sea of Okhotsk; but no matter.

The voyage that followed was remarkably exciting. It did not begin auspiciously. The ship was,

> of two hundred and forty tons burthen, with eight pieces of cannon and forty-three men, commanded by the Sieurs Esuryn and Korostilow; their lading was one hundred and forty-two sacks of flour, each containing one hundred pounds; two hundred barrels of brandy, each containing twenty-five pints. […] On our arrival on board we were received very roughly by the second-in-command, who, after having indulged himself in a set of invectives, caused us to be chained and confined before the mast, with orders to employ us in the meanest labour. […] On the arrival of the captain we were delivered from our fetters, and had the satisfaction to see our enemy punished with fifty strokes of the knout for having acted without orders.[17]

Once discipline had been restored, they set sail. Benyovszky, perhaps with tongue in cheek, writes that "The journal of our navigation is not sufficiently interesting to be given in detail; I shall, therefore, speak only of the leading circumstances"; and proceeds to give a very detailed and melodramatic account of the voyage. On the second day, a gale bore down on them, and the captain and all his men got themselves drunk (after all, there were 5,000 pints of brandy to hand). Their indisposition appears to have lasted a couple of days, during which the ship was at the mercy of a wild storm, with the wind veering in all directions. It was up to Benyovszky to save them all from destruction. The main-mast broke at three in the morning of the third day, swiftly followed by the mizzen-topmast, with a noise sufficient to arouse the captain from his stupor. He staggered out from his cabin, only for a part of the mast to fall on him and break his arm. The sailors, their heads filled with fumes, eventually appeared on deck to contemplate the damage. Benyovszky, man of action, organised them "to repel the danger" and the crew, salt of the earth, with hearty curses on their officers for ignorant and drunken wretches, swore that they would obey our orders. The Captain, who was likewise persuaded that he was indebted to our efforts for his preservation, and being afraid to put the command into the hands of his mate, whom he had hitherto kept in irons, declared loudly that he entrusted the conduct of the vessel to my care till he should be himself able to attend to it.[18]

On their fifth day at sea, the wind slackened and they found themselves off the coast of Sakhalin Island, considerably off-course. Benyovszky thought to land there and make his escape, but the crew, now quite sober, tended to disagree, and steered north-eastwards again. In desperation, Benyovszky played his trump-card with the iron and the garlic. To no avail. The wind changed and blew them in the authorised direction. On 1st December (Benyovszkian calendar) they arrived at the mouth of the Bolshaya River on Kamchatka.

"On the 2d, at high water, we entered the port; and in this place my command terminated."

But his command did not terminate for long.

Notes

1 Oliver, 1904 edition, p.30.
2 See Kropf, 1895, *passim.*
3 Benyovszky, 1790, Vol.I, p.1.
4 This and subsequent quotations from *ibid*, pp.1–5.
5 *ibid*, p.34.
6 Kropf, 1895, Vol.7, p.5.
7 *ibid*, p.34.
8 Cultru, 1906, p.160.
9 Belcour, 1776, pp.33–39 and *passim.*
10 Benyovszky, 1790, Vol.I, pp.41–43.
11 *ibid*, pp.48–49. The wording of this admission, we should note, is significantly different from the one related to Dresnay in Mauritius (see Chapter XIII, page 94, above).
12 *ibid*, p.51.
13 This and subsequent quotations from *ibid*, pp.54–60.
14 *ibid*, pp.61–71.
15 *ibid*, p.73.
16 *ibid*, p.74.
17 *ibid*, p.77.
18 *ibid*, p.79.

XV

KAMCHATKAN ROMANCES

"Entrails of Dogs and Rein-deer"

Baron Benyovszky's Leadership Qualities — Baron Benyovszky's Mastery of Chess —
Baron Benyovszky's Luck with the Ladies — The Amiable Afanasia Nilova —
The Good Mother — The Duplicitous Captain Stepanov —
Captain Tchurin's Troubles with the Ladies

We now open up several chapters of Benyovszky's *Memoirs* in which we can roam freely, untroubled by any contrary evidence from his contemporaries. He has the field clear to himself. Be prepared: you may find yourself wiping tears from your eyes, tears of joy and sympathy.

Having handed command of the ship back to the captain and his crew, still nursing sore heads, Benyovszky stepped on shore; the exiles were escorted into a yurt to await the arrival of a suitable representative of authority. Within a couple of hours an officer turned up at the head of a company of ten soldiers.

> The officer went first on board the vessel, and afterwards on shore, where he relieved our guard by his Cossacks. A certain something, which, according to his own expression, struck him at first sight of me, excited his curiosity to know who I was, which I satisfied laconically by answering, "a soldier, once a general, but now a slave." This answer surprised him, and, as he has since protested, conciliated his esteem. When he learned that my companions were likewise officers, he presented us with a dinner according to the custom of the country, which consisted of boiled fish, roasted fish, and fish powdered and made into bread. This cookery would have disgusted famine itself, but the thing which the most effectually overset my stomach was the drink; it was composed of fish putrified in water, the corruption of which gives the water a certain sourness.[1]

The menu rings true; the chivalric exchange between exile and officer, less so.

After dinner, the prisoners were taken up-river to the fortress at Bolsheretsk, a journey of some hours, in the course of which they encountered a small group of exiles; a brief conversation with these unfortunates immediately inspired Benyovszky to draw up a number of points of strategy aimed at securing liberty. We need not be astonished at the alacrity by which he arrived at his conclusions: these are, after all, his *Memoirs*. On the following day, the new arrivals were brought before the Commander, Mr Nilov, who gave them their orders:

1. That we should be set at liberty on the following day, and provided with subsistence for three days, after which we must depend upon ourselves for our maintenance.
2. That each person would receive from the chancery, a musquet and a lance, with one pound of powder, four pounds of lead, a hatchet, several knives, and other instruments and carpenters tools, with which we might build cabins, and that we were at liberty to choose our situations at the distance of one league from the town; but that we should be bound to pay in furs, during the first year, each one hundred roubles, in return for these advantages.
3. That every one must work at the corvée one day in the week for the service of government, and that we might not absent ourselves from our houses for twenty-four hours without the permission of the governor.
4. That each exile should bring to the chancery six sable skins, fifty rabbits skins, two foxes skins, and twenty-four ermines per annum.

While they digested these ordinances, the newcomers were offered temporary accommodation in the huts of the resident exiles. Benyovszky considered himself most fortunate to be billeted with Mr Khrushchyov, their designated leader. In Khrushchyov's cabin, they dined on fish, fish and caviar, and then settled down to a nightcap of brandy and tea. The host turned out to be a man of some learning:

> On the 5th, I arose and examined the whole cabin, which appeared to be very well furnished; but what surprized me the most agreeably was, an alcove of the same kind as that in which I slept, which was filled with French, Russian, English, German, and Latin books, placed in order. I found Anson's *Voyage* lying on a table, and began to read it with pleasure, but had scarcely finished the first page before Mr. Crustiew entered and embraced me. Our first conversation turned on this famous voyager, and my friend informed me that for six years past he had deliberated in his own mind on the means of quitting Kamchatka, and making his way to the Marian islands. The account of the island of Tinian, as described in that publication, had struck the imagination of Mr. Crustiew so forcibly, that the island, in his opinion, was nothing less than paradise.

And not merely was this a man of learning, but also of a keen awareness of Benyovszky's leadership qualities.

> From this turn of mind, I determined to acquaint him with the resolution of myself and my companions, at the same time proposing that he should join us. He joyfully accepted my proposition, and kneeling before me, immediately took an oath of fidelity and obedience.[2]

It really was quite extraordinary: a grizzled exile of some years' standing was completely bowled over by a few words from a mere youth, who was not even Russian, and who was probably still swaying from the sea-journey from Okhotsk. But that is just how things were in Benyovszky's universe.

With very little delay, a committee was formed of Benyovszky, his five companions, Khrushchyov, and someone mysteriously named as "Wasili, my old servant" – the last-named appears to have fallen fully-formed from the skies over Kamchatka and to have vanished again like smoke after this one mention in the *Memoirs*. When they were seated, Benyovszky gave them an extremely long speech (which was received "with veneration") and presented a number of "articles" of his proposed Society (For Escape); in no time at all, he was unanimously elected their leader, with Khrushchyov as his second-in-command. Khrushchyov then arranged to convoke a meeting of all the other exiles and recommend that they all join the Society.

Next, Benyovszky went off to pay his compliments to the commander. Nilov was so impressed by the multi-lingual Hungarian that he immediately appointed him as language-teacher to his son and three daughters, and excused him from all public work. And no sooner had these arrangements been made than they paid a visit on the Chancellor, Mr Sudeikin. The Chancellor was playing chess with the 'Hetman' of the Cossacks, a domestic scene which allowed Benyovszky to shine just a little more brightly: the Chancellor was losing the game, and, discovering that the Hungarian could play, offered him 50 roubles if he could win it. Benyovszky duly obliged. The hetman then offered Benyovszky good money if he could win games on his behalf against merchants of the town. It was the start of a whole series of chess-games played over the coming months against members of Bolsheretsk's finest, for daft amounts of money, all of which Benyovszky won without any difficulty at all.

In the space of two days, then, Benyovszky had recruited to his growing army of admirers: the resident exiles, the Commander, the Captain of the Cossacks, the Chancellor. It took barely another couple of days to recruit everyone else in Bolsheretsk.

First off, Nilov's gaggle of children: notwithstanding the fact that official records concerning Nilov only ever mention one son and no wife, we here find one wife, one son and three daughters. Amongst the three daughters, Benyovszky's *pièce de résistance*: the youngest girl, sixteen years of age and named Afanasia, a young lady of considerable charms and sensitivity.

Her questions convinced me that her father had given them some information concerning my birth and misfortunes. I therefore gave them an account of my adventures, at which my scholars appeared to be highly affected, but the youngest wept very much. She was a beautiful girl, and her sensibility created much emotion in my mind; but, alas, I was an exile.[3]

We shall see how the relationship between young exile and younger girl develops over the next few months: it is the very stuff of romantic fantasy. But before the lesson had ended, here was Nilov himself, delighted with the Hungarian's teaching methods; having now learned that he had single-handedly saved the *St Peter* from destruction upon the Sea of Okhotsk, he proposed to give him "a Kamchatka female slave, a sledge, and two dogs." Modestly, Benyovszky refused, but was obliged to return home with the bare minimum of a sledge and a chauffeur.

In the evening, the hetman and the merchants turned up on the doorstep, asking Benyovszky to establish a public school for the local children. No sooner said than done, with the stipulation that Nilov's children should also attend this school, to save the teacher the bother of having to traipse over to the commander's house every morning.

Benyovszky, in a moment of unadulterated pathos just as he was being elevated to local hero, decides to remind us of his wife and child: "The distressing image of a wife whom I loved, and who in my absence, in all probability, had given birth to an infant, presented itself constantly to my mind, and permitted me to receive no perfect satisfaction." His short bout of despondency was soon relieved by some profitable games of chess, followed up with music and dancing, and the circulation of "a few bottles" donated by Nilov himself. On this evening, the commander's wife, Madame Nilova, put in a first appearance and rather transparently offers up her daughter:

> During the whole entertainment, my scholar Aphanasia never quitted me but to join in the dance, which she did very gracefully; her mother came up to us once, and whispered to me, "I think your scholar will become your friend; have an eye over her: I am a kind mother." She spoke to me in very good German; and as it was the first time I had conversed with her I felt some embarrassment, but soon recollecting myself, I assured her of my respect and inviolable attachment.[4]

Madame Nilova, like her three daughters, was a complete fabrication. But, on the plus side, she had a romantic back-story, and Benyovszky entertains us with that. On the following day, while workmen were busy erecting the new schoolhouse (it took only a week to build), our hero went off to teach his new pupils German, French and Russian. While there he had another encounter with Madame Nilova.

When I was preparing to depart, the governor's lady arrived, and after dismissing her children, made me sit down beside her. She informed me, that she was the daughter of a Swedish colonel, exiled into Siberia; that her mother had changed her religion, and that she had married Mr. Nilow, at that time lieutenant-colonel, a worthy man, but greatly addicted to drinking, the excess of which rendered him brutal and insupportable; that she enjoyed no pleasure excepting that of seeing her family grow up around her, though at the present instant, after having suffered the mortification of seeing her two eldest daughters married to two officers who were addicted to gluttony and drinking in the most disgusting excess, she could not but lament the fate of the youngest, who was intended by her father to be married to a certain *kuzma* [*brute*], one of the most disagreeable persons in the universe. She therefore intreated me to endeavour to gain the confidence of the governor, and to use my utmost exertions to change this resolution. My reply to this good mother was, that I would do my best, and that at all times she should find me obedient to her commands.[5]

And then it was time for lunch.

It is hard to grasp just how swiftly Benyovszky conquered the hearts and minds of the residents of Kamchatka, both those who really existed and those who never did. There was no stopping him. The following days were filled with a wild round of teaching, playing chess, consorting with Afanasia in her bedchamber (entirely innocently), and partying. For a brief moment, it got serious: on the fifth day, Khrushchyov wheeled in a crowd of fifteen men, some of them exiles, some 'free,' who wished to join Benyovszky's secret Society. And then it was back to playing chess for roubles, partying, and – for light relief – hunting bears in a manly manner. Everything undertaken was done magnificently. Bystanders applauded. Gifts, bags of money, people: all fell at Benyovszky's feet; he was so flush that he even lent money to merchants to ease their debts.

There was of course a point to all of this: at the time of writing his *Memoirs*, Benyovszky was feverishly trying to find backers for his ambitious scheme to colonise Madagascar and turn it into the most profitable colony of the age. He had to demonstrate that he was the man who could soften the hardest hearts, engage with the most venal traders, gain the undying allegiance of rough soldiers and even rougher citizenry, conjure piles of gold from thin air and educate the uneducated. And it did no harm amongst his French audience that he was self-evidently a man for the ladies. He was Charm Personified – such a man could not fail in Madagascar. Your money is safe with him.

For twenty page-turning chapters, Benyovszky regales us with derring-do and romance. It would be unfair – to memorialist, publisher and public – to repeat everything here: those who gasp after adventure and entertainment can read the *Memoirs* for themselves. We shall simply clutch a small handful of silver threads to guide us safely through the relentlessly purple passages.

Afanasia Nilova, beautiful youngest daughter of Commander Nilov, sweet sixteen and threatened with a terrible marriage: the girl provided Benyovszky with an object for his sentimentality, which was quite right and proper in the late eighteenth century, and an incredibly useful addition to his tale of romantic adventure. From the moment the pair met, they hit it off. It might not have been obvious to everyone at first, although Afanasia's mother saw it quite clearly: she herself was a roiling pot of romance and tragedy. Having talked his way into being the designated language-teacher to the children of the family, Benyovszky found himself co-opted into the position of music-teacher as well. It was her mother who proposed this to him – on no rational basis at all. Our hero courteously acceded to the request, although "my whole knowledge of this art consisted in playing the harp." The harp would do nicely, confirmed Madame Nilova. Our hero, recognising that it would have been nothing short of a miracle to find a harp in Kamchatka, set out to make one, "though I had never handled any cabinet-makers tools." Luckily, the exiles were able to pool their resources: Khrushchyov "engaged to make the strings with the entrails of dogs and reindeer and Mr Stephanow promised to make all the iron screws." Job done. When the harp was presented to the family, despite its obvious weaknesses, the entire family was enchanted, and from that day forward, Afanasia was inseparable from her instrument.[6]

In return for these gifts, innocent young Afanasia then proposed to her father that he grant:

> the abolition of the sentence of my exile, and the necessary grace, in order that I might be employed in some charge under government, that her sincere desire of seeing me happy, and of partaking in my happiness, might be accomplished. At these words the governor flew into a rage, and loaded me with invectives, but the chancellor and Hettman remonstrated strongly against the injustice of blaming me for the sentiments of his daughter. They observed it was not impossible but that I might in future possess a charge under government, and in that case the governor could not do better to insure the happiness of his family. Their arguments at length had some effect on the governor, who became calm.[7]

Nilov then remembered an edict of the late lamented Emperor Peter, which allowed for the pardoning of exiles who uncovered plots against lawful government. Considering that Benyovszky had done something like that in the small matter of a poisoned sugar-loaf (a plot which, even had it occurred, had not actually been directed against the Governor; we shall return to it shortly), he felt able to sign an "act of absolution" to set the Hungarian free. He issued a note of pardon on the following day – an act which caused not a few raised eyebrows in the camp of the exiles, most of whom supposed, justifiably, that something rather suspect was in play. Benyovszky was placed on trial by the members of his Society, but a few well-chosen words had them on their knees begging for his forgiveness.

A rather unexpected side-effect of being set at liberty was that Madame Nilova put pressure on Benyovszky to marry Afanasia. But instead of coming clean and admitting that he was already married, the adventurer prevaricated. After a brief discussion with Khrushchyov and the priest, it was decided that he should go along with the deceit "for the purpose of supporting the common interest." But it goes absolutely without saying that he had something of a conscience:

> I resolved to do nothing which might injure my reputation. I therefore declared that I would put off this affair as long as I could, in order to gain time, and that I did not despair of obtaining their consent to defer the marriage till the month of May; at which period, it would be in our power to settle the business in another manner, I confess that in my own mind I felt the utmost regret and uneasiness, to be the instrument of distress to an amiable girl whom I tenderly loved; but the hope that she might, at some future period, be happier in a marriage more suitable to her situation, tended in some measure to render my reflections less afflicting.[8]

Over the next few weeks, he sometimes found himself in awkward social embarrassment as a result of his ambiguous position; but always managed to extricate himself with some sentimental statement. At the end of one evening spent playing chess, listening to the dog-entrail harp and generally enrapturing the company with fine conversation, Benyovszky was rewarded by an unusual proposal from Madame Nilova:

> great was my surprize, when the governor's lady introduced me into the chamber of Miss Aphanasia, where she took her leave, saying, I hope you will be prudent; but as it is proper you should be accustomed to live together, I thought you could not be better lodged than with my daughter; with these words she retired, wishing me a good night. Astonished as I was at this speech and manner of proceeding, so contrary to the customs of Europe, I had ample matter to form systems, but my charming companion did not permit me to employ my thoughts on meditations of this kind. She had so much to say and I to answer, that we passed the time without thinking of sleep, and I did not leave her company till eight in the morning.

Benyovszky sneaked home in the grey light of dawn, explained the situation to his fellow-exiles, and fell asleep in his own bed – only to wake at five in the afternoon and find Afanasia lying beside him: she "expressed the most lively apprehensions for my health, and declared that she would not quit me."[9] (This entire bedchamber episode, incidentally, was purged from the Victorian edition prepared by Captain Pasfield Oliver.)

No sooner had the Hungarian passed a couple of entirely platonic nights in Afanasia's company than her father began to appoint him into positions of official responsibility, even to the extent of asking him to draw up state documents. The mother, meanwhile, was having a house built for the happy couple, in expectation of their wedding at the end of May 1771. As the great day approached, young Afanasia was clearly in a heightened state of emotion; after Benyovszky had spent a few days away on official business, inspecting the surrounding countryside at the request of the Commander, Nilov received his report and then sent him in to see his daughter. "This beautiful and lovely young lady received me with those transports which the candour and openness of her disposition did not permit her to conceal, and her respectable mother bore a share in her joy."

And then they had dinner.

All of this romancing served one purpose: to bring Benyovszky further into Nilov's inner circle, to gain his absolute trust and thereby to make the planning of the Great Escape so much simpler.

The fact that neither Madame Nilova nor her daughter existed was entirely secondary to that purpose.

The wooing of Afanasia provided the basis of another dynamic to the plot: this was the rather entertaining rivalry between Benyovszky and Stepanov. Captain Ippolit Stepanov, we will recall, had travelled with Benyovszky from the far side of the Urals, and was one of the charmed inner circle, a founder-member of the Society. What Benyovszky did not realise was that this same man was a serpent, a man with little morality and even less loyalty. This realisation came as a shock to him and certainly to the avid reader, although Stepanov's cousin, Vasilii Panov, already knew the man's duplicitous character.

Stepanov was the trusted friend all the way through to page 165. But then he began to show his true colours. On 27th February, a meeting had just taken place, during which all fifty-nine members of the expanded Society had rubbed their hands in glee over the report that piles of weaponry had been secretly amassed in readiness for the escape.

> The meeting was on the point of breaking up, when Mr. Panow made a motion. He began by observing that the indiscretion of one single person would be sufficient to destroy all our hopes; for which reason he held it to be of the last necessity to resolve in this committee that the association should give up all authority into my hands, in order that, after having given so many proofs of my attachment to their interests, I might in future be dispensed from communicating my intentions respecting the measures I proposed to take, and the means which I intended to employ in carrying my plan into execution.[10]

All very sensible, one would have thought: Benyovszky as the absolute ruler, with no obligation to tell anyone what he was up to. What rational conspirator could object? But now the bombshell exploded.

> Mr. Stephanow opposed this motion; but it was agreed to by the society, so that Mr. Stephanow remained alone. In order to dissipate his confusion, I

declared that I would nominate him a member of my council, because, as he was the only one who mistrusted my intentions, he might superintend my actions. The meeting, however, opposed his nomination, at the instance of Mr. Panow, who declared that Stephanow had rendered himself incapable of any confidence on our part, and that it was merely with a view of excluding him from our secrets that he had made his proposition. [...] But he threatened, that if Mr. Stephanow did not consent to receive and submit to the future orders, till the day of our departure, he should hold himself obliged to employ every means in his power to come at the knowledge of his proceedings, and to expose him to the company.

Great was Benyovszky's astonishment at this revelation. He asked Stepanov to explain his position. This he duly did, "at the same time loading me with expletives," maintaining, amongst other completely untenable arguments, that there were others in the company better suited to leadership than Benyovszky; and finally challenging his glorious leader to a duel.

The duel that followed on the succeeding day went just as one might expect: drawing swords, they engage; Benyovszky immediately breaks Stepanov's sword; he steps back to show mercy; the wretch pulls out a pistol and fires it, grazing Benyovszky's arm; Benyovszky throws him to the ground; the wretch demands to be put to death, the hero refuses. All in a day's work for a gentleman.

The same evening, the unhappy Stepanov was brought before the committee and there he confessed the cause of his enmity. It was simple: Stepanov was in love with the ravishing Afanasia, and, to gain her hand, he would have to kill Benyovszky. After a few kind words from his rival, Stepanov "fell at my feet, begged a thousand pardons, and entreated me to forget all that had happened." Benyovszky thereupon explained that he had himself no intention of marrying the girl, and a gentleman's agreement was reached, whereby, at the time of the escape, Stepanov could carry her off himself. Bizarrely, Afanasia was then persuaded to go along with this, for the good of the conspiracy.

Stepanov's gratitude did not last long. About three days to be precise, when, "in the morning, I received a visit from Mr. Stephanow, who fatigued me with his meanness." These wild fluctuations on Stepanov's part, between eternal gratitude and protestations of loyalty on the one hand, and "invectives" and violent enmity on the other, lasted, we are led to believe, all the way to Macao. At the end of March, there was even a dangerous moment when Stepanov threatened to reveal all the details of the conspiracy to the governor – a threat which was finally ended by tying him up, gagging him and subjecting him to a mock execution.

But instead of arsenic and corrosive sublimate, I would only give him an emetic, the effects of which would lead him to believe his death near at hand. I assured the meeting that I was convinced that this crisis would produce his reformation, and that the instant would decide his fate, and convince him that life or death would depend on his repentance or perseverance in his criminal designs.[11]

This stratagem had the required effect: without even swallowing the "poison," Stepanov burst into tears, begged forgiveness, and fainted away (twice). The company was then quite appalled to learn that Stepanov "was already married to a wife then living in Russia." Not at all like Benyovszky, then. It took some time for Stepanov to recover from this ordeal: at the time of a visit some days later, Benyovszky found him "under the application of blisters, having been in a continual delirium for three days and nights."

Stepanov: a coward, arguably unbalanced, unfit for command, verging on the adulterous. We will have plenty more evidence of this over the coming weeks. No surprise, then, that it was Stepanov who caused all the trouble in Macao, arguing against Benyovszky's secret negotiations with the European traders, and generally causing a fuss.

Or – an alternative view: Stepanov caused problems in Macao, so it was necessary to show that he had always been of weak character and questionable reliability.

Whatever.

Benyovszky packed a phenomenal amount of activity into his few months on Kamchatka. We have seen him trouncing everyone at chess and effortlessly gaining the trust, loyalty, love and respect of the entire population of the peninsula. There were also a number of plots against his life to deal with, as we shall shortly learn; and of course there was the escape to organise. On top of all that, he made several trips out into the countryside, to prepare a full report on trade and industry, and to make detailed observations on human and animal life. This activity was requested by none other than Nilov, who had high hopes of becoming Governor in Okhotsk on the basis of it. Had any of this even been likely, Nilov must have been a little disappointed, because the report is short, the details are unremarkable, and most of it could have been gleaned from far more detailed accounts by people such as Bering, Coxe, Krasheninnikov and other travellers and scientists of the era – whose works, of course, were readily available in Europe at around the time when Benyovszky was preparing his *Memoirs*. Our Hungarian critic Kropf is suitably scathing: he could not imagine

> any period at which their value was more than a waste-paper dealer would have given for the paper they were printed on. [...] Moreover, few geographers would care to wade through scores upon scores of pages of love stories and other fiction in order to discover a few meagre geographical data, of which they would be loth to make any use on account of the tainted source from which they were obtained.[12]

Pasfield Oliver adopted the more gentlemanly critical method; he simply omitted all of the offending pages from his 1893 edition.

A lengthier description of Kamchatka, the Aleutian Islands and the Kuril Islands was included by Benyovszky at the end of his first "volume" – at the point where the voyagers have just set sail. There are thirty pages here – five summarising voyages of discovery made "to the eastward of Kamchatka," seven detailing a chart (alas, lost by the time of publication) which Benyovszky claims to have made of the Sea of Okhotsk, another five describing Kamchatka, and then more with lists and locations of the Aleutians, the Kurils, the Japanese islands and Sakhalin. Since he had never visited some of these islands, it must be supposed that he read up on them at a later date.

The purpose of the inclusion of these observations in the *Memoirs* was simply to prove to potential investors that the intrepid explorer knew what he was talking about when it came to trade and the exploitation of distant lands. Poor in quantity and quality they might have been, but they were an essential of the work.

Plots breed counter-plots. Apart from the machinations of the wayward Stepanov, there was a respectable sequence of minor plots against Benyovszky – which was only to be expected. The first one involved the trader Tchuloshnikov: this was the captain of that ship which had run aground the preceding August, resulting in the downing of tools by the hunters and crew; for reasons not entirely clear, the trader accused Benyovszky of inciting mutiny and threatened to denounce him to Nilov. The tables were turned when Benyovszky went and told Nilov of the trader's threats; Nilov, father of Afanasia, naturally took Benyovszky's side. That same night, Benyovszky was then set upon by Tchuloshnikov and his cousin "with two stout bludgeons and drawn knives." They should have known better: armed with only a stick, Benyovszky fought back, accidentally killing the cousin; the affray ended with the trader's arrest and imprisonment.

Just a few days later, things turned more serious. On the 1st January 1771, the exiles sat down to a modest celebration of the new year.

> We had received from several merchants, presents of tea and sugar, with which we regaled ourselves. But this pleasure cost us dear; for in a quarter of an hour after we were seized with violent cholics and vomiting. Mr. Panow was the first who assured us that we were poisoned, for he affirmed that he had observed many of the pieces of sugar tasted salt. In consequence of this supposition, each of us drank a large quantity of whale oil. It is impossible to describe our sufferings; some were affected more than others, and as to myself, who had only taken one cup of tea, I found, after I had taken the oil, that my pains disappeared with only a trembling in all my limbs. But my utmost exertions were required to attend my other companions, consisting of fourteen persons, many of whom vomited blood.
>
> During this crisis, several of our companions came to see us, who, when they found what had happened, made haste to bring a quantity of the rein deer's milk, which at last mitigated our pains, and caused them to go off with

a trembling of the limbs, excepting Mr. Csurin, who died in the night, and Mr. Panow, who continued scarcely alive. As soon as we had recovered our forces and began to reflect upon this event, we examined the sugar. I gave a piece to a cat, and another piece to a dog, wrapped up in part of a fish. Both these animals were strongly convulsed, and burst in the space of half an hour. This experiment convinced us that Mr. Casarinow, a merchant, had poisoned the sugar.[13]

Once the mess from exploding cat and dog had been cleared up, a sneaky plan was concocted. On the following day, Benyovszky visited the governor, related the incident and accused Kasarinov of having poisoned them. The commander then invited Kasarinov for a nice cup of tea. The suspect sugar-loaf made its appearance, Nilov pointedly informing his guest that it had been a present from Benyovszky. The merchant paled and said, actually, he did not feel thirsty any more, thanks all the same. Nilov pressed. Eventually Kasarinov confessed, was arrested, and had all his property confiscated; Benyovszky later successfully argued for leniency, and the unfortunate man was released and sent to the Kurils for two years.

One unlooked-for bonus from the Kasarinov affair was the uncovering of an agent in the ranks of the exiles. Kasarinov stated that a man by the name of Piatsinin had revealed the escape plot to him, and this, he tried to persuade Nilov, was the reason for his attempt on Benyovszky. Nilov was having none of it, and went off to his dinner. Benyovszky, on the other hand, went home, convened the committee, brought Piatsinin to trial and sentencing and, after a short blessing by the priest, the unfortunate man was led out and shot through the head. This was by no means the only traitor discovered in their midst – we have already seen Stepanov's attempts, which logically should have met with similar punishment: he was saved certainly because, in a rare nod to actual history, he had to be alive when they got to Macao. In February, while Benyovszky was being sledged around Lower Kamchatka surveying the countryside and hobnobbing with local chiefs, word arrived of another traitor.

On the 13th we reached the village of Kamenin, where all my projects would have been overthrown, if a lucky accident had not averted this most imminent danger. On the 14th, in the morning, I came out to direct Mr. Kuzneczow to send an express to our associates at Bolsha, to advise them of our return. As soon as I came out I was accosted by a native, who requested to be introduced to the governor, as he said he had a letter for him from an exile who had been taken ill, and was by that means prevented from waiting on the governor himself. I ordered this man to follow me, and went with him to Kuzneczow, where, after opening the letter, I saw it contained an account of the secrets of our union, from one of the associates named Levantiew. [...] Upon this information I ordered Kuzneczow to depart immediately with Ivan Kudrin, and dispatch the traitor. I then rejoined the governor, with whom I breakfasted.[14]

TRAVELLING IN WINTER KAMCHATKA.

FIGURE 15.1 "A Carriage Drawn by Dogs in Kamchatka" – lithograph for the 1790 edition of Benyovszky's *Memoirs.*

As it turned out, the miserable Levantiev was almost dead anyway: Kuznetsov returned reporting

> that Levontiew had declared his resolution to his cousin [...] who, not being able to dissuade him from it, had poisoned him in a glass of brandy, which they drank together: and that, on the arrival of Kuzneczow, this unhappy wretch was at the point of death. He confessed his intention to Kuzneczow,

and entreated, as a favour, that he would put him out of his misery, at the same time that he declared the society had nothing more to fear, since his letter was intercepted; because he had discovered his intention to no one but his cousin, who, faithful to his engagement, had poisoned him. This account gave me great satisfaction.

It was this treatment of Levantiev that provoked one of Stepanov's several tantrums, as we noted earlier. In passing, let us note the similarity of this episode – the waylaying of a messenger before Benyovszky is exposed – to the one back in Siberia, when the letter to Plenisner was switched. After this, would anyone trust a Siberian postman?

Lovers, acolytes, assassins, traitors, rivals, scheming mothers-in-law: all of human life was here.

In amongst all of these diversions, thankfully, a concrete plan was being laid for escape. There were several versions of the plan, each one better than the one before.

The first one that arose, if we discount the abortive hijacking of the ship from Okhotsk, was a proposal made by the mutinous employees of Tchuloshnikov. In December, the twenty-eight disgruntled men approached the exiles in a body, suggesting that they could increase the number of conspirators to such a size that they could easily seize a ship and make off. Benyovszky listened carefully, but finally decided that he could not trust them to keep their mouths shut; he politely turned them down. After desperate representations made by their leaders – throwing themselves at Benyovszky's feet in the approved manner – all twenty-eight were accepted into the company. But no immediate plans were hatched.

In early January, through the medium of Stepanov (he was in loyal mode at that time), another group of Kamchatkan residents made themselves known: the three apprentice navigators Izmailov, Bocharov and Lapin. These three, independently, had a plan to hook up with half–a-dozen hunters, seize a vessel and head off to the Aleutian Islands "to establish themselves there." Again, Baron Benyovszky made a note, but took no further action.

It was quite clear that the only way to escape was by ship. From early January, the conspirators started collecting weapons and "provisions sufficient for a voyage by sea of three months." As a subterfuge, Benyovszky had early on asked Nilov for permission to build a new colony for the exiles, some miles to the south of Bolsheretsk; any collecting of wood, provisions, weapons etc. could easily be attributed to the establishment of this new colony. By early March, the Swedish exile Meyder was able to inform the committee

that he had prepared one hundred cartouch boxes, each containing forty-eight full cartridges, and sixty other charges fastened to each; and that Mr. Crustiew had collected, or caused to be made, sixty knives, which might be used to advantage instead of cutlasses, as each of them was eighteen inches long and three broad: that sixteen pair of pistols and thirty-six hatchets had been purchased; and that Mr. Panow had caused one hundred pikes to be made.[15]

Also at that time, a request to Nilov for a proper ship to take them to their new village – a bold request, certainly – was regretfully turned down: *baydars*, large skin-covered open boats, would be provided instead. Not even Benyovszky would contemplate sailing the high seas in those. This did not prevent some of his more eager followers from suggesting a trip to the Kurils by *baydar*, where they would surely find a ship to take them to Japan, and then a Dutch ship to Europe.

While the search for a ship continued, the conspirators organised themselves. By mid-March, the following military structure had been established:

> On the 11th, the private meeting was held by adjournment, to appoint the order of service, in case we should be obliged to act by main force. It was settled as follows in three divisions.
>
> The left wing, commanded by Mr. Wynbladth. Mr. Kuczneczow, Stephanow, Sibaew, Bielsky, Lopcsow, With thirteen associates.
>
> The center. Myself chief. Mr. Panow, Ruimin, Meder, Srebernicow, Loginow, Baturin, With fourteen associates.
>
> The right wing, commanded by Mr. Crustiew. Archidiacre Protopop, The Prince Zadzkoy, Brandorp, Novozilow, Lapkin, Volkow, with twelve associates.[16]

It is a curious fact that a fair number of these twenty named leaders of the escape plan are never once mentioned by Ryumin, in his own detailed account of the voyage.

At length, Benyovszky announced the final plan: when the ship *St Peter*, which had brought them from Okhotsk, was ready to sail again in the middle of May, there would only be twenty-two crew aboard: an easy target for a disciplined and well-armed commando of exiles. They would infiltrate into the crew a dozen of their number who were not exiles, along with a couple of paying passengers of similar persuasion; tempt the captain to anchor just out of harbour in order to pick up some profitable contraband; at which point, the remaining exiles would paddle out and seize the ship.

By the end of March, all berths were booked, and crewmen placed. And then suddenly it all got easier.

The captain of the ship, Tchurin, approached Benyovszky with a sob-story. The captain, it seemed, was most unwilling to sail the ship to Okhotsk, because he had debts there which he could not pay; there was also the threat of a trial in the Admiralty court, on the matter of being in charge of a capsized ship, "the issue of which might condemn him to the mines." There was a real danger that Tchurin would pull out of his unwitting role in the plan, and the ship would end up captained by someone of stronger moral fibre, less susceptible to bribery in the form of contraband. In addition, there was a lady in the case: some "girl" for whom Tchurin had fallen and whom he refused to leave behind in Kamchatka. It is not certain whether this lady was his wife, or supplementary to his wife. Benyovszky took all this in his stride, and invited the captain to tea.

> After this confession, he begged me to have pity on his situation, and grant him my protection and advice. I promised to reflect seriously on his affairs, but observed, that it would require some time to consider maturely what was best to be done. I gave him my word, however, that I would clear him of his embarrassment; but at the same time, as a previous condition, I insisted that he should not mention his situation to any one, nor think of quitting the command of the vessel. He swore that he would comply with my directions, and thus we parted. But […] I called him back, to put a bag of five hundred roubles into his hands, with the compliment, that I begged him to accept of this advance to purchase a present for his lady. He refused at first, but I forced him to accept the present by declaring, that, if he persisted in his refusal, I should not believe he was really attached to my interests. He therefore accepted my present, and I was delighted at having made so good a bargain.[17]

All sorted. Benyovszky's winnings from chess had come in very handy indeed. It only remained to finish provisioning, have dinner, and wait for the ice to thaw.

Notes

1 Benyovszky, 1790, Vol.I, pp.81–88.
2 *ibid*, pp.89–98.
3 *ibid*, pp.98–100.
4 *ibid*, p.102.
5 *ibid*, pp.103–104.
6 *ibid*, p.113.
7 *ibid*, pp.124–125.
8 *ibid*, p.129.
9 *ibid*, p.141–143.
10 *ibid*, pp.165–166.
11 *ibid*, pp.197–201.
12 Kropf, 1895, Vol.7, p.243.
13 Benyovszky, 1790, Vol.I, pp.117–120.
14 *ibid*, pp.151–152.
15 *ibid*, p.164.
16 *ibid*, pp.180–181.
17 *ibid*, pp.201–205.

XVI

THE GREAT ESCAPE

"Twenty-two Bears Were This Day Salted"

Feverish Preparations – Izmailov's Treachery – Miss Afanasia's Red Ribbons –
Attack and Counter-attack – The Death of Commander Nilov –
Affecting Scenes with Widow – One Thousand Women and Infants –
Affecting Scenes with a Fatherless Girl – Final Preparations for the Voyage

"After dinner," wrote the commander of the plotters – this was after dinner on the 12th day of April, "I was seized with a violent cholic." The phrase *"After dinner…"* appears at least nineteen times in Benyovszky's journal, most of them relating to his time in Kamchatka. A regime of regular gentleman's mealtimes was clearly being observed.

Between the 10th of April and the 11th of May 1771, feverish preparations were made for the escape. So feverish, indeed, that Maurice Benyovszky had to spend some of them in bed. He wrote:

> After dinner I was seized with a violent cholic, succeeded by a fever, which forced me to go to bed. In the night I grew worse, which obliged me to send for Messrs. Crustiew and Panow, to whom I intrusted the care and superintendence of the company.
>
> On the 13th, Mr. Crustiew having acquainted Miss Aphanasia with my illness, she hastened to see me, and, as I was informed after my recovery, never quitted my bed-side, nor suffered any other person to attend me. The fever continued, without any regular period, during the 14th, 15th and 16th. On the 17th Mr. Meder bled me, and on the 18th he prescribed an emetic, by which treatment the fever left me on the 19th.
>
> On the 20th, I was able to quit my bed, and Miss Aphanasia informed her mother of my recovery, who came together with her other children, to congratulate me on the occasion. It was at this time I was informed of the

services Miss Aphanasia had done; I thanked her with the utmost sincerity, and was convinced that my gratitude affected her exceedingly. After the departure of Madame Nilow, though, her daughter staid with me.[1]

This affecting episode was immediately preceded by one which involved the treacherous triumvirate of Stepanov, Izmailov and Bocharov. Allegedly, Izmailov's two intimate friends Bocharov and Zyablikov had so much sympathy with Stepanov that they incautiously wrote a letter to him – a lengthy one at that, couched in flowery phrases, strangely reminiscent of Benyovszky's own style – promising to betray the "abominable chief" and "tyrant" to the authorities, and threatening to kill him given half a chance. Stepanov, at that time full of remorse, handed the letter over to his cousin Panov, and offered to deliver the counter-plotters to be sentenced to death; Panov, for his part, scuttled off to inform Benyovszky. Benyovszky, naturally, had a cunning plan: he drafted a letter for Stepanov to sign, indicating that there was nothing but sweetness and light between the two of them; the letter was sent to Bocharov and Zyablikov, inviting them to come along and see for themselves. This they duly did, and – to cut a long story short – they were immediately won over by Benyovszky, and signed up to the Grand Plot.

Izmailov, the nephew of Chancellor Novozilov, was now on his own. Benyovszky's prompt action immediately paid dividends, since Novozilov was at that very moment stirring up Nilov with his nephew's own report of Benyovszky's plot. Our hero challenged the chancellor for proof, and he made the mistake of calling Bocharov and Zyablikov as witnesses. An amusing scene followed, Izmailov's own letter to Novozilov was rubbished, the chancellor was made to look silly, and Nilov apologised profusely. On the following day, Novozilov came along to Benyovszky's HQ to apologise in person, promising never to doubt his word again. "We parted good friends."

Meanwhile, Captain Tchurin had whipped up a ship.

> On the 12th, I received a letter from Mr. Kuzneczow, wherein he informed me that Mr. Csurin was busy in fitting out his vessel, but that it was impossible to clear the ice during the present month: that he would answer for the taking of the redoubt, the fire of which would protect the ship, while the vessel in return would clear the approaches to the redoubt: that Mr Csurin was disposed to share our fortune at all risks, as he had his lady with him: and lastly, he concluded his letter by intreating me to facilitate the means of his female friend joining him.

Again, there is a little element of doubt here about the identities of Tchurin's "lady" and "his female friend." One suspects the worst.

While this was happening, Izmailov's campaign had picked up speed again. This time, the accusations revolved around the death of the traitor Levantiev, he who had (in our last chapter) written a letter to Nilov, exposing the plotters, for which he had been punished with poisoned brandy. The chancellor Novozilov, despite his earlier oath of loyalty and friendship, was back on Benyovszky's case. Conveniently, however, Izmailov informed Bocharov and Zyablikov of his thoughts, so Benyovszky was prepared for "an open attack." The first thing to do was to fetch Bocharov and Zyablikov and be sure of them; this was easy enough and soon the two men were on their knees, thanking him for his favour. Then, arms were distributed to the whole company, and a rota of guards established. Next, Benyovszky had to avoid being locked up: easily done when the daughter of the commander was on your side.

> Miss Aphanasia came to see me incognito. She informed me, that her mother was in tears, and her father had talked with her in a manner which gave reason to fear that he suspected our plot. She conjured me to be careful, and not to come to the fort, if sent for. [...] I tenderly embraced this charming young lady, and thanked her for the interest she took in my preservation; and as it appeared important that her absence should not be discovered, I begged her to return, and recommend the issue of our intentions to good fortune. Before her departure I reminded her to look minutely after her father, and to find me a red ribband in case government should determine to arrest or attack me, and, in the second place, that at the moment of an alarm she would open the shutter of her window, which looked to the garden, and cause a sledge to be laid over the ditch on that side. She promised to comply with my instructions, and confirmed her promises with vows and tears.[2]

The red ribbon idea turned out to be a stroke of genius. *Billets doux* poured out of the fort over the next few days, with and without red ribbons attached, including one on the 26th which advised Benyovszky that Afanasia's father "was more prejudiced in my favour than ever," and inviting him to an amicable meeting.

That letter was full to bursting with clippings of red ribbon.

For Nilov was by this time a very angry man indeed. He shouted at Madame Nilova, threatening to beat her, then he shouted at his children, and then something happened that got him really, really upset: Benyovszky kidnapped Izmailov and the chancellery secretary, Sudeikin, both of whom were about to be produced as witnesses to back up Novozilov's accusations.

This was the final straw for Nilov. He sent a detachment of Cossacks under the command of their hetman; Benyovszky and his company simply took them prisoner. The hetman sent a note back to Nilov advising him to negotiate peace-terms. Nilov was having none of it, and threatened Benyovszky with a death-sentence – a rather lamentable situation to arise between prospective father-in-law and son-in-law. In response, more soldiers were sent, who were likewise imprisoned. At this point, defence switched to offence, and various companies of the rebels, under the command of Benyovszky and Winbladh, moved on the fort. As they came within sight of it, an affecting scene occurred:

Before we met, I saw Mr. Stephanow, who, though scarcely able to walk, came armed, and had only time to tell me that he came to conquer or die with me. This resolution secured him my esteem; for tho' the poor man could scarcely support himself, he nevertheless did every thing in his power to encourage the associates.[3]

Fortunately, Stepanov did not have to sacrifice his life just then, since the defending soldiers fled at the first sign of trouble. Within minutes, as night fell, the fort was laid wide open, although some pockets of resistance remained.

What then followed was a scene of unmitigated tragedy:

As I heard a firing in the court, and saw that my comrades were fastening the petard to force the inner gates, I ventured to pass through a window which I found open. Madame Nilow and her children, at sight of me, implored my protection to save their father and husband. I immediately hastened to his apartment, and begged him to go to his childrens room to preserve his life; but he answered that he would first take mine, and instantly fired a pistol, which wounded me: I was desirous, nevertheless, of preserving him, and continued to represent that all resistance would be useless, for which reason I intreated him to retire. His wife and children threw themselves on their knees, but nothing would avail: he flew upon me, seized me by the throat, and left me no other alternative than either to give up my own life, or run my sword through his body. At this instant the petard exploded and burst the outer gate. The second was open, and I saw Mr. Panow enter at the head of a party. He entreated the governor to let me go, but not being able to prevail on him, he set me at liberty by splitting his skull.

No words can describe the unhappy scene this event produced: Madame Nilow fell at my feet, her daughters fainted, and the firmness of my mind was scarcely equal to the shock. I was ready to sink to the ground, when Mr. Panow seeing me in this situation obliged me to quit the apartment, and assured me that he would take care of Madame Nilow and her family.[4]

Thus ended the life of Grigorii Nilov. It may not have ended exactly as described. But the result was quite irrevocable. Sadly for him, the tearful family that gathered around his corpse was unlikely to have comprised anyone other than his son. The rest were spectres from Benyovszky's imagination.

The Hungarian, dripping blood all round the fort, rallied his men. Some half-hearted attempts by soldiers to re-take lost ground failed miserably, with fourteen Cossacks perishing under heavy fire. By three in the morning, the fort was secure, and "everything was in perfect order." Benyovszky arranged that Madame Nilova and her children should be bled to relieve their grief.

In the grey light of dawn, another challenge had to be met. The hetman had unluckily been freed from his prison, and had gathered all the remaining Cossacks on a hill overlooking the town. There were, we are told, "seven or eight hundred men."

Contemporary accounts, written by Russian officials[5] indicate that there may have been a total of around 300 military personnel on the whole peninsula, of whom 117 were based in Bolsheretsk. This was in 1773, at a time when the authorities had recently beefed up the military presence to avert any future outbreaks of enthusiasm by malcontents. The total population of Bolsheretsk was no more than 600 individuals, not counting dogs. Benyovszky himself set out the following numbers of the entire Kamchatkan population, "from the most authentic examination":

364	Soldiers
29	Land officers
422	Russian hunters
1500	Cossacks and their officers
26	Civil officers
82	Russian merchants
700	Descendants of liberated exiles
1600	Exiles of different conditions
8000	Male Kamchadales
2 or 3000	Female Kamchadales
40	Russian women
200	Women, descendants of the exiles
15963	Total.[6]

Presumably Benyovszky's "seven or eight hundred men," to whom he found himself opposed that night in Bolsheretsk, were drawn from the interestingly high number of "Cossacks and their officers." But given that even he states a few pages later that there was a garrison of 280 soldiers in Bolsheretsk, this number does seem a little inflated.

Notwithstanding these minor anomalies, Benyovszky came up with a sure-fire method of focussing the attention of the Cossacks and bringing them to surrender. It was so simple: round up all the women and children of the town, shut them in the church, and threaten to burn them alive if their husbands did not yield. No sooner said than done: "more than a thousand women, girls and infants" were locked up inside the church, and piles of wood and furniture set at all four corners, ready for a conflagration. To add a note of sombre threat to the whole scene, it was decided that Nilov's body should be placed in their midst: "the body of this unfortunate chief, whose life had been ever dear to me, was instantly carried to the place of destination."

In no time at all, the white flag was raised on the hill. The troops ran down and surrendered their weapons; some were locked up as hostages, the remainder threw themselves into the arms of their weeping wives and infants: a triumph of military strategy.

Having been wounded by Nilov, Benyovszky was bandaged up and told to take some rest. As he lay in the makeshift hospital, he was visited by the grieving widow of Nilov. "This worthy lady," as soon as she saw Benyovszky's suffering, forgot her own grief and very distinctly and very carefully pointed out that the Hungarian was in no way to blame for her husband's death. Not in the slightest. She had "with wonder beheld my forbearance, at the time when wounded by her husband, and in the most imminent danger of my life, I did not use my arms against him." Benyovszky – let us make it quite, quite clear – was innocent of any malicious intent.

The widow took this opportunity to make him promise to marry Afanasia.

> In this situation, urged by the necessity of calming the mind of an unhappy mother, whose virtue and firmness of soul I have every reason to admire, I promised all she required. She then embraced her daughter, advised her always to preserve the same attachment to me, and wished her every happiness; and at last hastily rising, she passionately exclaimed, you are the cause of the loss of her father, become her husband, and be a father to her![7]

On the 27th, Khrushchyov was packed off to the mouth of the river to seize their escape vessel, the *St Peter*. Various others took control of the armoury and the treasury, and Benyovszky suffered a little with his wound. As he lay there, Miss Afanasia turned up and advised him that Madame Nilova intended to depart in two days' time. To anyone else, this news might have seemed a little disconcerting: where on earth was she going, and how on earth was she going to get there? There was no ship. She would have to travel overland. Snow and ice still blocked such roads as existed. There is no word of anyone sensible accompanying her. Nonetheless, off she was going to go. But before that, Nilov was buried with great pomp and ceremony.

> After this ceremony I ordered Mr. Panow to persuade the archbishop, either by threatenings or promises, to preach a sermon in the church in favour of the revolution we had produced, and afterwards to receive the oath of fidelity, from all my companions towards me, upon the gospels at the altar.[8]

Benyovszky, thus cemented into position by religion, fell into a fever and delirium, where he remained for three days. During this time, Madame Nilova departed on her mysterious journey, along with her other children, all the preparations for the departure of the ship were completed, while Miss Nilova played nurse and mopped Benyovszky's brow.

On the 2nd May, when the Baron rose from his sick-bed, he gave orders for this and that, and turned his attention to the practical matter of funds: "The great quantity of furs which my officers found in the magazines, made me perfectly easy, as to the means of providing for the subsistence of all my companions on my arrival in Europe."[9] Then he interviewed eighteen new applicants for the escape. One name stands out here: Izmailov. For some reason, not explained by Benyovszky, Izmailov had decided he wished to come along, and was engaged in blaming the secretary of the chancellery, Sudeikin, for everything that Izmailov himself had done. He did this so remarkably well that the unfortunate Sudeikin was beaten up and left for dead in a ransacked house. As a precaution, Benyovszky had Izmailov clapped in irons – but this did not prevent him from putting him aboard ship when the time came. Could it be that Izmailov was taken along, rather than being left behind on Kamchatka, precisely because by 1784 the world knew – through the story of Captain Cook's voyages – that Izmailov had indeed been taken along?

On the 3rd of the month, there was a moment of rare honesty shared with the amiable Miss Afanasia. The girl turned up on the doorstep in floods of tears, clutching a letter. The letter was, of course, from that incurable turncoat, Stepanov. A rather touching scene ensued, which – alas! – we must share, at some length:[10]

> I opened the letter: it was written by Stephanow, who informed Miss Aphanasia, that after having been deceived and betrayed by me, she owed the most eminent vengeance to herself and family; to effect which he offered his services. He informed her that I was married, and consequently incapable of placing her in any estimable rank of life. He represented, that after this information, as she could never become my wife, she could not without dishonour follow my party: and he finished his letter by declaring, that he would efface her shame by my blood; for which purpose he waited only the re-establishment of his health, in order to offer his hand.
>
> This letter, at any other time, would have inspired me with pity for an unhappy man, who was rushing hastily to his destruction; but at that moment it affected me strongly. For I had proposed to defer my confession until I could procure a proper match for the young lady. In this state of astonishment she roused me out of my reverie, by saying, "Listen, my dear friend, do not afflict yourself: your Aphanasia will not be unhappy. She loves you, and will always love you. She cannot call herself your wife, but you may keep her as your child." Immediately after which she said, "Shall it not be so, my dear papa." This ingenuity and freedom of character, united to the heroic sentiments of so amiable a person, went to my heart, and I could not avoid paying the tribute to such elevated sentiments. I begged her pardon…

No, really: it all becomes a little too saccharine here. We must skip a few sentences…

> My words, though very ill calculated for my justification, were received with such interest as secured my pardon, which she pronounced by declaring, that nothing in the world could destroy her attachment for me. She added, that she would be contented to live in the country where I should fix my abode, and should enjoy perfect happiness in seeing me, and calling me father. Her hopes, she said, were to enjoy perfect repose in the bosom of my family, as she was resolved to renounce marriage intirely; and the only promise she requested of me was, to consider her as my own daughter, and permit her to change her cloathing, with a view that, when cloathed as a man, she might be less embarrassing to me.

Thankfully, at this moment "Mr. Panow interrupted our conversation."

Another typical scene with Stepanov followed: Afanasia denounced him; the serpent seized a pistol; he waved it about "furiously"; he was taken off to a darkened room to calm down. On the following day,

> Miss Aphanasia presented herself in the dress, and with the arms of a man, and the company named her *Achilles*. Her figure in this dress was charming, and she certainly had as much courage as it is possible for a woman to have.

And this is the very last time that Afanasia Nilova is mentioned in Benyovszky's *Memoirs*, until her death in Macao is recorded.

Between the 5th May and the 11th, final preparations were made for the voyage. Sundry persons, both male and female, exiles and citizens, turned up, just begging to be taken along. There were rumours of the other Kamchatkan garrisons taking up arms and marching against the rebels. On the 8th, "at six o'clock the vessel, having undergone a complete repair, was rigged, and twenty-two bears were this day salted as part of our sea-stock." Over the following two days, the vessel was fully loaded. On the 11th, the hostages were released and sent back to town.

Izmailov, as we have noted, was not sent back but brought on board; Izmailov's unfortunate victim, the secretary Sudeikin was also not sent back but, on the contrary, forced to embark to become the ship's cook. Like Stepanov, the later recording of actual events obliged Izmailov to be taken along on the journey, when it would have been far better to have abandoned him. Sometimes a man is not in control of his *Memoirs*.

And then, and at last: "On my arrival on board, I hoisted the colours of the confederation of Poland, which ceremony was attended with the discharge of twenty guns."[11]

The great voyage to Tinian, the island of liberty, had begun.

Notes

1 Benyovszky, 1790, Vol.I, pp.233–234.
2 *ibid*, pp.235–236.
3 *ibid*, p.242.
4 *ibid*, pp.243–244.
5 Schmalev, 1776; also Schlözer, 1780.
6 Benyovszky, 1790, Vol.I, pp.278–279.
7 *ibid*, pp.250–251.
8 *ibid*, p.256.
9 *ibid*, p.258.
10 All the following quotations regarding Miss Afanasia *ibid*, pp.258–260.
11 *ibid*, p.264.

XVII

THE FUR-TRADE

"All Join in Hating the Russians"

Lord Anson Discovers Paradise – Krasheninnikov Mistakes an Earthquake for Sea-Sickness – Birds, Plenty of – Murder, Rape and Kidnapping: Trading in the Aleutian Islands – Scurvy, Taxes and Baptism

But first, less of liberty and more of exploitation.

The northern seas that Captain Cook had explored were alive with inquisitive and acquisitive Russians. What lay to the east of Siberia was in the eighteenth century uncharted, uncivilised and, most importantly, uncolonised. It was all too tempting. For a period of almost eighty years, between 1725 and the end of the century, adventurous gentlemen from the Russian Empire – military, academic, mercantile, or simply mercenary – embarked upon voyages of exploration to map the coastlines and islands, investigate and civilise the native peoples, and seek out trading opportunities. They were, of course, not the first nation to engage in such practices. Great Britain had been sending ships into the South and North Pacific for some time. Captain Cook's epic voyages were but the most celebrated of dozens of similar, although largely shorter, voyages. France was not far behind, while the Netherlands, Spain and Portugal were old hands at such affairs.

Of all these voyages, it was the one undertaken by the approved British pirate Lord George Anson which had the most immediate attraction for Benyovszky and his friends. This was down to two factors: first, Anson's apparent inability to be vanquished by anyone or anything, while zigzagging around the Pacific; and second, the description of the island of Tinian, holiday destination of choice. In September 1740, George Anson had set off with a squadron of eight ships, crewed by men who were largely unfit for duty, being either decrepit ancients or raw untested youths. They were heading for the South Pacific, with explicit instructions to do as much damage to the Spanish war effort as they could, by 'interrupting' the trade between the East Indies and South America. In essence, this meant capturing Spanish trading ships, plundering them and making off home with the loot. Some might call this piracy; the British Admiralty certainly did not.

Poorly manned, poorly fed and setting off at the wrong time of year, it did not go well at first. By the time Anson's ships reached Cape Horn, the crews had already been decimated by sickness and scurvy, the food was rotten, and a sailor's life was unbearable. The passage round the foot of South America turned into an unmitigated disaster, with only Anson's ship making it into the Pacific intact.

Notwithstanding these setbacks, Anson spent the following three years cruising up and down the coast of South and Central America, harassing the Spanish settlements and any ship which came within sight, and also, for amusement, west and east along the Spanish trade-routes to the Philippines, capturing ships as they went. By the time this sole surviving ship returned to Britain in June 1744, Anson was immeasurably richer, his officers markedly less so, and the crew did all right for themselves; but the Spanish Empire, "that haughty nation," was considerably poorer. Which was the whole point. It was estimated that the capture of their final prize, a Spanish galleon, yielded over 35,000 ounces of South American silver and 1.3 million pieces-of-eight. Anson's chaplain Richard Walter, who compiled the book of the voyage, estimated the total profit from the entire venture at £1 million sterling (equivalent to around £185 million today): a labourer in Britain at that time might earn £32 in a year and a common seaman earned little more.

The human cost of this massive haul was quite astonishing: of more than 1,800 men who had set out in 1740, only 500 survived – and of those, only 188 men returned with Anson's ship. Scurvy had taken almost 1,300 men.

Benyovszky's reading of Anson probably skipped over the scurvy, the shipwrecks, the appalling conditions and rotten food (all of which his group on the *St Peter* were to experience for themselves) and concentrated on the description of the island of Tinian. For here, one was assured, there was "plenty of good water; there was an incredible number of cattle, hogs, and poultry running wild on the island, all of them excellent in their kind; the woods afforded sweet and sour oranges, limes, lemons, and coconuts in great abundance." Further, the island had "the air of a magnificent plantation where large lawns and stately woods had been laid out together with great skill."[1]

It was a place where Anson's bruised, battered and scorbutic crew could relax and recover. Anson's chronicler Richard Walter observed that

> our diseased in general reaped so much benefit from the fruits of the island, particularly those of the acid kind, that in a week's time there were but few of them who were not so far recovered as to be able to move about without help.

The clues were there: How To Prevent Scurvy. It took a few more decades for that message to get through to the British Admiralty. Captain Cook managed to stave it off with sauerkraut and malt, but his success was more down to general cleanliness and discipline than to the minimal amount of Vitamin C in pickled cabbage. The British Navy only finally adopted a policy of fresh fruit in the last decade of the century, and its robustly healthy crews were soon in peak condition to outfight the dastardly – and doubtless scurvy-ridden – French.

In the eyes of the exhausted crew of Anson's *Centurion*, Tinian was assuredly heaven on earth. It was hardly surprising that, thirty years later, the shivering masses of Kamchatka were intent on reaching it. No other island, possibly within striking distance, possibly not, could have matched their requirements better. (Paradise, alas, does not endure: in 1945 Tinian was the island from which the atomic bombs were flown to Hiroshima and Nagasaki. It now boasts a vast abandoned USAF airfield, two gas-stations and a casino.)

In the decade before Lord Anson set out on the high seas, the Russians had laboured hard at exploration. The Danish-born Vitus Bering, a captain in the Russian Navy, led the first expedition to Kamchatka in 1725. It was an exercise in self-sufficiency: they had to build their own ships when they got to Kamchatka, in order to explore the eastern coastline to the north. After three years, Bering had determined that the land-masses of Russia and America did not join up; the rather disappointing straits that separated them were named after him; he went off home. Immediately upon return, he set about organising a second expedition, bigger and better. Not all went well. The logistics of this expedition were such that the participants not only had to build their own ships, but even build their own shipyards to do so, DIY taken to extremes. Okhotsk was developed precisely for this shipyard: plenty of wood thereabouts, even if the ropes and sails, and all other supplies, had to be brought from Yakutsk. Around 3,000 labourers were sent eastwards to achieve the task. The members of the expedition found themselves straggled out across the vast distances of Siberia as they tried to reach their embarkation point. The land-route from Tobolsk to Okhotsk proved to be an extraordinarily difficult one. Although the expedition had begun in 1733, it was 1737 before Bering himself reached Okhotsk. A trio of academics from the Imperial Academy of Sciences in St Petersburg joined him. Despite these initial delays, the juggernaut of exploration was not to be halted and, by 1740, four ships were ready to sail; they stopped off long enough at Kamchatka to establish the settlement of Petropavlovsk, before heading northwards on a two-year round-trip which touched at the shores of Alaska and various points along the Aleutian Islands. Bering himself died of scurvy (or heart-failure) in December 1741, on an uninhabited island in the Commodore group which now bears his name.

While Bering and his ships were scouting up and down the Far North, Stefan Krasheninnikov, one of six students attached to the three academics, was deposited on Kamchatka in 1736. He was instructed to study and document all that could reasonably be studied and documented. By a series of unfortunate coincidences, Krasheninnikov was the only member of the original academic team who made it to the peninsula, although a professor of astronomy did pop by later; and so he had the field all to himself. His crossing from Okhotsk was rather of the quotidian sort:

barely out of port, "there was such a leak in our vessel, that the people below were up to their knees in water."[2] Most of the cargo was thrown overboard, and the pumps were manned non-stop for ten days. Having arrived at the mouth of the Bolshaya river, the sailors "mistook the tide," the ship ran aground and fell apart, "the planks quite black and rotten." For another ten days, passengers and crew camped upon the shore, awaiting relief from the fort, sheltering under bits of wood from the shipwreck. While they were there, an earthquake occurred but, as they were still suffering from the motion of the sea, it was barely noticed. The young student spent four years on Kamchatka recovering from this voyage. After further journeys, he finally returned to St Petersburg in 1745, where the fruits of his labours were published in March 1755, the same month that he died, in a book entitled *Description of the Land of Kamchatka*. This work attracted some interest, and it was translated into English in 1764.

The English translator, James Grieve MD, may fairly claim to being the grumpiest translator of his era (outdoing even Joseph Trapp MA, translator of Rochon). Despite having lived and worked in Russia for the preceding thirty years, he had no qualms about being critical: "the Russian language," he begins his introduction with no apologies,

> is rude and unpolished: other nations have with great care improved and refined their language by giving proper encouragement to men of learning and genius, but in that country literature has, on the contrary, been till very lately rather discouraged.[3]

So much for foreigners. But we English-speakers should be charitable:

> Great indulgence should be allowed the Author of this work: for though his manner is indigested, and his stile inelegant, abounding in digressions, and some uninteresting narrations, which obscure and confuse the more essential passages; yet he has communicated many very useful remarks.

So Dr Grieve did not waste his time translating any superfluous nonsense from the original work:

> the third part of this work has been most considerably abridged, as in treating of the manner, customs and religion of this barbarous nation [*of Kamchatkans*], it was loaded with absurd practices, idle ceremonies, and unaccountable superstitions. Sufficient examples of all these have been retained to shew the precise state of an unpolished, credulous, and grossly ignorant people.

The preceding two sections had also received the Grieve treatment: in the first, the Russian explorer had been so inconsiderate as to "minutely describe a great number of hills and rivers which did not serve to illustrate the subject." Grieve's index to the translated work is a masterpiece of laconic editing. Under the entry "*Birds*" there are the page-references for "*Plenty of*" (p.152) and "*Small, found at Kamchatka*" (p.162). Under "*Expeditions,*" the single entry "*Sent out*" (p.257). And under "*Wolves,*" two entries: "*Numerous*" (p.100) and "*Hurtful to the inhabitants*" (p.103).

Notwithstanding these caprices of its tetchy translator, the English edition of Krasheninnikov's book contained a vast amount of material on the geography, the natural history and the native peoples of Kamchatka, and a whole section on its recent 'conquest.' The geographical section covers Kamchatka itself, as well as details of the Kuril Islands, some of which Krasheninnikov visited himself, a brief account of the Aleutians, and a description – taken from the account of another of Bering's colleagues – of "America," being that part "which is now known from 52 to 60 degrees of north latitude." The natural history section looks in totally unacceptable detail at the soil, the "volcanos or burning mountains," metals and minerals, trees and plants, land animals and sea-beasts, fishes, birds ("*plenty of*"), and insects ("*swarms of*"). The section on the native peoples is wildly extravagant – it covers their language, their religion, their household goods and industries, their diet (mostly fish) – and shows clearly that the student from Moscow spent a great deal of time living and talking with them. There is an entertaining passage describing a celebration at which the hosts prepare "a liquor made of a large mushroom, with which the Russians kill flies. This they prepare with the juice of French willow"; fly-killer or not, this brew was clearly of the hallucinatory sort, and Russian soldiers were cautioned never to let any pass their lips. Krasheninnikov's summary judgement of the native population stops a little short of flattery:

> although their manner of living be most nasty, and their actions most stupid, yet they think themselves the happiest people in the world, and look upon the Russians who are settled among them with contempt: however this notion begins to change at present; for the old people who are confirmed in their customs, drop off, and the young ones are converted to the Christian religion.[4]

And yet, despite this, he presented an objective assessment of their way of life. His view of the Russian settlers was scarcely any better: "a people rude enough themselves [...] Their only want seemed to be that of brandy."

Kamchatka, barely discovered forty years earlier, had been well and truly conquered, much to the satisfaction of Imperial Russia. And now it was fully documented as well. Dr Grieve's translation of Krasheninnikov's book was itself translated into French in 1768. Now, in French or English, it was conveniently available to Benyovszky when he came to write his own memoirs.

It was in 1780 that William Coxe, himself no mean traveller in his role as secretary to the great and the good of his day, published a work in London entitled *Account of the Russian Discoveries between Asia and America*. This book provided an eminently readable overview of the voyages made by the Russian explorers and traders, from 1745 onwards, concentrating on the islands to the east of Kamchatka, the Aleutian and Fox Islands. Anyone wishing to learn of the brutal methods of early colonialism should profitably read it. Coxe also included two lengthy appendices: one described the Russian conquest of Siberia and some of the explorers who attempted to pass round the north-east edge of Asia from the north; the other appendix covered the state of trade between Russia and China, and included twelve pages, not to be missed, on "Tartarian rhubarb," its efficacy and its medical uses, and "its superiority over the Indian rhubarb."[5]

In the main body of Coxe's book, the voyages to the Aleutians of many unsung Russian heroes and villains are described. There are several episodes of high adventure: the heading for the chapter describing Alexei Drusinin's ill-fated voyage to Unalaska in 1763 reads: "*The vessel destroyed, and all the crew, except four, murdered by the islanders — The adventures of those four Russians, and their wonderful escape.*"[6] And, indeed, a reading of this same chapter does not disappoint. There are many episodes demonstrating appalling behaviour by the Russians — no worse and no better than their later equivalents in the conquest of middle and western North America, or the Europeans in Africa. The traders who followed up on the early exploratory trips lived to tell unedifying tales of trading, mistrust, mutual violence, rape, murder and kidnapping. In January of 1762, one set of traders "went with a party of twenty men along the shore; and, as they were attempting to violate some girls upon the island of Unyumga, were surprised by a numerous body of the natives." Two Russians were killed, three were wounded. This initial skirmish was followed up by others in which more men died on either side. This particular set of traders

> had behaved with such inhumanity towards the islanders, that they were brought to trial in the year 1764 [...] It appears also, that they brought away from Atchu and Amleg two Aleutian men and three boys, Ivan an Aleutian interpreter, and above twenty women and girls whom they debauched. Ivan and one of the boys [...] were the only persons who arrived at Kamchatka.[7]

The women all died in a mass-escape attempt, and the remainder, all bar Ivan and the boy, were subsequently pitched into the sea and drowned.

The very first group of traders who reached the Aleutians in 1745 under the command of Nevodsikov, angered by the refusal of the natives of the island to trade, summarily shot fifteen of them. The principal merchant,

> instead of punishing these cruelties as they deserved, was secretly pleased with them, for he himself was affronted at the islanders for having refused to give him an iron bolt, which he saw in their possession. He had, in consequence of their refusal [...] even formed the horrid design of poisoning them with a mixture of corrosive sublimate.

However, they retreated from this confrontation, only to find themselves shipwrecked; astonishingly, having come across a group of islanders who "treated them with great kindness," one of the crew "had the imprudence to make proposals to the wife of the chief."[8] It was to the eternal credit of the islanders that they forgave this band of unpleasant thugs and allowed them to be rescued a couple of years later.

While these particular voyages stand out for their cruelty, they demonstrated no more than the average behaviour of the traders. This is measurable by the fact that an "attempt to destroy the crew" by the natives of the Aleutian and Fox Islands was a theme common to many of these reports in Coxe. The people of Unimak Island "all join in hating the Russians, whom they consider as general invaders, and therefore kill them wherever they can."[9] Evidently, the Russian traders were not popular summer visitors. When they were not decimating the local wildlife, or raping the women, they were forcing the men to hunt for furs and deliver them up at well below their value. One early trader returned home, having traded for the skins of 1,040 sea-otters and 2,000 foxes. Taxes were arbitrarily raised on the islanders if the traders spent more than a season there. Some traders were there for several years – the voyage of one lasted from October 1762 to July 1766. It was common practice for the traders – and the natives – to ask for hostages to be delivered, in the hope of preventing bloodshed. The precaution was not always effective.

We will pick out one voyage as typical of these early encounters with reluctant trading-partners.[10] The ship of Afanasii Otcheredin, named *St Paul* like so many others, was hired by three merchants of Siberia, and left Okhotsk in September 1765. They reached Kamchatka twelve days later, and over-wintered at Bolsheretsk, finally departing for the Aleutians in August of 1766. No sooner had they arrived there than they came upon the wreckage of Drusinin's ship and learned from the locals that the crew had been murdered. The islanders took great delight in informing the new arrivals that the crews of two other ships had been disposed of in similar fashion in recent years. "This information occasioned general apprehensions" amongst the Russians. However, they had no choice but to stay put and do their best to keep friendly with the islanders. This tactic worked until the Russians made the mistake of asking them to pay taxes: "upon which they gave such repeated signs of their hostile intentions, that the crew lived under continual alarms." However, no attack was forthcoming, and the worst that happened to them in that first winter was that six crewmen died of scurvy, and several more were so weakened by the disease that they could not move from their hammocks.

In the spring they recovered, only to be attacked by "the savages," whom they repulsed with superior fire-power. The harvesting of furs then began in earnest; two boats were sent out further along the archipelago, and smaller parties dispersed from those. Results were not brilliant: two of the smaller parties were attacked and the men killed; the main party was subjected to several hostile attacks, losing several men.

By a stroke of good fortune, another trader turned up in the bay at this critical point, and between them they managed to prevail upon the inhabitants to knuckle under. In September, while they contentedly continued with their mission, a letter arrived from Unalaska, from the captain of a ship (yet another *St Paul*) of the Imperial fleet "in a secret expedition to those islands" who – most annoyingly – demanded a tribute of the skins which had been collected as tax from the islanders. This minor interruption, however, did not prevent this voyage setting off home, in May of 1770, with 600 otter skins, 756 black fox skins and 1,250 red fox skins. They arrived back at Okhotsk in late July, bringing with them, apart from the furs, "two islanders, whom they baptized. The one was named Alexei Soloviov; the other Boris Otcheredin. These islanders unfortunately died on their way to Petersburg; the first between Yakutsk and Irkutsk; and the latter at Irkutsk."[11]

There, in a nutshell, is the history of colonial trading.

Coxe was nothing if not thorough (he and Dr Grieve could never have seen eye to eye): his book contains a brief description, and the reported longitude and latitude, of each of the Aleutian and Fox Islands, he appends a table of the latitude and longitude of some of the principal places mentioned and their relative position to Moscow, Tobolsk and other cities. There is also an extensive list of the charts available at that time. And finally, for the explorer who wished to leave nothing to chance, a list of useful words in the 'Aleutian language' (the numbers one to ten, along with 'sun,' 'moon,' 'wind,' 'water,' 'chief,' 'man,' 'shield' and – of course – 'sea-otter').[12]

The books by Coxe and Krasheninnikov, stuffed with amazing facts, names of the principals and tales of adventure, are significant for our story, because they were both readily available in print in the period when Benyovszky was back in Europe, preparing his own papers and logs for publication.

With the name 'Otcheredin' tucked away at the back of our minds, let us now return to Benyovszky and his ship, as it sets out into the vast and briny unknown.

Notes

1 Anson, 1748, pp.304–319.
2 Krasheninnikov, 1764, p.279.
3 *ibid*, p.1.
4 *ibid*, p.180.
5 Coxe, 1780, pp.332–343.
6 *ibid*, p.80.
7 *ibid*, pp.65–67.
8 *ibid*, pp.34–35.
9 *ibid*, p.261.
10 *ibid*, pp.156–163.
11 *ibid*, pp.162–163.
12 *ibid*, p.303.

XVIII

A GENTLEMAN-PIRATE

Turnips, Garlic and Pirates

*A Full Ship's Complement – Many Provisions – Sailing to the Kuril Islands –
Avoiding the Kuril Islands – Arriving at Bering Island – Mutiny –
Mr Ochotyn the Pirate – Exchange of Civilities – Another Mutiny*

In his *Memoirs,* Benyovszky is pleased to record both the personnel aboard the
ship and the armaments and provisions carried. Under "myself, Count de
Benyowsky, Commander in Chief," and Khrushchyov as his second-in-
command, there were two watches of around thirty-six men, one led by Panov,
the other by Winbladh. Strangely, the treacherous Izmailov was named as one of
the leading men of Winbladh's watch. Stranger still, Panov had amongst his men
one "Mr. Contrathimaitre" – not a name that looks very Russian: it seems to be
the professional description of the bosun's mate rendered badly into French
(*contremaître*). Seventy-five persons "doing duty" along with "9 women and 12
passengers" – passengers? – totalled ninety-six on board. Along with them, they
had crammed in

> 8 Pieces of cannon, 2 Howitzers, 2 Mortars for bombs, 120 Muskets with
> bayonets, 80 Sabres, 60 Pistols, 1,600 lb. of gunpowder, 200 lb. Weight of
> bullets, 800 lb. Salted flesh, 1,200 lb. Salted fish, 3,000 lb. Dried fish, 1,400
> lb. Whale oil, 200 lb. Sugar, 500 lb. Tea, 4,000 lb. Damaged flour, 40 lb.
> Butter, 113 lb. Cheese, 6,000 lb. Different pieces of iron work, 120 Grenades,
> 900 Cannon ball, 50 lb. Sulphur, 200 lb. Saltpetre, 1,200 lb. [*of something else
> really important – a gap appears in the manuscript*], 36 Butts of water, 126 Chests
> of furs, 14 Anchors, and sundry cordage, with change of sails. One shallop
> and one canoe.[1]

On the first day, Benyovszky

caused divine service to be celebrated, according to the rites of the Greek church. Te Deum was chaunted, and afterwards the whole company renewed their oath of obedience to my orders: at five in the evening dropped down the river and moored at the entrance.

On the following day, the hostages were freed and they set forth upon the waves, stopping briefly to break up an ice-floe by firing a cannon ball at it; only 899 remained.

The moment when they all set off to sea comes as a breath of fresh air for the reader, who has by now been bludgeoned into a stupor by scene after scene of byzantine plotting, bloody vengeance, heavily-perfumed love-scenes and magnificent acts of Magyar-Polish chivalry.

The relief does not last long. No sooner has Benyovszky's ship left the shoreline of Kamchatka behind than it sets off on a voyage quite different in geography and schedule from the one described by Stepanov, Ryumin and Izmailov. Where these men reached the tip of Kamchatka, and turned rightwards to the south, Benyovszky's vessel turns sharp left, north-eastwards. Modestly, he suggests that his is the "seventeenth expedition" to set out from Kamchatka for exploration to the east – the first being Bering's in 1728.[2]

The intervening fifteen voyages noted by Benyovszky comprise a random assortment of voyages of discovery and trade, which Benyovszky suggests he studied in the archives in the Chancellery at Bolsheretsk. Most of them, quite coincidentally, had also been recorded by Coxe. These voyages were not always very successful: Bering undertook three expeditions over fourteen years – all lumped under "the first expedition" by our author – and died after a shipwreck; the third voyage listed by Benyovszky was undertaken by Nevodsikov who "left traces of unexampled cruelty behind him"; the tenth was made by a man named Stadenetsov who ran aground on the Aleutian island of Urumusir "where most of the people on board were cut off"; the eleventh also ended up on this island, where twenty-six crewmen were killed by the natives; the thirteenth included five ships, four of which were lost "by the ignorance of their commanders"; "the murders and robberies perpetrated by this armament on the inhabitants are incredible"; two-thirds of the men on the fourteenth voyage died of scurvy. The sixteenth and last voyage was the one which had later caused Captain Tchurin so much stress. The unfortunate Captain Krenitsin of that expedition "was drowned in the river of Kamchatka, by his crew, on his return, in the year 1770" – industrial relations had clearly reached a low ebb on that ship.

But there was no problem with obedience on Benyovszky's ship. The company acquiesced to his every suggestion. There was a brief debate about where they should go first. Benyovszky suggested mooring at one of the Kuril Islands, to collect yet more provisions and to bake bread. Having agreed wholeheartedly to this, the crew was a little surprised to find the ship sailing straight past the first of the Kurils. There was some dissatisfaction. "As they thought proper to threaten me upon my not attending to their demand, I put two under confinement, and determined not to come to anchor at the Kurelles islands, for fear of some mutinous consequences." Benyovszky had begun to make careful observations, quite properly, about wind-speed and direction, and their course. He noted on the 14th May that their course was south-east; without making a single comment on a change of direction, he noted on the 15th that their course was now north-east. So much for landing on the Kurils.

Their course remained generally north-eastwards for the following four days. On the first day, Izmailov made a "seditious proposal" to two Kamchadales, for which crime he was placed in confinement on a diet of bread and water. Here he remained until the ship anchored off Bering Island, the nearest of the Aleutian chain to Kamchatka, and some 500 miles north-east of the Kurils. Having established that the island was uninhabited, the company put ashore and began to bake bread, clean below decks and "air our provisions." The place where they had moored was unpretentiously given the name *St Maurice's Bay* "by my companions." In the south of the island, five crosses were quickly discovered, one of which bore the inscription:

> "To the honour of God and St. Nicholas, in the year 1769, on the 28th of April, this cross was erected by Peter Kreniczin, commander of the expedition sent for the discovery of California." This last discovery was not of any consequence, but the discovery of a species of turnips and very good garlick was extremely useful to us.[3]

While garlic and turnips were being gathered, another foraging party had returned to Benyovszky's tent with more interesting news: a cabin, a bath and a letter had been discovered. There were four barrels of whale oil and a pile of salted fish in the cabin. The bath was unoccupied. But the letter contained something of a surprise. It was written by a pirate; a gentleman-pirate of good European stock. It read as follows:

> Health to all those who may arrive on this island. I inform them that the ship *Elizabeth*, which left the port of Ochoczk in the year 1769, under my command, remained at this island a whole year, after having received much damage by tempests. After this long stay, being assured that all our attempts to put her into a situation to carry us home were useless, we broke her up, and built boats out of her materials, in which I am about to proceed on a voyage towards the island, which lies to the eastward, in hopes of finding some vessel, in which myself and crew may return. Written January 24, 1771.
>
> *Ivan Ochotyn, Captain. Baltasa Batakirow, Pilot*[4]

By astonishing good fortune, Benyovszky had heard tell of Mr Ochotyn. He was reputed to be a "man of family in Saxony" who had served in the Russian Imperial Army until his superior officers had been arrested and exiled, at which point, of course, he too had been arrested and exiled. Having found employment as a hunter operating out of Okhotsk, he soon managed to seize a ship and set himself up as a pirate, building an extensive network of contacts and allies amongst the Aleutian natives, mostly by marrying his comrades to local girls. Benyovszky adds a footnote which proves it all:

> The family of Mr. Ochotyn is known in Saxony by the name of Leuchtenfeld, and he referred, in proof of his assertion, to Baron Laffert, a Prussian officer, who was exiled to Kolima, and returned to Europe in 1760, in consequence of the pressing reclamation which was made by his Majesty the King of Prussia.

It is of little consequence that no one else apart from Benyovszky has ever made mention of this buccaneering gentleman. It is of equally little consequence that the name bears an uncanny resemblance to that of the trader Otcheredin who was mentioned by Coxe – of little consequence because Ochotyn and Benyovszky were kindred souls, fated to meet. The Hungarian penned an invitation to the Saxon, and the letter was posted through the door of the cabin. The very next day, five of Ochotyn's men turned up in a small boat, bearing a most civil reply (addressed to "the brave and intrepid commander of the vessel *St Peter*") suggesting a confabulation. Benyovszky sent back a gentlemanly acceptance, assuring his opposite number that "the conduct and behaviour of the famous Ochotyn have secured him my esteem for this year past." Meanwhile, both men detained the respective messengers as hostages. Just in case.

Before the two leaders could meet, however, a minor irritation had to be dealt with.

> Mr. Stephanow informed me that he had discovered a mutiny, by means of Alexi Andreanow. Upon examination I heard that Mr. Ismailow, with his friend Zablikow and fifteen others, had entered into an oath to seize the first opportunity, when the greatest part of the people should be on shore and myself on board, to secure my person, and afterwards return to Kamchatka; but, in case they could not carry this project into effect, that they should assassinate me, set fire to the vessel, and quit the island in the shallop. The deposition of Andreanow was confirmed by Popow and Rabalow. I therefore immediately armed those persons on whom I could place the most dependence, and afterwards mustered the whole company, to whom I exposed the authors of the plot. These were immediately put in irons, and carried on shore to be tried by a council which I nominated, and over which Mr. Crustiew was appointed to preside.

Nineteen of the company were made prisoners. On the very next day,

> at three o'clock my adjutant presented to me a memorial in the name of the whole company, requesting that Mr. Ismailow and the Kamchadale

Parenczin, with his wife, should be set on shore, and abandoned in the island, and that the others, who had been seduced by them, should be punished with fifty lashes, and afterwards restored to their functions, first renewing their oath of obedience. I complied with this general request the more willingly, as it was an object of great consequence to give an example and establish my authority by this proceeding.[5]

With the flogging out of the way, Benyovszky could concentrate on his new friend the pirate.

On the 23rd May, the two men finally met. Ochotyn was "a handsome figure, thirty-six years of age and spoke very good German and French." Civilities were exchanged and Ochotyn told Benyovszky his tale of adventure and escape. He had around 130 men at his disposal, and the full backing of the Aleutian natives. He intended to set up colonies on each of the islands, and establish a fiefdom for himself; to which end he proposed to "visit Kamchatka and Ochoczk, with the intention of utterly destroying these two establishments, and carrying off every thing which he might find suitable to his purposes." Ochotyn then suggested that he and Benyovszky join forces; Benyovszky regretted that he had to turn down this "project of eminent vengeance," putting forward the excuse that they had to get back to Europe with all speed; but promised that, on arrival in Europe, he would put in a good word for Ochotyn and secure the backing of some European power for the proposed colonisation. It sounded pretty lame, but Ochotyn fell for it. Any disappointment he might have felt was compensated by the presentation of 200 pounds of gunpowder and 100 of lead from the healthy arsenal of the *St Peter*. That same evening, Benyovszky and Panov paid a social visit to Ochotyn in his palisade, where they drank tea in the company of thirty-five of the pirate company, and sat up all night drafting letters addressed to European powers. (These letters never make another appearance in Benyovszky's *Memoirs*. For all we know, the ghost of Ochotyn is still out there, on his lonely island, just waiting.)

Early the following morning, replete with tea, they returned to the ship. Here they had a vote on where to go next. Benyovszky proposed going to China. The company shuffled off to talk amongst themselves. The following day, they shuffled back in again and announced that they did not wish to go to China, but rather

they were determined to seek a passage to the northward of Kamchatka, as the season, being summer, assured our success, and even supposing we should find insurmountable obstacles, we should be always able to reach the continent of America. To this representation, as I had understood from my intimate friends that the company was resolved to follow their plan in spite of me, I consented, because unwilling openly to oppose their decision. For a great part of the company, after having reflected on what had happened at Kamchatka, might probably have repented, and have been disposed to act treacherously towards me, as the neighbourhood of Kamchatka would facilitate all their attempts.[6]

It is at this point that things become even more rum than before. There was no reason for anyone to sail northwards; even supposing they could reach – or go round the top of – Alaska, no one had remotely whispered such a proposal before now. And here is Benyovszky who, a few days before, had refused point-blank to stop at the Kurils at the crew's request, for fear of mutiny, doing precisely what the crew now requested of him, for fear of mutiny; this being the same crew which was swearing oaths of loyalty to their commander on a daily basis.

None of it makes much sense. But it provided a handy trigger for the next stage of the Great Adventure.

Before they could set off, however, they had to deal with another minor inconvenience caused by the wayward Stepanov. Ochotyn wrote to warn Benyovszky that Stepanov had approached him with a proposal to join his pirate-crew. Ever the gentleman, Ochotyn advised Benyovszky to leave the island as soon as possible, to pre-empt any mass defections. Benyovszky announced their imminent departure to the assembled company, and Stepanov duly asked for a quiet word. The customary humiliation of Stepanov followed, ending in the troubled young officer throwing himself at Benyovszky's feet, "acknowledging himself guilty, and imploring my forgiveness, which I granted."[7]

Pausing only long enough to plant a cross to tell the world that Maurice August Aladar de Benyovszky had stayed on the island, the crew set sail on Wednesday, 25 May, heading northwards. Behind, on the shore, were Izmailov and Mr and Mrs Parantsin.

Also Mr Ochotyn, scratching his head at the direction his new ally had taken.

Notes

1   Benyovszky, 1790, Vol.I, pp.301–302.
2   *ibid*, pp.264–268.
3   *ibid*, p.307.
4   *ibid*, p.307.
5   *ibid*, pp.309–310.
6   *ibid*, pp.315–316.
7   *ibid*, p.317.

XIX

A VOYAGE NORTH

Seven Hundred and Forty Roots of Garlic Nearly the Size of a Child's Head

Of Maps and Mariners – Ice-floes and Terrible Ice-bergs – Mutiny –
America and its Many Treasures – With Friends on the Aleutian Islands –
Setting Sail for China – Another Mutiny – A Loss of all Water – Punishments –
An Hospitable Island, Unattainable – Fish-bread and Other Dried Fish Recipes –
Other Uses for Furs and Boots – Land Sighted!

In his 1893 edition of Benyovszky's *Memoirs*, Pasfield Victor Oliver, Sub-Lieutenant, RN provided an extremely useful map of our hero's voyage between Kamchatka and Japan. Oliver noted all the details provided by Benyovszky in his journal – course-bearings, place-names, longitude and latitude readings – then plotted them across a map of the North Pacific. Four voyages in total are marked out: the first is the one indicated by Izmailov's testimony, which is represented by a simple line leading south-westwards from Kamchatka, past the Kuril Islands and into the Japanese archipelago; the second is based on Benyovszky's latitude and longitude readings; the third is based on Benyovszky's course-bearings; and the fourth is based on Benyovszky's naming of the places he visited. The map has something of the air of a Jackson Pollock painting, with the last three lines diverging and converging up and down the coasts of Russia and of America, and criss-crossing various patches of empty sea in between. Oliver's rather ill-concealed implication is that Benyovszky had not a clue where he was supposed to be at any given time. (A more simplified map of the actual voyage is reproduced in Appendix IV.)

What remains surprising is that Oliver did not challenge Benyovszky's assertion of having been north of Bering Island at all.

One can only applaud Oliver's dedication to the task. One of the difficulties with interpreting the log of the voyage was that the longitude recorded by Benyovszky was relative to the longitude of Bolsheretsk itself, his point of departure. This was common practice at the time, since the technical equipment and expertise which allowed alignment with (say) Greenwich was not readily available – certainly not to some disorganised sailors who had just stolen a ship in the Russian Far East. In order to arrive at modern-day longitude readings, it is therefore necessary to add, or subtract, the position of Kamchatka from those logged: thus, "7 degrees, 56 minutes" was east of the position of Bolsheretsk (itself, 156 degrees, 16 minutes east) – that is, 164 degrees, 12 minutes east. A more complex calculation is required when finding positions to the west of Kamchatka, since Benyovszky used a relative position eastwards: "355 degrees, 8 minutes" meant 4 degrees, 52 minutes west of Kamchatka. Even taking into account those adjustments, the readings logged on the *St Peter* frequently do not locate a place with any precision on the map. Benyovszky is not to be blamed for this – the tools with which he had to work were almost certainly poor; many more experienced navigators of that time were only capable of approximating their true position.

So, poorly equipped and at odds over their destination, the captain, commander and crew set off northwards. They encountered snow, ice-floes and whales. On their second day out of Bering Island, "a whale, of very large size, came so near us, that I was obliged to fire at it. The second ball caused it to dive."[1] Eight hundred and ninety-seven cannon balls remained. On their third day, they bumped up against ice-floes "of enormous magnitude" which were covered with pieces of wood, and in the evening found themselves stuck fast between two pieces of ice, with their sails frozen solid. And they were only at a latitude of 58 degrees, in May. Such conditions were not unusual: ice would have been breaking up all the way from the Arctic Circle downwards. Even Clerke and King of Captain Cook's expedition were to encounter similar extremes of snow and ice, further south, in April of 1779.[2] While dodging in between the floes, Benyovszky grumbled about the "disagreement" of the Russian charts which he had, and made some random guesses at his position. On 28th May, he decided that he had reached Cape Olyutorsk (which he described as "Cape Apachazana").

Here, conditions took a turn for the worse. The log-entry reads:

> Sunday, May the 29th, a strong breeze and close cloudy weather, with a heavy swell from north-west, which frequently endangered us by driving large pieces of ice against the vessel. The considerable masses of these ice-drifts formed whole mountains around us, and threatened us with inevitable destruction, for the vessel being struck every instant by them was strongly agitated, and large masses of ice freezing to the ship's sides, and occasionally lifted out of the water by her motion, damaged her on all sides. Every roll was followed by an astonishing noise, occasioned by the rupture of these icy appendages. [...] About four in the morning the wind increased, and carried away our sprit-sail-yard; and about five we lost our foretop-mast. At six o'clock the vessel lay down on the larboard side, and the tiller could not be moved. Luckily for us, however, the arrival of day-light enabled us to see that part of the ice was jammed in between the rudder and the stern-post. I sent two of the company to beat it away, and afterwards we righted the

vessel. It was very fortunate that this accident did not happen in the night, as in that case we should have been lost without remedy. About noon the wind abated, and we perceived ourselves at the distance of two leagues and a half off shore, of which I took a view.

At seven hours and a half we had twenty-two inches water in the hold, which we cleared.

According to the report three sick. Latitude in, 59 degrees, 10 minutes; longitude in, 14 degrees, 34 minutes; wind west-north-west; current from north-east to south-west; course east, one quarter north.[3]

Barely five days into the voyage, the crew now decided they had had enough. The company requested an urgent meeting with the commander, to tell him that they no longer wished to head northwards. The commander reproached them for their want of confidence, told them gleefully that they would continue northwards just as long as it pleased him, and gave them an extra ration of brandy. Despite the brandy, or perhaps because of it, some rebellious souls took this decision badly. Soon, yet another plot was uncovered. Twenty-two of the crew had expressed a desire to be put ashore at the next convenient spot. To no one's surprise, Stepanov was behind it all. Great was the anger of the rest of the crew, who urged Benyovszky to throw the ringleaders into the sea. Mercy prevailed: the leaders were given twenty-five lashes, while their followers sheepishly apologised and went back to their posts. Panov, however, announced his firm intention to put his cousin Stepanov to death at the next opportunity. "This declaration, made in the presence of the whole company, produced an admirable effect".[4]

Despite the fact that his crew wanted to turn back and despite the fact that he had never wished to go north in the first place, Benyovszky continued his course northwards, encountering worsening conditions. The cold was so intense at 61 degrees latitude that all the water in the hold was frozen. By the 4th day of June, having battled through ice, hurricanes and whales, they reached 65 degrees and 20 minutes north: if one were to guess, this would have been Cape Anadyr, for just around the corner, on the authority of some native Chukchi who were idly hanging around to provide directions, was Cape Chukotski. Slightly north of the Diomedes Islands, Benyovszky found the ice-sheet impenetrable, just as Cook's expedition did in 1778 and again in 1779. He decided to turn eastwards and make for the Alaskan shores of America. After sailing for two days, with almost a metre of water (or ice) in the hold, they made land.

As soon as we had moored, I ordered twenty-eight associates on shore, to set up tents made of our sails, and at two and a half pm, I went on shore myself with Mr. Csurin, who having observed a place which promised to give us an opportunity of careening the ship, proposed to visit the spot. I therefore gave the necessary orders for unloading her cargo, and Mr. Csurin was charged to overlook and make the necessary preparations. Thirty-six of the associates, under the command of Mr. Panow were directed to undertake this, while the rest employed themselves in hunting, fishing and cutting of wood.[5]

Quite where this place was is open to debate. Benyovszky insisted it was the American mainland, but his longitude and latitude readings suggest that it was somewhere in the middle of the sea. If there needs to be a plausible location, then it was St Lawrence Island.

At this point, Benyovszky makes a rather startling blunder in his narrative of this supposed voyage into the deep north. Without any trace of embarrassment, he provides the following report from a scouting party sent out from their place of refuge, on the 7th day of June:

> Mr. Kuzneczow did not return till eight in the evening, when he informed me, that he had ascended the neighbouring mountain to the northward, and had discovered land to the north-east, but that to the eastward there lay an immense country with few mountains, and in many places without snow, and intersected by rivers. The approach of night not having permitted him to distinguish remote objects, he asked permission to take others of the associates with him to pursue his discoveries to the eastward; for he assured me, that he had observed signs of its being inhabited.[6]

If we consider that this place was at the same latitude as Reykjavik (or slightly further north than Anchorage), and that it was almost midsummer, when the sun sets at that latitude close on midnight, then the absurdity of "the approach of night" some considerable time before eight o'clock becomes apparent. The cynical critic might guess that Benyovszky had been reading some travellers' tales which had been set in months other than high summer. But that could be a harsh judgement.

Over the next few days, the crew beavered away at repairing the ship, a magnificent collection of 740 roots of garlic was stashed aboard, "nearly the size of a child's head," and the interrogation took place of an old native woman whose possessions convinced the travellers that they had indeed reached America. And then they set sail, heading ever southwards. Not a single piece of ice was spotted over the course of the next seven days, which is odd: barely a fortnight after great masses of ice had almost sunk the ship at similar latitudes, the sea was now entirely clear. Perhaps ship and crew simply needed no more excitement. During this time Benyovszky and his crew disagreed once more on priorities – the commander put into a bay and announced his desire to explore, his crew expressed a contrary aspiration to reach "some European establishment"; ever-consistent in his man-management, the commander acceded to their wishes and raised anchor. On the 18th of June, they had reached 55 degrees north. The Aleutian Islands appeared on the horizon. Time to let a little fresh air into their lungs:

> at two p.m. being desirous of inspecting the cargo, I caused the hold to be opened, out of which issued putrid vapours, doubtless from the corruption

of the skins. The women and sick, who were shut up below during the storm, were carried upon deck: they at first found themselves faint, but afterwards grew better.[7]

For a vessel which had been soundly repaired just a few days previously, it was not doing at all well: eighteen inches of water were pouring into the hold every hour and everyone was pumping like fury. Soon they had moored off one of the Aleutian Islands, where Benyovszky fully expected to meet up with friends and family of the pirate Ochotyn.

Winbladh and Kuznetsov were sent ashore to spy out the land and returned in the company of two Russians. This island, explained the Russians, was "the greater Kadik." We may take for granted that this was not the island of Kodiak, which was so far to the east that even Benyovszky would have had some difficulty explaining his presence there. It was more likely (all other things being equal) to have been one of the Andreanov Islands – perhaps Atka. The two scouts, finding themselves surrounded by suspicious armed natives, had hastily dropped Ochotyn's name into the conversation. This had immediately acted like oil upon troubled waters: "Ah, Mr. Ochotyn?" – everyone was wreathed in smiles. They all came back to the ship. After some more discussion, an escort named Salasiov was elected to guide them to the neighbouring island of "Urumusir", where Ochotyn's wife and in-laws lived. The guide provided Benyovszky with nuggets of useful local information, including the news that the mainland of America – "Alaksina" – was less than "40 leagues" away. This proximity would depend on your point of view, of course: Atka lies about 500 miles from the extreme western tip of the Alaskan Peninsula; the island of Unalaska fits the distance much better; but that is not where they were. Not even if they had been anywhere remotely near the Aleutians.

Two days later, after sailing past several islands, they reached Urumusir. No such island of this name exists, but from the positions given in the log (52° 25′ north, 28° 15′ east of Bolsheretsk) it might be supposed to be Adak Island. Or somewhere close by. But nothing is certain.

For the next five days, Benyovszky and his crew were richly entertained by the *tajon* or chief of the natives of this island. This chief was the father-in-law of Ochotyn; both he and Mrs Ochotyn burst into tears of joy when Benyovszky produced a letter from Ochotyn which he had carried all the way from Bering Island. Oaths, arrows and sundry other symbols of friendship were exchanged, along with considerable amounts of brandy and "at least two hundred pounds of tobacco" from the ship's provisions. A wild party ensued. At a high point in the proceedings, Benyovszky was presented with "an American," a young boy named Zacharii who had been captured by Aleuts. Unfazed, Benyovszky took on the extra passenger. Also in the midst of these celebrations, "fifty young women" from the island sneaked aboard for the purpose of "offering their services" to the crew: the commander felt unable to prevent this, and the young women stayed for a couple of days. When things calmed down a little, both crew and natives joined forces to make more permanent repairs to the ship, and prepare her for the next stage of the voyage. The *tajon* turned up on the last day, requesting that Benyovszky write a letter to Ochotyn, for no particular reason. Benyovszky duly obliged, with a splendid epistle which impresses by the airy way in which facts are ignored and patronising advice is handed out.

> Honourable Friend, After a painful and disagreeable navigation, in which I was compelled, by the obstinacy of my companions, to sail as far to the northward as 66 degrees, I have at last returned to the south, and have taken advantage of the winds to visit your island. [...] On my arrival, your friends and companions have given me every assistance to put my vessel into proper repair for a long voyage; and the islanders, from their example, have behaved with the utmost cordiality to us. [...] During the time of my stay, I have observed, with satisfaction, that the islanders are sincerely attached to you. I therefore recommend to you to avail yourself, as much as possible, of their affection; and for that purpose, I would advise you always to have a trusty party of these people near you; for among the Russians, who are with you, there will be some who will shew the disposition of the country. To place yourself out of danger of plots, you must keep your people in constant employment: and I take this occasion once more to repeat, that if I were situated as you are, with two or three vessels suitable to the undertaking, I would retire to the southward, where, doubtless, you will find islands, and the climate will second your attempts to establish a flourishing colony. The knowledge you have of the commerce of China, and the constant resource which you might have to your friends in the Aleuthes islands for furs, to supply this trade, could not fail to put it in your power to make an establishment of the first importance. Adieu, my friend, I wish you every prosperity, and you may depend upon my best exertions to cause some European power to accept your proposals. Signed MAURICE AUGUSTUS.[8]

With fond farewells to allies and young women alike, the crew unfurled the sails and the ship set sail on 27 June 1771. Their course over the next two and a half weeks led them steadily south-west.

In his version of events, the Baron went nowhere near the Kuril Islands; in the real version of events, he went nowhere hear the Aleutian Islands. If nothing else, a voyage of perhaps 2,000 miles, with stops for social visits, in a bare four weeks, in such conditions as are reported, was quite simply impossible. According to Izmailov, Ryumin and Stepanov, the ship had been moored at one of the Kuril Islands between mid-May and mid-June, doing nothing, with a total lack of imagination, while Benyovszky was battling his way up to the Arctic waters and down again.

This next leg of the voyage was full of incident. There were violent storms, mutinies (Stepanov, of course), a catastrophic loss of drinking water, a landing on an island which simply does not exist and near-starvation. Through it all, Benyovszky acted with composure and selfless discipline.

Let us begin with the mutiny, since from this stemmed many of the other travails to afflict the crew. On the second to last day of June, a strong wind shifted some of the cargo below decks, and six barrels of water were staved in. As a result, the daily water-ration had to be cut slightly. On the following day, who should come knocking on the commander's door, but tempestuous Captain Stepanov. He was making complaint and gesticulating inappropriately. What followed was a typical piece of Benyovszkian melodrama.

The problem, said Stepanov "filling the cabin with the grossest invectives," was that they all need more brandy in order to keep up their spirits. Benyovszky threatened to throw him overboard. Stepanov stomped off and began rabble-rousing, insisting that Benyovszky was fully aware of their position in the ocean but had "secret reasons" for not setting a course for dry land. Word came back to the commander that the mutineers were going to break open another barrel of water, *faute de mieux*. Steps were taken to prevent this, but they only succeeded in cornering the mutineers in a cabin containing three barrels of brandy; which they then settled down to empty. A few hours later, when the legless mutineers were rounded up and, as appropriate, clapped in irons or strapped to the mizzenmast, a terrible discovery was made:

> At one in the morning Mr. Wynbladth informed me, that the revolters, heated by the great quantity of brandy they had drank, and desirous of water, and at the same time not knowing what they did, had staved fourteen casks of water, which was entirely lost, and there remained no more than two casks and an half in all.

Stepanov was duly humiliated before the rest of the crew and obliged to serve as cook's assistant – clearly a position below decks that no one much wanted. Not that there was actually anything to cook.

> Stephanow was then brought to the main-mast to hear his sentence, and as he supposed I should condemn him to death, he was mean enough to implore my compassion, and still meaner after he had heard his sentence read. He thanked me for the pity I had shewn on this occasion. Mr. Panow, enraged at his pusillanimity, would have shot him through the head, if I had not prevented him.[9]

Truly, there was never a dull moment upon the *St Peter.*
Stepanov was going to be cook's assistant.
And now they were all going to die of thirst.
But no matter: the "associates" had their priorities in good order – Benyovszky noted approvingly that they voted to preserve all fresh water for "myself, the sick, and our female companions" and themselves to drink only such rain water and dew as they managed to collect in tarry casks.

On the second day of July, at a position recorded as "latitude 45 degrees, 57 minutes; longitude 11 degrees, 30 minutes" they found an island. The ship's boat was sent ashore with Mr Kuznetsov and a half dozen crew, but failed to come back before nightfall. The ship was being battered around at its anchorage by strong winds, and the crew demonstrated a deplorable lack of solidarity by suggesting that they abandon their shipmates and put out to the open sea. Benyovszky was having none of that. A crew-member seized a knife and tried to attack the commander; the latter pulled out his pistol, shot and wounded him; other hotheads amongst the crew rushed on deck, but "their impetuosity" was checked by the sight of some ostentatiously brandished pistols. Late in the evening, Kuznetsov finally returned. He reported that he had found several boats and a large ship at anchor; and some inhabitants "cloathed in the Chinese manner, in blue, with parasols." There were hogs (but no cattle), trees and water in abundance. There had followed a rapid exchange of greetings and presents (parasol, pipe, tobacco; sabre; knife), along with an invitation to stay. Kuznetsov explained he had to get back to the ship. The two parties took their leave of each other, the best of friends. Unfortunately, the winds had now become so contrary that it was not possible to make another landing and, with the crew glumly looking back to the receding shoreline, the ship set sail again.

A minor point of detail: at the longitude and latitude provided, there is no land of any sort within five hundred miles in any direction. Even allowing for some hefty mistakes in taking the positional readings, there is still no land of any sort. Perhaps the whole episode arose from hallucinations caused by lack of water?

Two days later, they took stock of their provisions. It did not look at all good:

> Our provisions consisted of six casks of salt fish, and two casks of dried fish; but the dried fish began to putrify by the heat, and convinced me that we could not use it much longer. All our biscuit was consumed, and our whole resource consisted in these two casks of dried fish, with two casks of rain water, and four casks of sweet water. I could not, therefore, depend on more than six or eight days provision, and fourteen days drink. The council determined to hold our course towards Japan, but to put in at any island we might come in sight of. This resolution was communicated to the whole company, who were very submissive, and consented to the decision, from the fear of hunger. Mr. Meder, having inspected our provision of salt fish, assured me, that in one or two days I should be obliged to throw the whole overboard; and, in order to turn it to the best advantage, he advised me to boil the salted fish to the consistence of a paste, and afterwards dry the paste into the form of bread, which might serve us in case of extreme need. I very much approved of this advice, and gave him charge to carry it into execution.[10]

On the following day, the crew came begging to be bled, that trusty medical solution to all problems from a headache to starvation. This request was perfectly acceptable. "In the morning Mr. Meder bled fifteen of the associates."

It turned hot. Very hot. The pitch melted off the sides of the vessel. They ate fish-bread. It was "harsh, sour and very salt." On the 8th July, the crew, contemplating their own mortality, either as a result of the heat or the fish-bread, or both, came in a body asking that Stepanov be forgiven for his past misdemeanours. Benyovszky agreed to receive Stepanov into the Society again. "This day Mr. Meder bled twenty of the associates." Stepanov was summoned and given a stern lecture. He asked to be allowed to acknowledge his fault and beg pardon in public. The judicious commander agreed. Mr Panov had his doubts and wagered that Stepanov would be up to no good within eight days. They counted the provisions again. Water was reported to be down to slightly more than three casks, with 900 pounds of dried fish. The company assembled to be told the bad news. Some bright spark demanded a re-count. It then appeared that there were now fewer than three casks of water, and only 460 pounds of dried fish. Much weeping ensued. It may have been from a heartfelt relief that only half as much dried fish remained. The number of men reporting sick rose to twenty-three.

On the 12th July, with reports of some crew-members on their death-beds, Benyovszky had a brilliant idea.

Being therefore obliged to apply my thoughts to the invention of an expedient, I fell upon that of boiling some skins of beavers, and seasoning them with whale oil. I communicated this idea to my friends, who received it with gratitude. To make a trial, I gave orders to scald and clean a skin, and then boil it. At six pm it was entirely prepared; and when I found that this ragout was capable of preserving us from dying with hunger, I immediately distributed it to the associates. The eagerness with which they set about preparing their meal, made them forget the danger we were in from the impetuosity of the wind, and it was not possible to employ them in any other service on board; so that the whole care of the vessel fell upon me and the officers. […] At day-break my companions thanked me for having employed my thoughts in procuring them some nourishment; and as there was no other provision on board, I caused some skins to be dressed for the sick. Mr. Meder informed me, that several of the associates had washed their shoes and half boots, and that, at the instant he was speaking, there were more than twenty pair in the pot.[11]

The recipe for boiled skins is not given: did they boil them in brine or in fresh water? And did Stepanov assist with the cooking?

Chewing boots and furs, the crew held on for several more days. The last of the water was shared out equitably. Benyovszky advised the crew that he really did not have a clue where they were. His readings confirm this: "latitude 32 degrees, 36 minutes; longitude 357 degrees, 15 minutes" – about 800 miles east of Yokohama. He did however know that they were "two hundred and forty, or perhaps three hundred leagues from the coast of Japan," and that their chances of reaching that land were a little shaky. Everyone got quite emotional, and the crew started queuing up to offer their dear leader a share of their rations. In particular, they pressed dried fish upon him. Noble actions all around, much applauded.

They headed for Japan. Quite why they had not done this earlier, is not explained.

On the 15th of July, at sunset, the look-out at the top of the mast cried out that he could see land. By the time someone else had climbed up it was dark, so the sighting could not be verified. The following morning dawned cloudy and nothing could be seen. But the combined efforts of a dog and a Native American soon reassured them.

> At this time my dog, Nestor, stood on the forecastle, continually barking, and snuffing up the air. Mr. Meder observing this circumstance, ran to me, and assured me, that he no longer doubted of the vicinity of the land, as he knew it to be usual for dogs to smell it. [...] At nine, Saccharie, my American, looking out ahead with the rest, called out, *Alaksina, Alaksina*, and pulled me towards the forecastle, saying in Russian, of which he had learned some few words, "Come along." When I came on the forecastle, he shewed me the place with his finger, continually repeating *Alaksina*, though none of us could discover anything. I called out to Mr. Kuzneczow, informing him, that the American saw land; but Kuzneczow replied, that he saw nothing. I therefore sent Saccharie to the mast-head, to shew him the place, and sent up my telescope. At half past nine, Mr. Kuzneczow at last called out land. On his assistance, I went up myself, and had the pleasure to see, at last, the prospect of our sufferings being mitigated.[12]

Their position was 32 degrees, 47 minutes in latitude, 355 degrees, 8 minutes in longitude (that is, 151° 24′ east of Greenwich). Which is about 800 miles east-south-east of Yokohama. In the middle of nowhere with no land in sight. But no matter. Their troubles were surely over.

Notes

1 Benyovszky, 1790, Vol.I, p.318.
2 Cook/King, 1834, Vol.3, pp.182–183.
3 Benyovszky, 1790, Vol.I, pp.320–321.
4 *ibid*, p.232.
5 *ibid*, pp.327–328.
6 *ibid*, p.328.
7 *ibid*, p.334.
8 *ibid*, pp.347–348.
9 *ibid*, pp.351–354.
10 *ibid*, p.360.
11 *ibid*, pp.366–367.
12 *ibid*, pp.370–371.

XX

THE ISLAND OF LIQUOR

"Namandabez!"

The Splendours of the Island of Liquor – Another Mutiny – Further Discoveries –
The Island of Usilpatchar – A Warm Welcome – Music, Tea and Religion –
An Agreement to Trade

Their troubles were surely over, for on 16th July they landed at the interesting island of Liquor.

"Liquor" – so-named by the voyagers "on account of the excellent water they found there" – had the whiff of Paradise about it. The description bears an uncanny likeness, at least in tone, and to some degree in detail, to the island of Tinian visited by George Anson. Hogs and goats abounded; there were "different fruits and plants of a delicious taste"; an abundance of fresh water; fish impaled themselves on hooks, just gasping to be eaten; there were coconuts, oranges and bananas. Had Ryumin been there, he would have fainted in rapture. And yet there was more, far more. A scouting party to the interior of the island returned in a state of great excitement: they

> brought pine apples and bananas, in great quantities, with several bundles of wood, with which, [*they*] assured me, the island abounded. But that which excited the greatest astonishment was some pieces of rock crystals, and stones, containing metallic particles, which were very heavy, and shone like gold. The sight of the crystal inflamed the imagination of my associates: they began to reason upon the circumstances, and concluded, that as the surface of the earth produced crystal, it doubtless contained diamonds at a greater depth. The mineral they had found, could be nothing, in their opinion, but gold.[1]

Benyovszky tried to reason that crystals and shiny rocks were no indication of diamonds and gold; but the desperate adventurers were having none of it; they were going to stop off here, dig for gold and then head for Europe with a fortune in their pockets. And yes: the moving spirit behind this covetous disregard of common sense and the greater good was Ippolit Stepanov. No sooner had Benyovszky turned his back on the ship for a moment than Stepanov led the worst of the company off into the woods to "take an oath." Hearing this, Benyovszky called a general assembly at which Stepanov spoke, "loading me with invectives, and threatening both myself and Mr. Panow with speedy death." Benyovszky, ever the master-strategist, challenged the mutineers to elect a new chief; it helped that "fifty-two companions" immediately sided with him. After the arrival of a deputation of Stepanovites who had decided to keep the status quo, just as long as they were permitted to dig for precious metal, a second meeting was convened, "at which I promised to discover the sentiments of my mind."

At this second meeting, Benyovszky resolved the difficulty by making a proposal no red-blooded man could refuse.

> The company immediately assembled, excepting Mr. Stephanow with ten associates, who were on board. I then represented to them, that no one among them could be more truly desirous of fixing his residence on this happy island, than myself, but that various reflections prevented me from adopting this resolution, and in order to shew them that they were well-founded, I declared to them, that our company consisting of a great number of men, and only eight women, the disproportion would hinder our union; and that, in fact, it was merely this want of women which had prevented me from making the proposal to them of fixing our residence upon the island: but at length, as I saw they had taken their resolution, I would acquiesce in their wishes, upon one single condition. Hereupon, they all cried out, "Hear, hear." I then declared, that my intention was to sail for Japan, and there make a descent near a town, from which we would carry off as many women as we could seize, together with cattle and grain. I concluded, by protesting, that if they would engage to second me in this project, I would promise to settle with them upon the island, to which we might easily return, and that one month would be sufficient for carrying the project into execution. I had scarcely finished my declaration, before they all exclaimed, "Long live our Chief, long live our General"; and they came one after the other to kiss my hand.[2]

Taking the final precaution of ferrying Stepanov to shore to serve out his imprisonment, "lest the madman fire the ship," the boisterous company busied themselves with loading the ship with fruit, water, hogs and goats and the "pintado bird," leaving the treasures of the earth for their return visit. Prior to their departure, Benyovszky took the precaution of letting the world know that he had been there.

> I gave orders to erect a cross, with the following inscription: "In the year 1771, on the 16th of July, the corvette St. Peter and St. Paul, anchored in the

harbour of this island, commanded by Maurice Auguste de Benyowszky, Magnate of Hungary and Poland, General of the Republic of Poland; made prisoner of war by the Russians, and exiled, by order of the Czarina, to Kamchatka, from whence he had the good fortune to make his escape, by the force of his courage. This island is not inhabited: it abounds with different wild fowl; the sea affords excellent fish, and its fruits and water are wholesome. It is situated in 32 degrees, 47 minutes latitude, and 355 degrees, 8 minutes longitude, from Bolsha, in Kamchatka."

Let us stop to contemplate this modest memorial. Disregarding the record of longitude, which is clearly wrong, two islands of the Izu group might qualify as a candidate for Liquor, lying within spitting distance of the latitude given. The larger of the two is Hachijo, which is around 4 miles long and 2 miles broad, and lies at 33° 05′ north. To the south is the tiny island of Aogashima, at 32° 26′. But... such indications of size as are given – several hours of cruising along the shores, states the record – would eliminate the smaller island. Hachijo is indeed an island of many natural charms; it would be churlish to deny the weary voyagers some respite on its shores. But it certainly was not uninhabited: indeed, the ship's complement would have been a little perturbed to discover it was a penal colony for Japanese exiles and hard-cases, with the requisite number of prison-guards. If we take into account the fact that neither Ryumin nor Stepanov even hinted at this place, and that Benyovszky stayed a week there without being accosted, then we must conclude, with regret, that Liquor did not exist. Benyovszky's carefully carved cross, therefore, was never to be seen by anyone else.

On Saturday 23rd July, they set sail, heading west-north-west. On the very first day out, it grew very hot and the crew complained of "excessive thirst." There was no pleasing them. Benyovszky told them to drink fruit-juice. After three days, they reached the Japanese coast, at a position of 33° 28′ north, 347 degrees from Bolsheretsk. This position was just as much in the middle of the ocean as the last place; but if we make allowances for the fact that, not uncommonly, longitudinal calculations went completely awry in the extremes of temperature and weather of long sea-voyages, a further 8 or 9 degrees to the west at the same latitude would bring them comfortably to either Shikoku Island or the Kii Peninsula. Or somewhere close. A day or two of sailing cautiously up and down the coastline suggested that they had reached an island. The company was all for landing, anxious to seize women, rustle cattle and perform other manly deeds. Benyovszky was more circumspect. Some sails came in sight. Benyovszky pulled out his perspective-glass and found that it was a whole fleet of boats. The boats did not approach. The voyagers found a sheltered bay and anchored, sending a party on shore to reconnoitre. Disappointingly there were no women, only a few abandoned fishermen's huts and a very large heap of fish-bones. Benyovszky "caused a sketch to be taken of the northern extremity of the island"; but, like several other maps and sketches mentioned by the author of the *Memoirs*, these were never delivered with the manuscript. Slightly disheartened by the midden, they sailed off again, westwards. More promisingly, on 28th July they encountered several Japanese ships and observed fires and lights on the coastline at night. They anchored once more and prepared to do business.

They had now reached the "Bay of Usilpatchar." As always with these renditions of Japanese names, a few misty shreds of doubt drift over the precise location. The nineteenth-century critic Kropf made it his business to hunt down the source of Benyovszky's every statement and kill it stone dead.

> As regards the name *Usilpatchar* given to the gulf in question by Benyowszky I find it is written *Usilpatéhar* in his MS. in the British Museum. And since he spells all his proper names according to the rules of Hungarian phonetics, it should be pronounced "Ushilpátéhár." The reader will at once discover that the name is of Benyowszky's invention, and merely a corruption of *Schiltpads Eylanden* (i.e., Turtle Island), shown on old Dutch maps, which he distorted in the same way as probably the name of Liqueyo (now Riu Kiu Islands) into Liquor.[3]

Kropf was of course entitled to his opinion.

The matter of identification may never be resolved. Benyovszky gives the latitude as 33° 41´, and his record of the longitude puts them at about 141° east ("345 degrees from Bolsha"). Ignoring the longitudinal record, we would guess that, if the ship was anywhere at all, then it was somewhere on the coast of Shikoku.

At daybreak, they found themselves surrounded by "near one thousand vessels, who were busied in the fishery." Few of the fishermen paid any attention, but those who did seemed to think the ship was Dutch. At length, some of the boats slung ropes aboard and towed them to another anchorage – in all probability intent on keeping the clumsy white men out of their fishing grounds. They accepted no thanks, indicating, by pointing to their own necks, that acceptance of gifts would be punishable by death. For the next few hours, the two sides eyed each other askance. Winbladh and Kuznetsov were sent ashore in a boat, clutching three beaver skins, six martens and a letter written in Dutch. After some nervous hours, they returned in the company of a Japanese gentleman who proceeded to address them in his native tongue.

> He came on board with confidence, and made a long harangue, every word of which was perfectly unintelligible to me. In order, however, that I might comprehend some part of it, I sent for Bocsarew, who had learned this language during the space of three years, at Irkuczk, in Siberia, from a Japanese, who had escaped shipwreck at Kamchatka, and after being taught the Russian language, at Moscow, was maintained by the senate to teach Japanese to the Siberians. Unfortunately it turned out that Bocharov had forgotten most part, and remembered only a few compliments, with which he regaled the Japanese.[4]

Now, is that not always the way with college-students?

However, Winbladh had excellent news. He made the following report:

> We found two hundred men on horseback, and an equal number on foot, armed with bows and lances, who likewise saluted us politely; but perceiving that we were desirous of repairing to the town or village we saw before us, they offered us horses; we mounted, and were thus conducted, in ceremony, to a castle at the extremity of a village, which is about one quarter of a league distant from the landing place. Here we dismounted, and were introduced into the court, in which we were very politely received by a person of distinction, who conducted us into an extensive hall, built on columns. Here we found another great man, seated on a sopha, who said to us *Fiassi guzarimas*, which we did not understand, and therefore we only saluted him, and made a sign that we did not comprehend him. The second words he spoke were. *To Golland,* which I understood, and made a sign that we were not Hollanders. Afterwards he said *To Sindzi,* to which, upon my making a sign that I did not understand him, he continued his questions. *To Pilipine, To Branki, To Masui, To Tungusi*; and as I had always answered in the negative, he beat a drum which was near him. Upon this signal several servants entered, to whom he gave orders, and immediately afterwards they returned with books and rolls of papers; he unrolled them, one after the other, and having at last found what he wanted, he made signs for me to approach, which I did. He then shewed me a chart, in which I distinguished Japan, China, the Philipine Islands, the Indies, and a tract of unknown land, nearly occupying the space and position of Europe. He took my finger, and directed me to place it on the map. I comprehended that he sought for the country from which we came. I shewed him Europe, which astonished him very much. He shewed his surprize, by crying out, *Namandabez* several times; and afterwards, as he seemed to doubt what he had learned, I availed myself of the assistance of the chart, and made signs to inform him, that the duration of our voyage, and the hard weather we had experienced, had exhausted us, and that we were in want of provisions.

(*Namandabez*, incidentally, is the Buddhist 'well, I never!' – *Namo Amida Butsu*: an understandable exclamation on encountering men from the other side of the planet)[5]. Benyovszky followed up this promising start by "shewing civilities" and slipping a couple of sable furs to the Japanese visitor. Shortly afterwards some small boats, groaning under the weight, brought provisions, which.

> consisted of twenty-five sacks of rice, four pots of soft sugar, four jars of tea, one jar of tobacco very finely cut, eight hogs, sixteen jars of preserved fruits, a quantity of onions, oranges, lemons, pine-apples, and other fruits, two casks of salt fish, six casks of a very agreeable kind of wine, and about fifty

fowls; but that which afforded the greatest pleasure to my companions, was the sight of three barrels of very strong spirits.[6]

Over the next few days, receptions and present-giving escalated, with lapsed interpreter Bocharov doing his utmost to facilitate communication. Where verbal understanding failed, both sides resorted to drawing pictures. By these means, Benyovszky was able to advise the "king" of the place that he was a "warrior of Europe." Some puzzlement was caused by Benyovszky's stature (lack of).

> By his gestures and signs, I understood that he wished to know why I was shorter than my people. In answer I caused a low stool to be brought to support my right foot, and then he saw me in my natural height, which likewise was some surprize to him. It was with much difficulty that I could make him understand, that in consequence of a wound in battle, my right leg was shortened four inches, which caused me to lean towards that side, and deprived me of so much in height.[7]

As well as providing civilised conversation, wines and good foods, the Japanese were itching to re-supply the ship. Supplementary to the considerable first load mentioned above, the voyagers now received a hundred sacks of rice, twenty hogs, twenty-six casks of water and two of spirits, and "a great quantity of fruits and dried fish, wine, and poultry." Dried fish they could have done without, but refusal might have caused offence.

At length, a *Bonze* or priest was introduced, who spoke "very good Dutch"; handy, since Benyovszky seems to have mastered that language as well. The Hungarian told the priest of his travels – but only one of those trimmed-down versions with which we are passing familiar: of being captured in Poland and sent to Kamchatka "from whence I had delivered myself with courage." He apologised for having landed in Japan, explaining that

> I had come thither with fear, on account of the relations the Hollanders had wickedly published, that the Japanese put the Christians to death. Upon these last words he replied, that it was true, that there was a decree of the Emperor not to admit any Spanish or Portuguese Christian into the country, but that the decree did not affect the Christians of other nations, who had never done harm to the empire.[8]

This last reassurance was rather convenient, since it suggested to Benyovszky's readership that Europeans would be welcome in Japan, for the purposes of trade. In point of fact it was also completely wrong; it was not until the mid-nineteenth century that the Japanese showed any signs of relaxing their restrictive policies on European traders of any religious or national persuasion.

The conversation between Benyovszky and the priest was interrupted by an invitation to visit the King, where they continued a discussion on Christianity and Buddhism over cups of tea, just like any other enlightened people of the world.

We will not fatigue ourselves by describing all the presents which were passed back and forth, the suppers and teas shared, the musical concerts attended ("the music and the song appeared to be not deficient in melody"), and the manner in which the crew "made themselves beloved by the natives." Benyovszky enjoyed himself so much that he was afflicted by a "violent head-ach." A highlight of the visit was the demonstration of Russian muskets and small cannon, which much delighted the King, the more so since he managed at his first attempt to shoot dead one of his own horses. At this success,

> he assured me, that I might make any request I chose, with the certainty of obtaining it. I availed myself of this favourable instant, to request permission, that I might return into his dominions, to open a trade under his protection. His answer surprized me, for he granted me this favour without hesitation; observing [...] that he not only granted me his protection in his dominions, but likewise would exert his influence with the Emperor, to obtain permission, that my vessels might enter all his other harbours.[9]

On the following day, as a very tangible symbol of this amazing trade-agreement, a "young gentleman" was handed over to Benyovszky, on the understanding that he would be returned home just as soon as the first merchant ships from Europe turned up in Japan. Fifty pieces of gold came with the young gentleman, to defray any expenses.

Like the "American" Zacharii, this young gentleman makes no further significant appearance in the *Memoirs*. He proved to be mildly useful for interpreting on two occasions a few days later. But, had he even existed, he certainly never saw his native land again.

And all good things must come to an end. On 2nd August, Benyovszky decided that they had better be moving on. He summoned his followers and reminded them of their agreed 'Plan A,' which consisted in seizing cattle and women, and returning to the Island of Liquor. The crew shuffled their feet and looked doubtful. Benyovszky then advised them that 'Plan B' was therefore in operation: they would head for China, return to Europe, sign up some European power, and return in style to Japan to establish a permanent colony. "These words were scarcely spoken, before the whole company cried out, that I might follow my own pleasure in all things, and they would punctually obey." And so, firing a twenty-one gun salute, they headed out to sea and headed south-westwards.

Barely a day had passed than the crew were whingeing again.

Several of the associates threw themselves at my feet, and intreated me to anchor again upon the coast of Japan, in order to procure them new opportunities of trading, and turning their furs to account. I granted their request the more readily, as I was desirous of becoming acquainted with the coast; but I promised to consent to their wishes on condition, that they should behave with the most exact subordination.

A close encounter with a ship followed.

> At sun-set, the weather appeared squally to the northward. At day-break we discovered an European vessel before us. I resolved to chace her, but I soon observed the Dutch colours; and as the vessel stood to the south-south-east, I pursued my course, and suffered her to go on unmolested.[10]

Quite in the tradition of George Anson; but how our hero could realistically have 'molested' that innocent ship, is not discussed.

On 4th August, they hit a storm and were forced into a bay on the coast. Their position was 33° 34′ north and 339° 12′ from Bolsheretsk (135° 28′ east), which puts them somewhere close to the island of Shikoku; or, in Benyovszky's log, "the port of Misaqui." ("Misaqui" appears at the southern end of the Izu Peninsula on the 1752 map of Japan created by the French cartographer Bellin – about 300 miles east of Shikoku; '*Misaki*' is the Japanese word for promontory.) At this anchorage, despite the best efforts of their Japanese passenger, the locals were not quite so welcoming, treating the ship and its crew with some suspicion. They handed over rice, water, fruit and "a very agreeable liquor," but simply made no effort to invite them to endless parties. Instead, three dour officials turned up demanding to know if they were Dutch or Spanish. Benyovszky considered it politic to appear to be Dutch and hastily scribbled a letter to be taken to the trading enclave at Nagasaki. It read as follows:

> Health to the officers in chief of the Factory of the Dutch East India Company.
>
> I acquaint you, gentlemen, that finding myself upon the coast of Japan, whither I was driven by a series of those incidents which often at sea compel the navigator to seek his safety wherever he can, I find myself in distress, which cannot be described; for which reason I have thought proper to address myself to you, and to request you to send me an interpreter, and assistance to conduct me to your port. My ship is a corvette, with near one hundred persons on board. An answer, if you please.
>
> I have the honour to be, Gentlemen, Your servant, Maurice August. Benyowsky.[11]

It should come as no shock to any reader that the letter which was actually written by Benyovszky had completely different words in it.

Notes

1 Benyovszky, 1790,Vol.I, pp.374–375.
2 *ibid,* pp.378–383.
3 Kropf, 1895, p.324.
4 Benyovszky, 1790, Vol.I, pp.389–391.
5 *"Fiassi guzarimas"* appears to be the polite introduction: 'My name is Hayashi.' *"To Golland... to Sindzi"* etc. appear to be the questions (in sequence): 'are you Dutch, are you Chinese, Spanish (*"Pilipine"*), Portuguese (*"Branki,"* 'Branco' being Portuguese for white; or possibly *Furanki* meaning French?), *"Masui"* (impenetrable), *"Tungusi"* (possibly Mongolian/Tartar). With thanks to Dr Astley and Professor Roberts for their hints and clues.
6 Benyovszky, 1790, Vol.I, p.392.
7 *ibid,* pp.396–397.
8 *ibid,* p.398. Although there is currently debate on the extent and purpose of the edicts restricting trade and contact with foreigners, it is generally acknowledged that the only Europeans granted any concessions were the Dutch, and this persisted at least until the 1850s.
9 *ibid,* pp.402–403.
10 *ibid,* p.407.
11 *ibid,* pp.410–411.

XXI

WHAT THE JAPANESE THOUGHT

"Foreign Paper with Horizontal Writing"

*Red-haired Foreigners – Trousers, Shirts and Snuff – Japanese Bureaucracy –
A Warning to the Dutch – Even Stranger: The Women Were Treated with Respect*

Eighteenth-century Japan was a supremely well-organised, civilised and literate place, so, while Benyovszky was erratically coasting their land, Japanese officials were taking careful notes.

The Baron appears in these reports under the name of "Hanbengoro" – 'han' being a rendition of the noble prefix 'von' or 'van,' and 'Bengoro' no more of an aberration than the Japanese names written down by our voyagers.[1] The reports, dated "in the eighth year of Meiwa" (1771), indicate that "Hanbengoro" had initially landed on the shores of the island of Shikoku. The crew had run out of food and were in a bad way, but the "daimyo of Hachisuka" took pity on them and supplied them with food and water. In return, Benyovszky handed over a couple of letters for the Dutch in Nagasaki.

The Japanese records[2] indicate that the place where the ship had landed was Sakinohama, a small town on the east coast of Shikoku, "on the eighth day of the sixth month" – that is the 19th July, which matches very neatly with Ryumin's date of 8th July (OS) – but not Benyovszky's 4th August. The residents of this town reacted very circumspectly – it was forbidden, after all, to have any truck with foreigners. When the foreigners insisted on coming ashore, every effort was made to give them what they wanted and then wave goodbye. And as a result of the possible threat of punishment, the several eye-witness accounts gave slightly different stories – most especially when it came to describing the goods which had been bartered with the "Red-hairs," in defiance of all edicts to the contrary. These ranged from a simple "some shirts" to a more precise inventory of: three cotton shirts, two pairs of cotton trousers, two pairs of red silk trousers, two yellow silk vests, one red and one blue silk vest, three scarves, six bundles of tobacco, a "sheet of foreign paper with horizontal writing on it," and one coloured picture. The foreigners also introduced the startled Japanese to snuff "which they inserted in their noses, and then put in our noses," and man-hugging: one of the Russians "placed his hand on Shinshichi's left shoulder and, spreading his chest, took Shinshichi's right shoulder with his right hand and pressed chest to chest, leaving absolutely no space between." All of this was disconcerting enough, but when it came to writing up the official reports, the rule about tangled webs of deceit came into play in a comedy of blame: higher officials refused to take away the trousers and shirts because they had not been mentioned in the initial report; the local officials countered with a valid complaint that "these are foreign things that we don't have the slightest idea about. The trousers and shirts all seem to be connected."

The locals were much relieved when the ship unfurled its sails and set off again four days later. According to the officials of Sakinohama, and at their suggestion, the ship initially sailed northwards up the coast to the small island of Oshima. Since the local officials there probably considered silence to be the best policy, we have no record of events there, although Ryumin's report (discussed earlier) also suggested a short move northwards. But we do know that the St Peter subsequently sailed south-westwards to land at the Satsuman island of Amami-Oshima, some 450 miles south-west of Shikoku. There they received a similar welcome from the "daimyo of Satsuma"; Benyovszky handed over four letters, "in sideways writing," along with a map.

Three of his sideways letters were apparently just expressions of thanks. All of them were delivered a month later to the Dutch at Nagasaki for translation. Thence, they made their way back to the archives in Holland. The final letter is fascinating (apart from anything else, it is postmarked with a real date and place):

> Highly Illustrious, High and Well-born Gentlemen, Officers of the Highly Esteemed Republic of Holland.
>
> Unkind fate, which has for some time been driving me here and there on the sea, has brought me for a second time into Japanese waters. I have come ashore here in the hope I might possibly meet with your high excellencies, and thus obtain help. It has been a great misfortune for me not to have had the opportunity of speaking to you personally, for I have important information to disclose. I have deemed it necessary because of my general respect for your illustrious states to inform you in this letter of the fact that this year, in accordance with a Russian order, two galliots and a frigate from Kamchatka sailed around Japan and set down all their findings in a plan, in which an attack on Matsma [Hokkaido] and the neighboring islands [...] has been fixed for next year. For this purpose a fortress has been built on the Kuril island nearest to Kamchatka, and ammunition, artillery and a magazine have been readied.
>
> If I could speak to you personally, I might reveal more than writing permits. Your high illustriousnesses may make such preparation as you please, but my advice, as an ardent well-wisher of your illustrious republic

and co-religionist, would be that you have a cruiser ready if you can. With this I further commend myself and am as sub-scribed, your most obedient servant

Baron Aladar von Bengoro

Army Commander in Captivity

20 July 1771 on the island Usma.

When I went ashore I left there a map of Kamchatka which may be of use to you.[3]

Now this is a surprise, and no mistake. Clearly, the dire warning about a planned Russian invasion was nothing more than a story invented for the Japanese and Dutch, something at which our hero was adept. The Russians had no such designs on Hokkaido; the northernmost Kuril Island was a very long way from Hokkaido; and even if there had been such a plot, Benyovszky was not going to be privy to it. Perhaps Benyovszky wanted to pre-empt any unwelcome Dutch interventions at sea, by posing as a friend? Or did he just want to stir up vengeful mischief against Russia? The Japanese, justifiably, were suspicious of him – they even surmised that the *St Peter* was one of the three Russian spy-ships mentioned. But for a while they took the warning very seriously.

So seriously, indeed, that a later Japanese historian suggested that Benyovszky had inadvertently kick-started Russian Studies in Japan.[4] Over the following years, various government advisers made their way to Hokkaido and the southern Kurils, looking for evidence of invading 'Red ainu' (Russians). They found little – the odd group of wet and miserable trappers, and some impudent merchants who had been nonchalantly trading in northern Hokkaido. Later still, in 1798, the Japanese strategist Honda Toshiaki wrote a book in which he mentions Benyovszky's arrival at Shikoku and Oshima, and his letters to the Dutch, as evidence of Russian aggression. (In a fit of uninformed optimism, Toshiaki also suggested that the Kurils were 'fertile,' and good for growing crops and fruit: you really cannot beat a good piece of travel fiction.) It was not until 1820 or so that any Russians and Britons became a nuisance: and those were simple whalers stumbling ashore.

As we shall see later, Benyovszky's story about invading Russians had diplomatic repercussions in Europe in 1776.

In the 1930s, the diary of a Yamanouchi samurai on Shikoku was unearthed by a Japanese professor and published by a Hungarian colleague (the diary has since been lost, probably in air-raids on Kochi in 1945).[5] It contained a drawing of a ship and a description of the strange manners of the foreigners on board.

The ship was described as having "a length greater than the width," a precision which should be savoured slowly. Its length was measured at "thirty fathoms" and it had three flags on its mast. Compare this with Nathaniel Barlow's reckoning of the ship at 50 feet in length: the only conclusion that can be drawn is that the tools of measurement were of some inexactitude. For further proof of this, consider the following description of the ship's crew: "the adult male height is three metres and a quarter, the women are two and a half metres, the 15–16 year-old males around one and a half metres high."

Remain calm. Suppose for the moment that we take the Hungarian word '*méter*,' which was used to translate the original Japanese text, to be a rather wild conversion of the standard Japanese measure, the *shaku*, which comes in at 0.3 of a metre. If we do that, of course, the conundrum veers rather giddily in the opposite direction.

Of course, ordinary Japanese people rarely saw foreigners. In a sobering counterpart to early European prejudices concerning non-Europeans, rumours abounded in Japan that people such as the Dutch were giants with cat's eyes, huge noses, red hair and no heels, who urinated by raising one leg like a dog. So, very tall men and pint-sized adolescents represented quite a moderate assessment.[6]

We move on to the remainder of the description, which seems more familiar: "their faces were red, and their bodies white." Northern Europeans on holiday, we are to understand. "Their noses are hooked and at least four inches long. Their clothes are made of damask, and their shoes of horse-leather."

On questioning the newcomers, the Japanese discovered that they were from "*Oren*," which should most probably be interpreted as Holland; such conversation as took place was conducted in Dutch, with translation into Japanese. These 'Dutchmen' engaged in quite peculiar practices:

> There is sometimes drumming on the ships, sometimes ringing bells, or blowing trumpets. In addition, they cried out what sounded like "*Kicsiren, Kicsiren*" – but we did not understand the meaning of this. Even stranger was the fact that they grasped each other's hands. But even stranger, it appeared that the women were treated with the respect afforded only to older men in Japan.

Some of these novelties of etiquette were quite enough to provoke one patriot, a man named Hansuke Tokide, to suggest blowing up the ship with gunpowder. To his everlasting disappointment, Hansuke could not come up with a good enough plan of execution.

In the spirit of pre-war Japanese-Hungarian Friendship, the original discoverers of this document suggested that "*Oren*" was in fact "Poland." But that link is tenuous at best. The drumming and trumpeting was probably related to time-keeping on the ship – summons to meals etc. The mystifying word "*Kicsiren*" means 'Christians' – but since it was illegal for Japanese citizens to meet anyone who was a Christian, the diary rather disingenuously claims not even to understand the word.

It is not certain that the ship was our *St Peter*; after all, there is no mention of the troublesome trousers. But there is a fair chance that it was.

And now we must bid farewell to the clear air of reality for a while, and stumble back into the smoke-filled *Memoirs*, nonsensical dates, indistinct places and all. We retreat back in time to "Misaqui."

The ship set sail from here on 5th August (now three weeks behind the timetable set by Ryumin and Stepanov) and continued westwards for five days. When they anchored again, the people they met here assured Benyovszky they were on the coast of Shikoku, in Tosa Bay. (Confused? This is where they really were before: but perhaps this is the landfall immediately after Sakinohama, at the small island of Oshima, Awa Province? Who knows?) Conversation was desultory. The Japanese young gentleman had already been completely forgotten about, and since Bocharov was clearly not up to the job, it was down to Benyovszky to establish communications:

> a young man said much to me, without being able to make himself understood; when, being out of patience, he repeated, "*To Hollandi, To Sindzi, Pu pu Tippo*," which I understood, and in answer, led him to the guns, and said, "*To Gollandi, pu.*" Towards noon the Japanese retired.[7]

On the 11th August, shortly after this informative exchange had taken place, the locals turned up in force. A nervous Benyovszky fired off cannon and muskets, which drove the Japanese to throw themselves on their faces or faint. A military officer who ventured on board indicated that he had come to arrest them. The foreigners acted dumb, and took away his scroll of authority; the poor man panicked, indicating that he would be put to death if he lost that piece of paper. It was duly returned, and the officer was sent home nervously clutching a beaver-skin and six sables.

This visit had just not been a success. Having terrified the natives, the *St Peter* weighed anchor and headed south-westwards.

But their Japanese adventures were far from over. There were women to meet.

Notes

1 Keene, 1969, pp.31–33; Lensen, 1971, pp.79–83.
2 Roberts, 2015, pp.97–102.
3 Keene, 1969, p.34. His translation from the original.
4 See Roberts, 2015, p.102.
5 See Mezey, 1939. Professor Roberts argues that the description may have been written forty or so years after the event, as an 'interesting local history' entry in the diary. Some of the patriotic embellishment is more likely of this later date.
6 Keene, 1969, pp.16–17.
7 Benyovszky, 1790, Vol.I, p.414. "*Tippo*" is probably *teppou* (a gun). Could "*pu*" be the sound of a gun? Benyovszky clearly knew what was going on, even if we do not.

XXII

THE RYÜKYÜ ISLANDS

"The Most Perfect Work of Living Nature"

*Collecting Tax-collectors at Takashima – Three Feet of Water in the Hold –
Shipwreck! – A Meeting of Christians – The Delights of Usmay Ligon –
Nicholas the Chief – Caressing Young Women – A Marriage Ceremony –
A Treaty – Fond Farewells*

According to the account passed along to us from Ippolit Stepanov, the ship arrived
at a Japanese island named "Usmaski" on or about the 20th July; this place "lay on the
28th latitude." According to Ryumin's account, on the 20th July they had arrived at
a place named "Usmaitsi." In both narratives, the previous port of call had been a
Japanese bay where they had received both supplies and hostility in equal measure.
Prior to that, they had been dallying in the Kurils, before wallowing aimlessly around
the North Pacific Ocean, hoping against hope that they would arrive somewhere
nice. Usmaski/Usmaitsi did indeed turn out to be somewhere nice.

Not to be outdone by these two narratives (of which, to be fair, he could have
had no knowledge when preparing his *Memoirs* for publication, the one being in
the travel-chest of a Dutch preacher in Indonesia, the other safely locked away in
the Imperial Archives in St Petersburg), Benyovszky arrived at the island of 'Usmay
Ligon' on 14th August 1771. It was the same place as that described by his fellow-
voyagers. It, too, was nice; very nice indeed. So nice that Ryumin and Stepanov
might not have recognised it.

But before reaching this second Paradise, there were two more adventures to
undergo. They took place at the island of "Tacasima," which is recorded as lying
at 30 degrees 38 north. By happy chance, there are actually islands here that might
fit the bill: Tanegashima at 30° 33´; or there is Toshima at 29° 50´; we discount the
large island of Tokashima at 33°. But take your pick. Unusually, the locals were
not keen to meet the courageous Baron: four small boats were spotted looking
dangerous.

I therefore anchored in twenty-two fathoms, between the small and the large island; but at a very short distance from the latter. Mr. Kuzneczow was immediately dispatched, with eight associates, and I sent the shallop after him. When we had entered the sound, which we at first supposed to be a bay, the small boat passed very near a large bark at anchor, whose crew shot at them with arrows, and at the same time near sixty boats put off from the shore, so that my people were in great danger. I was advised of this by two reports of the pateraroes which I heard, and I immediately weighed, and proceeded to support my detachment, by entering the sound. I soon perceived the state of affairs, and standing towards the great bark, I fired two shots into her, which drove all her people from the deck. The shallop then went along-side, and took possession of the vessel, while, on my part, I approached the shore, and anchored in four fathoms and an half, at the distance of half a cannon shot off shore, whither I likewise caused the Japanese bark to be brought, in which we found fifty-six men, four of them being *mimas*, or gentlemen; revenue officers of the Emperor. The lading of the bark consisted of tobacco, sugar, silk, varnish, porcelain, one hundred pieces of leather, some bales of cotton and silk, several chests of sabres, belts, and other articles of wearing apparel.[1]

Very similar acts of piracy took place, albeit on a far grander scale, during Anson's prowls back and forth across the Pacific; the prey there being Spanish treasure galleons. Benyovszky consulted with the young Japanese gentleman who was travelling with them, noting "with satisfaction" that he had been injured by an arrow; the young man, with commendable enthusiasm, confirmed that the attackers were "wicked and good for nothing" and that they should all be killed. (This, incidentally, was the young Japanese fellow-traveller's last useful act: he never appeared again, except to say farewell.) Further enquiries elicited the information that the four officers were tax-collectors who had been sent to "Tacasima and the island Nanghasaki" to collect revenues, and had only attacked Benyovszky because he had been attacking other tax-collectors in the smaller boats. It all seemed very believable, so Benyovszky spared their lives and put all the prisoners ashore.

Having won such a glorious naval battle, the voyagers decided that it would be best to take the captured ship, with all its treasure, along with them. They set off with the Japanese ship in tow, but gave up after a few miles, off-loaded the cargo to their own ship, then scuttled the Japanese one. "The cargo of this bark would have been worth three of four hundred thousand *livres*, French money, if we had been in Europe." What actually became of that haul of treasure is unknown. Like so many things, it is never mentioned again. Neither Ryumin nor Stepanov make any mention of these events, nor of the treasure. An oversight, no doubt.

No matter, we have no time for speculation – another crisis is upon us.

During the transfer of the treasure at sea, some of the underwater seams in the *St Peter* had opened, and water was pouring into the ship "with a noise resembling that of a river falling into the sea." Alarmed, the crew manned the pumps, but only managed to restrict the inflow to three or four feet of water in the hold. After several hours of excitement, they managed to find another set of islands. While attempting to enter a sheltered bay, a storm sprang up.

> I found the entrance dangerous; and perceiving the wind increasing, and disposed to be stormy, I was extremely alarmed, and lowered down the Japanese yawl, in which I went a-head with four associates, after having given orders that the ship should stand after us with all the sail she could set. At four we had a dreadful storm, the sea being all in a foam, and notwithstanding our efforts to keep a-head, the ship over-ran us; and to complete our misfortune, the yawl struck on a rock off the southern point of a bay, and overset, at the distance of about two hundred fathoms from the shore. I used the utmost exertions to reach the port by swimming, but the sea was so rough, that it was not till after the greatest exertions that I reached the shore, quite exhausted. I lost all recollection of what followed, until I was rouzed by my companions, who, having taken notice of the rock on which the yawl overset, sent the small boat to take us up. Loginow, one of the people who was with me, called to them, and they at last found me in a state of stupefaction, at the foot of a tree. The information I received from them, that the ship was at anchor in a good harbour, and that the island was inhabited, made me forget the past misfortune, and I pressed them to return; but understanding that three of my associates were still wanting, I engaged them to proceed in the search of these unfortunate men, of whom we found one, named Andreanow, alive, and the other two dead upon the beach. After this we embarked, almost life-less, and went alongside the ship, which was at anchor in four fathom water, and so deeply immersed, that I determined to run her aground upon a sand bank. At eleven, I was, by my own orders, carried on shore; for the fatigue had exhausted me so much, that I could not stir any of my limbs. My associates set up a tent, while others were employed in unloading the cargo; and Mr. Baturin undertook to bury the two people who were drowned.[2]

Benyovszky does not name the two unfortunate companions who drowned. Nor are their deaths mentioned at any other point in this, or any other, narrative.

Whatever: now they had reached Usmay Ligon at 29° north.

On the 15th August, after Benyovszky had recovered from his near-death experience, Mr Panov arrived with some good news:

> Mr. Panow informed me that we were on an Island inhabited by a people in a high state of civilization, from whom I was about to receive a visit. [...] I received them in the best manner I could, and was in hopes of making myself understood in the Japanese language, by means of Mr. Boscarew, whom I ordered to be called. All our efforts, however, were entirely useless. They only shook their heads, as a sign that they did not understand us: but one of

them presented a paper to us, on which I perceived some Latin letters. I received it with avidity, and it was with great pleasure that I read its contents in the Latin language to the following purport...[3]

At the risk of being accused of concealing facts, we shall simply summarise the contents of this remarkable paper. It seems that the islanders had been visited by four Jesuit missionaries in 1749. After the most satisfactory conversion of 260 islanders, three of the missionaries moved on to the next island, and one named Father Ignatio remained. The paper was Ignatio's last report before he expired in 1754. In it he had time to note that no merchant vessels, except those of China and Japan, ever visited these islands; all very promising. Benyovszky made sure to kiss the piece of paper and generally indicate that he was a good Christian gentleman. The islanders beamed.

On the following day, three hundred inhabitants, bearing parasols rather than weapons, presented themselves for inspection, and were easily persuaded to assist in the repair of the ship and the provisioning of the ever-hungry crew.

> In the course of an hour we saw several boats arrive, which brought mats and wood, and others with people on board, who came to build huts for us. Another party of the islanders arrived with rice, potatoes, bananas, sugar-canes, a kind of brandy, with provisions of fish, flesh, and fruit. These immediately set to work to cook for us all. Lastly, about noon, another party arrived with carpenter's tools, and gave us to understand that they were disposed to assist us, by working on board. I was desirous however that the company should have some rest, and therefore made signs that the work would not begin till two days after.[4]

Over the next few days huts were built; three meals a day were served, consisting of rice, meat, bananas and sweet potatoes; ship, sails and rigging were repaired; the cargo was dried out; and, as an innovation, a Russian-Japanese dictionary was prepared, which soon contained a hundred useful words or phrases. But for Benyovszky there was no respite:

> the island was exceedingly fertile; the climate though hot appeared excellent, and the people were independent. These were powerful motives to a man who was weary of being the sport of fortune: but unfortunately the hour of my repose was not yet arrived, and it was necessary for me to bear the burthen of the charge I had undertaken.[5]

The chief of the islanders introduced himself in "bad Portuguese" (which, nevertheless, Benyovszky immediately understood) as a native of the Vietnamese province of Tonkin; he had arrived there with the Jesuits and had stayed on. The chief gave Benyovszky the guided tour of the tourist attractions of Usmay Ligon, and various Christian sites of interest.

While he was doing that, Winbladh had made an excursion into the hinterland – and from his enthusiastic description, he must have had Ryumin in tow making an inventory:

> he had seen very handsome habitations and villages, and had observed large quantities of different fruits, such as cocoa nuts, oranges, lemons, pine-apples, bananas, water melons, sweet melons, grapes, potatoes, rice, maize, millet, peas, and other pulse; and that in the plantations he had seen bee-hives, sugar-canes, tobacco and cotton. He assured me besides that he had visited a manufactory of pottery and a distillery of spirits; and added that all the women in the villages were busied in making stuffs, either of silk or cotton. I verified this information myself the same day, and my stay upon this fortunate island increased my ardent desire to form an establishment there.[6]

The silks and cotton proved useful: Benyovszky immediately gave orders that the cloth should be made up into "shirts, frocks and trowsers," in order that the company should have "a uniform appearance." A uniform is a persistent – and of course very pleasing – theme in these adventures.

Benyovszky then busied himself with persuading the chief, christened Nicholas, that the formation of a trading-colony on this island would be beneficial to all. Nicholas was much taken with the idea, informed the other islanders, and they hastened to gather round and make approving noises: "this declaration was very agreeable to them, for they assured me that they would divide their possessions with us, instruct us in the manner of working and tilling the ground, and would give us their daughters in marriage."

However, even Benyovszky saw difficulties here: he frankly confessed that his company were not of the best quality, advising the islanders that he would have to go fetch more desirable settlers from Europe. This might take a couple of years. Luckily, the "estimable people" of Usmay Ligon had no problem with such a delay. Despite this resolution, there were still questions to be dealt with:

> They demanded, why I did not come among them, nor permit my companions to live with them in a cordial manner. I declared to Nicholas that my only apprehension was that our good intelligence might be interrupted by the inconsistency of my companions, who might displease the islanders by caressing their women. But he set my mind at ease in that respect, by informing me that they were at liberty to connect themselves with the girls, provided they abstained from the married women, who were known by a veil which covered them.[7]

The order went out: the men of the *St Peter* might mingle with the natives and caress the unmarried women. This instruction was well received. The men scampered off to do their leader's bidding. Thoughtfully looking after them, Benyovszky found himself in a fit of despair: he wanted to leave some men behind, but he saw that none of the present company would really do. He convened a meeting of the inner circle of trusted friends; they agreed that their colleagues were not desirable.

While that social dilemma was being debated, Nicholas and the islanders threw a party. It was the party to end all parties. There was food, drinking, dancing and wrestling. Lusty crewmen and compliant young girls paired off. Better still, Nicholas insisted that Benyovszky should be paired off as well. Benyovszky demurred; Nicholas insisted; Benyovszky caved in.

> At the end of our meal, the juice of sugar cane, which we drank, was mixed with a kind of spirit made from rice. This drink was very strong and exhilarating. From one subject to another, our conversation at last returned to the proposal made to me to choose one of their young women, which was again urged, and at last so strongly pressed, that I could not avoid saying that I was willing to make my choice at that time, but should reserve the accomplishment of my marriage till I returned. I had scarcely said this, before the chiefs arose, and the whole company disappeared, and left me alone with my friend Nicholas, by whom I was informed that the islanders were gone to nominate seven young women to be presented to me, in order that I might choose a wife from among them.[8]

At length the young women were led in: "three among them [...] might have disputed the preference with the most perfect work of living nature." Benyovszky was called upon to make a choice from "these charming objects." The lucky girl (named "Luminous Moon") turned out to be the daughter of the late Father Ignatio, one of three. For the sake of propriety, matters were so arranged that several of Benyovszky's friends and "one of our lady passengers" (could it have been the strangely elusive Afanasia?) stayed up all night with the happy couple, ensuring no hanky-panky.

Intimate relationships having now been established all over the island, Benyovszky deemed it best to formalise the trade-agreement. The two parties to the contract swore an oath before their common Christian God to adhere to all formal articles of agreement. In short: they would be friends; the islanders would clear a space big enough for two hundred houses on the south of the island, to receive the colonists; the colonists would recognise the laws and customs of the island. A written treaty was drawn up; Benyovszky reproduced it in his book, just in case there should be any doubt in the minds of potential investors, or of present readers.

> A Treaty, concluded between the chiefs and people of the islands Lequeio, and the Baron Mauritius Augustus de Benyowsky, in the name of the company under his direction. Contracted and signed on the 19th of August, in the year 1771, at the island Usmay Ligon, one of Lequeio.
>
> In the presence of God, who created the heavens and the earth. We, the chiefs and people of the island of Usmay Ligon, and the other Lequeio, of

the one part, and I, the Baron Mauritius Augustus de Benyowsky, of the other part, do stipulate:

That I, Mauritius Augustus de Benyowsky, do oblige myself, and do promise, upon my faith as a Christian, to return to this island, as soon as possible, with a society of virtuous, good, and just men, to dwell upon this island, and to adopt the manners, usages, and laws of the inhabitants.

And we, the chiefs and people, call to witness that God who created the heavens and the earth, that we will, at any time hereafter, receive our friend Mauritius, with all those who shall be his friends: that we will share with them our lands, and will assist them in all their labours, until their establishments shall be equal to our own; and, in the mean time, his friends, who remain with us, shall be considered as the children of our families, and treated as brothers.

Mauritius, in the name of the company of Europeans.

Nicholas, for the chiefs and people of Usmay, and the Lequeio islands.

In the timeless tradition of such things, Benyovszky also sealed the agreement with weaponry: "Accordingly I gave them eighty musquets, twenty barrels of powder, ten barrels of ball, six hundred Japanese sabres, six hundred lances, and twelve hundred different articles of iron work." All of which was most satisfactory. There was a brief interruption to play host to three Japanese ships which came sheltering in the bay: tea was served; perfect guests, not one Japanese trader batted an eyelid.

There only remained now the thorny question of leaving someone behind to watch their interests. Just as the ship was being loaded for the onward journey, five crew-members demanded to be allowed to remain on the island. Benyovszky was not keen, and tried to argue them out of their position. It was to no avail. Eventually, Benyovszky conceded, with the proviso that they did not try to recruit any of their comrades. They promised. Within the hour, at a general assembly, three more crew-members expressed a preference to stay. What was worse, Stepanov also wanted to remain and look after the Usmayans. Thankfully, the other stay-behinds refused him, stating that "they would not have an incendiary among them."

Leaving behind tearful islanders and eight bold, eager and unnamed men, the ship raised anchor at 10 o'clock on the 19th August, a good week's work well done.

Four days into the onward voyage, they encountered two Dutch ships, one of which demanded they show their papers. Benyovszky replied with four shots from a cannon and a peppering of musket bullets. "I then hoisted the colours of the Republic of Poland and continued my course due south."[9] The Dutch ships chose not to pursue them, surprised either by the cannonballs or the extraordinary sight of the Polish flag in the China Sea.

But the crew had been studying their books again:

Being underway, with all sails set, the associates, from the information they had found in Anson's Voyage, requested me to sail to the island of Formosa, in order that they might add the knowledge of this island to their other discoveries. Their proposition was likewise agreeable to myself. I therefore promised to carry their request into execution.[10]

Since they were already more than half-way to Formosa anyway, it did not disturb their course. And Formosa was to prove very exciting indeed.

Notes

1 Benyovszky, 1790, Vol.I, pp.417–418.
2 *ibid*, pp.421–422.
3 Benyovszky, 1790, Vol.II, pp.1–2.
4 *ibid*, p.5.
5 *ibid*, p.6.
6 *ibid*, p.9.
7 *ibid*, pp.11–12.
8 *ibid*, pp.14–15.
9 *ibid*, p.23.
10 *ibid*, p.24.

XXIII

FORMOSA

"An Inadvertence of the Count"

The Death of Three Associates – A Touching Death-bed Scene – The Massacre
of a Few Natives – A Formosan Prince – A Most Fruitful Alliance –
A Short War – Plans and Dreams – Trading with the Chinese –
A Vessel of Prodigious Magnitude – Arrival at Macao

"Latitude in 23° 22′; longitude in 325° 0′. Wind E. Current from the Southward, Course W ¼ S." For almost the first time since leaving Bolsheretsk, the log of Benyovszky's voyage shows a realistic position. Both latitude and longitude place the ship unquestionably on the east coast of Formosa, probably at Black Rock Bay, Taitung County. The date was Thursday 25th August 1771. Ryumin had stated that their arrival at Formosa was the 9th August; Stepanov put it slightly later, on the 13th. Benyovszky's date may be new style – i.e. eleven days later than Ryumin and Stepanov. Narratives are gradually beginning to link up.

Formosa was to be the scene of the voyagers' greatest triumph and of their most tragic moment.

First came the tragedy. There were warnings of things to come when they anchored in a "commodious" bay and sent the boats ashore with Kuznetsov, Winbladh and sixteen men. Four hours later, the scouts came paddling back in a panic, arrows protruding from three of them; they brought with them five prisoners, two of whom had been wounded by Russian musket-fire. Kuznetsov reported that they had encountered some villagers who had invited them back to their village for a meal. All went well until they returned to the boats, at which point the villagers – now "savages" – had rained arrows upon them; they had to fight upon the beach to make their escape. Uncharacteristically, Benyovszky thought it best to make a tactical withdrawal and, with five prisoners on board, he moved his anchorage further off shore. On the following day, they returned and found the inhabitants in peaceable mood, prostrating themselves at the Europeans' feet, begging for forgiveness. Several of the crew decided that they would now like to go and visit the villagers. Benyovszky, hearing of this "mutiny," went ashore with a guard and pursued them.

> I had scarcely made a few steps, before I heard a violent firing and horrible cries. The noise increased, and at last I saw my people retreating, and pursued by a number of blacks, who hastily followed them. When they came near me, they rallied, but no more than seven of them were armed, the others being entirely naked, with several arrows sticking in their bodies. I gave orders, therefore, for those who had no arms, to retire towards the vessel, and rallied the others; by whose assistance I stopped the crowd of islanders, among whom I observed several armed with our muskets. Unfortunately for them, they knew not how to use them; and as they were more advanced than the others, they were quickly destroyed by our fire. Only two of them escaped, who threw down their muskets to favour their flight. At the moment the Indians made their retreat, or rather fled, Mr. Kuzneczow arrived with twenty fresh companions, who chased them out of their village, and at last set fire to it in several places. After the total defeat of the islanders, the dead were counted; and it was found that they amounted to upwards of two hundred, without reckoning those who were wounded, and had fled.[1]

Not a bad day's work. Eight more crew were wounded in this rout, bringing the total to eleven. In compensation, over two hundred native islanders (now "blacks") were killed, plus two of the prisoners who had died in the interim. Just to make victory secure, seven boats belonging to the islanders were towed away, and an eighth, as yet unfinished, set alight.

The crew, some clapped in irons for their disobedience, the rest feeling sheepish, requested that Benyovszky find another anchorage. He obliged. They sailed northwards a little, much assisted by a coastal current, and anchored again. No sooner had they done so than "a prodigious number of islanders, of both sexes, appeared with poultry, rice, sugar-canes, hogs, oranges, and other fruits, which they exchanged with us for pins, needles, and other small articles."[2] Only beads and mirrors were lacking to make this a perfect cameo of Western colonialism. Benyovszky remained on his guard. Then a rather Quixotic figure turned up, clothed partly in European fashion, partly in native. This was Don Hieronimo Pacheco, a Spaniard from Manila, who had been living on Formosa these past eight years. Pacheco assured the voyagers that the villagers here were entirely to be trusted, the more so since those whom Benyovszky had just massacred down the coast were their deadly enemies.

Pacheco and Benyovszky exchanged gifts. The Spaniard was contracted to assist the ship and its crew while they stayed on Formosa. Watering holes were pointed out, and Mr Panov, with twelve crewmen, was sent off with barrels to replenish the supplies; out of caution, Pacheco sent along some armed villagers to guard them, in case of retaliation by the enemy. With these matters arranged, the two leaders settled down to serious chat about the governance of Formosa. Pacheco outlined some ideas for ridding the islanders of their Chinese masters by force of arms. Benyovszky was miles ahead of him: already "I had conceived the project of carrying his plan into execution."

And while they planned the downfall of the Chinese imperialists, a tragedy was unfolding at the watering-place.

It was only on the day after the crewmen had been sent out with empty barrels that Pacheco observed that they had not returned. No one else had noticed a thing.

> Mr. Kuzneczow immediately went with eight men, and returned about two pm. with the canoe and *periagua* in tow. As soon as I perceived them at a distance, I was surprized to see that some of them were covered with blood, and had arrows sticking in their bodies; and as I did not see either Mr. Panow or Mr. Loginow, I began to fear the worst. When the shallop came on board, Mr. Kuzneczow informed me, that Mr. Panow and Mr. Loginow were mortally wounded, and that John Popow was the first slain. After having received Messrs. Panow and Loginow, in order to give them every assistance, I enquired concerning the fact; and was informed, that Mr. Panow having visited the environs, and discovered no signs of any person being near, had been desirous of bathing, while the associates were at work, filling the casks; and that he himself had invited the others to follow his example. But he had scarcely laid aside his arms and cloaths, when he was attacked by twenty Indians, who shot at him with arrows; that Popow was one of the first who fell dead; and that afterwards Panow and Loginow fell, and all the others were wounded; and that certainly not one of them could have escaped, if Volinsky and Andre had not fired at the islanders from the canoe, into which they had retired. They added, that they dared not return on board and abandon Mr. Panow, who from time to time gave signs of life, as well as Mr. Loginow. They were in this situation when the shallop came to their relief.[3]

Panov lived long enough to gasp out a final noble farewell. Benyovszky modestly jotted it all down.

> "My brothers," said he [*Panov*] to his companions, "inform my friend, our commander, that my only regret at quitting life is, that I shall no longer be able to second and support his labours. Alas! he is very far from seeing their conclusion. Tell him, that I love him as my life; and that I should die contented, if I could have seen his merit and virtue recompensed. Intreat him in my name, not to revenge my death; but content himself with informing my brother of this misfortune. Take example, my friends, by me; if I had followed the advice of our chief and friend, I had still lived. Respect

and obey him as a father; and thou, unhappy friend, Stephanow, lay aside thy haughtiness, and that hatred which is concealed in the bottom of thy heart, against this worthy friend. Supply my place by thy fidelity to him." At these words I came forward; but my God, what a sight! He seemed to have recovered all his powers. He grasped my hand, wept, and embraced me, but was unable to speak for a long time. At length, he exclaimed, "Alas, dear friend! I shall soon be no more. I am myself the cause. But forgive me. My last wish is, that heaven may ever give thee friends like me. Thou art worthy of them, and happy are they who shall know thy worth, as I do: may heaven grant, that this land, which soon shall cover my bones, may be thy patrimony." The power of death interrupted his words, and deprived me of this dear and most valuable friend.[4]

Ivan Loginov, who "had paid the debt of nature a few instants before," spared his companions any lengthy speeches. Ivan Popov was already dead when they brought him back to the ship. All three were buried, with the islanders' permission, with great pomp. All that then remained was to wreak vengeance on those dastardly natives who had launched the attack.

Within about four hours, justice had been done. The crew started by executing the three surviving prisoners on the ship; then they boarded some native boats which had made the mistake of coming in close. Thirteen islanders were killed, and the remainder brought on board "and hung at the yard-arm." Benyovszky felt he had to intervene and call a halt, "but, alas!, I preached to the deaf." Unable to control them, he elected to direct operations instead. "I entered seriously into my business." Indeed he did. Jointly with Pacheco's men, they took a huge number of prisoners (643, to be precise) and killed improbable numbers more: "The killed were reckoned and proved to be eleven hundred and fifty-six. Our expedition being thus ended, without any of our side having received the slightest wound, I went on shore."[5] And then for good measure, they burned the village of their attackers to the ground. For the second time.

On the day after this little episode, the friendly party of islanders pitched in with heart and soul, constructing huts for the ship's crew. Pacheco announced that "a prince of the country," by the name of Huapo, was coming on a visit, since he had heard of Benyovszky's admirable exploits. The purpose of the visit was evidently to sign up Benyovszky and his mighty warriors for a campaign against the Chinese. According to Pacheco, Prince Huapo could muster 20,000 to 25,000 armed men. No mean feat, when one considers the population of Formosa as a whole was unlikely to be much more than 75,000: modern experts suggest that the total population on the east coast of Formosa would have been around 6,000 to 10,000 at most.[6]

Pl. XV. Vol. 2

() An . Affair of Retaliation upon the Island Formosa.

Vol. II. page 37.

Published as the Act directs Nov. 1st 1789. by i. Robinson & Partners.

FIGURE 23.1 "An Affair of Retaliation upon Formosa" – a lithograph appearing in the 1790 edition of Benyovszky's *Memoirs*.

While they waited for the Prince, some serious numbers were being discussed between the Spaniard and the Hungarian. Pacheco

> insinuated that it would be easy to conclude a treaty with this prince, to form establishments in his country, the productions of which consisting in gold, crystal, cinnabar, rice, sugar, cinnamon, silk, and particularly the most beautiful kinds of wood, might form advantageous branches of commerce;

in exchange for which they would receive a quantity of hardware, iron, and European cloth, to the profit of two hundred per cent, to the sellers.[7]

Already, the solemn trade-agreement with the people of Usmay Ligon was a distant memory.

Then an army general turned up, who had come to prepare for Huapo's arrival. He was no mean figure himself, arriving with magnificent tent, red carpet, dressed in a "long red *pautalon*" (a "close garment fitted to the body, and all of one piece from head to toe"), half-boots, white shirt, black jacket and a red surplice with buttons made of coral set in gold: quite the well-dressed man. He served pots of tea and offered bags of tobacco. And other refreshments: "at intervals, he caused betel and the areca nut to be presented to me, with a small quantity of lime, all which together I chewed, and found most execrable."[8]

On the following day, they chewed more betel, smoked more tobacco, and chatted of manly things. Benyovszky offered a demonstration of his cannon. A native boat was smashed to smithereens. The general was greatly impressed. There followed an exhibition of marksmanship with the muskets, which "induced him to spare no flattering expressions."

On the next day again, the Prince himself arrived with a splendid train of horsemen and infantry. Inevitably, the Prince turned out to be a magnificent specimen of manhood, strong, vigorous, lively, majestic, wise, intelligent etc., and – just as importantly – short: about the same height as Benyovszky. In no time at all, Benyovszky's ego had been thoroughly massaged:

> the Prince addressed me by our interpreter, assuring me, that I was welcome on the island [...] To this he added, that he had no doubt but that I was the person whose coming was announced by the Prophets, who had foretold that a stranger should arrive with strong men, who should deliver the Formosans from the Chinese yoke: in consequence of which he had determined to pay me a visit, and make me an offer of all his power and forces to support and obey me.[9]

Several pages of Benyovszky's *Memoirs* are now devoted to the traditional exchange of gifts and compliments, displays of military prowess, feasts and ceremonies cementing mutual friendship. Huapo was anxious to recruit Benyovszky to his cause; the latter was anxious to set up a trading-colony. Benyovszky stated his intention of returning first to Europe. The Formosan wanted to know whether he could leave some men behind; whether he could come back with reinforcements and armed ships; whether Benyovszky would accept the province of "Havangsin," complete with cities, towns and inhabitants for a trading-colony; and finally whether he could count on him to come on a punitive expedition against a neighbouring prince. To which Benyovszky replied: no, sorry; yes, 1,000 men and several ships, but – oh! – it will be expensive; yes, if you insist; and, finally, yes, he would come along for the military adventure. This expedition turned out to have estimable aims: the neighbouring Prince Hapuasingo, who was an ally of the occupying Chinese, had upset Huapo by trying to interfere in his affairs of government. Huapo had refused to yield any ground and the Chinese had immediately taken possession of Huapo's "finest and most fertile provinces." The plan now was to go and give Hapuasingo a good thrashing. It would only take a couple of days. "And the roads were very good." Benyovszky and his men were up for it.

Just here, for no apparent reason whatsoever, Benyovszky announced that Stepanov was now to be welcomed back into the fold, as "an equal." The perceptive reader will suppose that Stepanov has been raised up once more so that Benyovszky can cast him down again later. And so it shall prove.

In no time at all, Benyovszky had arranged his men. At first they were not keen, having better things to dream about than fighting in a local war; but their leader talked them round: there would be no trading-colony on Formosa if they did not participate in this little bout of physical exercise. It seems that the men, too, had forgotten all about Usmay Ligon, because they caved in quickly. There would be three troops – one under the leadership of Kuznetsov and Bocharev, with thirteen men; a second under Benyovszky and Stepanov, with sixteen men; and a third, under Winbladh and Baturin, with thirteen men. Cannon and musket were gathered. A horse was provided for every man, and some extra ones to carry ammunition. Huapo's army already contained 260 horsemen. It seems that horses were not in short supply.[10]

On the first day of September, the bold army set off.

Or, then again, it might not have been the first day of September. Benyovszky's first editor, Nicholson, feels obliged to point out a tiny chronological anomaly here:

> Here is an inadvertence of the Count, with regard to time. Under the date of August the 31st, are included the adventures of three whole days, as appears by the succession of the hours. It seems probable, that during his stay on shore, he kept minutes of the principal events, and afterwards divided them into day's transactions by memory; and that the present date should be September the 3d; a supposition, which, by including the three following days in one, agrees very well with the Prince's assertion, that Hapuasingo's capital was distant only a journey of one day and a half.[11]

On closer examination, Benyovszky appears to have furnished August 30th with two daybreaks, and the 31st with no fewer than three. An inadvertence indeed: but perhaps not one quite as innocent as Nicholson would have us believe.

On the first of September – or thereabouts – the bold army set off. A forced march of a couple of days followed. They were well provisioned by the locals who came out from their villages leading oxen laden with rice, fruit, and "several casks of a kind of brandy." Another village was found abandoned, but its pond was well stocked with tasty fish. On the third day, they met up with Huapo. He was late. "I took the liberty to remonstrate with him for his slowness; which he excused, by representing, that his troops being loaded with provisions, could not march so quickly."[12] At last, on the fourth day of the month, they came across "ten or twelve thousand men," mostly infantry, encamped in front of their capital, Xiaguamay. Their first assault was repulsed, with two hundred of the enemy left for dead. Benyovszky pursued them for two hours, by which time the sluggish Prince had at last deigned to put in an appearance. Benyovszky took charge of the reinforcements, beat back the foe. Stepanov, in a fit of unaccustomed glory, captured the rival Prince Hapuasingo "with four of his women, with whom he was endeavouring to make his escape." The enemy caved in straight away, Benyovszky played the gentleman with his captive and they sat down to wait – again – for Huapo, who was now away galloping instead of doing helpful things on the field of battle.

On Monday 5th September, Benyovszky told Huapo that, since the war was now over, he was setting sail for China. Huapo was distraught, as anyone would be. Benyovszky was firm. But after Huapo had begged, he agreed to leave behind one of his trusted associates, to prepare for a return visit with a fleet of merchant ships. The man chosen was "young Loginov," the (supposed) brother of the Loginov who had been killed a few days earlier; Huapo declared that Loginov would be appointed his "General of Artillery." A generous parting gift was received:

> The next morning I received the Prince's presents, consisting of some fine pearls, eight quintals of silver, and twelve pounds of gold. He apologized for the smallness of the present, on account of his distance from home, and because my precipitate departure prevented his making it more considerable. But with regard to myself, he sent me a box, containing one hundred pieces of gold, weighing in the whole thirteen pounds and a quarter; and gave orders to Bamini to accompany us with one hundred and twenty horsemen, to provide for our subsistence, Don Hieronimo likewise attended me as interpreter; and I gave orders for our departure at four in the afternoon.[13]

Not bad for three days' (or more, or less) work.

They marched back to their ship. It took two full days. The local inhabitants feted them all the way. Huapo's lieutenant, Bamini, pressed a necklace of pearls, some twenty-five pounds in weight of gold, and a large tent into Benyovszky's hands, and said farewell. Another example of Benyovszky's admirable leadership qualities followed.

> Being desirous of giving my companions a mark of liberality, I distributed among them the whole of the silver and gold by weight and I put the pearls and the box of gold, which had been privately given me, into the hands of my intimate friends, the officers and women. When the associates were informed, that I had kept nothing for myself, they proposed each to give me a half share of their possessions; but I refused and begged them to preserve

the whole, and to reserve their generous disposition for some future occasion, if I should find it necessary to apply to them for assistance; in which case I should not scruple to have recourse to them for a loan.

This conduct on my part seemed to elevate their minds, and gave me a perfect empire over them. And at this moment I was convinced, that though a man of genius may avail himself of his superiority over common minds, yet, an act of generosity at a proper time, is worth a thousand speeches, however eloquent.[14]

Having properly said thank-you for this generosity, his close companions then tried to persuade their leader to "fix his residence" on Formosa. Benyovszky demurred, citing personal reasons: "I had a wife who loved and was attached to me by the bond of marriage, and who probably at that instant had a child, as she was pregnant at the time of my departure." While his friends wiped away their tears, he then outlined his master-plan; it was grandiose, and clearly intended more for readers in Europe, than colleagues in Formosa.

I did not fail to represent, that a person on the spot could do more than a thousand written messages; and that, therefore, upon my return to Europe, I might reasonably expect to obtain the favour of some court, as we could assure them the greatest advantages; such as that of forming an establishment in the Aleuthes islands, to carry on the rich commerce of furs; to open the trade of Japan; to form an establishment on the islands Lequeio; and lastly, to establish an European colony on the island of Formosa. I expressed my firm assurance, that these propositions would insure our happy success; and that in case the European courts should abandon us, we should always have it in our power to carry our project into execution, by the fitting out of private vessels.[15]

This all-encompassing plan dazzled his immediate audience, and they bustled off to talk the rest of the company round: which turned out to be quite simple, although most had previously expressed a desire to stay on. In recognition of their easy malleability, Benyovszky agreed that they could stay on for a few more days, recuperating.

The respite gives Benyovszky the opportunity to launch into eight pages of "some notions and details respecting the island of Formosa, and the plan for forming an European colony there." The description of the geography, ecology and society of the island is summary. Our summary of his summary will consist in his words: "It is one of the finest and richest islands of the known world." A bit like Tinian, or Liquor, or Usmay Ligon, but writ large. Benyovszky provides us with geographical details of the entire island – something he certainly could not have found out from his week on the east coast. Equally, he describes the social hierarchy and political structures which would have been quite unknown to him as he sat down wearily to write up his notes on Friday the 9th of September.

Clearly, Benyovszky had compiled his report on Formosa in much the same way as he had compiled his report on Kamchatka – in Europe, and largely from other sources. There is no evidence from anyone else that a war – even a very small one – was fought on Formosan soil by the exhausted crew of the *St Peter*. It is highly unlikely that he had the time to strike up any agreements with local chiefs for trade, colonisation or arms purchases. And even if he had gleaned his description from the reports of other travellers, his numbers and facts do not always stack up. A modern expert on Formosan history has this to say of Benyovszky:

> In matters of which he could know little, such as the actual density of population on his eastern coast and into the mountains, he made incorrect assumptions that led to nonsensical claims concerning numbers of troops and followers, prisoners and slaves that could not have been true. In these areas the accumulation of claims is more damning than any one problematic claim, from huge villages and commanding armies to horse-hair (rather than dog-hair, which would be more tenable) clothing.[16]

Notwithstanding these minor objections to veracity and likelihood, Benyovszky proceeds to set out his "maxims" and plans for establishing a colony on Formosa. Its basis would be military "animated by glory," and the number of "councils" reduced to the absolute minimum: "Luxury must be banished" – except for "external marks of grandeur"; "Industry must be encouraged," an enlightened form of slavery would be tolerated, "libertinism" punished severely. And so on. Making the assumption that these founding principles would prove acceptable to both the funding European power and the local "people of condition," Benyovszky then sets out his demands for the financing and running of the new colony. A hefty 1,200,000 *livres* worth of merchandise was to be supplied, along with three armed merchant ships – this was reckoned to provide the basis for an initial three-year period, during which time Benyovszky would also be able to recruit 400 men and "two hundred foundling children of both sexes" every year, to keep the population growing nicely. In return, "a certain sum of money" (amount neatly unspecified) would be sent back to the European investors, who would have an absolute monopoly of trade with Formosa. Benyovszky already had a rosy vision of his future:

> These stipulations being thus fixed, I would repair to Port Maurice, where, conformably to the treaty entered into with the Prince Huapo, I would disembark; and, after having established a military post, I would repair to the capital of the province which has been ceded to me.[17]

"Port Maurice," for those who have not been paying attention, was the bay where they were currently anchored, to be named hereinafter in honour of Maurice Benyovszky.

The crew had had some R&R and their beloved leader had established his role as a founding-father. And so the voyagers began to load their booty on to the ship on the 10th of September. On the 11th, they made ready to sail. And just then ... our friend Stepanov made another scene. He asked leave to go on shore again. Benyovszky, fearing that "the wickedness of his character" might undo all their good works and credit, put the proposition to the company. They immediately vetoed the idea. "[*The*] unhappy man, urged by despair and rage, attempted to throw himself overboard; and by his outrageous deportment, obliged me, at length, to order him into confinement."[18] The weekly task of locking up Stepanov complete, they then weighed anchor and sailed out to sea, "the vessel making no water."

The *St Peter* sailed northwards to round the top of Formosa: a curious decision since Anson, their only reliable guide to the seas, had made for the far closer southern tip. But no matter: the scenery they saw was remarkably similar to that described by Anson. They crossed to mainland China and then coasted down to Macao. This final stage of their lengthy voyage was not devoid of incident: no sooner had they rounded the north cape of Formosa than they spotted "a large vessel"; they prepared to chase it, "but finding she outsailed us, I gave up the attempt." On 14th September they headed south-westwards, "according to the report, all well." On the following day, they sighted the coast of China and soon fell in with several fishing boats from which they bought some fish.

> Two Chinese among these fishermen, spoke a little Portugueze; and were at last persuaded to pilot us into Macao. They demanded for this service one hundred piastres; but in the mean time, requested leave to go on shore for their cloaths; to which I consented, on condition, that one only should go on shore, while the other remained on board. This agreement being made, they conducted us to an anchoring place.[19]

On the 16th, the pilot returned, having kitted himself out more respectably, and proposed to conduct them first to a port named "Tanasao," assuring them that the local mandarin was a good man.

Benyovszky was agreeable to the pilot's suggestion and they duly arrived at Tanasoa, where the Mandarin – or someone claiming to be him – interrogated them. Writing down Benyovszky's answers "with a hair pencil," the Chinese gentleman observed, with considerable understatement, that "he was surprised to see Hungarians arrive in China." But all was well: provisions were sought and given, and a small present of sable skins handed over to their host. On the next day, a bigger deal was struck, the Mandarin purchasing 150 beavers and 300 sables for the sum of 6,800 *piastres*; following their leader's example, the crewmen sought out merchants and "sold every scrap of bear's skin which they could collect." With the ready cash, sadly, the men did what men do: "in the night several Chinese vessels anchored near us, and my companions went on board them. They assured me, that every boat had several cabins, which were filled with girls, who sold their favours." However, on the following day "my companions were incommoded by the quantity of fruit they eat on shore, and six of them were taken with illness."[20]

We noted earlier that Benyovszky had originally suggested a less-than-warm welcome at Tanasoa. In his account to the Governor of Mauritius he had stated:

> Having however avenged the death [*of the three men on Formosa*], the winds being always contrary, I was forced to steer towards the continent of China, coasting along the little islands called Piscatoria; at last all our fresh water being exhausted, we were forced to enter Tanasoa, arms in hand, to repulse the Chinese who would not suffer us to fill our casks.[21]

No mention then of trading, presents, fruit, or girls. No mention, for that matter, of a spectacular war on Formosa.

We have also debated the location of "Tanasoa." Ryumin calls it "Tasona," Stepanov "Tschinchina." We should just be satisfied that, for once, the three accounts more or less agree. This was almost certainly a town on Dongshan Island, Fujian Province. "Piscatoria" refers to the Pescadores (Penghu) Islands off the west coast of Formosa.

They sailed on southwards. On the 18th, "eighteen of our people were this day sick, which I attributed to the spirituous liquor they had drank." On the 19th, the number of sick had reduced to eight: hangovers were abating. As men crawled out of their beds, one woman crawled in to give birth – "one of the women who was attached to Mr. Csurin, was brought to bed." On the following morning, they passed the mouth of the Pearl River:

> we saw a fleet, at the head of which was a vessel of prodigious magnitude, almost entirely gilt, and hung round with numberless streamers. My pilots informed me that it was the Canton fleet, which carried the revenues to Pekin. We counted one hundred and eighty-six vessels.

They were almost at Macao: time for Stepanov to form a cabal and make a nuisance of himself.

> Tuesday, September the 20th. This day I was attacked by a violent fever, for which the pilots advised me to eat an orange, roasted in its juice, with sugar, and a good deal of ginger; they prepared this remedy for me, and it produced a strong perspiration, which dissipated my complaint. Messrs. Wynbladth, Baturin, Gurcsinin, and Kuzneczow, with twelve others, were affected in the same manner. At eight pm. Mr. Sibaew acquainted me, that Mr. Stephanow taking advantage of my indisposition, had formed a party. [...] I went out of my cabin, where I found Mr. Crustiew engaged in a quarrel with Stephanow. I gave orders to seize the latter; and after receiving the information, that this wretch had proposed to the company, to sign an act of

complaint against me, to be delivered to the Governor of Macao on our arrival, I ordered him to be put in irons. This day we had twenty-two sick.[22]

On Thursday, the 22nd day of September 1771, the ship dropped anchor in the harbour of Macao. They had been nineteen weeks at sea.

Notes

1 Benyovszky, 1790, Vol.II, pp.28–29.
2 *ibid*, p.30.
3 *ibid*, pp.33–34.
4 *ibid*, pp.34–35.
5 *ibid*, pp.36–37.
6 Inkster, 2010, p.34.
7 Benyovszky, 1790, Vol.II, p.39.
8 *ibid*, p.40.
9 *ibid*, p.43.
10 Professor Inkster begs to differ: "all the evidence is that horses of any sort remained very rare indeed on the east coast and in the mountains and forest areas." Inkster, 2010, p.35.
11 Benyovszky, 1790, Vol.II, p.53.
12 *ibid*, p.54.
13 *ibid*, p.58.
14 *ibid*, pp.59–60.
15 *ibid*, pp.60–61.
16 Inkster, 2010, pp.37–38.
17 Benyovszky, 1790, Vol.II, p.68.
18 *ibid*, p.70.
19 *ibid*, pp.71–72.
20 *ibid*, p.73.
21 Rochon, 1793, p.223.
22 Benyovszky, 1790, Vol.II, p.75.

XXIV

MACAO

"This Proposition, so Evidently Interested, Disgusted Me"

Politeness from the Governor – Sudden Deaths – Negotiations with the French –
Perfidious Albion – Uninteresting Dutchmen – Incorrigible Stepanov –
Winbladh Forgiven – Booking of Passages

On Thursday, the 22nd day of September 1771, the ship dropped anchor in the harbour of Macao. They had been nineteen weeks at sea.

Well, not exactly.

They had set off from Kamchatka on the 12th of May, according to the Russian or old-style calendar. They had arrived in Macao on the 11th of September (OS), or 22nd September (NS). The old-style date is the one given by Ryumin. It may also have been the one given by Stepanov. The new-style Gregorian date was that given by observers at Macao – Nathaniel Barlow and Bishop Le Bon. The ship had therefore been at sea for eleven days less than Benyovszky implies. All very innocent and understandable perhaps – except that Benyovszky manages to fill out all the extra days with danger and excitement; and even sneaked in some more by pumping five days' worth of derring-do into two days on Formosa. There are no dates missing in his scrupulous log.

They had been just over seventeen weeks at sea.

Well, not exactly.

One might be seduced into thinking that they had spent eleven (according to Ryumin) or twenty-five days (according to Stepanov) ashore on the Kurils. Stepanov's chronology may itself have been doctored by Ebeling who assures us that Stepanov was unreliable, if not mad.

Let us content ourselves with saying: they had been at sea quite a long time. For those who seek chronological comprehension, we have provided a cross-comparison of dates in Appendix II.

Not wishing to arrive quietly in Macao, Benyovszky fired off a twenty-four gun salute, and hastened ashore to meet the Portuguese Governor. "He received me with great politeness." There was not the slightest sign of a raised eyebrow after Benyovszky "had acquainted him with my misfortunes and my deliverance." Permission was given for the ship's complement to rent accommodation. Not everyone was so polite, however:

> several persons of the magistracy, who were present, expressed some suspicions of me; for which reason, to prevent debates, I thought proper to put my vessel as a deposit, in the hands of the Governor; reserving only for each of my companions, the necessary arms, such as guns, pistols, and swords, which I likewise deposited in the castle. After this convention, the Governor charged M. Hiss, a gentleman of French extraction, but settled at Macao for some years, to assist me in my affairs, and serve as interpreter.[1]

We noted earlier, from Nathaniel Barlow's account, that Benyovszky had been suspiciously secretive about anything connected with his supposed route from Kamchatka. Scepticism about Benyovszky was not easily dispelled.

But then a rather unfortunate event occurred – the deaths of a fifth of the ship's crew.

> At six pm. the guard having come on board, I caused all my people to go on shore. For the first day, my companions lodged in a public house, and the excess and avidity with which they devoured the bread and fresh provisions, which they were now supplied with, cost thirteen of them their lives. These died suddenly, and twenty-four others were seized with dangerous illness.[2]

Curiously, Benyovszky expended no energy in his *Memoirs* in lamenting the loss of so many lives. He expressed no great surprise that it should have happened. But if we are to believe his preceding accounts that the only sick people were those who had partaken of too much fruit or Chinese liquor or women in the previous week, and that everyone was well fed and rested after their holiday on Formosa, then these sudden deaths from overeating ought to have given him pause for reflection. Not a bit of it – there was accommodation to arrange, trading to be started, lobbying to be done, smart uniforms to design and commission. And there were financial worries, too – perhaps a little unanticipated for a man who had been hoovering up gold and jewels all the way down the coast of Japan and Formosa. Benyovszky describes these leadership concerns in some detail:

> September the 23d. M. Hiss having found two convenient houses, I hired them, and went to reside in them with my companions. This day I dined with the Governor [...] On my return home, I found all my people commodiously lodged, and an apartment compleatly fitted up for myself; the Governor having supplied the furniture out of his own house. [...] I gave

orders to clothe my companions uniformly, in red and white, as well as the officers; and the Portuguese ladies undertook to provide the apparel for our female fellow travellers. When the accounts were made up, these charges were estimated at eight thousand piastres, and the monthly expence for lodging and provisions, amounted to six thousand two hundred piastres.

On the 24th, [...] three more of my associates died, and their conversion was published throughout the town. In the evening, a Dominican priest, and friend of the Governor, named Zunitta, came to me, and offered every assistance in his power; and as I thought I might dispose of my furs by his assistance, I proposed the business to him, and he consented to take them. I therefore put into his hands four hundred and eighty dozen ermines; and he agreed to pay me for each beaver fifty piastres, for each sable six piastres, and for every dozen of ermines eight piastres; which produced the sum of twenty-eight thousand four hundred and forty piastres: the whole, and only remains of so considerable a fortune, as I had brought from Kamchatka! a scanty pittance, scarcely enough to pay the expences of putting into Macao.[3]

All readers can sympathise with Benyovszky: at 8,000 *piastres* of capital outlay on accommodation and uniforms, and 6,200 *piastres* per month living expenses, 28,440 *piastres* would only last about three months, without any thought of purchasing passage to Europe. Of course, in the heat of the moment, he had forgotten the 6,800 *piastres* he had been paid for furs in Tanasoa. And the value of the cargo (400,000 *livres*) he had filched from the Japanese tax-collectors at "Tacasima." And the considerable amount of money he and his crew had been given on Formosa. And he also forgot to mention the fact that the furs were mostly stolen property in any case, and not his to sell. But obviously his concern was that he was not going to reach Europe a rich man. A journey that had started out as an escape to liberty had turned into an accountancy nightmare.

Putting his disappointments behind him, Benyovszky gave orders for Stepanov to be released. Again. "The town" (persons unknown) gave the Hungarian baron a present of 1,000 *piastres* along with forty-two pieces of blue cloth, and twelve of black satin (purpose unknown). All that was requested in return was a copy of his journal for their archives. Benyovszky was no idiot, however: "I promised the deputies, that I would give them an historical extract, as I could not act so much to the prejudice of my own interests, as to deprive myself of the merit of my manuscripts."[4] He then went out to dine with the Bishop. Between them, they agreed that a French ship would return them to Europe.

And then:

On the 25th, Miss Aphanasia paid the debt of nature. Her premature death affected me greatly, and more especially as it deprived me of the satisfaction of repaying her attachment, by her marriage with the young Popow, son of the Archimandrite, to whom I had given the surname of my family. This day I dispatched Mr. Crustiew with letters to the Directors of the French

> Company, containing my reclamation of the protection of the colours of his Most Christian Majesty. He returned on the 29th, and brought me a very favourable answer, and the assurance of my passage, which news was very acceptable to me.[5]

An astonishing little passage this: two brief sentences to announce to the reader the death of a young girl who had been the focus of so much sentimentality and intrigue barely four months earlier, followed – without even a pause for breath – by an account of his most satisfactory negotiations with the French. It is perhaps the closest that Benyovszky came to admitting that Miss Afanasia never actually existed.

Enough of sentimentality: enter Perfidious Albion!

> October the 3d, 1771. A certain Mr. Gohr, Captain in the service of the English Company came to see me, and made me offer of services on the part of the Directors, and a free passage to Europe, provided I would bind myself to entrust my manuscripts to the Company, and engage to enter into their service, and make no communication of the discoveries I had made: this proposition, so evidently interested, disgusted me; but I was contented to answer, that I was very sensible of the obliging offer he had made; but that, as I had accepted those of the French Directors, it was not in my power to change my determination: that with respect to my entering into the service of the Company, it did not appear to me to be so easy; because it was not only necessary that I should be assured of a superior station, but that in the mean time all my people should be provided for; and that our common lot, and the execution of several projects should be secured. My answer surprized Mr Gohr, who took his leave in an affected manner: the moment after his departure, I learned that Mr Stephanow had accompanied him; and from thence I inferred, that I should still find new causes of discontent on his part, which accordingly happened, as will appear in the sequel.

For all Benyovszky's outrage, Mr Gore's approach on behalf of the British East India Company could not have been unexpected. Nor can that, on the following day, of a Dutchman:

> On the 4th of October, I received a letter from Mr. L'Heureux, Director for the Dutch Company. He sent me a present of cloth, wine, beer, brandy, salt provisions, and two thousand *piastres*. His letter and presents were accompanied with the offer of a passage for me to Batavia, and the assurance that I should be received into the Company's service.

Benyovszky expressed less disgust and cheerfully remarked that, "as he made the same proposal as the English, I refused the acceptance of his presents, except the liquors."[6]

But the dastardly British were not so easily put off:

> On the 6th, Mr. Jackson, an English merchant established at Macao, arrived with Mr. Beyz: they renewed the propositions made by Mr. Gohr, and shewed me full powers, signed by the English Council at Canton, to regulate the conditions of my engagement, and to offer a present of fifteen thousand guineas.

Benyovszky thereupon upped the stakes by stating his conditions:

> The first *sine qua non* was, that the Company, in consideration of my consigning my manuscripts, and entering into their service, should grant me a pension of four thousand pounds sterling, reversible to my children; and that they should settle on each officer a pension of one hundred pounds, and each associate thirty pounds; and that they should give me every assistance in forming establishments beyond China. On this first condition the Plenipotentiaries acknowledged, that they had not sufficient authority to conclude with me, and retired, after begging that I would well consider their offers.[7]

Benyovszky did not feel called upon to express any disgust whatsoever on this occasion – doubtless he was just a little disappointed that the envoys did not have full authority to agree to his conditions.

But trouble was brewing.

> This evening the Governor informed me, that the four English gentlemen had been with him, and that he thought several of my associates were gained by the English. In fact, these gentlemen, piqued at their want of success, raised embarrassments among my people, in which Mr. Stephanow was of wonderful service to them.

And so it came to pass. Stepanov was on the brink of another episode.

On the 12th October, M. de Robien, the representative of the French Company at Canton, announced that there were two ships prepared to take them all to France. But on the very same day, Kuznetsov advised Benyovszky that Stepanov had secretly agreed to deliver all of the ship's papers and journals to the British, for the sum of 5,000 pounds sterling. Benyovszky immediately emptied his chest and gave all his papers into the safe-keeping of Bishop Le Bon. Next, he summoned all the survivors of his company and wondered aloud how they could be discontented, since he had shared with them all the booty from the Formosan War. Almost before he had finished, Stepanov "loaded me with invectives" and accused Benyovszky of concealing from the company even greater treasures than those distributed on Formosa.

He then excited the companions to throw off my authority, by assuring them that he would secure them a large fortune the instant they should determine to put my papers in his hands, and follow his party. The infamous plot of this wretch was nothing extraordinary; but when I understood that he was supported by Mr. Wynbladth, my ancient Major, the companion of my exile, and my friend, I was incapable of setting bounds to my indignation, and could not avoid declaring, that their proceedings were highly disgraceful; and to confound them, I displayed their secret projects to the company, and justified my words by shewing Mr. Jackson's letter, which convinced them that Messrs. Stephanow and Wynbladth, under pretence of serving the company, were desirous of securing the five thousand pounds to their own use. They were highly irritated, and threatened them; but Stephanow preserved a party of eleven, with whom he went to my lodgings; and while I remained in conversation with my friends, he seized my box, in which he supposed my papers were deposited. As soon as I heard of this outrage, I went to his chamber, followed by twenty associates; and as he refused to open the door, I broke it down. On my entrance he fired a pistol at me, which missed. In consequence of this attempt, I gave orders for seizing and keeping him in strict confinement; and as it was necessary likewise to secure Mr. Wynbladth, I went to his chamber; but he had retired into the garden, armed with a pair of pistols and a sabre. I determined to shut him in, being convinced that he could not get over the walls on account of their great height. This whole affair passed without the least alarm without, as the doors of the house were shut.[8]

Intriguingly, this episode dovetails quite nicely with Ryumin's deposition on the crisis in Macao: so it may even be true. It is probably well that these stimulating scenes took place behind closed doors; the Chinese authorities in Macao were not noted for their tolerance of misbehaviour on the part of their trading-partners – and would have taken a dim view of some vagabonds who had just turned up on a scruffy little ship.

Within twenty-four hours, Winbladh, abandoned and dripping in the garden under heavy rain, requested forgiveness. Not wishing to risk any more danger and excitement, Benyovszky had him locked up in the "Governor's Castle" alongside Stepanov. And then, exhausted, the commander fell ill. From 22nd October until the 18th November, he lay in a fever in the Governor's quarters. While he was there, seven more of the voyagers died. He provides a list of all "those who died at Macao"; it is headed up, naturally, by Miss Afanasia du Nilov. For those interested, his full list can be found at the end of Appendix I. "The great number of deaths in so short a time, gave me a very unfavourable opinion of the climate of China."[9] And it was not just the Grim Reaper who had taken advantage of his illness: the scheming British had not been idle either. Disgruntled at his refusal to do business, they had reported Benyovszky to the Chinese authorities in Canton, claiming that he was a pirate and a deserter from the Russian Empire; for their part, the Chinese authorities demanded either that Benyovszky be surrendered into their hands, or that he leave port immediately. Some letters were sent back and forth, an "imperial officer" turned up in a magnificent boat to suggest that "he was informed of the falsity of the insinuations against me, and hoped to convince me of the justice, which the Chinese knew how to render to heroes like me." And in the end the whole affair petered out.

The falling-out between Benyovszky, Winbladh and Stepanov is presented in the *Memoirs* as the result of Stepanov's usual machinations. We will recall two different views of this unpleasantness. Ryumin, in his final report, suggested that Benyovszky himself had provoked an incident by insisting that the voyagers all reject their Russian faith, revealing that all his previous remarks about the Grand-Duke Paul were just nonsense, before announcing that he was going over to the French; which was not quite what the voyagers had been expecting. To compound this, there was an allegation of Benyovszky's rape of "the Kamchatkan serving-girl of Churin's." It is a difficult accusation to substantiate. The people who told that story were interested in painting as black a picture as possible of the Hungarian. Major Winbladh − we must imagine him to be a bluff sort of character, honest, unassuming, and downright trustworthy − remonstrated with his old comrade-in-arms, on both the financial and the criminal matter; but to little avail. Benyovszky was more skilled in the art of back-stabbing and plotting than his adversary. The result was that both Winbladh and Stepanov ended up in the custody of the Portuguese Governor, leaving the field clear for Benyovszky to exert pressure on his crew for the return of his precious log-book.

Having thus rendered all dissenters harmless, the glorious leader was able to concentrate on the primary tasks of selling off all that he could, and making ready for the final leg of his escape to Europe. Just then, lest we forget about him, "my Japanese traveller" popped up again, having been ill since their arrival in Macao. "His recovery was very agreeable to me, as his person interested me strongly."[10] Not so strongly, however, that he was ever mentioned again; nor is there any indication that the unfortunate young man travelled with them to Europe. He was either abandoned to his fate in Macao, or he never existed at all.

On the 10th December, all the survivors from Benyovszky's company were assembled and told to prepare to return to Europe. "They consented, and submitted entirely to my orders." They did not have much choice. Next, Winbladh was forgiven and released from confinement;

> but as I could not place the same confidence in Mr. Stephanow, I paid him four thousand *piastres*, with leave to go where he pleased. He immediately took part with the Hollanders, whose director, M. L'Heureux, expecting to derive some information from him concerning our voyage, received him, and sent him to Batavia.[11]

An expensive ticket, but one Benyovszky was entirely happy to pay for. Money was suddenly no object.

Notes

1 Benyovszky, 1790, Vol.II, pp.76–77.

2 *ibid*, pp.76–77.

3 *ibid*, pp.77–78. The priest "Zunitta" may be the same as the priest "Surida" who later advised the governor of Mauritius about "a child dressed as a priest."

4 *ibid*, p.78.

5 *ibid*, p.79.

6 *ibid*, pp.79–80.

7 *ibid*, p.80.

8 *ibid*, pp.81–83.

9 *ibid*, p.84.

10 *ibid*, p.86.

11 *ibid*, p.87.

XXV

MAURITIUS

"I Could Not Believe That He Had Discovered such Agreeable Countries"

Of Gloves, Hats and Needles – Financial Problems – Taking Ship to Mauritius –
A French Charlatan – The French King is Interested – An Uncle, a Spouse, a Son

Money: very confusing in the eighteenth century. In 1773, Wyndham Beawes Esq., "His Britannick Majesty's Consul at Seville," published the sixth edition of his book on foreign trade. Its title alone was worth the cover-price:

> *LEX MERCATORIA REDIVIVA: or, the Merchant's Directory. Being a Complete Guide to all Men in Business, whether as Traders, Remitters, Owners, Freighters, Captains, Insurers, Brokers, Factors, Supercargoes, or Agents. Containing an Account of our trading Companies and Colonies, with their Establishments, and an Abstract of their Charters; the Duty of Consuls, and the Laws subsisting about Aliens, Naturalization and Denization. To which is added, a State of the present general Traffick of the whole World; describing the Manufactures and Products of each particular Nation: and Tables are given of the Correspondence and Agreement of the European Coins, Weights, and Measures, with the Addition of all others that are known. Extracted from the Works of the best Writers both at Home and Abroad; more especially from those justly celebrated ones of Messieurs Savary; improved and corrected by the Author's own Observations, during his long Continuance in Trade. The whole calculated for the Use and Service of the Merchant, Lawyer, Senator, and Gentleman.*

In sheer scope, it is unlikely that anyone could produce a similar volume today. Which is our loss.

Beawes' mighty work covered every aspect of foreign trade that a gentleman might encounter, from captains to supercargoes, from ballast to wrecks, lighthouses to pirates, quarantine to war and peace. There is a section on "Arbitrators,

Arbitrament, Arbitration Bonds, and Awards," and another "Of Usury." Of particular interest are his sections on "The Par of Monies" (exchange-rates) and equivalences of weights, measures ("The Correspondency of the Length of a Foot in divers Places") and coins ("both Real and Imaginary" – ten pages of them).

Of trade with Russia, there is not much said, and nothing whatsoever about the exchange-rate of the Russian rouble. However, in the several pages dedicated to "commerce with Muscovy," a most impressive list of imports into Russia is provided, "by an ingenious gentleman, whose Remarks may be depended on." Here, amongst itemised alcohol, cloth, metals and oil imports, we find the fact that Russia imported "Gloves, Men's and Women's, 2632 dozen," "Hats, 310 dozen," "Needles, 16,500,006" (either the Russian clerks were most pernickety, or the stray 6 is a printer's error). All imports came to a total value of 3,300,923 roubles.

From the lengthy sections on coins and exchange-rates, two things stand out very clearly indeed: that there was no standardisation and that there was no currency control. Any one place on the planet could have several different trading currencies. In the age before nation-states were in vogue, any one tract of land could have completely different domestic currencies. This was the case even in Spain and France. The world, when it traded, used Dutch or Spanish equivalents. But what you got for your money was perfectly random. Mr Beawes notes quite placidly that Spain "exchanges with London, a Dollar or Piece of Eight, for an uncertain Number of Pence." This remark is then followed by a passage of especial delight describing Spain's other rates of exchange:

> With *Brabant, Flanders, Holland, Zealand* and *Hamburgh* [*it exchanges*] its Ducat of 357 Maravedies, for a Number of Groots; with *France* for so many Maravedies against the French Crown, or the Pistole for so many Livres &c, with *Portugal*, the Ducats for Crusades, or a Pistole for a Number of Reas; with *Novi*, an uncertain Number of Maravedies for the Crown Mark; with *Venice* the same, for a Ducat Banco; with *Florence*, ditto for the Ducat of 7½ Livres; with *Leghorn* the same for the Dollar; with *Milan* the same for the Ducat of 115 Soldi; with *Naples* the same for the Ducat of 10 Carlins; and ditto with *Palermo* and *Messina* for the Florin of 6 Tarins.[1]

Mr Beawes does spend some time explaining how much in gold or silver the main European currencies might be worth. And gets himself into such a tangle with fractions, that he is obliged to mop his brow and follow it up with several pages dedicated to "Problems," such as a despairing school-pupil might have faced not so many years ago.

> We have found in $210\frac{866}{1663}$ *English* Crowns of 5 Shillings Sterling, as much pure Silver as in $213\frac{99}{326}$ *French* Crowns of 6 Livres; or 1 Crown of 6 Livres has as much fine Silver as $\frac{22432024}{22728249}$ of an English one of 5 Shillings, but the working of this with so great a Fraction being very troublesome, it may be changed for a less Fraction that shall be almost of the same Value.[2]

Thus, when we are faced with a world of real and imaginary currencies, where exchange-rates were largely undocumented, it is hard to put a value on any one transaction. Some cursory research would reveal that, at the end of the eighteenth century, a French Crown (or six *livres*) was worth around five British shillings, and that a Spanish dollar was worth 4 shillings and sixpence in British money; further, that a Russian rouble was worth around two French *livres*, and slightly more than four British shillings. It is also possible to find the equivalent value of the main currencies in gold – the French *Louis d'Or* was worth ¼ ounce (Troy) of gold; in pounds sterling, the same amount of gold was worth a guinea (1 pound and one shilling). But that does not help us much with the *piastre* or *livre* in China.

Equally problematic is any attempt to compare the value of money in 1771 with the value of money in the twenty-first century. As a very, very rough guide, one British pound of 1775 would have been worth around £19 sterling in 1975 and (perhaps surprisingly) around £130 sterling in 2011. But what does that tell us? Living conditions have changed beyond recognition, diets have been transformed and the quantity and quality of material possessions are beyond recognition. The ordinary British people of 1775 were certainly far poorer than those of today, but not necessarily by a factor of 130.[3]

All of which renders a little pointless any deep analysis of Benyovszky's financial position in Macao. If, in Tanasoa, he sold furs to the value of 6,900 *piastres*, then that might have yielded £153 in British money. But he was in China, so the exchange-rate was entirely irrelevant. If, as he reports in his *Memoirs*, he sold the brave ship *St Peter* to a Portuguese merchant for the princely sum of 4,500 *piastres*, then that was only about £100. It may have been all that it was worth: built of fir, leaking, battered and – worst of all – stolen, it was unlikely he was going to get a better price for it. Stepanov noted that the ship had been sold for 3,960 Guilders. Sir, that is just plain confusing! One supposes that he got that figure from his Dutch friends, while sailing to Batavia. However, since the Dutch Guilder was worth around 1¼ *livres* (at a notional exchange-rate only) his figure may not be far out.

The cost of shipping Stepanov off with the Dutch was put by Benyovszky at 4,000 *piastres*, while the sum of 115,000 *livres* was required for the passage of the remaining forty-eight to Europe. This was perhaps equivalent to 21,300 *piastres* – all else being equal, an economy-class ticket. On top of that, Benyovszky was outraged to find, on 1st January 1772, that he was required to shell out a further 450 *piastres* to hire three sampans to take him and his group down the river to board their French ships.

We have to accept some of what Benyovszky tells us about how much money he received, and how much he spent. He declares a total income of around 42,000 *piastres* and total outgoings of 52,450 *piastres*: all in all, not a discrepancy which would have pleased Mr Micawber. We will recall that he also claimed to have captured the cargo of a Japanese merchant ship, which had a value of around 55,000 to 75,000 *piastres*, but ruined his accounts by never mentioning the haul again, let alone selling it. In June, he had had sanguine hopes of selling all his furs in China for "near a million *piastres*," a figure increased randomly to "a million and a half," and then dramatically revised downwards to 25,000 in August. In the end, he claims to have sold furs to the value of 35,200 *piastres*.

But in the final analysis, he spent what he could and no more. The tickets home emptied his purse, which put him in a really bad mood. In the second week of January he reports, "I was employed in liquidating my accounts; and after having settled every thing, I found myself totally destitute."[4]

With the ship sold and Stepanov neatly shipped to distant shores, all the adventurers had to do was wait for the French ships. On the 14th of January, the company boarded their expensive hired sampans and arrived at the mouth of the Tigu River – the Bocca Tigris strait which guards the entrance to the Canton anchorage at Whampoa – where they sat on their hands for a full week before the two promised French ships arrived. The group split evenly between the *Dauphin* and the *Laverdy* and set sail, arriving at Mauritius on the 16th March. Benyovszky was quite exhausted by then, particularly since the French pestered him for seven full weeks with questions "respecting my discoveries during my former voyage." Luckily, the Governor of Mauritius gave him a very warm welcome, sending out a boat to bring him ashore, putting him up in his own house, and taking him on official trips round the island.

Not long afterwards, the French explorer Yves-Joseph de Kerguelen turned up, on his way home from a voyage of exploration across the Southern Hemisphere. Benyovszky was unimpressed:

> The arrival of Lieutenant Kreguelin [*sic*] was a great relief to me. For this navigator having returned from a voyage to the Southern lands, gave employment to all the politicians and idle talkers of the island; who before his appearance, had no other object but myself. I became acquainted with this officer; but from what I had myself seen in the North, I could not believe that he had discovered such agreeable countries, as he asserted to exist on his Southern continent.[5]

This criticism seems a little rich, coming from a man who had just invented several candidates for Paradise on Earth. But, as it transpired, Benyovszky was entirely justified: the noble and adventurous Kerguelen had sailed across the Southern Indian Ocean and had spotted a distant island through a triple curtain of snow, hail and fog. On closer examination, it turned out to be a large land-mass, which he assumed was the fabled southern continent. He named it 'France Australe,' landed to claim it for France, promptly lost sight of his companion-ship, and sailed for home. (His fellow-captain, after realising that he in turn had lost Kerguelen, headed eastwards and claimed Western Australia for the French in March 1772; he then limped on to Timor and Batavia, and then back to Mauritius where he and many of his crew expired, victims of scurvy and typhoid.) Back in France, meanwhile, amidst a little controversy which echoed the doubts faced by Benyovszky in

Macao, Kerguelen had persuaded his Royal sponsors that he had discovered a land of plenty.

Kerguelen was a man who seemed to specialise in locating desolate and not very useful islands – an earlier voyage saw him mapping the location of Rockall in the North Atlantic. On his return voyage to the Southern Ocean in 1773, he was a little disappointed to realise that he had discovered only the Desolation Islands, an archipelago of gale-swept, rain-sodden, cold and barren islands named thereafter the Kerguelen Islands – but, on the plus side, still a French possession today. His return to France in 1774 was less triumphant than in 1772: he was court-martialled on a number of counts (including that of smuggling aboard his 14-year old mistress) and sent to prison for four years.

Kerguelen was found out. Benyovszky was not. It makes all the difference.

According to Benyovszky's chronicle, the French ships continued their journey from Mauritius on 4th April. According to Ryumin, it was the 24th March. The discrepancy is that between the old-style and new-style calendars. Ryumin was happy to stick to the best and true Russian calendar, Benyovszky had reverted to decadent European habits. On the 12th April, they stopped briefly at Madagascar, where Benyovszky stepped ashore for two days and gave it the benefit of his colonialist's eye. The rest of his journal is remarkably skimpy – only three short sentences after leaving Madagascar, they had arrived in France, on 18th July 1772 (all dates NS, hereinafter). At Port Louis he started writing letters to Paris, and on 2nd August, received an invitation from the Duc d'Aiguillon who invited him to pay a visit. This was no less a person than the French Minister for Foreign Affairs. All went well – his stories about Formosa began to pay off.

> On the 8th of August, I arrived in Champagne, where the Minister then was, who received me with cordiality and distinction, and proposed to me to enter into the service of his master, with the offer of a regiment of infantry; which I accepted, on condition that his Majesty would be pleased to employ me in forming establishments beyond the Cape. [...] In the course of the month of December, the Duke d'Aiguillon proposed to me from his Majesty, to form an establishment on the island of Madagascar, upon the same footing as I had proposed upon the island Formosa; and I at last complied with the desire of this Minister, to whom I shall be ever bound in gratitude, as well as personal esteem and attachment.[6]

And there was also something of a bitter-sweet family reunion.

> In France, likewise, I had the happiness to find my uncle, the Count de Benyow, Commandant of the castle and town of Bar, Commander of the Royal Order of St. Lazare, and Chevalier de St. Louis. The assistance of this worthy relation, and the benevolence of his Majesty, put me in a condition to send an express into Hungary, to enquire after my spouse and child. She

arrived at the end of the year; but she had the misfortune to see her son expire, at the instant of the arrival of my courier. An event which was the more affecting, as I was then in a situation to provide for him very advantageously in France.

This was the son (Samuel) whom Benyovszky had never seen. He mourned him with much the same words as he had mourned "Miss Aphanasia du Nilov." The nobility of the uncle, we must remind ourselves, was fictitious.

Between September 1772 and March 1773, Benyovszky negotiated with the French government, on the explicit instruction of Louis XV, "to make a considerable enterprise on the island of Madagascar." It is clear that some of the stories which later appeared in the *Memoirs* were now going the rounds of ministerial buildings in France. With military and diplomatic backup, Benyovszky expected to achieve or surpass in Madagascar all that he had achieved in Japan and Formosa on his own.

The project could not possibly fail.

Notes

1   Beawes, 1773, p.761.
2   *ibid*, p.388.
3   House of Commons, 2012.
4   Benyovszky, 1790, Vol.II, p.88.
5   *ibid*, pp.89–90.
6   *ibid*, p.91.

XXVI

MADAGASCAR – THE PROJECT

Good War Against Bad White Man

Madagascar: The Hope of all Frenchmen – The Benyovszky Volunteers –
Mauritius Proves Unhelpful – Of Kerguelen and Cabbages – Of Trade and
Commerce – Of Health and Death – Of Blameworthy Colleagues –
Of Diplomacy and War – King of Madagascar

Benyovszky presents the contract with the French government as if they had been head-hunting him to lead an expedition to that island of riches. In reality, the final agreement between the two parties was the result of sheer hard graft on Benyovszky's part, aided by more than a dash of starry-eyed ignorance on the part of the French Foreign Minister.

The case for doing something about Madagascar was, for the French, quite compelling. They had been eyeing up this vast island for some time, since it had untapped riches which – if nothing else – would make it a splendid staging-post for ships travelling between France and the Far East. In 1732, the French East India Company had succeeded in establishing a couple of trading-posts on the east coast of the island, and these were visited regularly by ships sent from Mauritius. But the Madagascans were not entirely compliant – some years they would do business, other years they would attack the traders. In 1739, for example, in an event echoing that which befell the *St Peter* in Formosa, two dozen Frenchmen were killed when they landed for fresh water. Despite all their best efforts, the French proved incapable of gaining more than a toehold upon the island. When the French East India Company's fortunes vanished in a puff of smoke at the end of the Seven Years' War in 1763, control of trade in Mauritius and Madagascar was handed back to the French Crown. The government then renewed attempts to bring the natives round to a more modern way of thinking. Fundamental to the modern way of thinking was the slave-trade.

In 1768, a man with clear ambitions stepped up to the mark. This was the Count de Modave, a soldier with several years of valuable experience in oppressing refractory natives in the hot climes of India. Having paid a brief visit to Madagascar on his way home, he persuaded the Minister in Paris to send him back with troops, workers and money, to sort things out once and for all. His plans sounded very similar to those of Benyovszky a few years later. "The success of this project," he argued blithely,

> will recover all of our losses in Asia and America, and at the same time guarantee our trade with the Indies and put us in a position one day to take the most terrible and complete revenge on our enemies.[1]

The island, it seemed, contained mines just bursting with iron and gold, innumerable herds of cattle roamed the plains, the harvests were bountiful and the islanders themselves would provide an endless reserve of deep-sea sailors. In September 1768, Modave disembarked at the trading-post of Fort Dauphin (present-day Tolanaro) at the southern end of the island, and proceeded to rent some land from the local chiefs. And then, in the heat and humidity, it all went downhill really fast. Disease had claimed the lives of 21 of his 130 men by the end of the first year, the number of cattle purchased was negligible, and his appeals for more men, weaponry and funds went unheeded. After only thirteen months, the little colony was evacuated again. In the following years, Paris pondered the experience, attributing the failure sometimes to the man, sometimes to the location, sometimes to the ambitious scale of the project.

And there things were left until Maurice Benyovszky turned up.

Benyovszky's *Memoir Concerning the Expedition to Madagascar*, which forms a significant part of the Nicholson edition of 1790, begins with the following bold and accusatory words:

> As the success of every remote enterprize which is intended to form an establishment of Europeans, is dependant always on precise orders and instructions, as well as preparations and well-founded operations, made in consequence of a knowledge of the country, and proportioned to the advantages which are proposed to be obtained, I think it necessary to give an account of the circumstances which preceded my arrival on this island. Circumstances which prove, that notwithstanding the very scanty means which have been afforded me, I have succeeded in forming treaties of friendship and alliance with the greater part of the inhabitants of this extensive island; and, consequently, that if I had not been, as I may say, totally abandoned by the Minister, which was the source of the miseries, diseases, and mortality, to which myself and my people were exposed; the island of Madagascar, at this day in alliance with France, would have formed a power, capable of supporting her colonies of the isles of France and Bourbon, and defending her establishments in India, as well as securing new branches of commerce to that kingdom, which would have carried immense sums into the royal treasury.[2]

We shall not fill the following pages with Benyovszky's account of the preparatory negotiations with the French Foreign Minister Duc d'Aiguillon and his colleague the Count de Boynes, Secretary of State for the Navy. Those anxious for such excitement are encouraged to consult Benyovszky for themselves. Suffice it to say that Benyovszky tempered the unrealistic expectations of the government with some hard-nosed proposals of his own (a "Plan" enshrined in seven succinct "Articles"); and that, from the very start, Benyovszky had serious doubts as to whether the plan could possibly succeed. This part of his *Memoirs*, of course, was written some years after his stint on Madagascar.

By December of 1772 an agreement had been reached. A company of around 240 "Benyovszky Volunteers" would be established, whose task it would be to sail to Madagascar and by means of "good example and the power of religion" bring the islanders to their senses. The Minister had by now been thoroughly convinced of Benyovszky's suitability for overseeing such a strategy: had he not done so in Usmay Ligon and Formosa? Pay-rates were carefully worked out (the Commandant was to receive 22 *livres* per day – 8,000 per annum – increased by ministerial decree to 12,000 in April 1773). More importantly, designs for uniforms and flags were also agreed on. Three months later, fully funded and elegantly clad, Benyovszky returned to Lorient to make the long journey southwards.

His company of volunteers sailed in three ships: one group left in advance on board *L'Etoile*. We are not advised just who these bright-eyed volunteers were, but no doubt they were of an adventurous disposition – a later report described them as "boys, blackguards and shoe-blacks." Benyovszky – along with his wife and his wife's sister "Mlle. Henska" – sailed on 22nd April on board the *Marquise de Marboeuf*, and a third group followed some weeks later on the *Laverdy*. Amongst the company was the Swedish doctor, Magnus Meyder, who had escaped from Kamchatka along with everyone else. There is no word of how he later fared, but one would suppose that, at the age of 79, he did not last long in the conditions the company were to meet in Madagascar. There is also a suggestion that bluff old Major Winbladh had been signed up, but that, due to illness, he never set off southwards. He retired to Sweden instead. A sensible man.

The voyage was perfectly run-of-the-mill. Scurvy ravaged crew and passengers, and one of Benyovszky's lieutenants was dead before they even reached the southern tip of Africa. They ran out of food, and had to put in to False Bay for several days. Finally, they limped into port at Mauritius on 21st September.

On the five months of the voyage, Benyovszky did not remain idle. He divided his time between training his troops, and drawing up grandiose plans for the conquest of Madagascar (by means of intelligent alliances, not selling arms to the natives, and the construction of impregnable forts), and for the expansion of trade (coffee, cotton, sugar, pepper, slaves…) and industry (shipbuilding, mining, distilleries, tanneries…). And, we must suppose, getting to know Mme Benyovszky again after a long separation – a new son briefly pops into the narrative a short time later.

No sooner had the Company of Benyovszky Volunteers arrived in Île de France (Mauritius) than the whole scheme began to unravel. The Minister in France had not thought to inform the Governor's office on Mauritius of his agreement with Benyovszky. Worse, he had completely fudged the issues of how Benyovszky would be provisioned during the first period of colonisation, how he would communicate with Paris, and whether or not Mauritius would have any control at all over the Madagascar colony. Worst of all, no one in Paris appears to have considered that a trading-colony on Madagascar would be in direct competition with the traders based on Mauritius. The new Governor of Mauritius, M de Ternay, had taken over from Dresnay in August 1772; unlike his predecessor, he was not a great admirer of Benyovszky, and remained entirely impervious to the Hungarian's winning ways. Ternay and his lieutenant, Maillart, immediately started to write furious letters back to Paris, seeking clarification on Benyovszky's project and position, demanding to know whether the adventurer's daily requests for stores, men and weapons had any justification, and bitterly protesting against the way in which this bunch of would-be colonists had been dumped on them unannounced.

Maillart himself became so fed up with Benyovszky within a few weeks that, in a letter sent to Boynes on 27th December 1773, he had this to say:

> I would guarantee to you today that, even if one could find the only man capable of making an extraordinary project succeed, that man would fail miserably in the one which M. Benyovszky has dreamed up. I do not draw back from telling you that, not only will this officer do nothing useful for the service, but that he will do it at the cost of many men and the King's gold. He has set no limits on his ambitions except those of his desires – and his desires have no limits. I would add that he will end up destroying all that remains of a peaceful relationship with those people amongst whom he is going to establish himself, and he will end up closing, perhaps forever, all those doors through which we might succeed in establishing a solid presence in Madagascar.[3]

He may have had a point. But he also had his own interests to defend, after all.

By happy coincidence, another person passing through Mauritius at this time was the explorer Kerguelen. He had arrived there from France on 29th August, on his second voyage to discover France Australe (no more successful than the first, it turned out). He, too, had cause to complain of both Ternay and Maillart, whose only interest in his voyage was in charging him exorbitant sums for repairs and stores, and off-loading the worst of their unemployed sailors on to him. When he left Mauritius again two months later, optimistically gazing eastwards, Kerguelen described both of them as "my enemies." While in port he was witness to some of Benyovszky's specific troubles.

Notwithstanding all this unpleasantness, Benyovszky proceeded to execute the original plan. In November, he sent thirty of his company across to occupy the small island of Maroce in the Bay of Antongil, in the north-east of Madagascar. In

December, the final 100 members of his company turned up from France. Paying little heed to those who advised him not to move his remaining men until the worst of the wet season was over in late March, Benyovszky took all his men over to Antongil where they arrived mid-February.

We have the unaccustomed luxury of having more than one account of Benyovszky's activities. We have, in fact, four reports of his residence on Madagascar. Firstly, we have Benyovszky's racy account, as reproduced in his *Memoirs*. We have also, from the pen of the same man, a collection of reports sent back to Paris, and carefully unearthed for us by the French historian Prosper Cultru. We have letters sent back to Paris by Maillart – he was never going to give up. And we have the reports of two government inspectors who were sent out from France in the summer of 1776, Paris having finally been poked into a state of alarm by some of the things they were hearing. It will come as no surprise to learn that these accounts tell different tales. Even Benyovszky's *Memoirs* and his letters tell two different tales.

But let us begin with Benyovszky himself.

> As soon as [*we*] had come to anchor, I sent the small boat on shore, to bring the earliest news of the situation of my detachment, and the disposition of the islanders. The shore was lined with chiefs, who expressed the greatest satisfaction at seeing me; a circumstance which gave me no small pleasure.[4]

A good start? Not at all.

> But these agreeable ideas were much diminished, upon entering the palisade which enclosed my men, and which, for want of effects to pay the blacks, they had been obliged to construct themselves. This hard work, at their first landing in an extremely hot country, had exhausted and reduced them to the most deplorable state. The commanding officer and surgeon were both ill, without assistance or medicines, and under the necessity of keeping a continual guard day and night against the natives, who had made an irruption upon my feeble detachment with a number of armed men: and notwithstanding their weakness, they had defended themselves with such firmness, that they took seven prisoners from a chief named Raoul; but whom, by a stroke of policy, they had thought proper to send back without any ransom. All these circumstances […] had almost entirely exhausted the detachment.

Benyovszky set about retrieving the situation. The island of Maroce was promptly renamed to the 'Île d'Aiguillon'; the trading-post was named 'Louisbourg'. The natives were won over by presents, and they set about constructing proper huts for everyone to live in. Then they turned their attention to draining the swamp. Last, but not least, the fresh troops were disembarked and cannon set up.

No sooner had things settled down than a visitor turned up. And yes, it was Kerguelen again. On this, his return journey, he was somewhat battered and bruised, bearing the slightly embarrassing news that he had not discovered very much of use. Kerguelen noted in his account of his voyages that he had several reasons for calling in at Antongil, in preference to Mauritius, not the least of which was the certainty of finding fresh meat, rice, lemons and other fresh fruit there. It goes without saying that he had no wish to tangle with Maillart again. But, less selfishly,

> I knew that M. de Benyowsky had established himself on Madagascar and that I would render a great service to the King if I were to hand over to this commander all the things which I had on board which would be of use in such an establishment.[5]

Here is Benyovszky's account of Kerguelen's visit:

> On the 23d, his majesty's frigate L'Oiseau, commanded by a Lieutenant, and his majesty's vessel Le Holland, commanded by Mr. Kerguelen, having anchored in the road, with two hundred of their people sick, I gave them every assistance in my power; and more particularly an abundant supply of refreshments, by means of which their health was speedily restored. On the 25th of the same month, his majesty's packet Le Dauphin, commanded by Mr. Feron, an attendant on the expedition of Mr. Kerguelen, anchored likewise in the road.[6]

Here, on the other hand, is M Kerguelen's version, taken from his *Voyages*. Reaching Madagascar with ninety-eight men dangerously ill with scurvy, and a further fifty also afflicted, he met the Hungarian.

> M. le Baron de Benyowsky, who commanded this area, needed many things, as I had foreseen; and I supplied them to him – gun-carriages, bricks for an oven, iron tools; I gave him shirts and blankets for his people, who lacked everything; finally I had my carpenters build him a store for his provisions.
> Although the Bay of Antongile was the one place in Madagascar where one found the best herds of cattle, I had great difficulties in getting any, because M. le Baron de Benyowsky was at war with several chiefs or kings. However, I managed to get hold of some, by the efforts of M. Kavuel de Mery, who was acting as officer.

The fresh meat and lemons almost instantly cured those of his crew who were not in the "third period" of the illness – those needed a further six weeks of rest and fresh veg.

> I was obliged to re-embark about twenty of the sick, in the hope of getting them to the Cape, where they might successfully be treated; in any case, they

did not wish to stay in Madagascar, and M. de Benyowsky only had a poor surgeon and very little in the way of medicines, as one can see from this extract from a letter he sent to me on 20th March:

"I have received, Sir and dear friend, the letter which you did me the honour of writing. Very many thanks for all the proofs of friendship which you have given during your stay here. Be advised that my gratitude and my attachment will only end when I die. I am sorry about the Surgeon. I only have one, and that is certainly not enough. I repeat my earnest request that you should inform the Minister of all my needs and that you tell him about all the ill-will of M. Maillard, who wanted to sacrifice my people. I have the honour to be &c, signed the Baron de Benyowsky."[7]

Kerguelen left Madagascar on 2nd March and reached the Cape of Good Hope on 7th May. He had already lost fifteen men to scurvy on the voyage from Kerguelen Island to Madagascar, he lost a further ten during his stay at Antongil, and another ten on the way to the Cape. (It is a little ironic that the islands which now bear his name are also home to an anti-scorbutic plant which also bears his name: the Kerguelen Cabbage – more properly *Pringlea antiscorbutica* – was noted in later years for its excellent healing powers on malingering seamen.)

But whom to believe? The man Benyovszky who had such an elegant pen, or the explorer Kerguelen who had failed to discover Australia or even a cabbage? Certainly, Kerguelen had no axe to grind with Benyovszky, no reason to malign him, either then or later – in fact, he viewed him as a fellow-victim of the Mauritius mafia. But, within just a week, could Benyovszky really have fallen out so badly with the natives that they were already refusing supplies? It strains, perhaps, credibility.

A hint of what may have happened was provided by the Abbé Rochon. Admittedly writing after the event and with no strong desire to show Benyovszky in a good light, he describes the arrival of the colonists in stark terms:

Benyowsky arrived in the bay of Antongil, with a military establishment, calculated to terrify the natives. The soldiers of his legion wore sabres of an enormous size, their girdles were trimmed with pistols, and it seemed as if their arms, caps, and uniforms had been purposely invented, to frighten the poor savages out of their wits.[8]

What happened next is also the subject of two accounts completely at variance with each other. According to Benyovszky, several of the local chiefs accepted his invitation to come to a meeting on 1st March to discuss "friendship and alliance" and the thorny question of the colonisation of their lands. Once he had put his proposals to them – all were entirely reasonable – he was pleased to observe their reaction:

they all set up shouts of joy; and said, they could not doubt the good intentions of the king, as he had sent ships and troops to them, in preference to the other provinces, to support them against their enemies; that they acknowledged him from thenceforth as their friend, and should consent to cede to me the land upon which I had begun to form my establishment, provided I entered into an oath not to construct fortresses. With respect to the land I required up the country, they said they would consider of it; but that they required an oath, by which I should acknowledge that I had no right over them, and would confine myself to the simple title of their friend, in which quality I should assist them against their enemies.

Having acceded to the propositions, we celebrated the oath to ratify our union. This ceremony, which they call *Cabar*, was seconded by an entertainment, in which they drank a cask of brandy I distributed among them. My friends then returned to their own villages, where they celebrated new festivals, in testimony of their joy at having gained the friendship of the king of France.[9]

Oaths and brandy notwithstanding, these new friends turned up in dead of night a week later (long after Kerguelen had sailed away) and robbed the stores. An unmannerly disagreement of several days' duration followed, culminating on 12th March in an offensive by the colonists, armed with cannon and muskets, who drove the islanders out of their village and, in the time-honoured manner, "reduced it to ashes, and destroyed their works. This stroke restored the tranquillity of the establishment."

Kerguelen's account reads a little differently. Writing in 1775, while Benyovszky was still on Madagascar, he expands on his dealings with the infant colony:

I applied to M. de Benyowsky for some cattle, but he was only able to supply me with 4 in 10 days. I needed at least one every day for the sick. All the negroes retreated at the sight of the war-apparatus and cannon which M de Benyowsky had unloaded; they did not want to sell him anything at all, and the war-chiefs were holding continuous assemblies (which they named 'palavers') to agree on how to attack him. I decided to send my boat to the villages 4 or 5 leagues further up the coast, to try to barter for chickens and cattle which were so necessary. M de Kavuel [...] sent back 5 cattle on the first expedition, 8 on the second, and then as many as I wanted. He went himself into the villages, taking with him only one or two sailors, with no fear, even when often surrounded by 300 or 400 negroes, armed day and night, and who only wanted to talk about M de Benyowsky whom they named 'the bad white man.' All of these people said to M de Kavuel that they would give us anything we needed, and would refuse nothing to the ships, but that they would give nothing to the Baron de Benyowsky, and that they were only awaiting our departure before attacking him: all the chiefs came to visit me aboard, even the enemies of M de Benyowsky. They brought me chickens, rice and cattle as presents, as '*salam.*' They repeated continually that they would refuse everything to M de Benyowsky and that after our departure they would make 'good war' against him. I said everything that I could to them. But chiefs, men, girls, women and children, they all repeated M Baron de Benyowsky, 'bad white man.' I told the Commander what these islanders were thinking, and he replied that he would defeat them and he asked me for reinforcements. I gave him 12 volunteers whom I had plucked from amongst the worst of the legionnaires who had been given to me at Île de France to replace the men I had lost on the voyage from France. [...] When I was getting ready to leave, M. de Benyowsky wrote me a letter which his Major, M de Marigny delivered. After thanking me a thousand times for all the help I had given him, he advised me that on the previous day two warrior chiefs had come as far as his entrenchments and fired some shots into his camp. Also that these chiefs had a strong stockade armed with small cannon at a league's distance, and that he feared an attack from them after I had left. He begged me, in short, to give him help, and to burn this village as soon as possible. I made the necessary dispositions, and in the night I disembarked eighty armed men. M. de Benyowsky had sent in my boats 50 of his volunteers, commanded by his major, but they were mere boys, blackguards, shoe-blacks of the Pont Neuf. They had not even landed when the whole village was in flames. Our fellows had sprung on shore at once, and not finding anyone, had set fire to all the houses. We knew that the chiefs and inhabitants of the village had been warned by the very negroes who served M de Benyowsky's camp.[10]

Benyovszky and Kerguelen did not see eye to eye on much. But at least they agreed on how to deal sensibly with mutinous natives. And both commanders had poor-quality men under their command; amusingly, Kerguelen used the situation to off-load the worst of his.

Again, one would have to ask the question: how had Benyovszky apparently managed to alienate the locals so much in the space of so few days, to the extent that matters had to be settled with fire and sword? Was such a thing possible? Benyovszky's own account of his time on Madagascar suggests that this state of affairs cannot be discounted. One could, if one were so inclined, reduce his narrative of 160 pages to a couple of sentences: endless negotiations with local chiefs, resulting in oaths of eternal friendship; endless troubles caused by said chiefs reneging on their promises or by new chiefs showing up with a host of warriors. It was not, as the Count de Modave had adequately established five years earlier, an easy task persuading the Madagascans to become well-behaved trading-partners. Indeed, it was not until 1885 that they finally succumbed to French blandishments – and ten years later to their guns.

It would be too easy to become deluded by the extensive and persuasive prose of Benyovszky's official account. For all his faults, he could write a swaggering tale, and did so in the section of his *Memoirs* entitled 'A Full Account of the Particulars Relating to the Royal Establishment at Madagascar.' But in order to make some progress in this document, and through the two years and ten months which he spent on Madagascar, we shall merely extract some illustrations of his main themes.

First, trade and commerce.

On the 28th May 1774, newly settled in, Benyovszky sent a letter back to Ternay and Maillart on the Île de France (Mauritius). It contained

> a statement of demands of things, which the establishment could not dispense with; and among others, filtering stones, medicines, surgeons, and some blacks, accustomed to the service of the hospitals, together with persons capable of over-looking the preservation of his majesty's store-houses, and also flour and liquors. At the same time I demanded of those gentlemen, articles of trade; and assured them, that if I received those articles, I should soon be in a situation to procure them nine hundred thousand pounds of white rice, and three thousand oxen; and that it was of the greatest importance to the service, that they should send me two galliots for the exportation and importation of rice and merchandize from the chief to the out-settlements, as well as to carry my detachments, which had hitherto been obliged to repair to the place of their destination by land, across marshes, which had greatly contributed to their destruction. To these demands, I added that of a reimbursement of the sum of ninety-six thousand one hundred and sixty-six *livres*, which I had myself advanced to the treasury of Madagascar, upon the requisition of the officers of the administration; which sum had been employed in purchasing various kinds of merchandize, with eatables, drink, and medicines, of which the general magazine was entirely destitute: and, lastly, I observed to Mr. de Ternay, that the deplorable situation of my troops scarcely permitted them to perform the ordinary services; for which reason I requested him to order me a supply of men, and to permit the officer, whom I sent directly for that purpose to the Isle of France, to raise soldiers, workmen, and engage with such inhabitants as might be willing to come with them.[11]

This is a fairly typical example of the Baron's method of doing business with Paris and Mauritius: extravagant promises of goods to be delivered by him, in return for sums of money and a long shopping-list of necessities.

Second, health.

In July 1774, many of the colonists were sick with disease. Several had sneaked aboard ships heading for home. Benyovszky's own health suffered, as did that of his son. We have not heard of this son before – clearly, it was not the one who died before his mother reached France, but a recent arrival. Like other similar losses described by Benyovszky, mourning seems to have been swift:

> My health, which had been unsettled for a long time, now began for some days to experience the most dreadful attacks. My only son Charles Maurice

Louis Augustus, Baron de Benyowsky, died of the country disorder on the 11th of this month, at seven in the morning, to my extreme regret; and on the 12th, Mr. De Marigni, my major, for whose life I had been so greatly apprehensive, died at ten in the morning. He was equally lamented by myself, and all the officers of my corps. My fever became every day more violent, and forced me at last, to repair to the Plain of Health.[12]

As a direct result of this loss, Madame Benyovszky retreated to Mauritius, only to return some months later, when it was politically useful for her to do so.

Third, blameworthy colleagues.

Benyovszky had several bêtes-noires during this period of his life, not the least of whom was his quartermaster, a man by the name of M des Assisses. The unfortunate Assisses was the Stepanov of Madagascar. It was he who promised one thing and delivered another, he who fouled up the accounts and he who failed to make all necessary reports.

The continual chagrin and disquiet which I suffered, destroyed my health, and reduced me to such an extremity, that the surgeons despaired of my life. In the height of my illness, the Sieur des Assisses requested my officers to meet at his habitation; and on their refusal, he waited upon them, and declared that he had particular orders from Mr. Maillart to seize all my effects and papers, in case my life was in danger; and that in consequence of the evident danger in which I then was, he requested them to assist him in carrying his orders into effect. [...] At the moment, however, in which the Sieur des Assisses condemned me to death, a favourable crisis dissipated my disorder, by a spontaneous evacuation of bile, and placed me entirely out of danger. Great indeed was my surprise, when my officers came to express their joy on my convalescence; and when I heard at the same time, from their report, of the conduct which this chief storekeeper had adopted with respect to me, I immediately sent for him, and reproached him for his conduct. Confounded as he was at the disclosure of his proceedings, he avowed, in the presence of my officers, that all which he had hitherto done, had been founded on particular instructions of Mr. Maillart. He at the same time put into my hands these instructions, which might more properly be called a defamatory libel, of which I immediately sent a copy to the Minister, addressing my packet to him by the Chevalier Grenier, Commander of his Majesty's frigate the Belle Poule.[13]

Benyovszky then proceeded to accuse Assisses of purloining seventeen casks of wine from the stores, for consumption by himself and cronies; and alluded to his "conduct with the women." Benyovszky's blackening of the name of his quartermaster sits at odds with another batch of his letters which were all written in the very same month – and more amicable letters it would be hard to find.

Little presents of food were being exchanged between the pair, and Mme Benyovszky frequently asked her husband to pass on to Assisses *"mille choses obligeantes."*[14]

Fourth, negotiations or war with the natives.

Many and lurid are the descriptions of diplomatic negotiations, of treacherous breaches of agreements, and of open war in the *Memoirs*. An entire section is devoted to a 'History of the War against the Seclaves,' which resounds with more than a few echoes of the famous three-day war on Formosa. Reduced to its essentials, this describes an offensive against the untrustworthy Sakalava people, the largest of the Madagascan clans, which had been a thorn in Benyovszky's side for several months; in May of 1776, the Hungarian veteran decided that enough was enough; he marched out with his own troops (45 volunteers, 26 slaves, 25 workers) alongside 4,000 natives supplied by the more friendly clans of the island, and, by dint of brilliant generalship, knocked some sense into the recidivists; within three weeks, the Sakalava were at his door begging forgiveness and seeking "peace at any rate."

As a direct result of this famous victory, the assembled chiefs of the island made a startling proposal in mid-July. It was nothing less than to recognise Benyovszky as the god-given King of Madagascar, a descendant of the ancient family of Ramini. It was, of course, none of his doing. He was minding his own business when a delegation of chiefs was announced. They were worried that their dear colonist was about to be shipped back to France. Three of the chiefs sat down, but their leader, one Raffangour,

> remained standing, and spoke the following words, which I here give accurately:

> "Blessed be the day which brought thee into the world. Blessed be thy parents, who have taken care of thy infancy; and blessed be the hour in which thou didst set thy foot upon our island.
>
> The Malgagos chiefs and captains, whose hearts thou hast gained, who love thee, and are faithfully attached to thee, have received information that the French King intends to appoint another in thy place; and that he is angry with thee because thou hast refused to deliver us to his slavery: they have therefore met, and have held cabars, to decide upon the manner in which they should act, if this should prove true. Their love and their attachment for thee, have obliged me, in this circumstance, to reveal to thee the secret of thy birth, and thy rights over this immense country, all whose people adore thee. Yes, I myself, Raffangour, reputed the sole survivor of the family of Ramini, I have renounced this sacred right, to declare thee the only true inheritor of Ramini. The spirit of God, which reigns over our cabars, caused all the chiefs and captains to make oath, that they would acknowledge thee their *Ampansacabe*; that they would no more

quit thee, but preserve thy person, at the price of their lives, against all the violence of the French."[15]

Naturally, all of this came as a bit of a surprise. Benyovszky found himself in some embarrassment. Was this not the second time in his life that his person had been foretold by supernatural means – just like the 'Prophets' cited by Prince Huapo on Formosa? He asked to mull over their proposal. It then emerged that an old woman of the island was convinced that Benyovszky's mother was one of their own. What further proof was required? Benyovszky modestly accepted the honour. A considerable number of meetings, assemblies and ceremonies followed over the course of July and August (interrupted briefly by a visitation from two government inspectors, with whom we shall deal shortly). In the final celebrations in October, no fewer than 50,000 Madagascans were prostrate before their new king (a quick revision upwards from 30,000 just two pages previously). Meanwhile their women were swearing oaths to Madame Benyovszky, announcing that they would obey all of her orders in respect of decent family life. A final set of oaths was sworn:

> In presence of our people, having consumed the sacrifice, and made the oath of blood, we proclaim, declare, and acknowledge Mauritius Augustus for our supreme chief *Ampansacabe*, titles extinct since the decease of our holy family of Ramini, which we revive in him and his family. It is for this reason that, having consumed the sacrifice, we submit inviolably to his authority.[16]

And so on. This was all written down – conveniently – "in the language of the country, with Roman letters" and signed by all the "great men" of the island.

If it had not been completely true, it might have been hard to believe.

On this highest of high notes, Benyovszky uses words strangely familiar to us to announce to his faithful people that he has to return to Europe, "in order to conclude treaties of commerce and friendship with any European nation whatever." Stopping only to "purchase the cargo of a private vessel, of the value of forty-five thousand *livres*, for which I gave one hundred and twenty-eight slaves"[17] he boarded ship on the 14th December 1776, and set sail again for Europe.

His emotions ran unusually high:

> At this single moment of my life, I experienced what the heart is capable of suffering, when torn from a beloved and affectionate society to which it is devoted. At length I went on board, not without paying a tribute to nature, which I had never experienced during the most dreadful sufferings of my tyrannical exile. The north wind at length began to blow afresh; and towards evening I set sail for the Cape of Good Hope, at which place I proposed to freight another vessel, to carry me to France. This voyage may probably give birth to happy circumstances, such as my wishes have formed, in favour of the settlement at Madagascar, and may perhaps repair the faults committed by the minister.[18]

Alas, the King of Madagascar never got around to documenting the dashing of those happy hopes.

Notes

1 Cultru, 1906, p.42.
2 Benyovszky, 1790, Vol.II, pp.93–94.
3 Cultru, 1906, p.64.
4 Benyovszky, 1790, Vol.II, p.114.
5 Kerguelen, 1782, pp.82–83.
6 Benyovszky, 1790, Vol.II, p.117.
7 Kerguelen, 1782, pp.84–85.
8 Rochon, 1793, pp.241–242.
9 Benyovszky, 1790, Vol.II, p.118.
10 Kerguelen, 1782, pp.154–155.
11 Benyovszky, 1790, Vol.II, pp.133–134.
12 *ibid*, p.135.
13 *ibid*, pp.150–151.
14 Cultru, 1906, pp.91–92.
15 Benyovszky, 1790, Vol.II, p.244.
16 *ibid*, p.269.
17 *ibid*, p.277.
18 *ibid*, pp.281–282.

XXVII

MADAGASCAR – THE REALITY

"Everything Is Rotten"

Secretaries and Orphans Required – Doubtful Inspectors – A Strong Lack of Evidence – What Could Be Done with 40 Million Livres and 12,000 Men

So much for Benyovszky's authorised history of his three years on Madagascar. To describe everything that is said to have occurred would be fruitless: it would take a book all of its own; we already have one; his own words should suffice for anyone interested. A refutation of all that went on would also require a book of its own; and in 1906, the French historian Cultru undertook that task with considerable energy and zeal. Some of what Cultru unearthed can briefly be mentioned here: these are the letters which Benyovszky sent back to Paris on a regular basis, and which paint a picture slightly different from the one described in the *Memoirs*. Here, there are no wars, no sickness – only triumphs.

At the end of March 1774, six weeks after his arrival on Madagascar, Benyovszky wrote to Aiguillon to account for his activities so far.

> The place I have chosen, sir, is the healthiest, without fear of contradiction, on the whole island. To assure myself even more of its wholesomeness, I have ordered that all the marshes around it be dried, and I have established several fresh-water springs. The port is one of the most magnificent that one could hope to find in these regions. To control it, I have built batteries, and I will establish piers and a pontoon for the loading and unloading of ships. [...] Since the 9th November 1773, until today, I have lost only 9 soldiers and 4 sailors, 3 of the former managed to kill each other, before my arrival here, and 1 drowned; there are therefore only 5 deaths by sickness, and libertinage is almost certainly the cause of those. [...] The discipline of my troops and the order which reigns, since my arrival, has dazzled the natives

of the country. All the chiefs of this part of the island have taken an oath of loyalty, acknowledging themselves as subjects of His Majesty.[1]

Appended to this rosy picture was a list of requests for additional men and materials. Not much, really: just

> a ship of 600 tons, loaded with wine, brandy and flour, 200 recruits, 6 carpenters, 2 blacksmiths and 2 masons, 3 officers of the rank of captain – to command the different outposts, 2 surgeons with medicines, 6 12-inch mortars and 16 cannon, along with munitions, 2 chaplains, and an assortment of tools.

At the beginning of September, the picture was rosier still. In a report to Boynes, Benyovszky announced that eight outposts had been established up and down the east coast, each under the command of an officer, and fully-manned, and that a road had been built over to the west coast. His report to Aiguillon later that same month was bullish:

> Posterity will read with much pleasure the history of the revolution in Madagascar. It will learn that a body of men, comprising 237 individuals, reduced by sickness and exhaustion to 160, has subjugated an island which is 800 leagues in circumference [...] Today I can count that 32 provinces of the island of Madagascar are subject to our establishment, whose chiefs pay an annual tribute which will cover the costs of my troop. Apart from this tribute, I have procured a revenue of 150,000 *livres* and expect to realise a profit of 4 million francs annually, provided that M. de Boynes can send the necessary trading goods.

The admission that seventy-seven men had been lost does not quite square with his letter of March. But no matter.

Attached to this new letter was a further shopping-list (a 300-ton ship, a 150-ton one, 12 cannon, 6 mortars, 30 blunderbuss, 24 breech-loading cannon, anchors, flags, hand-mills; also a second-in command, 4 captains, 1 warehouseman, 4 subalterns, 15 secretaries, 4 priests, 4 doctors, 4 master-carpenters and 12 assistants, 2 master-masons, 2 blacksmiths, bakers, gardeners, tanners, coopers, butchers, farmers, 60 orphans of both sexes aged between 2 and 15) – all of which were "absolutely necessary" for the success of the enterprise.[2]

In May of the following year, Benyovszky proudly announced that the "vast kingdom of the Seclaves" (those very same Sakalava with whom he had just waged a short, sharp war) had "finally submitted to our government." There was, perhaps understandably, no mention of a war – merely that the chief of the Sakalava had turned up keen to sign a treaty. Madagascar was now in the bag. The place was a treasure-house of natural resources, just crying out to be exploited – rice, coffee, wheat, cattle, slaves, men to employ as soldiers and sailors, not to mention the mines "of which every province is full." Since November of 1774, he had only lost six men. He ends this letter with the rather plaintive remark that, since Mauritius was not sending him any supplies, "I have bought a two-masted coastal trader for the service of his Majesty. The money for this came to me from China, proceeds of the sale of the galleon from Kamchatka which I sold at Canton."[3]

This is the same money which the Baron, earlier in his *Memoirs*, was moaning that he did not possess. It must have been in his back pocket all along.

But even in these gleaming reports back to Paris, the tarnish of real life could not help showing through. In a letter of October 1775, he had this to say:

> At the end of last year, I had the honour of forwarding my accounts to M. de Boynes by the ship *Postillon*. Since the departure of this vessel, the commanders of the Île de France have left us in a state of utter abandonment [...] They have not blushed in using the most ignominious calumny to blacken my reputation. And every refusal of help has thrown my troop into the deepest despair, which I have only been able to alleviate with the greatest trouble, myself and my officers sacrificing all our essential items, wardrobe and furniture to raise money to pay the troops. In such a state as this, we await assistance, or a recall home.[4]

Either because of this lament, or because of a stream of carping letters from Mauritius, where supplies normally imported from Madagascar were running low, the French Ministry finally decided to do something. Both Aiguillon and Boynes were gone, sacked for general incompetence in June 1774. Their successors had become aware that there was a significant difference between the two sets of reports from the Indian Ocean. While Benyovszky was, on the one hand, insisting that his men were generally fit and healthy, there was the contrary report from the captain of a ship which visited Louisbourg in July of 1774 (this ship also temporarily evacuated Mme Benyovszky back to Mauritius) which stated that, of 237 troops, 180 had died, and of 22 officers, 12 had died. At that time, Benyovszky was claiming only forty-nine dead. A year later, Benyovszky himself had reported that he had only ninety-two survivors from all the troops who had landed there – inclusive of sundry reinforcements which had arrived between times (Kerguelen's astute off-loading of twelve troublesome crewmen was typical of such reinforcements). Maillart on Mauritius was almost apoplectic in his wrath that Benyovszky had been refusing to provide a list of the dead, so that families in France could be notified.

The Abbé Rochon had a far better grasp of local conditions than any of the would-be colonists. His description of northern Madagascar is colourful, but falls short of being seductive:

> [*Benyovszky*] chose the bay of Antongil as the chief place of his residence, but from the beginning of October to the beginning of May, pestilential fevers ravage and desolate that district. No doubt the murderous vapours

which rise from the marshes and woods, are the real cause of this fatal epidemical scourge: the inflammable air, and the putrid particles which rise copiously from the stagnant waters corrupted by the decayed parts of vegetation, change, during calms and great heats, the goodness of the atmospheric air. In that season, the air is rarely refreshed by quick sea-breezes, and the Northern winds carry those exhalations along the coast, and their pernicious effects are completed by calms and a constant drought. The natives know but little how to preserve themselves from this danger; by remaining in their hovels amidst a thick smoke, the most robust, and the most sober of them frequently fall victims to the violence of the distemper; it is therefore no wonder that the Europeans, forced to pass the winter on this coast, perish by a contagion which even cuts off those who are the most accustomed to the climate.[5]

On top of disease and climate, Benyovszky also had to contend – blindfold – with his enemies on Mauritius; and these did not merely comprise the Governor and his lieutenant. Pierre Poivre was a government administrator on Mauritius between 1767 and 1772, charged with building up agriculture and the economy; he was an ardent horticulturalist and an even more ardent critic of the Hungarian. Poivre had encountered Benyovszky when he had first passed through Mauritius, en route from Macao. In a letter to Rochon, he did not mince his words when coming to a judgement:

We have seen swarms of locusts devouring in an instant abundant harvests; we have seen two terrible hurricanes threaten this island with total subversion; Madagascar always served to compensate the mischief done by those awful scourges: henceforth the Isle de France has lost all resources, it must fall and perish, if similar scourges should again happen to spread disolation over these fields. Under the government of Benyowsky, Madagascar will no more be the support of this settlement; in our future misfortunes we must only hope for precarious and distant relief. I was much habituated to the success of cheats and adventurers, but the success of Benyowsky overwhelms me with confusion, the more so, as I have written a letter on his account to the minister. I well know that oddities are pleasing, that they amuse the multitude and raise their credulity to the highest pitch of excess; but how could I imagine that a stranger just broke lose from chains and prisons at Kamschatka, and sunk into contempt by his own writings, should obtain an important charge without my approbation? Strongly attached, in virtue of my office, to the welfare of this colony, I ought, the first time he spoke to me about Madagascar, to have excited in him a desire of dethroning the Mogul [of India]; his request would undoubtedly have been complied with, and we should thus have got rid of him.[6]

Assailed on all sides by claims and counter-claims, the French Ministry for once took a sensible decision. In the summer of 1776, Paris did not send reinforcements, supplies or munitions, it did not even send any orphans: it sent two government inspectors, Bellecombe and Chevreau. These two gentlemen arrived in mid-September, stayed for a fortnight, and reported back on what they found. Their inspection was thorough. They visited all of the available outposts which Benyovszky had – or claimed to have – established. They opened the doors of every hut, poked inside every barrel.

Their report was damning. We shall not replicate it in full, only provide extracts from one document. This was an order for building works drawn up by Benyovszky in 1774, and annotated (*in italicised text*) by Bellecombe and Chevreau.[7]

Louisbourg – Terrain elevation. 600 fathoms long, by 180 and 120 broad, 4 feet high; the river and the sea rising 18 inches at high tide. *This earthwork could not be verified.*

18,000 days of labour, construction of palisades and cabins including the hospital.... [*total value:*] 13,440 livres. *All of these buildings have been thrown up in haste and have no solidity. They no longer exist: everything had to be renewed last year.*

Construction of Fort Louis with an elevation of three feet above the surrounding terrain: 3,600 livres. *There is a fence of about 1,500 or 2,000 uprights, with 3 or 4 cabins to house 25 men. Warehouse, armoury, sentry-post – all standing.*

The road from Fort Louis to the town, next to the sluice-gate: 1400 livres. *There is a small path: we saw no sluice-gate. It must have been destroyed.*

Dredging of the natural canal for bringing fresh water... 1350 livres. *Expenditure cannot be verified.*

Île d'Aiguillon – Opening of a canal 83 fathoms long, one fathom wide and 3 feet deep – 1,150 Livres. Removal of trees to establish the garden: 700 livres. *There is only the very smallest trace of both of these works.*

At the Bay of Convalescents, four cabins for the sick, the bakery, one house and two cabins for slaves suffering from smallpox: 960 livres. *There is no sign of any building at this bay. We were told they had been burned down by the negroes.*

Construction of road from Louisbourg to Angontsy, through woods, marsh, mountains and rivers, 34 leagues long. 260 men employed for five months, making 69,000 days 29,250 livres. Other: 23,810. Item, the road from Louisbourg for 28 leagues across marsh and plains, 80 men employed for 73 days... 5,840 livres [*Total:*] 58,900 livres. *Very considerable expense, utterly useless, and we were not able to verify it. We never saw any roads anywhere.*

Drainage works ... 68,000 livres. *All the drainage ditches are works which cannot be verified since they are not visible, or only very little.*

Buildings on the Plain – ditches, cabins, hospital ... 3,400 livres. *These buildings, situated on the left bank of the river, are abandoned and completely rotten.*

Fort Auguste ... *Everything is rotten, uninhabitable in the rainy season.*

Trading-post at Rammonier, ditto at Angousavé... *There was never anyone in these outposts...*

Trading-post at Antoguin, with a square palisade, two stores and a field for cattle: 488 livres. *Monsieur Corby remained at this outpost for two months and then abandoned it.*

Establishment of a post at Manahar: 1,252 livres. *It is unoccupied.*

Construction of a road from Mahaler to Angontsy: 103,228 livres. *This outpost is to the north, on the coast. But we think that carriage of exports to Louisbourg could be done only by sea and that these expenses for a road are a pure loss.*

Improvements at Tamatave and Foulepointe. *We never saw anything new built at Foulepointe nor at Tamatave. Everything is old and fallen into ruin and cannot have been repaired.*

Construction of a road to open up communication from Angouan to Monigano, and of a fort on the Plain of Maherony... 146,584 livres. *This is the plain where the Fort St Jean is situated; this is a very small fence of stakes about 4 feet high with a little ditch which one can step across; there are some huts inside and out. It is entirely rotten.*

One item alone stands out in this catalogue of criticisms and missing evidence: *"The garden does exist and seems well-maintained."*

Accompanying Bellecombe and Chevreau was Commander de la Pérouse, who made his own report. (This was the same Pérouse who eleven years later dropped off Lesseps in Kamchatka; he would have been greatly tickled by the echoes of the Benyovszky affair there.) The words he used, and the situation he describes, were no different from those of his colleagues: poverty, misery, rotten wood, empty storehouses and overgrown fields.[8]

I arrived at Foule Pointe on the 17th of September 1776. The population of the villages adjacent to the harbour was reduced to one half of the former number; bloody wars had isolated the whole country: the crops had been destroyed, and agriculture was given up to such a degree, that we could scarcely obtain three hundred pounds of rice. The want of all other provisions was equally great and distressing. My surprise could hardly be described. I had been in the same place three years before; trade and agriculture were then flourishing, and the markets afforded plenty of every thing; ten large ships received a complete cargo of rice, yet this immense quantity of an article of the first necessity made not the smallest change in the price of value. These ships all sailed to the Isle de France, which three successive hurricanes had plunged in the greatest distress. All the crops were lost; a dreadful famine menaced the whole colony; they felt its precursory calamities, when the sudden arrival of the ten ships loaded with rice, rescued the inhabitants from misery and despair. If in this circumstance, like in many others, Foule Pointe has saved Isle de France, these hopes had now completely vanished. The fields laid fallow, all commerce was at an end. The despotism of Benyowsky had spread terror and alarm throughout the island.

Pérouse remained entirely unimpressed by Benyovszky's achievements. The principal town and its environs seemed hardly to merit anything other than contempt:

> [*Bellecombe*] seemed satisfied with the military position of the place chosen by Benyowsky for his principal settlement, to which he gave the name of *Louisbourg*. But if the place is easily to be fortified, there can be none more humid and unwholesome. Louisbourg is situated on a kind of cape, which projects into the sea, to the distance of three hundred fathoms, the ground on which the houses and magazines are erected, rises hardly four feet above the level of the waters when the tide is strong. It acquired this level by heaping one load of rubbish upon another. All the land adjacent forms a marsh covered by high water.

As for the "Plain of Health" on which Benyovszky had established facilities for the colonists to recover from all the tropical sicknesses daily assailing them – it clearly breached advertising guidelines:

> Benyowsky spoke to us in the highest praise, of the happy locality of this spot truly rural, but we found it did not deserve its name. The Plain of Health appeared to us an unwholesome place, encompassed by mountains, whose great elevation stops the clouds, and condensates them into rain.

A lengthy interview between Bellecombe and Benyovszky was also documented by Pérouse, and one gets a refreshing sense of reality from the Hungarian's reported answers:

> [*Bellecombe*] asked him why he had left off sending rice and bullocks to Isle de France. The wars I was obliged to sustain against the natives, answered Benyowsky, have deprived me, and still deprive me of provisions of the first necessity. How could I in such a situation, send provisions to Isle de France? You must be sensible of the impossibility. I find it likewise an easy talk to justify the wars I have carried on. I convene a *Palabra*, I make advantageous proposals to the natives; they not only reject them, but insolent chiefs dare to threaten me; they go farther, the signal is given to put me to death – several muskets are fired upon me. I escape, miraculously as it were, from this imminent danger, gallantly supported by my soldiers, I disperse the rabble, and frighten them by the fire of artillery from the fort.

Bellecombe then suggested that Benyovszky convene the unruly natives one more time to persuade them of his peaceful intentions. After much argument and with bad grace, Benyovszky did so. It was not a great success, partly because the Madagascans were already weary of meetings, partly because Bellecombe's own approach appears to have been unduly patronising:

> The *palabra* met on the second of October 1776; it was not numerous, and only attended by six chiefs and one hundred and fifty islanders. Mons. de Belcombe renewed the treaty of peace, exhorted them to apply themselves to husbandry, and to avoid every subject of dissention. The natives seemed quite motionless, and insensible of all professions of friendship and assurances of benevolence. Benyowsky seemed much dissatisfied at this silent disapprobation of his conduct.

Benyovszky himself makes no mention of this meeting. On that very day, his own *Memoirs* reveal that he was busy with paperwork, preparatory to his return to France. According to the same *Memoirs*, however, two days later a whole collection of chiefs assembled and poured out their protestations of undying attachment. On the 6th of October six chiefs did indeed turn up with their men, much as Bellecombe reported. But on this day, and for several days following, no fewer than fifty thousand natives swore allegiance to Benyovszky, with all the enthusiasm requisite to please a God-King.

It really is surprising how two perceptions of the same event can vary so much. It is well that Bellecombe and Pérouse did not witness all these jollifications: they might have felt that their critical report was being petty.

Before departing, Pérouse himself had a long chat with Benyovszky. The former's remark that "France would get very little of use out of this colony" met with a refreshingly frank and unapologetic reply from the colonist:

> You are right, he replied, but a lesson costing two million *livres* is not too dear to teach the Minister that one could not do anything small-scale on Madagascar; but if one could provide two million a year, with six hundred (supposing four to five hundred new recruits every year) men, the colony could make good progress in twenty years. I then suggested to him that, at four thousand leagues from France, one would not choose a country where five out of six men die within two years, where those who survive are weak, convalescent and incapable of military or agricultural work. As an example, I pointed out his eighty men who had no idea how to handle a rifle or do military exercises. He admitted himself that he had not been able to instruct them, because they were continually in the hospital. [...] I asked M. de Benyowszky what his plans had been when he arrived on Madagascar. He replied: "To force the people to do what the King [*of France*] wished; but he had never fully understood the intentions of the government in this respect; besides he knew it was no easier to conquer a colony in the face of enmity than to form a new one altogether."[9]

Pérouse was not impressed by "this vindictive man," and remained

> astonished at the degree of confidence granted to the projects of that
> adventurer. I remained convinced that the 40 million livres and the 12,000
> men which were to be sent to him over twenty years, if his plan was adopted,
> would simply be added to the loss which France had already made.

Bellecombe and Chevreau seem to have been a little less hard-headed than Pérouse. As a parting shot, Benyovszky persuaded both of them that he had in his past life been a priest, a page and a midshipman. They swallowed this amusing autobiography whole.

Notes

1   Cultru, 1906, pp.66–67.
2   *ibid*, pp.73–74.
3   *ibid*, p.77.
4   *ibid*, p.79.
5   Rochon, 1793, p.237.
6   *ibid*, pp.236–237.
7   Cultru, 1906, pp.168–175.
8   Rochon, 1793, pp.242–256.
9   Cultru, 1906, pp.179–180.

XXVIII

EUROPE AND AMERICA

"I am Ready to Offer Your Country...
My Blood, My Knowledge and My Courage"

In France – In Austria – In France Again – In Bavaria – In Croatia –
In France Again – In America – In France Again – In London – In America Again

And there, at last, Benyovszky's several autobiographies terminate. All that we have for the last ten years of his life are the biographical reports of others, who – incomprehensibly – did not cast him in the most glorious light. Let us follow the trail.

Benyovszky had two perfectly valid reasons for leaving Madagascar in December 1776. The first was that his health had suffered quite dramatically during almost three years on the island – like everyone else who had arrived there full of hope in early 1774, he had been assailed by scurvy, malaria and other diseases of a tropical nature. His family, too, had undergone much. And by now he must have realised that his attempts to build a thriving colony on the sandy foundations of dreams and fiction were doomed to failure. So when he applied to Bellecombe and Chevreau for leave of absence, they were quite happy to accede – on the understanding that someone else would look after the colony in his absence. The two inspectors left the island on 6th October, dropped down the coast to Foulepointe and then made for India, from where their report made its way back to France. It was a long time indeed before the recommendations of their inspection reached Paris (April 1778). That gave Benyovszky a good few months to hot-foot back to France and see what he could salvage from the wreckage before the damning report arrived.[1]

Left in charge of what remained of the various trading-posts was one of his few surviving colleagues, the Chevalier Sanglier. The final stages in the history of the colony were all downhill. When the inspectors' report arrived, the government was swift to act: an order of 22 May 1778 disbanded the "Volunteers" and transferred all remaining members of the company into a branch of the Colonial Army. In the interim, a revolt of the troops based at the Foulepointe outpost (they had not been paid for some time) ended in the deaths of seven during a manhunt, with the remaining three clapped in irons. The winding-up order from France arrived in June 1779, and was immediately executed by the new Governor of Mauritius: all remaining soldiers were removed to Fort Dauphin, there to stew forgotten and unpaid for almost three years. By 1781, of the sixty-nine men who had been rounded up, only Sanglier and forty-eight others remained alive. These survivors were shipped out to Mauritius in January 1782.

But, by then, Benyovszky had cashed in. He arrived in France in April of 1777. Officials were a little surprised to see him, but not unduly concerned. Taking advantage of the prevalent ignorance, the returning hero pressed home his demands. He asked for – and was granted – the Croix de Saint Louis; he asked for, but was regretfully refused, the rank of Brigadier; he asked for all his accounts to be paid, and received an immediate advance of 50,000 *livres* before anyone even bothered to check them over; he asked for his back-pay, and received 100,000 *livres* without delay. He even had the brass to present the government with a new plan for the colonisation of Madagascar: this would have ceded the island to Benyovszky for thirty years, assuming the usual annual tribute from the French King of funds, materials and human resources. In return, the Benyovszky Company would provision French ships and send back annually 1,200 head of cattle and rice to the value of one million *livres*.

Unfortunately, this grand plan was neither approved nor rejected. It meandered across a few desks and then vanished into the archive.

Such ministerial apathy may be explained by a curious incident which took place in July 1776. That summer, the Russian Ambassador to London, when on a visit to Paris, let slip a remark that Russia and Britain were planning a project which "would stun Europe": in essence, the two countries were plotting to invade Japan. A Russian expert named Jean-Benoît Scherer, recently returned to France from employment in St Petersburg, became aware of this diplomatic leak. He immediately sent a memorandum to the French Foreign Minister claiming to know the full detail of this project.

In outline the stunning plan was this: the British were to despatch Captain Cook to Kamchatka, where he would supervise the assembly of a Russian naval invasion force. The Russians would provide 14,000 marines and all ships, Cook the maritime know-how. Russia would then invade Japan, while Britain would distract the Prussians – who might potentially invade Russia from the west while its back was turned – by arranging a small war with them. The ultimate goal was to enrich both Russia and Britain, with the added bonus of an eastern bridgehead from which to launch possible invasions of California and the west of the Americas.[2]

Does any of this sound familiar? It should do: Scherer cited the principal authority. "It was Baron Benyovszky who provided the proof of all this for us. He had found secret orders, sent from St Petersburg, in the chancellery of the Kamchatka government, to which he had had full access for several weeks." Further proof, should it be needed, lay in Cook's imminent departure for his third voyage (which would take in the Russian Far East), the continuing machinations of Britain, Russia and Austria around a 'Triple Alliance,' and the real clincher: the Russians had established an academy in Irkutsk where kidnapped Japanese mariners were busy teaching Japanese to Russian soldiers. In the meantime, the Japanese were defenceless, their Emperor having melted down all the country's weapons to help construct new palaces. It was the perfect conspiracy.

What to do? Scherer had the answer: the French naval man-of-the-moment, Bougainville, was to be despatched with two ships to Japan, carrying arms and a warning for the Emperor. He was to stop off at Madagascar to pick up the one man who was an expert in the field: Benyovszky. The icing on the cake was that, along the way, Benyovszky could establish those long-cherished trading-colonies in Formosa, Usmay Ligon and Kunashir (one of the Kuril Islands), all independently of Japan. France would then have a toehold in the North Pacific, and an ally in the Japanese Emperor. What could be better?

Clearly, Scherer had a passing knowledge of an early version of Benyovszky's stories and of the material the Hungarian had lodged with the French Ministry in 1772. But since he had returned from Russia after Benyovszky had left for Madagascar, the pair had never met: which is a shame – had they teamed up, the course of world history might have been so different. At all events, the French Foreign Minister, Vergennes, was galvanised into action by Scherer's memorandum; he scuttled off into his archives and spent several days reviewing the material. But at length he decided that the story was without foundation. Perhaps the dispiriting reports coming out of Madagascar and Mauritius inclined him against the Benyovszkian thesis. (At all events, Captain Cook was in the clear – in 1779, all French naval ships received instructions not to molest Cook's ships if encountered on the high seas.[3])

None of this excitement, we guess, was relayed to Benyovszky on his less-than-glorious return from Madagascar. But he knew not to stand still. Already, he had written to the Empress Maria Theresa in Austria, to ask pardon for having abandoned his native land to fight in Poland in 1768. Implicit in the request was the idea of doing some profitable business back home. The pardon was granted and our adventurer made haste back to Hungary, where he received the coveted title of 'Count' which he had been borrowing these several years past. Returning briefly to France in early 1778, the new Count tied up some loose ends: when his company was disbanded in May, the French government rather confounded expectation by giving him compensation – he was made Brigadier and given a pension of 4,000 *livres*, with yet more back-pay, as well as a one-off lump-sum of 151,869 *livres* (budget-heading unclear – maybe in settlement of his claims from the previous year). With these little matters resolved amicably, Benyovszky promptly sought permission to go and join the Austrian army. The ministers appeared to have no problem with that, and even agreed to continue to pay out his pension until he deigned to come back to France.

Thus, with pockets bulging and a smile upon his face, Benyovszky left France in August and arrived home just in time to get involved in the War of the Bavarian

Succession (also known as 'The Potato War'), a minor spat which had broken out in July 1778 between Austria and Prussia, with all the other continental powers poking their noses in. It was not a particularly profitable war for anyone; thousands of troops of both sides died for very little national honour or advantage. Benyovszky's younger brother Emanuel was already involved in the military operations; big brother gleefully joined in. According to his own correspondence, Benyovszky

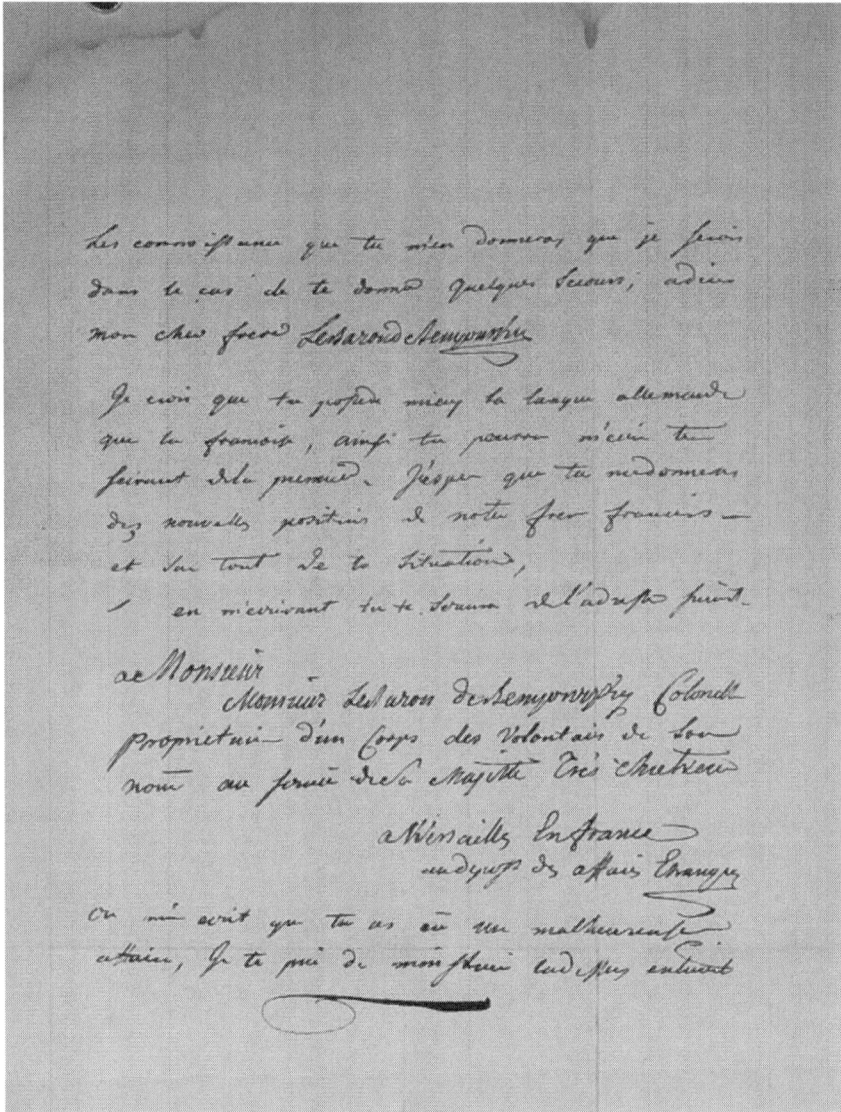

FIGURE 28.1   The final page of a letter written by Benyovszky to his brother Emanuel, advising him to "avoid dissipation."

served as Colonel with great distinction between September and January – on one occasion capturing 822 prisoners. As with the Polish campaign ten years earlier, no other accounts can verify his claims: *tant pis*. He resigned his commission in May 1779 and headed for his Hungarian homeland. Eager to spend his cash, he bought a small estate at Vietzka.

But he did not remain in retirement for long. Already he had scented another business opportunity.

The port of Fiume (present-day Rijeka) on the Adriatic coast was the only sea-port available to the Hungarian half of the Empire. Count Benyovszky suddenly expressed an interest in Fiume and all its dealings, and in March of 1780 presented a memorandum to the Imperial Chancellery. The plan outlined here was to expand trade through the port – specifically agricultural products from Hungary and Croatia – and turn it into Hungary's very own gateway to the Mediterranean, in direct competition with the Austrian rival of Trieste not far to the north. The Emperor Josef II saw no harm in it. Benyovszky got the job. From the end of 1780, he laboured away on the Adriatic coast. Much of his labour consisted in proposing fanciful plans and borrowing money from gullible investors. He met with little success on the first part, but more on the second. The only thing that grew was his pile of debt. He sent to Paris to demand another 83,000 *livres*. Paris refused. To keep himself afloat, he borrowed 30,000 Austro-Hungarian florins from one fellow-Count (who was astute enough to charge 11% interest on the loan), another 35,520 from another Count, and 5,000 from others unnamed. (If, like the estimable Mr Beawes, we may be permitted to keep a track of monetary values here: a pair of men's riding boots cost just over one florin in 1770; the same amount could buy you twelve chickens or 160 eggs. Seventy thousand florins was therefore a lot of chickens.) After a while, the Counts pressed for their money back. Benyovszky had to mortgage his new estate at Vietzka. Finally, he skipped the country at the end of 1781, leaving in his wake a bemused business partner, a crowd of creditors and some disconsolate unpaid employees.

He made his way to France.

But by now France was having nothing more to do with him.

He sailed to America to try his luck.

He felt encouraged to cross the Atlantic, first, by the fact that another younger brother, Ferenc, had established himself as a soldier there in 1779 (this brother had a colourful career as mercenary across the globe, before dying, impoverished, in 1789).[4] Second, there is strong evidence that the American ambassador to Paris, Benjamin Franklin, had been introduced to Benyovszky, and had provided him with letters of introduction to the leaders of the young revolutionary state. On his arrival in America in early 1782, Benyovszky tried to find a post in the army, advising George Washington that he was "ready to offer your Country (of which I am ambitious of becoming a citizen) my blood, my knowledge and my courage."[5] A young country could surely ask for no more. Washington was less enthusiastic. He wrote back politely, advising the Count that, with the British surrender at

Yorktown the previous October, the War of Independence was effectively over and officers were already being stood down. Despite the depressed state of the mercenary job-market, Benyovszky was not discouraged; he immediately came up with a plan for forming a "foreign legion" of volunteers to serve in the new country (Supreme Commander: Count Benyovszky). This new approach found some favour with Washington and various generals, and, with slight modifications, came very close to gaining approval from the Board of War. Alas, it failed at the final hurdle.

(There is a legend that Benyovszky had managed, in all his activities, to fit in an active stint in the American War of Independence. However, research has shown that this was not our Maurice, but his brother Ferenc, who was some seven years younger. Young Ferenc had not much of a war – echoing his older brother's experience in Poland, he managed to get himself captured and sent back to France; an alternative version of events suggests that the boy deserted.[6] But another good story sprang up in later years: this suggested that Benyovszky married in America, fathered another three children there, and was murdered in 1809 in Texas. Sadly, this one too, although entirely fitting for the man and his interesting autobiography, was not true.)

Rejected in America, Maurice headed for the island of Haiti.

But when he discovered that the newly-installed French Governor of Haiti was none other than M de Bellecombe, the inspector from Madagascar, he could only bury his head in his hands. No gainful employment was to be found in the Caribbean, although Bellecombe – perhaps out of pity – did ask him to take some official despatches in his luggage when he sailed back to France.

France took delivery of the letters, but was still having nothing more to do with the postman.

Certainly, he was still a Brigadier, and still had his 4,000 *livres* pension. His attempts to persuade the new French Foreign Minister to fund a second trading expedition to Madagascar initially gained some traction; the Minister consulted his adviser, wondering vaguely if they should give this chap another chance? In the end, however, the request was lost as it passed up and down the corridors of power. France was in any case eyeing up Indo-China as a more promising colony.

In desperation, Benyovszky sailed to Britain.

He arrived there in October or November 1783, and was joined by his wife. She had followed him north and south, east and west throughout, and now had at least one child in tow – daughter Roza was born in 1779 and a second daughter, Zsofia, was still a babe-in-arms.

When news reached Paris that their pensioned Brigadier was looking for backers in London, there was some consternation and much wild speculation. Marshall Dumas, one-time Governor of Mauritius, wrote to the Minister to suggest that they might be under threat of a 'Theodoric project.' This slightly obscure reference was to the German adventurer Theodor von Neuhoff who had contrived to be elected King of Corsica in 1736, before fleeing to Britain, where he married the daughter of the Earl of Lucan, fell into debt, then cleared his debts by mortgaging his kingdom to British creditors. Could history be repeating itself? Could the British now have designs on Madagascar? There were rumours that the Hungarian had already left Britain with five ships and a large host of 'volunteers,' all set to found a trading-colony under the Austrian flag.[7]

The Minister shrugged in the Gallic manner, and passed Dumas' letter down the line. As a precaution, a memorandum was sent to Mauritius, instructing the authorities to establish communication with Benyovszky if he should turn up, and, at the very least, keep him away from the east coast of Madagascar.

In reality, far from making a triumphant return to the Indian Ocean, our Madagascan Theodor was getting nowhere fast in London. On Christmas Day 1783, he composed a "Proposal to His Britannic Majesty" suggesting terms of trade and mutual support between his colony on Madagascar and the British in India. He may even have presented these plans to the British government; but if this was the case, the British government was not buying from any foreign Johnnies. He did, however, manage to persuade a leading member of the Royal Society of London, Jean-Hyacinth de Magellan, to lend him a large amount of money to fund an ill-defined trading project; as collateral, Benyovszky handed over the lengthy manuscript of his *Memoirs*. In London, he also picked up a number of business associates, minor nobility and ex-military men, more or less unemployable, and exclusively impoverished. All were dazzled by the prospect of trade in hot climates. Some may also have been impressed by a document which Benyovszky now produced: it was signed by the Emperor Josef, dated 20th September 1783, and in cod-Latin granted Benyovszky the right, under Austrian protection, to exploit and govern the island of Madagascar. He had a flag of convenience: all he needed now were some financial backers. The ones in London had enthusiasm, but no money.

America was the place.

Benyovszky sailed again to America.

He left for Maryland on the *Robert and Ann* in April of 1784. A cargo worth around £4,000 was on board, paid for by the dupe Magellan, intended for trade in Madagascar. Eight or nine of his new associates accompanied him, mostly French or mid-European. Arriving in Baltimore in July, he found half-a-dozen more. And – at last! – two amongst them had money: Messrs Zollichofer and Meissonier, owners of a "respectable commercial house." A contract was drawn up between Zollichofer and Meissonier, on the one part, and Benyovszky and everyone else on the other (several of the men named on Benyovszky's side were already dead, and one – Mayeur – was still languishing oblivious in the humidity of Foulepointe. Luckily, no one looked too closely at the names). The deal was fairly simple: a "Society" would be established between all partners, effective for six years; Zollichofer and Meissonier would put up the money and a 450-ton ship, the *Intrepid*; in return, the ship would be loaded with "healthy negroes," to be sold at the Cape of Good Hope or Haiti, and the money would be credited to the Society. The main aim of the Society was, explicitly and unashamedly, trading in slaves. The investors would receive back all of their initial investment from the first voyage, plus 100% of the profits, then 50% of all profits in years two to six, and the town of "Mauritanie" would become the property of the Society forever.

The project could not possibly fail.

Notes

1   For all information on this period of Benyovszky's life, see Cultru, 1906, pp.131–132.
2   Lefèvre-Pontalis, pp.440–443.
3   Cook/King, Vol.3, 1834, p.448.
4   Kunec, 2010, p.46.
5   *ibid*, pp.47–48.
6   *ibid*, pp.43–44.
7   Cultru, 1906, pp.146–147.

XXIX

RETURN TO MADAGASCAR

"Give Me One of Your Pistols
and I'll Follow You"

Unforeseen Problems on Arrival – The Death of Benyovszky –
The Re-appearance of Benyovszky – An Unwilling Guide –
The Death of Benyovszky

In the spirit of hope, therefore, the *Intrepid* sailed from Baltimore on the 25th October 1784. Aboard were sixty-two people, four of them women – but Mme Benyovszky stayed behind this time, pregnant again. The two main investors very wisely stayed behind as well. An American army captain by the name of Paschke was a member of the company, and it was he who documented the voyage.[1] Their cargo consisted in the main of gunpowder (three hundred barrels), cannon (twenty) and rifles (fifty-five crates of twenty-five each). And then some agricultural and building tools. And plenty of brandy. One night in late December, the ship ran aground on the coast of Brazil, near the Cap de Saõ Roque. With some difficulty, and after throwing overboard ten cannon, it was refloated. They had to stop for repairs and provisions, but it was not a welcoming shore. Two of the minor investors jumped ship and went home. After a delay of two months, they set out to sea again, and in early May sailed round the Cape of Good Hope. By then, rations had been cut by half, and they had run out of meat (by an oversight, they had brought no furs to chew). On 22nd May 1785, they stopped off at the Mozambican port of Sofala, and took on water and food. Three weeks later, they crossed to Madagascar and, unable to go any further, dropped anchor close to Cap St Sebastien in the north-west of the island.

Benyovszky felt he was now on home territory. A local chief appeared on the shore, with two hundred of his people. They were happy to sell some cattle to the weary voyagers. An oath of friendship was duly sealed in blood, with the ship's guns celebrating merrily in the background. It was agreed that they could set up huts and a store, and bring off the remaining cargo. After a couple of days,

Benyovszky sent a man across the island to seek out M Mayeur, the sleeping partner of the contract, asking him to send 250 tribesmen by return, who would be armed and undertake the dirty work of rounding up a shipload of slaves. In the middle of all this, the chief of the Sakalava was spotted glowering in the trees, suspicious: was this not the same bad white man he had been fighting just a few years earlier? Benyovszky tacitly admitted it was by setting up three of his cannon behind some trenches and posting a guard.

On 1st August, the Sakalava chief returned with a thousand of his men. A nervous Benyovszky attempted to seal a pact with him. The chief demurred, explaining politely that it was too late in the evening for such things; would tomorrow do? But he did bring along some baskets of rice and demanded brandy in return. There was none to hand. Paschke was sent back to the ship for a spare barrel. No sooner had he reached the ship than he heard shots and saw, in the darkness, the flashes from gunfire. The crew panicked and wanted to sail off immediately; only with difficulty were they persuaded to wait until daylight. Daylight arrived. The ship fired signals. There was no reply. They kept this up until midday. Through a telescope, they could see that the huts and storehouse had been destroyed. The shore was crowded with islanders and not a single white skin was in evidence. There had been thirty-six members of company and crew on land. Assuming the worst, the ship sailed away, and after taking sixteen days for the 400-mile crossing, reached the port of Ibo on the coast of Mozambique. Here, in unseemly haste, the ship was sold off in favour of the investors. The ship's company dispersed.

There was much rejoicing in that part of the world. It was a Frenchman who bought the *Intrepid*, and he reported the glad news of Benyovszky's demise to the latest Governor of Mauritius, the Vicomte de Souillac. In turn, the Vicomte lost no time in relaying this back to Paris. Everyone rubbed their hands with satisfaction.

M. le Vicomte was a little premature.

In January of the following year he had to send a follow-up report, advising that Benyovszky had returned from the dead and was fortifying a small post at Angontsy (near to modern Ambohitralanana), situated on the coast barely 50 miles round the corner from his old stomping-ground at Antongil. He had not only managed to fend off the Sakalava, but had also transported all his men and some of his stores round the coast by canoe. Here he had set down in mid-October and was occupying his time in ransacking the stores and re-establishing old connections with local chiefs. It appeared that he had with him only fifteen of his original company, the rest having expired from one thing and another, or fled.

M le Vicomte got to hear of all this when a routine patrol ship returned from Madagascar, having encountered some of Benyovszky's men at Foulepointe. The ship's captain tried to persuade the local chief to hand over the intruders, but the local chief refused to help either side. The commander of the unwelcome guests was a German baron by the name of Adelsheim; under the captain's nose, he waved a document signed by Josef II of Austria, granting Madagascar to Benyovszky.

M le Vicomte was not amused. But it was the wrong season of the year to be despatching troops to the island. He instead sent orders to Mayeur, holding the fort at Foulepointe, to arrest Benyovszky or, at the very least, to refuse to give him any help or provisions whatsoever. The Hungarian, in the meantime, sent a letter over to Mauritius, advising the French not to interfere with his activities: was he not, after all, the *Ampansacabé*, the King of Madagascar?

M le Vicomte fumed. Blithely disregarding the fact that Madagascar was not in fact French territory, he made plans to root out the intruder who was compromising such trade as was still possible with the Madagascans. In early May a ship loaded with sixty soldiers, veterans of the Indian campaigns, was sent from Mauritius with the explicit aim of arresting the Hungarian and sending him back to France. The ship picked up an unwilling Mayeur at Foulepointe, to act as guide and interpreter, then sailed northwards to land the troops. They arrived at Angonsty just before dawn on the 24th May 1786.

Events then unfolded very swiftly. Forty soldiers and their officers were disembarked and they crept more or less quietly through the forest. Despite their caution, they attracted the attention of guards who were skulking in the trees. Shots were fired, cannon-fire was returned. The French commander suggested to Mayeur that he go ahead and parley with Benyovszky. Mayeur's reply was both succinct and sensible: "I certainly will not. He would hang me. Give me one of your pistols and I'll follow you." They tiptoed onwards until they reached an enclosure. It had been abandoned. They found no trace of anyone, only a path leading off into the forest. They followed the path and came across a small settlement: this must be 'Mauritanie.' As they checked their rifles and powder, Benyovszky spotted them and ran shouting into a small wooden fort raised a little above the surrounding ground. Around ninety of his men waited in defensive positions. The French troop advanced cautiously. Benyovszky fired a cannon. Shots were exchanged. The commander of the French troops ordered an assault. No sooner had they started running forward than Benyovszky was observed firing a rifle and immediately dropping it. His hand went to his left breast.

Two minutes later he was found lying dead.

There were no other fatalities; only one French soldier was injured. Eight white prisoners were taken: Baron Adelsheim, a French nobleman by the name of Brossard, four American sailors and two unnamed Frenchmen. Most of the locals had already vanished into the forest; but they came back the following day, bringing with them Mme Adelsheim and "an old Portuguese woman from Rio."

Benyovszky did not leave much from his final voyage to Madagascar: 200 *piastres*; hardly any provisions or munitions; a briefcase with three documents. One of the documents was a treaty dated 3 October 1776, giving Benyovszky full powers, as *Ampansacabé*, to negotiate in Europe on behalf of the islanders. Another was dated 28 March 1784 in London, appointing Mr Magellan as European plenipotentiary for the company. The third, dated August 1785, appointed Chevalier Hensky as Secretary of State and Lieutenant-General of Madagascar. M Hensky, we suppose, was a relative of his wife; unfortunately, he had perished some time before.

Benyovszky also left a widow. In Baltimore, Mme Benyovszky received a letter from Benjamin Franklin on 11th May 1786, who – choosing his time rather badly – enquired after her husband. Some months thereafter, learning of her husband's demise, she and her two daughters returned to Hungary, taking up residence in the village of Vietzka, near Beckov. (She was now known as 'Countess Anna Susanna de Hönsch.') It is there that she died in 1826 at the age of 75.

The village and fort of Mauritanie were destroyed. Benyovszky was hastily buried. The French troops, having carried out an entirely illegal mission to everyone's satisfaction, went back to Mauritius.

The King of Madagascar was dead.

Note

1   All quotes hereinafter from Cultru, pp.147–159.

XXX

HISTORIES

Perfidious Mutilations in Counterfeit Editions

Three Volumes Printed in Beautiful Characters – A Severe Illness –
Several Mishaps – A Fever of Translation – Wickedness, Jealousy and Credulity –
A Monstrous Character – Operas, Films, Parodies, Musicals – And Coins

Dead, but not entirely forgotten.

The Parisian philosophical *Journal Encyclopédique* of the late eighteenth century always ran reviews of recent publications. More cosmopolitan in outlook than the vast majority of today's journals, the literary section reported on books from all over Europe. In the July 1784 edition, for example, there were notices of a dozen books published in France (with subjects ranging from the education of the deaf and dumb, to some shocking and spicy *causes célèbres* revealed by a famous solicitor), three from Britain (including *A General Synopsis of Birds* by the renowned ornithologist John Latham, and a review of Nathaniel Halhed's *Grammar of the Bengal Language*), four from Germany (of specific interest was *Historia Febris Hecticae – A History of the Hectic Fever,* by Wenceslas Trnka, Professor of Pathology at the University of Bude, in Hungary. It is pleasing to note that Trnka listed seven cures for this tubercular malady; no claim, however, is made for any of the cures being successful), two from Holland (one of which was a timely condemnation of Symphysiotomy) and three from Spain (including a new Spanish translation of the Montpellier Catechism).

By far the longest notice in this same edition of the *Journal,* sandwiched between birds and Bengal, was a prospectus for the publication by subscription of the Count Benyovszky's *Memoirs.* This book was to appear in three volumes, and the sales pitch ran as follows:

Memoirs, Voyages and Discoveries of the Count de Benyowsky, Born a Magnate of Hungary, one of the Chiefs and a Marshal of the Confederation of Poland &c,

proposed by subscription, in 3 volumes, in quarto, with almost 60 copper-plate engravings. The first volume, according to a Prospectus printed in London, will contain the private life of the author, the details of his military service in the Imperial armies, his entry into the service of the Republic of Poland, a summary of the revolution and of the war of this republic against the Russian, an account of the sufferings of M. de Benyowsky after being made prisoner of war, a description of the interior of Russia, with an exposé of the domestic troubles of that Empire, the author's voyage to Kamchatka, to which he was exiled, &c, some remarks on Siberia, an exact description of this distant land, with maps and plates relative to it, the voyage of the Count, by sea, from Okhotsk, Siberian port, to Kamchatka, a description of this peninsula, the history of the exiles in this same country, the enterprise formed by the author to form a party and regain liberty, an account of the fortunate revolution by which he made himself master of the capital and of the port of Bolsha, with 59 men against 280 soldiers and 700 militia. This volume will be supplemented with 12 or 14 copper-plate engravings.

So far, so tempting for the reader in search of tales of exotic places. And it gets better.

The second volume will contain the *Extracts from the Memoirs of all the Voyages and Discoveries made by the Russians in the Northern Ocean, which M. de Benyowsky found in the Chancellery of Kamchatka,* his departure from the port of Bolsha on board the corvette *St Peter and St Paul*, his voyage into the Polar Sea, the discovery of the straits situated between the two capes, that of Tartary named Csukocskoy, and that of America called Allaksina, the description of the Kuril Islands and the Aleutian Islands, which he sailed past, several discoveries on the islands and lands situated between Kamchatka and California, putting into port in Japan, some details of that Empire, and an account of his stay on one of those islands, a description of the islands of the Kings and of Legueio, the landing of the author on the island of Formosa, a description of this island, his arrival on the coast of China, his stay at Macao, his return to Europe, passing through the Ile de France and Ile de Bourbon, putting in to port on the island of Madagascar, and then his arrival at Port de L'Orient, where he disembarked. In this volume, there will be around twenty copper-plate engravings.

Dear reader, please pause to take a breath after that volume, described all in one sentence, for the third one is just as good:

The third volume will offer the history of the Count from his reception in France, his entry into the service of this Monarchy, details concerning the mission with which he was charged by Louis XV, to establish relations of trade and friendship with the inhabitants of Madagascar, his departure from Europe on this mission, an account of his activities on Madagascar, a description of the island, the history of its morals, usages, customs and riches, a reliable census of its population, details on the division of the provinces and governments of its king, princes and chiefs, the treaties concluded by the author with the natives of the country, the events which he experienced during the five years employed in civilising this nation, which gave all of its trust and friendship to him. In this last volume there will be approximately 24 copper-plate engravings.

Having thus wound up the reading public to a fever-pitch of excitement, there followed the technical details, the small print, some esoteric notes on copyright protection, and a heartfelt blast against piracy. All of which give an interesting insight into the publishing business of the eighteenth century.

> *Conditions.* The three volumes, printed in beautiful characters and on good paper, will each have more than 300 pages. It will be published in two editions, one in French and the other in English: the larger number of subscribers for one or the other will decide which edition appears first.
>
> The total price of the subscription, one should add, will be 3 guineas, half to be paid when subscribing, the other half on receipt of the final volume. The receipts will be signed and initialled by the editor (M. Schreiber, Engineer Officer) or by the booksellers, named below, with whom one can subscribe [...]
>
> As soon as the sum of the subscriptions is sufficient to cover the printing expenses, then printing will begin. These *Memoirs* are already prepared for publication, and, once started, the printing will continue without interruption. One expects that the public will be eager to hasten the publication of a work which is perhaps the most interesting and most singular that has ever appeared in this genre.
>
> Since there are booksellers in the other main cities of Europe who are in correspondence with those in London, one has deemed it unnecessary to open this subscription other than in the capital of England, at the premises of: Sr. J. Robson of Bond-Street, White of Fleet-Street, P. Elmsly & T Cadell in the Strand.
>
> At the end of the 3rd. volume, a list will be provided of certain marks which are to be found in every copy, but which no one would suspect without being warned, and which, by consequence, the counterfeiters will not be able to imitate. These marks will constitute the identity of the original London edition, and will assure the public that there have been no changes unfaithful to the original, nor any of those perfidious mutilations with which counterfeit editions of this work cannot fail to be filled, despite all the protestations to the contrary of the interested parties in this piracy.[1]

In July 1784, Benyovszky was already in America, hoodwinking the citizens of Baltimore into financing his next trip to Madagascar. He had no further part to play in drumming up subscriptions for his book. As it happened, the required minimum financial backing was never attained, and the publication project was shelved.

William Nicholson, who finally published the *Memoirs* in 1790, takes up the story:

> About the latter end of the year 1784, Mr. J. Hyacinth de Magellan, FRS *etc*, a gentleman well known in every part of Europe, by the philosophical correspondence he has for many years carried on with the first literary characters, shewed me a printed paper in French, containing proposals for publishing the memoirs and voyages of the Count de Benyowsky, in three volumes, by subscription: a design that was afterwards given up. The Count was not at that time in England, but had departed upon a private expedition to the island of Madagascar; in the fitting out of which, Mr. Magellan had advanced a very considerable sum. This expedition was not, however, attended with success: Mr. Magellan determined therefore to publish this work; and accordingly disposed of the copy of the present proprietors, at the same time that he engaged to communicate the transactions of the Count, from the conclusion of the present Memoirs to the time of his death. An unforeseen event rendered him incapable of performing this engagement: for soon after Christmas, 1788, he was attacked with a severe illness, which affected his memory so much as to prevent his attending to any literary pursuits, and has continued ever since.[2]

Magellan – more properly João Jacinto de Magalhães – descendant of the famous explorer of the same surname, was a Portuguese physicist and polymath who had made his home in London and become a respected member of the Royal Society. His publications were many and varied. Displaying that special naivety particular to people of genius, he managed to get himself tangled up with the adventurer Benyovszky and parted with his money to fund a pie-in-the-sky expedition to Madagascar. As Mr Nicholson notes, in something of an understatement, the expedition "was not attended with success." But, struck down by illness at the age of 68, Magellan was unable to proceed with his scheme to recoup his investment by other means. Nicholson, a young physicist and chemist in frequent correspondence with the Royal Society, took up the challenge. Why he should have felt enthusiastic enough to do so, is not known. There was certainly no professional interest in what Benyovszky had been up to. It is likely that he simply felt an obligation to his old friend Magellan.

The printing of the work was not unattended by further mishap. The "proprietors" of the material to be published – friends and relatives of Magellan – were persuaded by Nicholson to lodge all the manuscripts and drawings in the British Museum "a place peculiarly calculated for the security of the public in such cases." The manuscript is still stored there. However, several of the drawings and maps which Benyovszky had carefully prepared, "were lost by a fire that consumed the house of Mr. Heath, the engraver." (James Heath, a well-regarded and busy engraver, lost most of his property, money and many other engravings in the fire. It took him some time to recover his business.) Nicholson was not greatly concerned at any of these losses – "they consisted chiefly of views and figures." Neither was he particularly impressed by the drawings which did survive the fire: another drawing which vanished was one of the *St Peter*. It showed a ship "differing in no respect, either in hull or in rigging, from a European ship," and so was without much interest; however, "I fear it has been irrecoverably mislaid, among other papers of no value." Even those which did survive mischance were not all printed. Nicholson mentioned an engraving of the shipwreck upon the "Liqueio Islands": "as it is evident that neither the Count, nor any of his companions, could have taken a drawing of the incident," he chose to omit it as merely ornamental. Similarly, a drawing of the coast of Formosa is so lacking in "notes of bearings, distance etc," that it was deemed superfluous.

Sadly, those plates which did make it into the volumes were not particularly impressive either. In Volume I, there are views of various rocky headlands purporting to be *inter alia* Bering Island, Kamchatka Point, the Kurils, the Cape of "Alaksina" and so forth. Benyovszky's sketch-maps of Japanese bays are provided – but Nicholson had to improve the one of the so-called Bay of Usilpatchar: "NB This sketch has neither scale nor compass. The Editor has inserted the Compass upon Conjecture." There is a small plate (No. V) of a rather cute, almost medieval-looking ship with two masts, which contrasts rather oddly with the more robust, three-masted vessel depicted in an action-filled engraving of "An Affair of Retaliation upon the Island Formosa." Volume II is bursting with maps of bits of Madagascar, some taken from the maps drawn by other French surveyors, some proudly inscribed as the work of "Rosières, Officer acting as Engineer." The latter are maps, slightly idealised, of the settlements founded by Benyovszky. All the plates are inscribed with the date of publication – 12th November 1789.

In editing the *Memoirs*, Nicholson was keenly aware of contradictory evidence and contemporary criticisms. He took the time to compare this narrative with the story which Izmailov told to Captain Cook, and came down firmly on the side of Benyovszky, whose account he described as "an authentic journal." And while noting in passing that "the Count's skill in navigation, whatever eminence it may have procured him in Kamchatka, appears to have been very moderate,"[3] he was prepared to overlook the lack of accuracy as to longitude, as being quite common even amongst experienced navigators. He did remark in a footnote that "the Count does not appear to have reached America in that latitude [54º]," but was not greatly perturbed by this glaring inaccuracy, even although latitude was rarely miscalculated by any navigator of even very moderate skills. His considered judgement was that the entire story was generally sound, despite doubts expressed by others:

MEMOIRS AND TRAVELS

OF

MAURITIUS AUGUSTUS COUNT DE BENYOWSKY;

MAGNATE OF THE KINGDOMS OF HUNGARY AND POLAND, ONE OF
THE CHIEFS OF THE CONFEDERATION OF POLAND, &c, &c.

CONSISTING OF HIS MILITARY OPERATIONS IN POLAND, HIS EXILE INTO KAM-
CHATKA, HIS ESCAPE AND VOYAGE FROM THAT PENINSULA THROUGH THE
NORTHERN PACIFIC OCEAN, TOUCHING AT JAPAN AND FORMOSA,
TO CANTON IN CHINA, WITH AN ACCOUNT OF THE
FRENCH SETTLEMENT HE WAS APPOINTED
TO FORM UPON THE ISLAND OF
MADAGASCAR.

WRITTEN BY HIMSELF.

TRANSLATED FROM THE

ORIGINAL MANUSCRIPT.

IN TWO VOLUMES.

VOL I.

LONDON:

PRINTED FOR G. G. J. AND J. ROBINSON, PATER-NOSTER-ROW.

M,DCC,XC.

FIGURE 30.1 Frontispiece of the first edition of Benyovszky's *Memoirs*.

Of this singular character, many and various have been the opinions. Those whose interests led them to oppose him have spared no accusations against him; and their accusations are of the strongest and even the most horrid nature. [...] Yet while he lived, he was never without enthusiastic admirers, and warm friends who readily exerted themselves, against every risque and every calumny, to serve him. If it were expected that I should give my opinion, I would declare, that I have not yet seen any thing against him which will not bear two interpretations [...] For these reasons it is that I would suspend my opinions.[4]

A sensible approach, one would agree, for a scientist. In the interests of providing a full story, Nicholson provided a potted history of Benyovszky's second voyage to Madagascar and his subsequent demise. And in the interests of good marketing, he did not reproduce such letters, found in Magellan's collection of papers, as were written by people hostile to Benyovszky.

The Nicholson edition was printed in London early in 1790 ("for G. G. J. Robinson and J. Robinson, Paternoster Row"), in handsome quarto format; another edition was printed in Dublin, by Porter and Jackson. A French edition followed in 1791, in handy pocket-sized octavo, printed by Buisson in the Rue Hautefeuille. Even in the midst of their great Revolution, it was hoped that the French would retain their enthusiasm for a 'good read.' And then the Germans caught up. Caught up and overtook everyone: a translation appeared in Berlin in 1790, with another edition from the same publisher four years later. Meanwhile, the brothers Christoph and Johann Ebeling of Hamburg had rushed out their own edition in 1791, keeping neck and neck with editions – all pirated – which appeared in Leipzig and Tübingen in the same year. The German public proved insatiable for Benyovszky – further editions of the above followed thick and fast, along with slimmer "edited highlights" volumes – seven or eight editions in total before 1796. The Poles brought out their own translation in 1797, and further editions appeared there over the next decade. Benyovszky Fever gripped Europe for a couple of years: yet more editions appeared in France, Austria, Holland and Sweden in the years 1791 and 1792. In 1807 a Slovak edition appeared. But it was not until 1888 that a Hungarian translation was published.

A Russian translation, it should come as no surprise, remained elusive. Only in 1822 did the historian Berg even note the existence of Benyovszky, when editing Ryumin's journal. His reference to the *Memoirs* – and his view of those who read them – is a little disparaging:

This event [*the escape from Kamchatka*] was described by Benyovszky himself in his *Voyages et Memoires de Maurice August Comte de Benjowski, Paris 1791*, and was translated into English, German and other languages. In this work Benyowsky presented himself as an extraordinary hero, and assailed Russia and its then government with the most unjustified slander and presented all his actions in an extremely favourable and false light. Many of our

GEDENKSCHRIFTEN

E N

R E I Z E N

D E S

GRAAVEN VAN BENYOWSKY

DOOR HEM ZELVEN BESCHREEVEN,

NAAR DE ENGELSCHE VERTAALING UIT HET
OORSPRONGLYK HANDSCHRIFT OVERGEZET.

EERSTE DEEL.

TE HAARLEM,
B Y A. L O O S J E S, Pz.
M D C C X C I.

VOYAGES

ET MÉMOIRES

D E

MAURICE-AUGUSTE,

COMTE DE BENYOWSKY,

*Magnat des Royaumes D'HONGRIE et DE
POLOGNE,* etc. etc.

CONTENANT ses Opérations militaires en
Pologne; son exil au Kamchatka, son Evasion
et son Voyage à travers l'Océan pacifique, au
Japon, à Formose, à Canton en Chine, et
les détails de l'Etablissement qu'il fut chargé
par le Ministère François de former à Madagascar.

TOME PREMIER.

A PARIS,
Chez F. BUISSON, Imprimeur-Libraire, rue
Hautefeuille, n° 20.

(1 7 9 1.)

Neuere

Geschichte

der

See- und Land-Reisen

Vierter Bnd.

Begebenheiten und Reisen
des Grafen
Moritz August von Benjowsky,
von ihm selbst beschrieben.

Zweyter Band.

Aus dem Englischen übersetzt
von
C. D. Ebeling,
Professor am Gymnasium in Hamburg.

und
Dr. J. P. Ebeling,

Mit des erstern Anmerkungen und Zusätzen,
wie auch einem Anhang

aus
Hippolitus Stefanows
russisch geschriebenem Tagebuche
über seine Reise von Kamtschatka nach Makao.

Mit Landkarten und Kupfern.

Hamburg, 1791.
bei Benjamin Gottlob Hoffmann.

HISTORYA PODROZY

Y

OSOBLIWSZYCH ZDARZEN

SŁAWNEGO

MAURYCEGO-AUGUSTA

HRABI

BENIOWSKIEGO

SZLACHCICA POLSKIEGO
i WĘGIERSKIEGO,

ZAWIERAIĄCA W SOBIE:

Jego czyny woienne, w czasie Konfederacyi
Barskiey, — wygnanie iego nayprzód do
Kazanu, — potym do Kamszatki, — wale-
czne iego z tey niewoli oswobodzenie się, —
iego podróż do Kalifornii, potym przez
Ocean spokoyny do Japonii, — Formozy,
— Kantonu w Chinach, — założenie przez
niego osady na wyspie Madagaskarze, z zle-
cenia Francuzkiego Rządu, — iego na tey
wyspie woienne wyprawy, uznanie iego na
reszcie Naywyższym iey Rządcą.

z Francuzkiego tłómaczona.

TOM IV.

EDYCYA NOWA,

w WARSZAWIE,
w Drukarniach połączonych GAZETY WAR-
SZAWSKIEY i Sukces: TOMASZA LE BRUN.

1806.

FIGURE 30.2 Frontispieces for the Dutch (top left), French (top right) and German (bottom left) editions of Benyovszky's *Memoirs* of 1791 and the Polish (bottom right) edition of 1806.

countrymen, who unfortunately know foreign languages better than they know that of their Fatherland, read this absurd fiction of this Count and believed it blindly. Kotzebue made a play out of the novel, which was not only performed in the German Theatre here, but was even translated into Russian and went to three editions! The careful researcher [*i.e. Berg*] into the history of Russian navigation and geographical discoveries has been so fortunate as to get access to the true reports of the deeds of this boastful hero and share them with us, in order to illuminate this fascinating event in our recent history and simultaneously to destroy the construction of slander, lies and self-praise which had been erected by wickedness, jealousy and credulity.[5]

The publication of the *Memoirs* attracted immediate critical interest on both sides of the English Channel. First into the field was a review of the Nicholson edition, which appeared in *The Gentleman's Magazine* of 1790. The reviewer settled himself down at the start with a waspish comment:

> It must be acknowledged that, independent of the Count's character, as drawn by his own pen, which represents him as little influenced by a regard to truth, or indeed any principle of morality whatever, his accounts favour much of romantic embellishment and exaggeration.[6]

And then proceeded to accurately summarise the contents of both volumes. One curious anomaly crept in to an otherwise faithful review: having briefly described the death of the hero in Madagascar, the reviewer observed that "his wife, whether Polish or Japanese is not certain, who had born him a son, and was at this time pregnant, appears to have been with him, and was probably involved in the fate of his party." One can applaud the reviewer's stamina in reading the 822 pages end-to-end, and therefore forgive this lapse of concentration. To make up for the misidentification of the spouse, the reviewer showed himself to be quite familiar with other books covering similar geographical areas, and cited likely sources for those copper-engraved plates which had finally made it into the book. "The charts of harbours on the coast of Madagascar," he wrote, "are found in Mr. Dalrymple's Collection from M. d'Apres; and as they do not essentially differ from these engravings, it is probable the Count had them from the same quarter." Other plates – depicting people in sledges, Japanese dignitaries on the march, and the method of preparing manioc root have, he judged, "hardly the merit of novelty to help the sale of the book. [...] Others more conversant in books of travels may possibly discover other conformities." His final judgement of the author is reasonably damning: "we cannot acquit [*him*] of many violations of morality and integrity."

Not long after this, there appeared a review of the English edition in the *Journal Encyclopédique* of February 1791. The French critic was not kind.

> Right from the start of the first volume, one notices so many small inexactitudes, so many faulty memories, such an inclination to state as a

certainty anything which does not even look plausible, such a long list of dangers faced, such good fortune in escaping them, that one would have to be extraordinarily gullible to avoid being assailed by a host of doubts about the veracity of these tales. The second volume does not dispel these doubts, since on every page one comes across so many things which are not impossible, but are quite improbable, or at least are contradicted by the accounts made by every other known traveller.[7]

In a lengthy review, running to twenty-four pages, the reviewer does his best to present the outlines of Benyovszky's tale, but finds himself obliged to cast doubt on the factual accuracy at every turn.

A side-swipe at Benyovszky came just a few months later, in July 1791, in a review in the same journal of Alexis Rochon's *Voyages*. When it came to summarising Rochon's views on Benyovszky, the reviewer vented his spleen. Talking of the appointment of the Baron as the official French colonist of Madagascar,

> we shall limit ourselves to stating that this is a typical example of those ministerial abuses which were only too common in the Ancien Régime. [...] There were no absurdities, no vexations, no horrors which M. de Boynes' favourite did not permit himself, and one can see in the account by our author the tragic repercussions of the caprices and influences of the French ministers of the old regime. Characters as monstrous as that of the Satrap Benyowsky can only take things to such a level of excess if allowed to do so by that most puerile of human sentiments – vanity.

The reviewer rounded off his remarks with the following post-revolutionary reminder: "Let us not forget: it was thus that our millions and our morals were compromised before our Era of Liberty."[8]

One gets the impression that this was not a good time to publish the *Memoirs* in France. Feelings about him there clearly ran high; this may have been one reason why the 1784 Prospectus had not been successful. When the French edition was finally published, later in 1791, the *Journal* limited its notice to a shortened version of the title, its price – "Two volumes in octavo, comprising approx 960 pages. Price: 8 *livres* bound, plus 9 *livres* postage" – and no review at all.

A more private criticism was expressed in Germany. The German satirical writer Heinrich von Bretschneider was not greatly taken with Ebeling's edition, nor with Benyovszky himself. Of the "invented island of Usmay Ligon," Bretschneider observed:

> This is supposed to lie in Japanese waters. Since B. invented it, is it any wonder that the great geographical expert Prof. Ebeling in Hamburg, looked in vain for any mention of it in other books, and supposed it to be either a slip of the pen or a printer's error?[9]

We have earlier noted Bretschneider's comments on a 1780 rough draft of Benyovszky's great work, that "there was already something unbelievable in those papers, and some things quite suspicious..."

Poorly received by the critics, then. But what do critics know?

These few uncharitable voices of doubt and dissent were drowned out by the ringing of cash-registers. Here was a story of adventures, exotic travel, romance, war and high political drama. What was not to like? Benyovszky's adventures were avidly lapped up across Europe, and championed with considerable enthusiasm. In Germany, the Ebelings were not going to put up with any criticism of their man from anyone – hence their summary dismissal of Stepanov's diary, which

> is written with a bias: thus the author will already be known to the readers of this book and his words should be compared to Benyovsky's story, which he mostly confirms. [...] Readers will of course not forget who Stefanov was, and what character he displayed throughout, however mercifully he was treated by the Count, who was always ready to forgive him.[10]

There was a slow uptake of enthusiasm for Benyovszky in his native land – slow, but gradually growing, and then persistent. Despite some initial interest in translating the *Memoirs* into Hungarian in the heady days of 1790–1791, it was not until a century later that such an edition appeared. Vilmos Voigt has provided an excellent overview of the growth of Benyovszkiana in the nineteenth century.[11]

Mention has already been made of the enthusiasm of Kotzebue, and his tempestuous dramatic interpretation of the *Memoirs*. His play was closely followed up by another written by Goethe's brother-in-law, Vulpius, whose *Graf Benjowsky. Ein original Trauerspiel* was first performed in 1794. In New York, as early as April 1799, a play written by William Dunlap was

> brought out with great expense and care. Receipts first night 800 dollars. The audience were much gratified, and expectation, though on tip-toe, fully satisfied. [...] Mr. Barrett's Stepenoff was good, and Mrs. Barrett, though not youthful enough for the heroine, played it with truth and force.

Mr. Cooper, who played Benyovszky, was not mentioned in this critique, but Mr Bates, who played the Hettmann, "as usual said any thing but what was put down for him."[12] It was, in fact, a modest success. This play was also put on in Boston. But maybe not Baltimore.

Apart from the usual biographies, there were also a good number of novels and instructive "stories for young people" – and as many operas as you could hope for. The first Benyovszky opera appeared in France in 1800 and was performed in Austria four years later. It was based on Kotzebue's play; but in the Vienna Hoftheater production the main character underwent a name-change from Benyovszky to "Edwinsky." Anti-French feeling was at that time running high in

FIGURE 30.3 Flier for a performance of the Hungarian opera of 1848.

FIGURE 30.4 Opening bars of Ferenc Doppler's score for the 1848 opera.

Austria, and the mere suggestion of having a character on stage who had seen service in the French Army would have had the censor reaching for his red pen.[13] An English opera followed in 1826, also basing itself on Kotzebue's play. Both of these operas even spawned their own music-hall parodies, a sure sign of popular success. Not to be outdone, the Hungarians produced their own opera in 1848, complete with Cossack dancers and chorus.

Between 1850 and 1890, a host of historical novels rolled off the printing-presses. In 1889 there appeared the utterly uncritical and enthusiastic Hungarian edition of the *Memoirs*, a four-volume publication (by some quirk of publishing logistics, it appeared not in strict numerical order), prepared by the prolific novelist and writer, Mor Jokai. Jokai was the Father of Hungarian Romantic History, the Walter Scott of Budapest: his collected works run to 100 volumes. He was a man who managed to focus the aspirations of the growing movement for independence from Austria upon the Hungarian 'national' history. The bursts of interest in Benyovszky and all his works tended naturally to coincide with upsurges of political nationalism or radicalism. The initial wave of enthusiasm, in and after 1790, fed on the bourgeois radicalism which swept Europe in the wake of the French and American Revolutions, and the Hungarian Count was undoubtedly seen as a figure standing up to feudal oppression in Russia and France. In the late nineteenth century, the maturing Hungarian national movement found its very own national hero in Benyovszky, and this led to an upsurge in books and novels about him. More recently, the break-up of the Soviet sphere of influence, and the consequent splitting of Slovakia out of Czechoslovakia, has understandably led to a renewed interest in the iconic historical figures of the region. Benyovszky's birthplace, Vrbové, historically in Hungary, now lies firmly in Slovakian territory.

And interest never died down. The good Captain Pasfield Oliver, something of an expert on Madagascar and Mauritius, indulged his later retirement years in editing the *Memoirs*. Despite major reservations about Benyovszky, Oliver had sufficient patience and dedication to provide the British reading public with not one, but two editions of the book. The first was published in 1893, with a properly critical introduction, the second edition appeared eleven years later and contained a full bibliography. Oliver's wide reading allowed him to identify some of the sources for the Count's many tales of exploration and pirates; he attempted to identify some of the Japanese islands and ports of call. But such dedication to the editorial task did not blind him to some of Benyovszky's faults. His damning judgement was this: "At that time Europe was teeming with adventurers, plausible, amusing, and good-looking, but wholly unprincipled Don Juans, who would fight under any leader where plunder was to be gained. Such an one was Benyowsky."[14]

In more recent years, there has been other more academic activity. In 1987, a Benyovszky conference was organised in the Hungarian town of Erd, at which a number of papers were delivered. Japan and China have recently been taking an interest in our man. In Washington in 2000 an exhibition was held, entitled *Count*

Maurice Benyowsky. An 18th Century World-traveler from Slovakia. In a surreal turn of events, given what Benyovszky actually did in Madagascar, the honorary consul of the Republic of Madagascar in 2006 presented his credentials in Budapest, referring to Benyovszky and stressing the importance of "Madagascan-Hungarian friendship." There is today a street named the *Rue Benyowsky* in the Madagascan capital Antananarivo. A society for promoting Madagascan-Hungarian friendship had already been set up earlier in the decade, and was instrumental in 2004 in arranging the Hungarian publication, with critical apparatus, of Benyovszky's own version of the events in Madagascar. Seven years later, the Society organised a Benyovszky Memorial Day, to celebrate 265 years since his birth and 225 since his death; it was a significant cultural event, involving libraries, media companies, academics and politicians from Hungary and beyond. Films and TV-programmes have appeared in recent years: in 1975, there was a popular thirteen-part Hungarian TV-series (Benyovszky would have been pleased – his name appears on the writing credits); in 2009, Hungarian TV aired a programme on Benyovszky and Madagascar; 2013 saw a musical with dance-routines. For the anniversary year of 2016, a Hungarian 'Memorial Committee' was set up to organise another conference and an exhibition, campaign for a postage-stamp and stage another musical (and also debate whether Benyovszky was Hungarian or Slovakian).

Not every modern assessment of Benyovszky has been uncritical. In 2007 the Hungarian historian Vilmos Voigt poured cold water upon Benyovszky's account of his time in Madagascar:

> [*it*] is truly a personal work and takes reality only as a starting point, it is neither a work of *belles-lettres* nor an ethnological description. Besides, Benyovszky did not have the talent for either of these. Obviously he could not draw well either, and he did not think of noting down even a short list of words from the remote and strange languages. He was really interested in only one person: himself.[15]

These comments about the Madagascar journals apply equally well to the totality of the *Memoirs*. Given this sober judgement and the sheer amount of factual material available which easily contradicts Benyovszky's many claims, one might scratch one's head over the popular and uncritical fascination with Benyovszky in his homeland(s). It is almost as if Robinson Crusoe were still being celebrated as a real historical person. But turn that bemusement on its head: Robinson Crusoe and Maurice Benyovszky appeal to the hidden adventurer in us all. The tales might be tall ones, but why should they not also be popular?

Books, films, TV-dramas, exhibitions, conferences; operas; parodies of operas; and, in these modern times, websites.[16] And, of course, coins. On the two hundred and fiftieth anniversary of his birth in 1996, the National Bank of Slovakia issued a commemorative 200-crown (7 Euros) silver coin, showing Benyovszky's head on one side and a ship on the other. The PR material relating to the striking of the coin read as follows (in the Bank's authorised translation):

Count Moric Benovsky (20.9.1746, Vrbove − 23.5.1786, Madagascar), a typical representative of the period of the Enlightenment, the development of transport and trade, exploration of unknown regions, French colonel, Ruler of Madagascar, and the first Slovak author of a best-seller, was involved in the history of various countries. After being captured while fighting for the independence of Poland, he was deported to Kamchatka, where he organized his escape. His voyage to Macao was the first known voyage from the north-east to the south-east shores of Asia. The King of France entrusted him with an expedition to Madagascar, where he unified part of the island, and the local tribes granted him the title of 'King of Kings.' Upon his return to Austria, he attempted to build a fleet of ships for overseas trade. After this failed, he became a general in the American army, and organized another expedition to Madagascar, where he fell in battle with the French in 1786. His travel memoirs were published in London in 1790, and have so far appeared in at least 20 editions in more than ten languages.[17]

And every word of the above is said to be authentic.

Notes

1 *Journal Encyclopédique*, July 1784, Vol.58, pp.364–367 (author's own translation).
2 Benyovszky, 1790. Vol.I, pp.i–ii.
3 *ibid*, p.ix.
4 *ibid*, p.xviii.
5 Berg, 1822, pp.56–57.
6 *The Gentleman's Magazine*, 1790, Vol.60, p.725.
7 *Journal Encyclopédique*, February 1791, Vol.71, p.451.
8 *Journal Encyclopédique*, July 1791, Vol.72, pp.482–483.
9 Meusel, 1816, pp.112–113.
10 Ebeling, 1791, p.283.
11 Voigt, 2007, *passim*, and specifically pp.102–103.
12 Dunlap, 1833. pp.96–97.
13 Albrecht, 2008, pp.219–220.
14 Oliver, 1893 edition, p.52.
15 Voigt, 2007, p.100.
16 For example, www.benyovszky.hu
17 www.nbs.sk/en/banknotes-and-coins/slovak-currency/slovak-commemorative-coins/silver-200sk-coin-commemorating-the-birth-of-benovsky

XXXI

A FINAL AUDIT

"A Very Fair Claim to the Title of Adventurous"

He Was Not an Explorer – A Wretched Farrago – Heroes and Heroines All –
Extraordinary Achievements – An Ignominious Murder

Benyovszky: explorer, developer of trade and transport, French colonel, American general, best-selling author? Let us conduct a final audit.

Explorer?

It is fair to say that Maurice Benyovszky did not do much exploring. The voyage he made down the Kurils and Japan was one of escape. The voyage he made to the north-west coast of America and the Aleutian Islands was a complete invention. Certainly, he visited places that very few Europeans had ever seen before. Had he been a true explorer, and stuck to the facts, his *Memoirs* would have been a far better book. As it is, he rarely had anything true and new to tell the world. He was of that interesting sub-species, the retrospective explorer. When he prettied up his account of his many adventures, several years after the event, he relied without acknowledgement on the records of those who had gone before – or after – him. All fair enough: but he undermined the whole thing by inventing places and people and episodes that had no basis in reality.

It is beyond the scope of this present book to determine exactly which episodes, names and locations Benyovszky 'borrowed' to flesh out his *Memoirs*. Suffice it to say that a number of his critics – from 1790 onwards – have convincingly proposed a series of maps, charts, travellers' tales and expedition reports which echo with strange familiarity in Benyovsky's account.[1]

Arguably, our inadvertent escapee Ivan Ryumin did a far better job as an explorer. Vague though his records are in respect of locations (but remarkably accurate on dates), they are alive with curiosity and descriptions of places which he really did visit. He even went to the trouble of naming his companions. All of which was sadly lacking in the Count's journals. Did Benyovszky bother to count the number of streetlights in Paris? We think not.

Developer of trade and transport?

No one can deny that he wanted to develop trade. Commerce was the air that he breathed. In these our modern times, trade and transport are usually presented as benefits to society as a whole (even if the naked facts frequently contradict this idea). But it is disingenuous to imply that Benyovszky was some kind of enlightened socio-economic benefactor. The main purpose of his reminiscences was to cajole the potential investors of Europe and America into funding trading trips that would make him, Benyovszky, rich and famous. The French discovered this to their cost in Madagascar.

French colonel and American general?

Benyovszky liked to be seen as an experienced military man, whose bottomless reservoir of strategic genius demonstrated that small numbers of skilled Europeans could so easily subdue large numbers of Asian and African people. This was the purpose of his extra, and entirely fictitious, five years of youth. It was the purpose of the lengthy narration of his exploits in the war between the Polish rebels and the Russian Imperial armies; of the over-elaborate uprising in Bolsheretsk; of that most remarkable war in Formosa… not forgetting the countless military victories in Madagascar. The waging of war was, after all, the necessary foundation for the colonisation of Africa, Asia and the Americas. Whether Benyovszky was really a consummate soldier, or just thought he was, is wide open to debate. Mention is made on our coin of the 'battle' in which he fell in Madagascar – it was unfortunately no more than a rather shabby assassination. As for being a French Colonel – that is pitching it low: he was a French brigadier, according to his pension-rights. And an American general? Nope.

Best-selling author?

That, certainly. If one reliable measure of a best-seller is the number of gaping holes in the plot, then the *Memoirs* measured up. And then some. His book is in places clumsy, in places awash with scented romance and courtliness, here exciting, there numbingly improbable. And, in the final analysis, revelatory not of the big wide world, merely of Benyovszky's own big wide personality. He was indeed the first Magyar and/or Slovak best-selling author. There is nothing wrong with any of that: the public at the end of the eighteenth century clearly wanted all this and more. What kind of kill-joys are we, 225 years later, to scoff at their preferences?

The man clearly had an eye for plot: just consider the almost-global reactions to his wondrous tale about the Russian invasion of Japan.

It is only a shame that Benyovszky spent so much time on invented adventures and so little time on the events and adventures he actually experienced. His book might still have been a best-seller today.

So what remains?

In 1895, the Hungarian critic Lajos Kropf, had this to say:

> Enough remains to give our hero a very fair claim to the title of adventurous. […] A faithful record of his experiences would have made a very readable book; the wretched farrago he has produced, though it sets up claims to being considered a work on history and geographical discovery, is neither one nor the other.[2]

Kropf hit the nail on the head: stripped of all the imagined episodes, of all the romanticising, of all the plagiarisms, and of the self-aggrandisement which struts across every single page, what the crew of the galliot *St Peter* achieved was still – to paraphrase *The Gentleman's Magazine* – extraordinary.

The unsung companions – Stepanov, Ryumin, Izmailov, Tchurin, Loginov, Bocharov and all the others, both men and women – fully participated in every moment of a daring voyage from Kamchatka. Some sought liberty, some sought a better life and some simply sought adventure. They sailed three or four thousand miles in an overcrowded ship across an uncharted sea, they worked hard at survival, they experienced hunger and thirst, boredom and despair. Arguably, they sailed farther than any Russians had sailed before them, on a journey that took them half-way round the world. But they held together as a crew to the very end. Many of them lived to tell the tale, some died, some found liberty or a kind of paradise and some came home again. And on top of all that, they had to put up with the close company of Benyovszky, clearly a man with a very high opinion of himself.

Heroes and heroines all, and just as deserving of a book as their leader.

As for Maurice Benyovszky himself, he may have been an insufferable companion, but his achievements speak for themselves. At the age of only 24, he took a leading role – alongside Ippolit Stepanov – in the preparations for escape from one of the most inhospitable outposts of the Russian Empire. Elected their leader, he guided some seventy desperate men, women and children (and Nestor the dog) in a leaky ship, with no reliable instruments or crew, down the chain of the Kuril and Japanese islands. This was a route which very few Westerners had followed before him – the most notable exceptions being Spanberg and Walton, in ships belonging to the Bering expedition in 1738; but even those who had been there left little in the way of maps or descriptions.

He encountered communities which were quite unused to the sight of Europeans and – for the most part – he managed to avoid bloodshed. After an exhausting and perilous journey of more than four months, he reached the port of Macao with the loss of only three men. Even men as experienced as Captain Cook could scarcely boast as much.

Once in Macao, he proved himself entirely capable of negotiating with hard-bitten European traders for the return of the surviving voyagers to French territories. Once in France, still aged only 26, he appeared so self-confident before the Parisian sophisticates of the Ancien Régime that he persuaded a set of wide-eyed ministers to fund an expedition to Madagascar.

His plans having misfired badly in Africa, and then failed in Croatia, he still did not give up. In the hopeful – perhaps gullible – young United States, he succeeded in garnering more financial backing for his rampant ambitions. His ignominious murder by French troops before he had even reached the age of 40 may simply have anticipated the date of his death in Madagascar; or it may not. What else he might have achieved – and what other exciting tales he might have invented for us – can only be imagined.

Notes

1   Oliver's 1893 edition, pp.47–52, lists a fair number of the sources. Even Nicholson's first edition conceded that material had been borrowed from elsewhere. Kropf, Cultru, Inkster, Voigt and others have added to the list.
2   Kropf, 1895, p.482.

APPENDIX I

Voyagers and Family

1. A Consolidated List of the Voyagers

The story of the voyage is as much about the ordinary people who sailed as it is about the Hungarian adventurer who led them. We have therefore set out below two lists of the participants in the voyage from Kamchatka to Macao. The first, which is the more accurate one, is a consolidated list of names mentioned by Ryumin,[1] or in the documentation prepared by Sgibnev,[2] or *en passant* by Benyovszky (it should be noted that Benyovszky, where he uses the same surname, frequently uses a completely different forename from our other two sources). The second (Section 2) is a list of names mentioned by Benyovszky alone – and these are principally people who died in Macao.

A.S. Sgibnev was a Russian archivist who in 1876 examined documentation of the investigations which took place in Siberia in the immediate aftermath of the mass-escape. This stated that there were sixty-three male and seven female voyagers, but included two possible duplicates. Thirty-two of the people are not named, but grouped as 'workmen' or 'workers' – if one were so inclined, one could match these unknowns with names in Ryumin's list. The overall figure of seventy is agreed with by both Ryumin and Stepanov. In the list below, the four entries marked with an asterisk are names listed by Sgibnev, but not by Ryumin.

According to Benyovszky, and depending on which version of his story one believes, there were anything between sixty-two and ninety-six voyagers. Around fifty were actually named, but at least half of those seem to be mis-named.

Ryumin was anxious to tell us where individuals ended up: his comments are also provided below; the present author's comments are italicised.

Surname	Forename	Designation
Andreyanov	Alexei	"Prisoner"
	Remained in Port Louis, Mauritius	
Andreyanova	Agafya	Wife of Andreyanov
	Remained in Port Louis, Mauritius	
Baturin	Asaf	Former convict artillery regiment, exiled by order of 13 June 1770
	Died on the ship from Canton to Mauritius	
Benyovszky	Maurice	Hungarian adventurer
	Colonel in the service of the French	
Bereznev	Gerasim	Cossack sailor
	Where he is, is not known *Returned to live in Okhotsk*	
Bocharov	Dmitrii	Apprentice navigator
	Now in Paris *Returned to live in Irkutsk and made a career as an explorer*	
Bocharova	Praskovya Mikhailova	Wife of Bocharov
	Died in Macao	
Brekhov	Igor	Koryak
	Now in Paris *Returned to Kamchatka*	
Gromov	Nikolai	Banished by the decree of 13 June 1770 Workman of the merchant Kholodilov
	Died on the ship from Canton to Mauritius	
Izmailov	Gerasim	Apprentice navigator
	Left on Kurils *Returned to Kamchatka and made a career as an explorer*	
Khrushchyov	Pyotr	Former guard captain who was exiled by order on 6 December 1763
	Captain in the service of the French *Probably remained in Mauritius*	
Korostelev	Dementii	Bolsheretsk garrison soldier
	Died in hospital in Lorient, Brittany	
Kosakov	Andrei	
	Remained in Port Louis, Mauritius	
Kosakov	Ivan	
	Now in Paris *Returned to live in Irkutsk*	
Kosakov	Kondrat	
	Died in Macao	
Kosintsov	Nikita	
	Remained in Port Louis, Mauritius	
Kostromin	Fedor	Merchant
	Died in hospital in Lorient, Brittany	
Krasilnikov	Sidor	Kamchadale
	Died of scurvy in hospital in Mauritius	
Kudrin	Ivan	Merchant
	Remained in Port Louis, Mauritius	
Kuznetsov	Grigorii	"Peasant" exile
	Lieutenant in the service of the French *Probably travelled to Paris and then accompanied Benyovszky to Madagascar*	

Surname	Forename	Designation
Kuznetsov	Jakob	Merchant
	Died of scurvy in hospital in Mauritius	
Loginov	Ivan	Manufacturer
	Killed on Formosa	
Loskitov	Igor	
	Now in Paris *Returned to live in Irkutsk*	
*Lapin		Merchant
	[Fate unknown – not mentioned by Ryumin; possibly identical with Oblyupin?]	
Lyapin	Vasilii	Prisoner
	Reached Paris *Returned to live in Okhotsk*	
Maschinskoi	Ivan	
	Died in Macao	
Medaev	Ivan	
	Now in Paris *Returned to live in Irkutsk*	
Meyder	Magnus	Admiralty doctor who was exiled by order on 6 December 1765
	Doctor in the service of the French *Possibly travelled to Paris; accompanied Benyovszky to Madagascar*	
Moskalev	Ivan	
	Came to Paris *Returned to live in Irkutsk*	
Muchin	Alexei	
	Now in Paris *Returned to live in Irkutsk*	
Novozhilov	Ivan	Exile
	Died in Macao	
Novozilov	Stefan	
	Remained in Port Louis, Mauritius	
Oblyupin	Kosma	
	Left sick in Mauritius, now come to Paris *Returned to live in Irkutsk*	
Odorin	Andrei	
	Died of scurvy in hospital in Mauritius	
Panov	Matvei	
	Died in Macao	
Panov	Vasilii	Guards Lieutenant exiled by order of 7 June 1770
	Killed on Formosa	
Parantsin	Alexei	Kamchadale
	Left on Kurils *Returned to Kamchatka*	
Parantsina	Lukerya	Parantsin's wife
	Left on Kurils *Returned to Kamchatka*	
Perevalov	Mikhail	Bolsheretsk garrison Corporal
	Died in Macao	
Piatikin	Kondratii	
	Now in Paris *Returned to live in Irkutsk*	

(Continued)

Surname	Forename	Designation
Popkov	Martin	Kamchatkan
	Died in Macao	
Popov	Ivan	Tax-collector
	Killed on Formosa	
Popov	Leontii	
	Remained in Port Louis, Mauritius	
Popov	Pyotr	Banished by the decree of 13 June 1770
		Workman of the merchant Kholodilov
	Died on the ship from Canton to Mauritius	
Popov	Prokotii	Kamchatkan
	Now in Paris *Returned to Kamchatka*	
Popov	Zakhar	Aleut
	Died in Macao	
Potolov	Vasilii	Cossack sailor
	Remained in Port Louis, Mauritius	
Pudakov	Jakob	
	Died in hospital in Lorient, Brittany	
Pyatsinin	Andrei	
	Died in hospital in Lorient, Brittany	
Ribrikov	Vasilii	
	Remained in Port Louis, Mauritius	
Ryumin	Ivan	Chancellery clerk, who was sentenced to deprivation of rights
	Now in Paris *Returned to live in Tobolsk*	
Ryumina	Ivana	Wife of Ryumin
	Now in Paris *Returned to live in Tobolsk*	
Sakarina	Juliana	"Mate's wife" – *by implication, the "Mate" was one who died*
	Remained in Port Louis, Mauritius; married Khrushchyov	
Samoilov	Ivan	
	Died in Macao	
Sarakanov	Pyotr	Banished by the decree of 13 June 1770
		Workman of the merchant Kholodilov
	Died on the ship from Canton to Mauritius	
★Savelev	Alexei	"Peasant"
	[Fate unknown – not mentioned by Ryumin]	
Semilev	Timotei	
	Where he is, is not known	
★Semyachekov	Timotei	Prisoner
	[Fate unknown – not mentioned by Ryumin – possibly identical with Semilev?]	
★Shabaev		Manufacturer
	[Fate unknown – not mentioned by Ryumin]	
Sofronov	Pyotr	Cossack sailor
	Now in Paris *Returned to live in Okhotsk*	

Surname	Forename	Designation
Stepanov	Ippolit	Army Captain who was exiled by order of 7 June 1770
	Arrested in Macao *Died in Batavia*	
Sudeikin	Spiridon	Clerk, Nilov's former secretary
	Reached Paris *Returned to live in Tobolsk*	
Tchuloshnikov	Alexei	Totemist clerk
	Remained in the command of Benyovszky *Probably accompanied him to Madagascar*	
Tchuloshnikov	Mikhail	Merchant
	Died of scurvy in hospital in Mauritius	
Tchurin	Maxim	Navigator
	Died in Macao	
Tchurina	Nastasia Fedorova	Daughter of Tchurin
	Died in Macao	
Tchurina	Stepanida Fedorova	Wife of Tchurin the navigator
	Died in Macao	
Trapeznikov	Efrem	
	Died in hospital in Lorient, Brittany	
Tserebrinkov	Jakob	
	Now in Paris *Returned to live in Irkutsk*	
Turchanin	Aleksander	Exiled by order of 22 September 1757
	Died in Macao	
Ustyuzhinov	Ivan	Son of Kamchatkan priest
	Remained in Port Louis, Mauritius *Joined Benyovszky in Madagascar; returned to Nerchinsk, Siberia in 1789*	
Volbinin	Gregorii	Sailor from Okhotsk
	Died in Macao	
Winbladh	August	Exiled by order of 18 July 1770
	Remained in Port Louis, Mauritius, because of the disease *Later returned to Sweden*	
Zyablikov	Filipp	Apprentice navigator from Okhotsk
	Died in Macao	

*Names listed by Sgibnev, but not by Ryumin.

2. Names Mentioned only by Benyovszky

Surname	Forename	Designation	Fate
Juska	Alexis		Died at Macao
Kazakov	Stefan		Died at Macao
Kuzmika	Ekaterina	Girl-friend of Jakob [?] Kuznetsov	Died at Macao
Lapsiev			Volunteered to remain on Usmay Ligon
Levantiev	Kasimir		Died at Macao
Loginov		Younger brother of Ivan Loginov	Volunteered to stay behind on Formosa as General of Artillery
Lubimoi	Yakov		Died at Macao
Maschinskoi	Andrei		Died at Macao
"My Japanese traveller"	"Young gentleman" picked up in Shikoku		Abandoned in Macao
Nilova	Afanasia	Daughter of Commander Nilov	Died at Macao
Nolinkin	Georgii		Died at Macao
Novozilov	Gregorii		Died at Macao
Panov	Georgii		Died at Macao
Perevalov	Nikolai		Died at Macao
Perevalov	Ivan		Died at Macao
Perevalova	"Madame"	"Wife of Perevalov"	Died at Macao
Pottosiov	Zacharii	"The American," 12-year old boy picked up in Aleutians	Unknown
Rabalov		Discovered Izmailov's mutiny	Unknown
Sipskoi	Boleslaus		Died at Macao
Tchodin	Lavrentii		Died at Macao
Voronov	Georgii		Died at Macao
Zacharka	Alexei		Died at Macao
Zadskoi	Eraklii	"Prince"	Died at Macao
Zarskoi	Nikolai		Died at Macao
Ziran	Alexander		Died at Macao

3. Benyovszky's Family³

Maurice Benyovszky

Known as: Moric Agoston Aladar; Maurice August; 'Count' or 'Baron'
Baptismal name: Mattheus Mauritius Michael Franciscus Seraphinus
Born: Vrbové, Hungary, 20 September 1746; Died: Madagascar, 23 May 1786

Father

Samuel Benyovszky. Born 28 January 1703, Nagyszombat in Trnava region, Hungary; died 25 October 1760, Vrbové

Mother

Rozália Revay de Trebosztó. Born 4 June 1719, Cifer in Trnava; died 26 July 1760, Vrbové

Siblings

- Marta. Dates unknown
- Ferenc. Born 1753?; died?
- Emanuel. Born 1 April 1755; died 1789? (in USA)

Half-sisters (daughters of Rozalia's first husband József Pestvármegyei)

- Borbála
- *Two other sisters, details unknown*

Wife

Anna Zusanna Hönsch. Born 18 October 1750, Poprad, Hungary; died 4 March 1826, Beckov, Hungary

Children

- Samuel. Born 9 December 1768, Poprad; died 22 September 1772, Poprad
- Charles Maurice Louis Augustus. Born 1774? in Madagascar?; died 11 July 1774, Madagascar (*non-verifiable details provided by Maurice himself*)
- Roza. Born 1 January 1779, Beczko, Hungary; died 26 October 1816, Vieszka, Hungary
- Zsofia. Dates unknown

Notes

1 Berg, 1822, pp.109–110.
2 Sgibnev, 1876, pp.540–541.
3 All the places mentioned here as being situated in Hungary in the eighteenth century are now in Slovakia.

APPENDIX II

Dates and Places

1. A Tentative Outline of the Journey from Kamchatka to Paris

All dates are new style (eleven days after old style)

23 May 1771	Departed from Bolshaya River, Kamchatka
29 May – 9 June	On Simushir, Kuril Islands
19 July – 23 July	At Sakinohama, Shikoku, Japan
23 July – 25 July	On Oshima island, Awa Province?
31 July – 11 August	On Amami-Oshima island, Satsuma Province
27 August – 1 September	On Formosa
8 September	Arrived at Dongshan Island, Chinese mainland
22 September	Arrived at Macao
14 January 1772	Departed Macao for Bocca Tigris (Humen Strait)
22 January	Departed for Mauritius
4 March – 24 March	On Mauritius
7 July – 27 March 1773	At Lorient, France
15 April	Ryumin et al. arrived in Paris

2. Cross-References of Dates of the Voyage from Kamchatka

On the (old-style) dates mentioned by...

...Ryumin (all dates OS)	...Stepanov (all dates OS)	Benyovszky claimed...	NS★
12 May 1771 departed Kamchatka	12 May departed Kamchatka	12 May, left Kamchatka	23 May
29 May abandoned Izmailov on Kurils 6 June at sea	18 May to 12 June at anchor at one of the Kuril Islands	20 May arrived at Bering Island	31 May
		21 May Izmailov put ashore	
		29 May heading north-east towards Tchukchi Territory	
		5 June at the mouth of the Anadyr River	
		12 June near 'America'	
15 June at sea		17 June coasting down the Aleutians	28 June
		21 June arrived at the Aleutian island of Urumusir	
		29 June departed Aleutians	
8 July arrived at the Japanese island of Shikoku	8 July arrived at Shikoku	4 July put in at an unknown island	15 July
12 July departed Shikoku		7 to 15 July at sea	29 July
		18 July arrived at Liquor Island (non-existent)	
20 July arrived at "Usmaitsi" island (Amami-Oshima) 31 July departed "Usmaiovski Bay"	19 July anchored in a bay at "Usmaski" (Amami-Oshima) ...until 1 August	22 July, departed Liquor	2 August
		28 July to 10 Aug in or around Shikoku	8 August
16 August arrived at Formosa	14 August landed at "Termora" (Formosa)	14 Aug arrived at "Usmay Ligon" (Amami-Oshima)	25 August

(Continued)

On the (old-style) dates mentioned by... (continued)

...Ryumin (all dates OS)	...Stepanov (all dates OS)	Benyovszky claimed...	NS*
17 August Panov, Popov and Loginov killed	(15?) August three crew-members killed	19 August departed Usmay Ligon	
		26 August arrived at Formosa	6 September
		29 August three crew-members killed	9 September
		30 August to 13 September on Formosa, engaged in war	10 to 24 September
21 August departed Formosa	20 August departed Formosa, heading for China	13 September departed Formosa	24 September
26 August off the coast of China	26 August off the coast of China	15 September off the coast of China	26 September
28 August Chinese mainland – "Tasona"	28 August arrived at "Tschinchina," stayed there for five days	16 September arrived at "Tanasoa" (Chinese mainland)	27 September
12 September arrived at Macao	22 September (*NS date provided by editor Ebeling; OS is 11 September*) arrived at Macao	22 Sep arrived at Macao (*this date verifiably correct, NS*)	1 October
4 January 1772 departed Macao		14 January departed Macao (*all dates now NS*)	14 January
11 January departed for Mauritius		22 Jan departed for Mauritius	22 January

*Benyovszky's date rendered as new style.

APPENDIX III

Bibliography

1. Books Referred to in the Chapters

Albrecht

Carol Padgham Albrecht, *Music in Public Life: Viennese Reports from the Allgemeine Musikalische Zeitung, 1798-1804*. PhD dissertation, Ohio, 2008.

Alexander

John T. Alexander. *Catherine the Great*, Oxford, 1989.

Anson

A Voyage Round the World, by George Anson Esq. [...] compiled by Richard Walter, MA. (*2nd edition*) London, 1748.

Beawes

Wyndham Beawes, *Lex Mercatoria Rediviva; or, the Merchant's Directory etc*, Dublin, 1773.

Belcour

François Auguste Thesby de Belcour, *Relation ou Journal d'un Officier François au Service de la Confédération de Pologne*, Amsterdam, 1776.

Benyovszky

Memoirs and Travels of Mauritius Augustus Count de Benyowsky, Magnate of the Kingdoms of Hungary and Poland, One of the Chiefs of the Confederation of Poland &c. Translated and edited by W. Nicholson, London, 1790.

Berg

V. I. Berg, *Flucht des Grafen Benjowsky aus Kamtschatka nach Frankreich*. In: St Peterburgische Zeitschrift, Vol.1, St Petersburg, 1822.

Cochrane

Narrative of a Pedestrian Journey through Russia [...] to the Frozen Sea and Kamtchatka, by John Dundas Cochrane, London, 1825.

Cook/King

The Three Voyages of Captain James Cook Round the World, edited by Captain James King: Vol.2, London, 1821.
Ditto. Vol.3, London, 1834.

Coxe

William Coxe, *Account of the Russian Discoveries between Asia and America*, London, 1780.

Critical Review

Critical Review, or Annals of Literature. Vol. 23, London, June 1798.

Cultru

Prosper Cultru, *Un Empereur de Madagascar au 18ième Siecle: Benyowszky*, Paris, 1906.

Dunlap

William Dunlap, *History of American Theatre*, Vol.II. London, 1833.

Ebeling

C. D and J. P. Ebeling. *Neuere Geschichte der See- und Land-Reisen, Vol.IV. Begebenheiten und Reisen des Grafen Moritz August von Benjowsky [...] wie auch einem Auszug aus Hippolitus Stefanows russisch geschriebenem Tagebuche*, Hamburg, 1791.

Gentleman's Magazine

The Gentleman's Magazine and Historical Chronicle, Vol.52, London, 1772.
The Gentleman's Magazine and Historical Chronicle, Vol.60, Part 2, London, 1790.

Gilbert

William Gilbert, *De Magnete, Magneticisque Corporibus, et de magno magnete tellure, etc*, London, 1600.

House of Commons

House of Commons Research Paper (12/31): *Inflation: the Value of the Pound 1750–2011*, London, 2012.

Inkster

Ian Inkster, 'Oriental Enlightenment: The problematic Military Experiences and Cultural Claims of Count de Benyowsky.' In: *Taiwan Historical Research*, Vol.17, No,1, pp.27–70. Taiwan, 2010.

Journal Encyclopédique

Journal Encyclopédique, Vol.58, Part 5 (ii), Paris, July 1784.
Journal Encyclopédique, Vol.71, Part 2 (i), Paris, February 1791.
Journal Encyclopédique, Vol.72, Part 5 (xx), Paris, July 1791.

Keene

Donald Keene, *The Japanese Discovery of Europe, 1720 to 1830*, Stanford, 1969.

Kerguelen

Yves-Joseph de Kerguelen, *Relation de Deux Voyages dans les Mers Australes et des Indes*, Paris, 1782.

Krasheninnikov

S. Krasheninnikov, *History of Kamtchatka, and the Kurilski Islands, with the countries adjacent.* (J. Grieve transl.) London, 1764.

Kropf

L. L. K[ropf], *Mauritius Augustus Benyowszky*. In 'Notes and Queries', Series 8, Vols.6 and 7. London, 1895.

Kunec

Patrik Kunec, *The Hungarian Participants in the American War of Independence.* In: Codrul Cosminului, XVI, No.1, pp.41–57. Suceava, 2010.

Lefèvre-Pontalis

Germain Lefèvre-Pontalis, *Un Projet de Conquête du Japon par l'Angleterre et la Russie en 1776.* In: Annales de l'École Libre des Sciences Politiques, Vol.4, Paris 1889, pp.433–457.

Lensen

George Lensen, *The Russian Push Towards Japan*, New York, 1971.

Lesseps

Barthélemy de Lesseps, *Journal Historique du Voyage de M. de Lesseps*, Paris, 1790.

Matthews

Owen Matthews, *Glorious Misadventures: Nikolai Rezanov and the Dream of Russian America*, Bloomsbury, London, 2013.

Meusel

J. G. Meusel, *Vermischte Nachrichten*, Erlangen, 1816.

Mezey

Isztvan Mezey, *Az igazi Japan*, Nippon-Magyar Society, Budapest, 1939.

Oliver

Memoirs and Travels of Mauritius Augustus Count de Benyowsky, &c. Edited by Samuel Pasfield Oliver 1893.
Ditto. Edited by S. P. Oliver 1904.

Roberts

Luke Roberts, *Shipwrecks and Flotsam: The Foreign World in Edo-Period Tosa.* In: Monumenta Nipponica, Vol.70, No.1, 2015. pp.83–122.

Rochon

Alexis Rochon, *Voyage to Madagascar and the East Indies* (transl. from French by J. Trapp), London, 1793.

Ryumin

Ivan Ryumin, *Zapiski Kantselyarista Ryumina o priklyutsheniyach' ego s' Beniovskim.* In: Siberian Archive. St Petersburg, 1822.

Schlözer

August Ludwig Schlözers […] *Briefwechsel.* Erster Theil, Heft I–VI, 1776. 4. Auflage, Göttingen, 1780.

Schmalev

Timotei Schmalev, 'Neueste Nachrichten aus Kamtschatka […] June 1773.' In: *St Petersburgisches Journal*, Vol.I, April 1776, pp.18–25 [Partial reproduction of article also translated by Schlözer, above].

Sgibnev

A.S. Sgibnev, *Bunt' Benyovskavo v' Kamchatke v' 1771.* In: Russkaya Starina, Vol.XV, St Petersburg, 1876.

Sobel

Dava Sobel, *Longitude: The True Story of a Lone Genius Who Solved the Greatest Scientific Problem of His Time*, London, 1996.

Stein

V. I. Stein, *Samozvannoi imperator Madagaskarskii (M. A. Ben'ëvskii).* In: Istoricheskii Vestnik No.7, St Petersburg, 1908.

Voigt

Vilmos Voigt, *Maurice Benyovszky and his "Madagascar Protocolle" (1772–1776).* In: Hungarian Studies, Vol.21, Part 1, 2007.

2. Principal Editions

This list is drawn mostly from the bibliography in Captain Oliver's edition of 1904. Listed in chronological order.

- *The Memoirs and Travels of Mauritius Augustus, Count de Benyowsky. Written by Himself.* Translated from the original manuscript (by W. Nicholson). 2 vols, 4to. London, 1790.
- *The Memoirs and Travels of Mauritius Augustus, Count de Benyowsky. Written by Himself.* 2 vols, 8vo. Dublin, 1790.
- *Des Grafen Beniovsky Reisen durch Sibirien und Kamtschatka über Japan und China nach Europa.* (Translated from the English into German by D. M. Liebeskind, with notes by Joh. Reinh. Forster.) 8vo. Berlin, 1790. Reprinted 1794 and 1806.
- *Voyages et Memoires de Maurice-Auguste, Comte de Benyowsky.* Paris, 2 vols, in 8vo, 1791. (Edited by J. H. Magellan and F. J. Noel.)
- *Grefwens Mauritz August von Beniowskis Lefnadslopp och Resor af honom sjelf beskrefne* (ed. Samuel Ödmann), 8vo. Stockholm, 1791.
- *Des Grafen Beniovsky Reisen durch Sibirien und Kamtschatka über Japan und China nach Europa,* Übersetzt von Geo. Forster. Leipzig, 1791.
- *Des Grafen Beniovsky Reisen durch Sibirien und Kamtschatka über Japan und China nach Europa.* Aus dem Englischen übersetzt von C. D. und J. P. Ebeling. Hamburg, 1791. Vols 1 and 2. Reprinted 1797.
- *Des Grafen Beniovsky Reisen durch Sibirien und Kamtschatka über Japan und China nach Europa.* 8vo. Tübingen, 1791.
- *Gedenkschriften en Reizen des Graaven van Benyowsky* [...] Dutch translation, four volumes, Haarlem, 1791/1792.
- *Des Grafen Beniovsky Reise. Aus dem Englischen übersetzt und abgekürzt.* Vols i–ii. 8vo. Reutlingen, 1796.
- *Historya podrozy osobliwszych zdarzen Maurycego-Augusta slawnego hrabi Beniowskiego szlachcica polskiego i wegierskiego...Z Franczuzkiego tlomaczona,* vols, i–iv. 8vo. Warsawa, 1797. 2nd edition, ib. 1802. 3rd edition, ib. 1806.
- *Pamatné Prihody Hrabéte Benowského* [Slovak edition] translated by Samuel Cercansky, 8vo. Bratislava, 1808.
- *Vie et Aventures du Comte M. A. B. résumés d'Apres les Mémoires ...* Par N. A. K[oublaski]. Bibliothèque des Écoles Chrétiennes, 2eme series, 1 vol. Tours, 1863.
- *Benyovszky Moricz eletrajza sajat emlekiratai es utleirasai* [Translated from the English edition of 1790 by M. Jokai]. Kepekkel, terkepekkelf, etc. 8vo, 4 vols, Budapest, 1888–1890.
- *The Memoirs and Travels of Mauritius Augustus, Count de Benyowsky.* From the translation of his original manuscripts (1741–1771) by William Nicholson, FRS, 1790. Edited by Captain Pasfield Oliver. 8vo. Illustrated, p.399, with map of voyage, London, 1893.

- *Dziennik podrozy i zdarzen hrabiego M. A. Benoiwskiego na Syberyi, Azyi i Afryce* [Polish translation]. Four parts, Krakow, 1894.
- *Memoirs and Travels of Mauritius Augustus Count de Benyowsky, etc.* Edited by Captain Pasfield Oliver, London, 1904.

3. Other Critiques, Biographies and Histories

Listed in alphabetical order of author.

- Assendelft de Coningh, Cornelis Theodoor van. *Mijn Verblijf in Japan.* ('My Visit to Japan') Amsterdam, 1856. [Specifically pp.155–160].
- Barquissau, Raphael. *Les Chevaliers des Isles,* La Réunion, 1990.
- Cseke, Zsolt. *Benyovszky Móric és a malgasok földje.* Pecs, 2012
- Cultru, Prosper. *De Colonia in Insulan Delphonam vulgo Madagaskar. A barone M. A. de Benyowszky deducta.* Paris, 1901.
- Dvoichenko-Markova, E. *Benjamin Franklin and Count M. A. Beniowski,* Philadelphia, 1955.
- Ferard, Paul-Louis. *Benyowsky. Gentilhomme et Roi de fortune.* Paris, 1931.
- Flacourt, Etienne de. *Histoire de la Grande Île de Madagascar.* Paris, 1913.
- Hunt, William R. *Arctic Passage: The Turbulent History of the Land and People of the Bering Sea 1697–1975.* New York 1975.
- Janko, Dr. Janos. *A Grof Benyovszky Irodalom Anyagarol.* In: Szazadok xxv. Budapest, 1891.
- Janko, Dr. Janos. *Grof Benyovszky Moricz mint foldrajzi kutato. Kritikai megjegyzesek Kamcsatkalol Makaoig tett utjara.* Budapest, 1890.
- Kropf, Lajos. *Art. Grof Benyovszky Moricz.* Szazadok, Budapest, 1894.
- Kukulski, Leszek Oprac. *Pamietniki; fragment konfederacki. Maurycy Beniowski.* Warsaw, 1967.
- Landelle, Guillaume Joseph Gabriel de la. *Le Dernier des Filibustiers, le Roi des Rois (Benyowsky).* Paris, A. Cedot. 1857 (1858).
- Laut, Agnes C. *Vikings of the Pacific. The Adventures of the Explorers who came from the West, Eastward.* London, 1905.
- Orlowski, Leon. *Maurycy August Beniowski,* Warsaw, 1961.
- Paseniuk, Leonid, *Pokhozhdeniia barona Beniovskogo: Istoriko-biograficheskii ocherk.* In: 'Kamchatka', pp.109–166, Petropavlovsk, 1978.
- Paseniuk, Leonid, *Miatezhnaia sud'ba skital'tsa.* In: 'Belye nochi na reke Mamontovoi', pp.194–302, Krasnodar, 1988.
- Sieroszewski, Andrzej. *Maurycy Beniowski w literackiej legendzie,* Warsaw, 1970.
- Smith, Herbert Greenhough. *The Romance of History: Masaniello, Prince Rupert, Benyowsky etc.* London, 1895 [specifically pp.55–92].
- Teixeira, Manuel. *O Conde Benyowsky em Macau.* Macau, 1966.
- Thalloczy, Lajos. *Gr. Benyovszky Moricz Haditengereszeti es Kereskedelem Politikai Tervei (1779–81).* Budapest, 1901.

- Vacher, Paule: *Contribution à l'histoire de l'établissement français fondé à Madagascar, par le baron de Benyovszky (1772–1776)*. Tananarive, Faculté des lettres et des sciences humaines, 1970.

4. Plays, Operas, Fiction and Films

Much of this information is taken from Voigt. Listed in chronological order.

- August von Kotzebue, *Die Verschwörung auf Kamtschatka*, 1792. Play. Published Leipzig, 1795.
- Christian August Vulpius. *Graf Benjowsky. Ein original Trauerspiel in fünf Aufzügen* (Leipzig, 1795). Play, first performed in 1794.
- Rev. William Render, *Count Benyowsky; or, the conspiracy of Kamtschatka. A tragi-comedy, in five acts, by Baron Kotzebue*, ... Translated from the German, London, 1798. (Also Dublin, Edinburgh and Cork, 1799.)
- Benjamin Thompson, *Count Benyowsky; or, the conspiracy of Kamtschatka*. Trans. from the German of Kotzebue. London 1800. (Also printed in: *The German Theatre*, Vol.2, London, 1801.)
- William Dunlap, *Count Benyowski*, New York, 1799. A play.
- François Adrien Boieldieu, *Die Verwiesenen auf Kamtschatka*, opera. Libretto by Alexandre Duval, based on Kotzebue (1800). Performed in 1804 in German (Vienna – directed by Georg Treitschke) and in 1813 in Polish.
- Count Joseph Gvadanyi, *Ronto Palnak, egy magyar lovas kozkatonanak és Grof Benyovszky Moritznak elete. Pozsony*, 1807. An epic poem.
- James Kenney, *Benyowski, or the Exiles of Kamschatka*. An operatic play following the plot of Kotzebue's drama. Performed in Drury Lane, London, March 1826.
- Ferenc Doppler, *Benyovszky vagy a kamcsatkai száműzöttek*, 1847. A Hungarian opera: libretto by Rudolf Köffinger; music by Ferenc Doppler. Music published 1855.
- József Gaal, *Gróf Benyovszky Móric élete és viszontagságai*. 1857. A novel for young people.
- Luise Mühlbach, *Benyovszky*, 1866. Four-volume novel in German. Translated into Hungarian, 1866.
- Vilmos Radó: *Benyovszky Móric élete és kalandjai*, Budapest, 1889. Several reprints.
- N. G. Smirnov, *Gosudarstvo solntsa*, Moscow, 1928 (reprinted 1992).
- Dénes Barsi, *Madagaszkár királya*, Budapest, 1943.
- Kurt Martens, *Graf Benyowsky verachtet den Tod*, Berlin, 1944. Novel.
- Miklós Rónaszegi, *A nagy játszma*, Budapest, 1955. A novel for young people.
- Igor Ciel (director), *Vivát Benyovszky!* 1975. Slovak-Hungarian TV film series.
- Árpád Thiery, *Benyovszky gróf*, Budapest, 1993. Novel.

- Zsolt Cseke, *Benyovszky Móric és a malgasok földje*, 2009. 6-part documentary for the Hungarian TV channel Duna-Televízió.
- *Benyovszky*, a Ballet and Musical, performed at Kosice, Slovakia, 2013.
- Irina Stanciulescu (director), *Benyovszky, the Rebel Count*, Hungary 2012 and 2015. Film.

APPENDIX IV

Maps

Two maps are included here.

The first is a very simple sketch map made by the author of the present book. It shows roughly the route of the *St Peter* as it made its way from Bolsheretsk on Kamchatka to Macao. It would not have met with Benyovszky's approval, showing as it does not a single enticing island of paradise, nor indeed tracing any of his daring exploration of the Alaskan lands. A great failing.

The second is a map created for Mor Jokai's 1891 Hungarian edition of Benyovszky's *Memoirs*. It shows all the travels of Benyovszky, from his capture in the Polish wars, right up to his demise in Madagascar. An almost complete circumnavigation of the world is indicated. Jokai took Benyovszky entirely at his word. Everything is exactly as it should be. Much better.

We have already referred to another map, not reproduced here, which is just as entertaining as Jokai's – but for different reasons. As described above at the start of Chapter XIX, the map created by Captain Oliver for his 1893 edition of the *Memoirs* plots the initial stages of the voyage of *St Peter* – from Bolsheretsk into the Bering Sea and down as far as the Kurils. The voyage is traced in four different ways: first, "Benyowsky's true course according to Ismiloff;" second, "The Count's track according to his lat. & lon. positions;" third, "Benyowsky's probable route according to his bearings;" fourth, "Benyowsky's course according to his account of places visited." Oliver was a man committed to his trade. But his dedication clearly forsook him, for he made no attempt to plot the voyage through Japanese or Chinese waters. The line of the third route heads off southwards at the edge of the map, with an arrow and Oliver's laconic note: "To fictitious I. of Liquor." Those interested in this map can track it down in Oliver, or view it on-line at the author's website – www.andydrummond.net/benyovszky

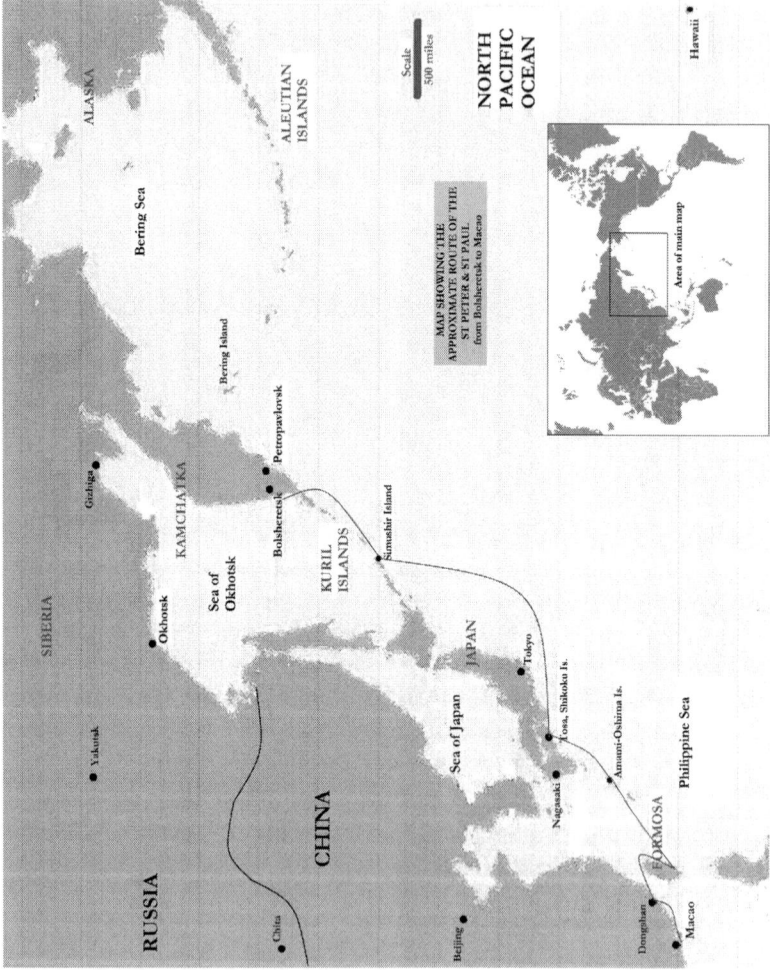

MAP A.1 A simple sketch-map of the path of the *St Peter* across the North Pacific, from Kamchatka to Macao.

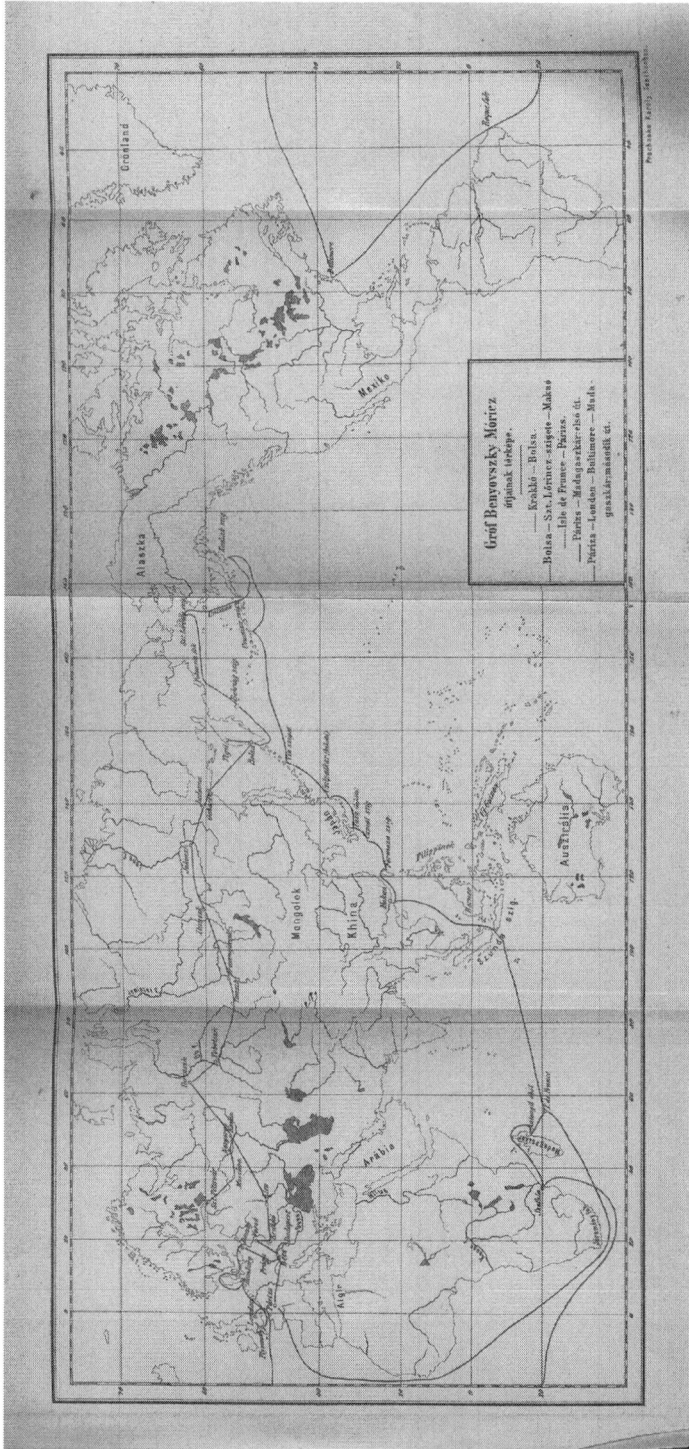

MAP A.2. An outline map of all Benyovszky's putative journeys, taken from the 1891 Hungarian edition of Benyovszky's works (ed. Jokai).

INDEX

Taylor & Francis eBooks

Helping you to choose the right eBooks for your Library

Add Routledge titles to your library's digital collection today. Taylor and Francis ebooks contains over 50,000 titles in the Humanities, Social Sciences, Behavioural Sciences, Built Environment and Law.

Choose from a range of subject packages or create your own!

Benefits for you

>> Free MARC records
>> COUNTER-compliant usage statistics
>> Flexible purchase and pricing options
>> All titles DRM-free.

REQUEST YOUR **FREE** INSTITUTIONAL TRIAL TODAY

Free Trials Available
We offer free trials to qualifying academic, corporate and government customers.

Benefits for your user

>> Off-site, anytime access via Athens or referring URL
>> Print or copy pages or chapters
>> Full content search
>> Bookmark, highlight and annotate text
>> Access to thousands of pages of quality research at the click of a button.

eCollections – Choose from over 30 subject eCollections, including:

Archaeology	Language Learning
Architecture	Law
Asian Studies	Literature
Business & Management	Media & Communication
Classical Studies	Middle East Studies
Construction	Music
Creative & Media Arts	Philosophy
Criminology & Criminal Justice	Planning
Economics	Politics
Education	Psychology & Mental Health
Energy	Religion
Engineering	Security
English Language & Linguistics	Social Work
Environment & Sustainability	Sociology
Geography	Sport
Health Studies	Theatre & Performance
History	Tourism, Hospitality & Events

For more information, pricing enquiries or to order a free trial, please contact your local sales team: www.tandfebooks.com/page/sales